DRUMMING UP
DIALOGUE

DRUMMING UP DIALOGUE

•◆•

**The Dialogic Philosophies of Martin Buber,
Fred Iklé, and William Ury Compared and
Applied to the Babukusu Community of Kenya**

Patrick Wanakuta Baraza

iUniverse, Inc.
Bloomington

Drumming Up Dialogue
The Dialogic Philosophies of Martin Buber, Fred Iklé, and William Ury Compared and Applied to the Babukusu Community of Kenya

iUniverse books may be ordered through booksellers or by contacting:

iUniverse
1663 Liberty Drive
Bloomington, IN 47403
www.iuniverse.com
1-800-Authors (1-800-288-4677)

ISBN: 978-1-4620-1620-4 (sc)
ISBN: 978-1-4620-1621-1 (e)

Printed in the United States of America

iUniverse rev. date: 08/22/2011

For my beloved mother,
Sabina Nelima.

CONTENTS

Acknowledgments

This book belongs to many others as much as to me. Literally every page contains the traces of the encounters that inspired *Drumming Up Dialogue*, both small and large—a conversation with a friend, a remark by an elder, a reader's suggestion, someone else's inspired writing on a particular subject, and a multitude of experiences with my people, the Babukusu of western Kenya. Words are unable to express my deepest gratitude to all those who have supported me and enriched this book.

Very special thanks to Dr. Hilary J. Martin, Dr. James A. Noel, Dr. Hamid Algar, and Dr. William R. O'Neil, for their time, effort, guidance, and support on this book. For all the years of friendship and for financial and moral support, no words can express the debt I owe Frederick Scheetz and family. Paul and Connie Zimmerman have been my very special friends through the past several years, providing me a home away from home. Connie Zimmerman designed the cover and edited my first book, *Rival Claims for the Soul of Africa*, and Paul was indefatigable in helping me through the labyrinth of visa issues in order to allow me to live here in Spokane and teach at Gonzaga University.

Thanks to Dr. John Marshall James, recently deceased, who was an astute reader, editor, and critic but also incomparably supportive. He made the struggle to complete this manuscript not only possible but also pleasurable. My debts to him, both intellectual and personal, have no end. And then, thanks to Brother Martin Fallin, who read my original text, and to Stacy Gonzalez and Harry Bright, who spent countless hours correcting my English grammar, as well as providing me with the kind of encouragement and support that only love can bring.

Prologue

Archeologists would have us understand that Africa is, by increasing evidences, truly the birthplace of humanity. It should not surprise us that, among the more primitive societies, there is a most basic and effective cultural means to keep the peace among those who would acknowledge the wisdom of doing so. Does the Bukusu way of dialoguing hold a key to human survival?

Drumming Up Dialogue attempts here to work through the thinking of three leading writers in the field of conflict management, examining first a twentieth century writer and ending with the work of a twenty-first century philosopher and a demonstration of contemporary, progressive thinking. The progression moves from Martin Buber, to Charles Iklé, and on to William Ury, who describes what it is that the Bukusu people do so well.

Let it be said here that, among the traditional Bukusu, one of the means of transmitting messages from village to village is a drum. Utilizing variations in beat and tenor, the drum conveys precise meanings that cannot be mistaken. All that is expected of good newspaper reporting is transmitted—who, what, why, when, where, and how are all conveyed in Bukusu dialogue.

The people who are the focus of this study are the Babukusu of Bukusuland. *Babukusu* is the plural and refers to the entire cultural nation of more than several Bukusu peoples. *Bukusu* refers to the people of the land by location of the people. The origin of these titles refers to the ancestor from whom Babukusu claim descent. The term *Omubukusu* is the singular for a Bukusu person; *ba* is the plural, and *bu* refers to the place. The term *Bubukusu* also may refer to the countryside itself.

The Bukusu are a nation of over one million people living in the farming region of southwestern Kenya near Lake Victoria, Mount Elgon, and the Ugandan border. This community has always been religiously oriented. The community's belief in one God, whom they call *Wele Khakaba* (God the giver), long predates African contact with Islam or Christianity. An African is profoundly and incurably a believer, a religious person. To him or her, religion is not just a set of beliefs but also a way of life and the basis of culture, identity, and moral values. Religion is an essential part of the tradition that helps to promote both social stability and creative innovation. Religion permeates all aspects of African life.

Over the last one hundred years, the Babukusu have interacted with European, Christian, Arab, Swahili, and Asian Muslim cultures. Even as Bukusu people have become Muslim or Christian converts, they have remained rooted in their culture. For the traditional Bukusu, religious beliefs and behaviors continue to shape the daily lives of the entire community, even as converts attend their places of worship. It is unfortunate that Christian and Muslim religious leaders and groups there will show a hostile attitude to such bifocal life. Consider how Islam has relegated Bukusu traditional religion to "ignorance" and Christianity would call it mere "paganism"; in either case, it is seen as savage. So today, Bukusu Muslims and Bukusu Christians are persuaded that their Bukusu spiritual tradition is a fossil and not anything of importance in their changing lives. Consequently, the Bukusu people who continue to follow their traditional religious practices are barely tolerated; they are discounted and demeaned by their mainline brethren for being superstitious, naive, and outdated.

The leaders of the larger Babukusu are not considered as equal partners in interreligious dialogue with members of the Christian and Islamic populations because Bukusu religious tradition has neither formalized text nor religious hierarchy. Because the traditional religion has no formal written traditions and no sacred text—as do the Muslims with the Qur'an and the Christians with their scriptures—the Babukusu depend strictly on their oral tradition, which must ever be revisited by the community to find the right response to the issue of the moment and place. When others fail to honor the Babukusu oral tradition with dialogue, that system has no real strength to cope with the larger world that descends on the people from beyond their own.

Religious intolerance on the part of Babukusu Christians and Muslims toward their traditional brethren has led to conflicts regarding issues such as initiation and circumcision, land rights, the role of women, and polygyny. When converts from one cultural belief system to another are poorly assimilated, the most extreme result may be the extinction of the more elemental cultural way of life. Conflicts and unsatisfying assimilation do occur in Africa wherever these forces and belief systems clash. Therefore every faction of the Babukusu society needs to understand and respect the Babukusu traditional religion in order to facilitate positive interactions with Islam and Christianity.

This book's focus, then, is on the Bukusu people of western Kenya. It does not compare or contrast Bukusu history and culture with those of any of the other ethnic groups of Kenya, much less with those of other African peoples, except for occasional research comments from the components of our three-legged stool—Martin Buber, Fred Charles Iklé, and William L. Ury. *Drumming Up Dialogue* builds the case for the necessity of dialogue that is the Bukusu people's own. The focus is on the Bukusu traditional religion, primarily as it has evolved in the second half of the twentieth century.

Represented here is one of the few studies of the Bukusu people and the only one addressing their religions. The study is undertaken with that methodology peculiar to the West that seeks to comprehend Babukusu storytelling by way of cultural study. In this way, the Western mind may come to understand the life of the community that is the heartbeat of Bukusu culture. Theirs is that traditional mind-set, in which time is a purveyor of lessons and looking back provides a far more potent education than seeking meaning in the future. This sensibility can be translated into English by saying that the Bukusu have a focus on the past and the "imminent now"—a concept that exists within the African perception of time, which is entirely different than that of the Western perception. In traditional African cultures, time is a chain of events that have occurred, those that are taking place now, and those that are inevitably or immediately, "imminently" to occur. In order to be actual, events must be experienced. For example, the Bukusu people live with elephants in their part of Africa. The people are well aware, therefore, that elephants take eighteen to twenty-two moons[1] to gestate their young—that a year and a half must always pass and then the elephant will give birth, as has always been the case. The people have always understood the baby elephant's birth to be not so much in the future but still within the "imminent now"—time already lived and experienced. In other words, the birth is an event that has once been experienced. Since traditional Africans can have "active interest in events that lie in the future ... out to perhaps two years" or that seem "inevitable," John S. Mbiti, a Kenyan scholar and authority on African traditional religions, thinks such events lie within "the horizon of what constitutes actual time."[2]

The book will begin with a discussion of the Bukusu people of western Kenya, followed by the history of Islam, Christianity, and Bukusu traditional religion. It will then move into strategies of dialogue based on Martin Buber's philosophy of dialogue, Fred Iklé's principles of negotiating dialogue, and William Ury's techniques for conflict resolution, applying dialogic principles to the Bukusu model.

I am a Bukusu elder and leader, a Roman Catholic priest, and a scholar of Islam; I have worked with the political and religious hierarchy in Kenya, as well as with the poorest of the poor in its vast, arid deserts. Currently I live in the United States and teach both Islamic Civilization and African Catholicism in the Department of Religious Studies at Gonzaga University in Washington State. I revisit Kenya and family there in Bukusuland at least once each year. Much of the data for this book has come from my early personal life and from ongoing contact with my people, as well as with those in all of Kenya and the whole of Africa. I hope that the ideas and contributions of the Bukusu people will come through loud and clear, as if being drummed in language that is unmistakable.

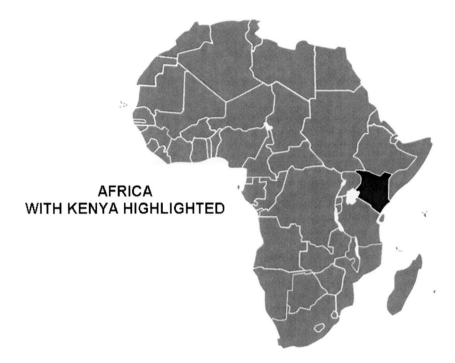

AFRICA
WITH KENYA HIGHLIGHTED

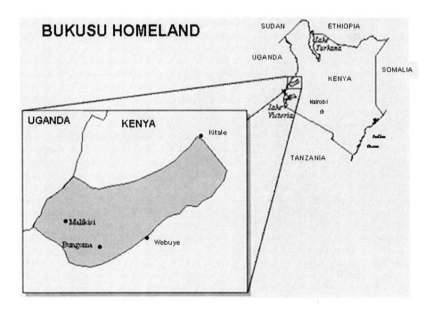

BUKUSU HOMELAND

PART I

THE CONTEXT OF DIALOGUE:
THE BABUKUSU OF WESTERN KENYA

CHAPTER 1

•◆•

THE GEOGRAPHY AND ANCESTRY OF THE BUKUSU

To appreciate the Bukusu people today, one must consider the general background of the geography where they reside, as well as several important components of their culture, including:

- Their language and the role of oral literature
- How their rites of passage are organized
- The hierarchy of their leadership
- The structure of their burial practices

The Bukusu people live largely in Kenya's Western Province.[3] They live within a triangle formed by three great features of this geographically exuberant part of the continent—Lake Victoria, an enormous body of fresh water; the Rift Valley, an ancient but still disruptive catastrophe to the earth's surface that runs from Palestine to southern Africa; and Mount Elgon on the Kenya-Uganda border.

Lake Victoria or Victoria Nyanza (also known as Ukerewe, Nalubaale, Sango, or Lolwe) is 68,800 square kilometers (26,563 square miles), of which Kenya claims only 3,785 square kilometers (1,461 miles). Africa's largest lake and the largest tropical lake in the world, Victoria Nyanza is the world's second largest freshwater lake and the third largest of all the lakes in the world, exceeded in size only by Russia's Caspian Sea and North America's Lake Superior.[4] Lake Victoria creates a unique local climate. As the water evaporates, the forming clouds meet the cold air streaming from the mountain ramparts that surround the lake, resulting in heavy rainfall, particularly on its eastern shores and on Mount Elgon.

Ethnically, the Luo people on the lakeshore lowlands; the Luhyia on the sugar lands north of Kisumu; and the Gusii people in the fertile Kisii hills, southeast of Kisumu, constitute the densely populated region.

Kenya, an independent republic on the coast of the Indian Ocean, forms part of the east African region. Sudan and Ethiopia bound it to the north, Somalia to the east, Tanzania to the south, and Uganda and Lake Victoria to the west.

Kenya's population comprises many ethnic groups, cultures, religions, and languages. According to archeological findings for Kenya today, human history started 2.5 million years ago. Presently, over forty million people live in Kenya, distributed very unevenly throughout the country's geography, as the northern and northeastern regions are arid and barely hospitable for human settlement.[5] Most Kenyans dwell in the highlands, where the climate is mild. The urban populations constitute nearly 25 percent of the nation and are concentrated in a few large cities. The rural population is confined to the fertile areas sustained by agriculture. The unemployment rate is 40 percent.[6] Kenya's human diversity is a positive resource, but it also has been a source of conflict, as was observed during 2007 and early 2008 in the aftermath of the country's presidential election.

Despite leadership's efforts to inspire Kenyans, the idea of a united people with a common destiny has not been popularly acceptable. The truth is that, for Kenyans, as for the people of several other African countries, "unified" applies first to one's own group before it can be applied to a nation. Many Kenyans, especially those who have not had the privilege of receiving formal education, do not readily understand the concept of a nation-state. To illustrate, an arbitrarily chosen border split the Maasai land between Kenya and Tanzania more than one hundred years ago. The imaginary line of that border resulted in violence against the Maasai people, tearing their lands asunder. However, their collective memory retained and still retains the notion of "one people" alive in spirit and in determination. I here remind the reader of what it means for traditional peoples who live in a time reference that maintains them in the imminent now. The notion of the past is forever present with the Maasai people. In critical moments, the family stands on the experience of the past.[7] Thus, the Maasai of Kenya find it difficult to understand why an imaginary line impedes the way to their cousins, the Maasai of Tanzania. This is why, their thinking goes, you should never trust a straight line on a map, as it was probably put there with a ruler by someone from far away and for his own gain, not taking anything else into consideration.[8] Is it any wonder, then, that so many of Africa's traditional peoples, as a result of the insensitivities of colonization, still seem to lie bleeding, having been clawed by those rampant lions symbolized in the heraldries of the crowned regents of Europe's Holy Roman Empire, even as that empire fell away?

The beginning of Kenya's history as a modern-era political entity came with the region's inclusion in the occupation of the British Empire in the late nineteenth century. Cultural regions within Kenya were established as a British protectorate. By 1920, Kenya had been made a full colony.[9] The name *Kenya* comes from a mountain peak in the central highlands that the *Kikuyu* people[10] called *Kirinyaga*, which means the "Mountain of Whiteness," and which is now commonly known as Mount Kenya. With its perennial mantle of snow, the mountain traditionally is revered as home to the omnipotent deity, *Ngai*. The Supreme Being is the source older than any time reference imaginable, said to be "dreamtime" or "time before time"—that is, the source from which the imminent now of life ever flows back to deity itself.

Kenya is a cultural microcosm of all Africa. People from many parts of the continent have been migrating to Kenya for centuries, all of them bringing distinctive features of their own cultures and languages to create a colorful mosaic of humanity. Three distinct language groups are found in present-day Kenya—the Bantu,[11] the Cushitic,[12] and the Nilotic.[13]

Paradoxically, the smallest group, the Cushitic-speaking Kenyans, occupy the largest area. These nomads of the north, who roam over almost half the nation, make up only 3 percent of Kenya's total population. The remaining 97 percent of Kenyans are Bantu- and Nilotic-speaking groups. The remainder speaks Cushitic languages. These three languages bind together the whole nation, comprised of more than forty different ethnic groups.

All those peoples who migrated to Kenya over the last four thousand years have assimilated something of the culture of those who were already there and have affected that culture with their own in a process of mutual influence going back nearly to the earliest *Homo sapiens*.[14] Over the centuries before the arrival of Europeans, three great migrations moved into the area now defined as Kenya—the largely, but not exclusively, agricultural Bantu; the pastoral Cushitic speakers; and the pastoral-agricultural Nilotic people. The small groups of hunter-gatherers who lived in this then sparsely populated region were enveloped as the conflicting tides of people ebbed and flowed, leaving eddies and whirlpools of their intermingling that comprise today's cultures.

By the time of colonial rule, the ethnic groups were given distinct and rigid boundaries by European administrators, who were too ready to separate them by "tribe." The word *tribe,* as defined by P. H. Gulliver, professor of African anthropology at the University of London, means "any group ... distinguished by its members on the basis of cultural-regional criteria." Linguistic and anthropological studies continue to reveal that such European presumptions have been far from true.[15]

The resultant population spectrum includes some minorities, such as Indians, Arabs, and Europeans. This is the reason Kenyans speak more than one language. The native tongues persist, but Kiswahili is the common language for all of east and central Africa. Kiswahili is a mixture of Bantu, Arabic, Portuguese, Spanish, Hindi, English, and German that developed as a *lingua franca* for trade between the different peoples. The word *Swahili* was used by early Arab visitors to the coast and means "the coast." Ultimately, Swahili came to be applied to the people of the coast and to the language itself.

To demonstrate the contribution of others to the Swahili culture, take the Swahili words for the numbers one through ten, respectively: They are *moja, mbili, tatu, nne, tano, sita, saba, nane, tisa,* and *kumi,* all of which stem from the Arabic language. The Swahili also absorbed words from the Portuguese, who controlled the Swahili coastal towns between AD 1500 and AD 1700.[16] Examples of the words that the Swahili language absorbed from the Portuguese include *leso* or *kanga* for a kind of cloth; *meza* for table; *geresa* for prison; and *pesa* for peso, or money. The Swahili language also borrowed some words from the languages of the later English and German colonials on the east African coast. Swahiliized English words include *baiskeli* for bicycle, *basi* for bus, *penseli* for pencil, *mashine* for machine, and *koti* for coat. Swahiliized German words include *shule* for school and *hela* for German coin.

Swahili is the language for the people of the east African coast. Longtime interaction with other people bordering the Indian Ocean spread the Kiswahili language to more distant places, such as the islands of Comoro, Seychelles, and Madagascar, and even farther beyond to South Africa, Oman, Yemen, and the United Arab Emirates.

Trade and migration from the Swahili coast during the nineteenth century helped to spread the language to the interior, particularly in Tanzania and Kenya. It also reached Somalia, Uganda, Rwanda, Burundi, Congo, the Central African Republic, and Mozambique. Christian missionaries had to learn Kiswahili as a means of social communication to spread the Gospel in east Africa. In this way, the missionaries also helped to spread the Kiswahili language. In fact, Dr. Johann Krapf, a German Anglican missionary in east Africa, as well as an explorer, a linguist, and a traveler, prepared the first Kiswahili-English dictionary.

Throughout colonial times, colonizers used Kiswahili for communication with the local inhabitants. The colonial administrators pioneered the effort to standardize the Kiswahili language. The Zanzibar archipelago was the epicenter of culture and commerce. Therefore, the colonial administrators selected the dialect of the Zanzibar town, Unguja, as the standardized Swahili. The Unguja dialect (*Kiunguja*) was adopted for all formal communication in schools, mass media, books, and other publications. Now, Kiswahili is the most widely spoken language in East Africa, as is recognized by many world institutions. It is one of the languages featured on the BBC, Radio Cairo, Voice of America, Radio

Deutschewelle, Radio Moscow International, Radio Japan International, Radio China International, Radio Sudan, and Radio South Africa. The Kiswahili language is also making its presence known in the world of song, theater, movies, and television programs. For example, the lyric for the song entitled "Liberian Girl" by Michael Jackson contains the Kiswahili phrase, *"Nakupenda, pia nakutaka mpenzi we!"* (I love you, and I want you, my dear!). The celebrated Disney movie *The Lion King* features several Kiswahili words, including *simba* (lion) and *rafiki* (friend) as the names of the characters. The Kiswahili phrase *hakuna matata* (no troubles, or no problems) also appeared in the movie.

In Kenya, Kiswahili is an official language that serves as the communication link among Kenya's many ethnic groups. Currently, Kiswahili is playing an increasingly vital role in the daily commercial, political, cultural, and social life of the region at every level of society. Kiswahili has always been an important language among the military and the police; however, English is also an official language of Kenya, a remnant of British imperialistic nationalism (more politely called "colonial rule"), and continues to be the key to one's social advantage today.[17]

Western scholars often divide Kenya's population into indigenous ethnic and language groups.[18] By percentage of the total population, these are the Kikuyu (22 percent); the Luhyia (14 percent); the Luo (13 percent); the Kalenjin (12 percent); the Kamba (11 percent); the Kisii (6 percent); the Meru (6 percent); other Africans (15 percent); and non-African Asians, Europeans, and Arabs (1 percent).[19] A large portion of the country (60 percent) is arid and semiarid, inhabited by people whose livelihood is derived solely from small, pastorally based income. These peoples include the Turkana, Rendile, El Molo, Pokomo, Borana, Maasai, Pokot, Somali, Endo-Marakwet, Samburu, and Oromo (Galla).

Western scholars also will divide the population based on religious affiliation: Protestants, together with Anglicans constitute 38 percent of the population; Roman Catholics, 28 percent; those following indigenous beliefs, 26 percent; Muslims, 6 percent; and others, 2 percent.[20]

Whether referring to culture or religion, these statistics assume that such identity categories are mutually exclusive. The reality is that indigenous religions and indigenous cultures are not easily distinguished as exclusive from one another. Mbiti affirms: "Religion permeates into all the departments of life so fully that it is not easy or possible always to isolate it."[21] Mbiti continues, "Because traditional religions permeate all the departments of life, there is no formal distinction between the sacred and the secular, between the religious and the non-religious, between the spiritual and the material areas of life."[22]

In the African understanding, the world is not fragmented but remains whole as a symbolic paradigm of the sacred. There is no perceived division between the physical and the spiritual. Because a person can think it, so it can be. The physical can indeed be a channel for the spiritual, as opposed to something "corrupt" that stands in opposition to it. Divine worship, therefore, would not be regarded as an activity one should separate or isolate from other activities. Life, as lived, is a sacred "activity" in and of itself. One worships as one breathes.[23] Africans who follow Islam or Christianity will often retain beliefs and practices from an indigenous African religious tradition. It is not unusual for an African Christian to participate in a Christian ritual by going to church on Sunday and then participate in an African religious ritual later on. African people throughout the world have a worldview that is conceived as a universal oneness. In other words, African worldview is "holistic." The term *holistic* here refers to a conviction that there exists a fundamental interconnectedness of all things in the universe. Indeed, there is an interconnectedness of all things that compose the universe. The African cosmos is like a spider's web; its least element cannot be touched without making the whole of it shake. Everything is connected and interdependent. "This interconnectedness," French social psychologist, Erny Pierre explains, "is conceived as a kind of 'vitalism' or life force which pervades all of nature: rocks, trees, lower animals, the heavens, the earth, the rivers, and particularly man, who is a vessel for this oneness which permeates and infuses all that is."[24]

With that understood, let's begin by taking a brief look at the interactions between the Bukusu people and the social situations in the modern Kenyan state.

As noted earlier, *Babukusu* is the plural and refers to the entire cultural nation of more than several Bukusu peoples. The word *Lubukusu* means the language that the Bukusu people speak.

The *Abaluhyia* is a political designation for an even larger umbrella group, of which the Bukusu are a subset. The Abaluhyia is comprised of seventeen different groups, or subnations, that speak four Luhyia dialects: Lubukusu, Luwanga, Lulogoli, and Lunyala. The diversity of pronunciations and intonations—the lexical vanity even—among Luhyia dialects is accounted for by the common factors accompanying their emergence. The differences that distinguish each cultural group and its language are the result of unique characteristics acquired in different places and at different times in history, and expectedly so, since these small units were ethically and particularly inwardly focused.

Their mythical national ancestor, *Mubukusu*, is said to have lived at a place called Embai in Karamoja, which is in present-day Uganda. Under the pressure of the Teso people, who were then his enemies, Mubukusu and his sons were forced to migrate in a southerly direction, settling down again somewhere to the east of Mount Elgon. Upon their arrival, the Babukusu found that the country was practically uninhabited, with the exception of such minor peoples as the Ng'oma, Lago, and El Kony. The Babukusu occupied the location. Their only threat was from the Maasai, who occasionally came from the east to raid their villages and steal their cattle. Today, the Babukusu inhabit the Bungoma district of the Western Province of Kenya, which is bordered by the Kakamega and Vihiga districts in the east, Mount Elgon in the west, the Transzoia district in the north, and the Busia and Amagoro districts in the south.

The Bukusu nation is made up of many clans. Dutch anthropologist Jan de Wolf provides a definition of the word *clan* that is useful in describing the Babukusu people: "It is a social unit, which consists of all the patrilineal descendants of a common ancestor who do not marry each other."[25] All members of Bukusu clans speak the same language and share one culture. Both the mother's and the father's clan membership socially defines each Bukusu child or adult; however, traditionally, the adult male lives in the father's clan village.

The Bukusu people live 250 miles northwest of Nairobi. Their homeland is abundantly blessed with many rivers and streams that nourish the rich grassland. The land is fertile and conducive to agricultural use. In the early years of the twentieth century, the Babukusu lived on millet and small livestock. Now they grow corn, beans, tomatoes, potatoes, and a mixture of green vegetables for food as well. They grow coffee, sugarcane, and tobacco for cash. They also have the typical livestock of peasant farmers—cattle, goats, sheep, and poultry.

For a visitor traveling to the homelands of the Bukusu people, the scenery in the Rift Valley is breathtaking. The approach via road or rail from Nairobi winds gently up through the highlands and suddenly approaches the edge of the Great Rift Valley, which drops about six thousand feet to a ribbon in the Rift Valley floor below.[26] Looking at the floor of the Rift Valley from the escarpments, one sees that the scenery reflects a typical African savannah of tropical character, with numerous umbrella-shaped acacias, aloes, and wild figs growing in clusters among grasslands inhabited by elephants, lions, giraffes, zebras, hyenas, and many other large mammals. A sense of human presence emerges as the Bukusu *kraals*, or cattle enclosures fenced by thorn bushes, come into view. Herds of cattle graze on the sparse pastures. The scanty banana groves, the corn and millet fields, seem barely arable from a distance, not revealing that the greater part of the Bukusu homeland on the edge of the Rift Valley is one of the most fertile and economically advanced regions of Kenya.

The road requires one's full attention. It is on the narrow paths that frequently cross the winding roads traveled by hundreds of people, mostly women and children. Some will be chewing pieces of sugarcane while walking down the road to the local markets, carrying on their heads or backs produce such as maize, sugarcane, and bananas. Women form a long trail, water pots balanced on their heads; they adjust the babies strapped to their backs and set out for home, into the setting sun, toward the thin smoke plumes of the villages.

Women maintain the water supply for their homes and for their extended families. They also carry firewood, the most important source of domestic energy for the family, sometimes trekking several miles to collect it. At night in the village, the villagers often dance around the campfire, and sometimes this develops into a trance, one of the principal elements of Babukusu spirituality. As the people circle the fire, one of them eventually falls into a trance. In this altered state of consciousness, the Bukusu people believe they can cure the sick and communicate with the dead and absent relatives. Numerous herds of goats, sheep, and cattle graze on either side of the road, and now and then these animals awkwardly dart in front of a car while the herd boys run for cover or just look on passively from a safe distance.

The roads meander over the hills and through the flat-bottomed valleys, going through a lush, beautiful land of gardens near Webuye Falls, traditionally known as *Mwikhupo*. It is one of the most densely populated regions of Kenya. The majority of Bukusu huts, with their low, circular mud walls and their peaked straw roofs, still look exactly as they did in 1883 to explorer Joseph Thompson, the first European to visit the district.[27]

Juxtaposed with this rural simplicity are numerous indications that the Bukusu homeland has undergone some great changes. Passing through Bukusu villages, one spies a red brick house with a thatched grass or corrugated iron sheet roof standing conspicuously among the mud huts. It likely belongs to a teacher, trader, chief, successful local farmer, or *matatu* owner (one who owns a "three-penny taxi").[28] Pastures and homesteads are fenced with barbed wire and "No Trespassing" signs, signifying that the owner is adopting a more European or American attitude toward private land ownership. At the crossroads are shops, stores (*dukas*), and kiosks, owned by enterprising Bukusu men and women who have learned trading skills from Asian or Arab traders. They sell cigarettes, matches, kerosene, soap, sugar, candles, salt, safety pins, thread, and the like.

Farther on, toward the former European settlements of Kitale and Eldoret, the road turns off in a westerly direction through Bukusu country along the foothills of Mount Elgon, or *Mount Masaba*, as the Babukusu call it.[29] The eighth highest mountain in Africa and the third greatest volcanic peak of east Africa, after Mt. Kilimanjaro and Mt. Kenya respectively, this mountain dominates the skyline of the Kenya-Uganda border. In addition,

Mount Elgon has the largest base area of any freestanding volcano in the world.[30]

Although Mount Elgon is a scant fifty miles from the equator, it has snow upon its fourteen thousand-foot high crater wall during cool weather. The climate of Mount Elgon shows a bimodal pattern of rainfall, with the wettest months being May, June, and July. The forest zone of the slopes of Mount Elgon receives maximum rainfall, important to the mountain's role as a water tower for several million people living around it.[31] The Bukusu people share this benefit.

In the rainforest that covers the vast slopes of this enormous volcano, one can find many of Africa's animals, from the common elephants, buffaloes, bushbucks, leopards, monkeys, hyraxes, and antelopes, to the rare and shy pangolin. According to the Bukusu people, *Mount Masaba* is the sacred home of God.

To understand and appreciate Bukusu people and their homelands, it is crucial to analyze the pressures operative in their interactions with others— that is, to understand the dynamics of their neighborhood relationships. The Bukusu are one of the seventeen Kenyan subtribes of the Luhyia Bantu language and cultural group of east Africa. The neighbors of the Bukusu people are Banyore, Gisu (in Uganda), Idakho, Isukha, Kabras, Khayo, Kisa, Manyala, Marachi, Nandi (Kalenjin), Saamia, Tachoni, Teso, Tiriki, Tura, Wanga, and Watsotso; each speaks a different dialect.

However, newfangled challenges of neighborliness and relationships keep multiplying. How can one deal with these new relationships in a way that preserves the integrity of the communities? Good neighbors are still good neighbors, and long-term relationships are as important today as they were many years past. Some refer to the old saying, "Good fences make good neighbors." Good neighbors are cultivated just like the crops we grow. No matter where you farm or what you grow or raise, good neighbors make all the hard work infinitely more enjoyable. You can't put a price tag on the feeling of being part of a community. That's what rural community life is all about. Long-standing relationships are worth far more than the money that changes hands. If we cultivate our neighbors and work hard to stay in touch with them, we'll benefit, they'll benefit, and ultimately—since every thread in the fabric of our community is important—we all benefit. There is a Quaker saying: "To have a friend, be one." So it is for the Bukusu: To have good neighbors, they must be good neighbors themselves.

In Africa, streams, springs, and watering holes are considered to belong to the area, rather than to the individual who claims to own the surrounding land, and all may use them freely. Similarly, rights to fishing, although it is of little economic importance in most areas, are held collectively. In addition, neighbors usually graze their cattle over fallow fields and along the verges of paths and may collect thatching grass and firewood from the same areas. As these economic considerations indicate, the emphasis in neighborly relationship is on friendship and mutual assistance.

Local neighbors, as well as kinsmen and women, recognize the important rites of passage of the individual, bringing small gifts at birth, circumcision, marriage, death, and even after. An example widely practiced is that of setting a portion of an evening meal aside for the ancestors, who spiritually enjoy the meal with the family. Yet the very intensity of a relationship between neighbors can go awry and put distance between them. In a neighborly setting, disputes among close relatives can occur over the distribution of land and cattle, as well as over the exact boundaries of adjacent plots. Conflict can also arise when the cattle break loose from their ropes and ravage a neighbor's field.

A number of different indigenous groups border the Babukusu. The Kalenjin people live on the northern and eastern slopes of Mt. Elgon, on the Ugandan border.[32] The Kalenjin are sometimes referred to as the "Elgon Maasai," since they were the original occupants of the foothills of Mount Elgon. The Kalenjin are very proud of their customs of cultural identity, including the custom of female circumcision, which distinguishes them from their neighbors.

To the northwest of the Bukusu homelands are the *Gishu*. The Gishu inhabit the western and southern halves of Mount Elgon. However, they have a close cultural tie to the Bukusu people. The present distinction between the two peoples appears to have developed as a result of the partitioning of the clans by the British colonial administration when they established a border between Uganda and Kenya in 1904.[33]

In the eastern part of the Bukusu homelands, along the upper reaches of the Nzoia River, live the Tachoni, a small nation that already maintained close relationship with the Babukusu in pre-colonial days. The Tachoni account for their origins as a people suggests that their ancestors emigrated from Egypt. They speak a Luhyia dialect that is similar to the one spoken by the Babukusu. Unlike the Bukusu people, the Tachoni perform both male and female circumcision rite.

To the west of Bukusulands live the Nilotic Teso. A distinguishing characteristic of the Teso is their removal of the two front teeth of the lower jaw in both men and women. The ritual operation is performed at age fourteen. The teeth are knocked out with an axe struck against a piece of wood held behind the teeth, or extracted with a hooked iron implement designed for the purpose. The Teso people of Kenya are among the few Kenyan tribes that do not traditionally circumcise their males as an initiation to manhood. Instead, in Teso traditions, initiation traditionally involved the removal of six front teeth—three each from the upper and lower jaws. The performing of this ritual served both an aesthetic purpose and as a rite of passage. Records kept of the prevalence of the tribal custom of extracting lower central incisors indicate that this practice is rapidly dying out.

To the south of Bukusuland, along the middle reaches of the Nzoia River, live the Wanga people, whose leader was Nabongo Mumia. Nabongo is one of the most influential kings in the history of east Africa, coming after the Baganda kings of Uganda. The Wanga people claim that their earliest ancestors lived in west Africa. Gideon S. Were, former historian at the University of Nairobi, observes, "The distinguishing factor of the Wanga is the ritual killing of their elderly *nabongo* [king], wrapping the corpse of the dead nabongo in a newly killed bull's hide."[34] The Wanga kings are not allowed to die a natural death. Should the Wanga king become too old to rule or should he fall sick beyond recovery, he is strangled by the *wachero* (clan elders) using a rope.

To the south of the Bukusu homelands are the Kabras. They claim to have come from the west. The Kabras appear to be closely related to the Tachoni, with whom they frequently intermarry. Their languages are very similar. The Kabras also share cultural traditions and beliefs with the Bukusu people; for example. the manner in which they perform male circumcision rites is similar.

The Khayo, Marach, and Holo, who live to the southwest of Bukusuland, claim to have come from the Soga area in Uganda. The Khayo have since mixed significantly with their northern neighbors, the Nilotic Mia, or Teso.

The Logoli people to the south of Bukusu territory say that they came from south of Lake Victoria. They live in the Vihiga district, in the western province of Kenya.

To the south and southwest of the Bukusu homelands live other Luhyia peoples; these include the Tiriki, Banyala, Bachocho, Banyore, Bakisa, Bamarama, Idakho, and Isukha inhabit the Kakamega district of western Kenya. The regional area of these groups, where the land rises to about five thousand feet, is extremely beautiful. It is the "evergreen" region of Kenya.

CHAPTER 2

•—•

THE NEED FOR BUKUSU CULTURAL
SENSITIVITY WITH NEIGHBORS

B y 1895, colonization had forced tribes in Africa to close in on each other's lands. In the northwest, near the town of Kimilili, the Kalenjin had their primary homeland. The Babukusu were forced to come live among them. In this area of Mount Elgon, relations between the Babukusu and the Kalenjin people are still unsettled over land ownership. At one time, the Kalenjin referred to the Bukusu people as *kitosh*, or "mean-spirited people" or simply "enemies," because the Bukusu methods of fighting were ruthless.[35] The Bukusu considered *kitosh* to be a serious insult. After bitter battles and great losses, a third party, the colonial British government, stepped in and convinced both sides to drop the issue of *kitosh*. Out of that situation appears the concept of a third party to a dialoguing between two opposing forces. Here was the source of what these peoples would take as their own principle for conflict resolution; even though the principle of applying congenial dialogue, even with one's enemy, was already known to them within their own tradition, the notion that a third party could ensure the success of the dialogue process was added.

In contrast, the Tachoni and the Gishu have historically gotten along well with the Babukusu. Jan de Wolf, as research assistant to Dr. Günter Wagner, reported that the Bukusu regard the Gishu, Tachoni, Kabras, and

Nyala as friendly neighbors. These groups speak a Luhyia dialect, which is not very different from the one spoken by the Bukusu. These groups maintain regular marriage relations with the Bukusu people, even though the Bukusu rule or custom stipulates that one marries within the same group (Bukusu), though not within the same clan.[36]

The Babukusu looked upon the Teso, Wanga, and Khayo as their traditional enemies.[37] In the case of such long-standing adversaries, it was customary to marry only women from adversarial clans who had been captured as children during war and who had then been brought up under customary Bukusu ways of life. This was traditionally the only exception that allowed Bukusu people to marry outside the tribe. This custom no longer applies. According to this understanding, when circumstances change the sociopolitical landscape, any contemporary culture will evolve. But how can this evolution most equitably be guided?

In his essay, "National Liberation and Culture," Amilcar Cabral, the Guinean revolutionary leader and scholar of sociology, writes: "Culture is simultaneously the fruit of a people's history and a determinant of history, by the positive or the negative influence which it exerts on the evolution of relationships between man and his environment, among men or groups of men within a society, as well as among different societies."[38] Africa's cultures are incredibly instructive because they are so complementarily diverse. Every African country is a mix of tribes, each with its own unique language and culture. Countries as small as Uganda may be home to more than thirty tribes. Much of Africa's cultural activity centers on the family and the ethnic group. Art, music, and oral tradition serve to reinforce existing religious and social patterns as immutable.

The notion of a Luhyia culture may sound rather improbable, if not ridiculous: How can a culture so diverse exist? The purpose of this study is to affirm that ethnicities and other forms of cultural differences among such people as Luhyia of western Kenya do coexist. The Luhyia people, through their long traditions of managing their ethnic diversities, have developed a superculture that brooks all diversities by reaching understandings through dialoguing; the result, a common unity—that is, community.

To understand the study of any culture, it is necessary to define the terms *culture*, *ethnicity*, and *culture of diversity* so as to minimize any ambiguity among them and to realize transparency and goodwill as demonstrated in dialoguing about them.

According to Constancio Nakuma, professor of Romance and Asian languages at the University of Tennessee, Knoxville, "The term *culture* is generally used to denote a dynamic process of social organization, marked by a collective effort of members to survive and prosper in their total environment."[39] Therefore, culture is first and foremost a continuous process that must be experienced personally. Professor Nakuma's experiential view of culture implies that much of the cultural experience is essentially of a subliminal nature, which would explain why it is difficult to describe culture with any degree of precision.[40]

Nakuma goes on to explain the concept of culture as consisting of all the mentally preserved "snapshots" of that process that inform the current process and shape evolution. Snapshots fall into the category of elements that make up the cultural heritage of a people.[41] The elements of culture of which members are generally conscious usually include rituals, which are behavioral patterns classified as either acceptable or unacceptable. For example, among the Bukusu people, marriage within the same clan is regarded as incestuous and unthinkable, while among the Somali and Arab communities, marriage between relatives is acceptable.

John S. Mbiti, in observing the elements of culture that a society seeks to impart to its members through education, asserts, "In African societies, the birth of a child is a process which begins long before the child's arrival in this world and continues long thereafter. It is not a single event, which can be recorded on a particular date. Nature brings the child into the world, but society creates a child into a social being; a corporate person."[42]

David Cohen, professor of anthropology at the University of California, Berkeley, affirms, "To become acknowledged as responsible members of society, young people need to understand where childhood ends and where adulthood begins and what their society expects of them."[43] The initiation of the young is one of the key moments in the rhythm of individual life, which is also the rhythm of the corporate group, of which the individual is a part. A rite of passage that marks a time when a person reaches a new and significant change in his or her life is something that nearly all societies recognize and often hold ceremonies to commemorate. These ceremonies are held to observe a person's entry into a new stage of life and can be anything from a high school graduation ceremony to a birthday party to a funeral. Most rites help people to understand their new roles in society. They can also help others learn to treat people who have experienced certain rites of passage in new ways.

For the Bukusu people, the most effective place for the initiation of the young is the wilderness. It is a neutral place that is detached from the areas with which the young person is familiar, and it is a place that provides the necessary challenges or adventures to promote personal growth. In the wild, initiates learn many things, including matters relevant to sexual life, marriage, procreation, and family responsibilities. The act of rejoining with their families after initiation represents their rebirth, or reintegration.

How does one describe a people? Obviously, we do not use terms like *red* or *yellow*, and there has been some debate about whether *black* is acceptable. Along the same lines, there has been discussion as to whether *white* is or should be more acceptable than other color designations. Obviously, having high regard for each person on his or her own merits, regardless of color, is most acceptable. Cultural identification is more important than what one does as an individual. And when we focus specifically on questions of "ethnicity," we take measure of a person all the way from the individual self to his or her role as a member of the community, with the emphasis on community. Ethnicity, therefore, denotes a group of individuals who consider themselves, and/or are considered by others, to share common characteristics that differentiate them from other collectives within a society. Ethnic groups develop distinct cultural behaviors, and they can be identifiable in terms of religion, politics, occupation, and language. Because ethnicity is based on cultural differences, it is social in nature. Therefore, ethnicity refers to the *perception of shared heritage*. An ethnic group is, in essence, a self, and on the other hand, a perceived community of people who believe that they share a common tradition that their neighbors do not share. For example, male circumcision and the process that goes with it are distinct among the Bukusu community; their neighbors do not fully share it.

In addition, ethnic groups tend to be defined on the basis of communal interests rather than on the basis of individual interests. For example, membership in the Bukusu community can be construed as membership in an ethnic group whose values include religion, the practice of circumcision, and other lesser values. The vast continent of Africa is so rich and diverse in its cultures that there exist many different cultures not only from one country to the next but within each individual country.

CHAPTER 3

•◆•

BABUKUSU SYMBOLIC IDENTITY:
THE THIGH OF AN ELEPHANT

The Babukusu have come to classify themselves figuratively as "Thigh of an Elephant." The thigh of an elephant is highly revered for its strength and power. This metaphor is used to distinguish the Babukusu cultural identity from that of other Kenyan cultural groups. According to the Bukusu historian Makila, the thigh of an elephant symbolizes the common destiny and solidarity of the Babukusu, based on the sociopolitical tenets of six main clan clusters that comprise the Bukusu nation—the Basilikwa, Bamalaba, Banambayi, Bamwalie, Baneala, and Bakikayi. Each one of these clans has its own historical baggage within it members' personal behaviors and memories, telling of wars; adventures; migratory movements; calamities; place names; encounters with alien ethnic groups; and, be it particularly noted, the assimilation of strangers and their customs.

Genealogical background and clan histories are summarized precisely in traditional stories, indicating what great men and women or controversial personalities in the past a particular clan boasts of, and what political and military achievements a clan may thereby claim. The history of the meaning behind "the Thigh of the Elephant," and the Bukusu people's identification with it, is made clear by the way they introduce themselves.

The names of clan clusters, like those of individual clans, are revealed through self-introduction. The Bukusu people have a typical way of introducing themselves that does not require the help of a third party. There are two stages of self-introduction—the declaration of one's personal name and ancestry (*Khukhwitacha*) and the declaration of one's clan peculiarities, making a claim to clan affiliation and origins (*Khukhwilaa*).

Strictly speaking, according to Makila, self-introduction developed to serve three purposes in Bukusu society. First, it enables people, even today, to observe the rules of exogamous marriages. So, consider how it is natural and common for boys and girls to fall in love at first sight. As a precaution against the possibility of their being too closely related, it became customary for strangers to first establish the grounds of their kinship before pursuing a love relationship. Secondly, self-introduction brings together new acquaintances at public functions, such as dancing sessions and funeral ceremonies.

The third purpose of self-introduction is to discover and identify aliens in the community. In earlier times, life was harsh and precarious. Strangers who appeared in one's territory might be spies or enemies who were intent on invading the community. Much as it was not safe for people to venture into strange lands, it was not safe for total strangers to be admitted into village society unless their origins were thoroughly known; unknown persons could not be allowed in until their ethnic origins, as well as their mission in the host community, had been established. Trepidation and suspicion were so prevalent that a stranger was always treated as an intruder until and unless he proved himself no threat through adequate self-introduction. This is not to imply that strangers have always been chased around or treated with hostility in Bukusu society. Quite the opposite is true. A code of conduct exists whereby the Babukusu are required to treat genuine strangers cordially, provided that such strangers have no destructive intentions toward the community.

By expressions of indivisible unity, courage, and bravery, "the Thigh of an Elephant" symbolized the warmth and nobility of the Babukusu. Among themselves through self-introduction, each person has always been expected to express firm loyalty to the Thigh of an Elephant. Nothing in the philosophy of the Thigh of an Elephant admits anything of elitism or racial purism. When aliens are assimilated into Bukusu society, they have two options for affiliating themselves with the group: One is to found a subclan within an existing clan, and the other is to be accepted into an existing clan.

Self-introduction is somewhat tedious. A person states his or her own name and the names of his or her parents and then declares his or her maternal and paternal ancestries (*Khukhwitacha*). By declaring his or her personal ancestry, the individual makes claims as to the past achievements of the paternal clan in the clan's collective memory (*Khukhwilaa*). Through ancestral claim, anyone may learn a person's clan and peculiarities. When a stranger declares his origins, others learn his clan group or "gate." *Khukhwitacha* and *Khukhwilaa* are terms that point to broad relationships, such as that between the clan and its nation. *Khukhwilaa* reveals clan origins in terms of cooperative achievements, migratory movements, and common ancestry. When a person makes utterances of *Khukhwilaa*, the person is considered to be doing so under oath. It is normal for a Bukusu individual to boast or swear in truth by the honor of his mother. This is to say that sons are psychologically closer to their mothers by sentimental attachment than they are to their fathers. For this reason, within the Bukusu people, a mother commands the highest degree of respect and esteem in the heart of her male child. If one wants a Bukusu person to lose control of his reason, one has only to insult his mother in his presence.

When declaring one's clan cluster, one would, for instance, say, "*Ese wa Namurwa, Papa basilikwa barwa be Mbayi,*" which means, "I am the son of Namurwa (in other words, Namurwa is my mother); my father belongs to the cluster of clans that lived in Mbayi and descended from Silikwa." Alternatively, a woman makes a declaration in the name of her father.

Self-introduction among Bukusu people is not a means of providing the audience with entertaining talk. The claims and declarations of the speaker answer several questions that a listener would otherwise have made an effort to ask, including what the speaker's affiliation is with the Thigh of an Elephant, meaning, of course, within the Bukusu fold. A Bukusu person might say publicly, "*Ese omusilikwa, omurwa we Mbayi, omunianiambi, omusila matakho, owakenda ne chikhendu sikanda, ne chimuka mumabeka,*" meaning, "I am Omusilikwa, the heroic fighter of Mbayi, who had a slim backside and walked with pride (retreated proudly), carrying bundles of raffia palms and a bunch of milk gourds over the shoulders."[44] Another example of self-introduction goes, "*Ese Omwilifuma, maande, khafumbi, khafweli, bisela, munyanye owatikitia likulu lia mwenyamwenya; owakwila ekhumbo wenyokhela libeka.*" This means, "I am Omwilifuma [clan], who created clouds and tickled the sky until it smiled. He fell on his elbow and rose by the shoulder."[45] Self-introductions among the Bukusu people are so significant that, to understand them, one has to pay close attention to what goes on in introduction dialogue.

The following section takes up the theme of the "clan," setting it in the context of Babukusu clan membership. A clan is a solidly related group of people with identity. Apart from being a member of an individual family, every Bukusu person acquires by birth his or her membership in another and larger social group, the clan. The Bukusu nation is made up of several clans, each of which is an independent group.[46] Clans in Africa are the central unit of administration, with clear political, cultural, and religious structures; they are found in rural areas, not in cities.

Although every Bukusu clan claims to have descended from the common ancestor *Mubukusu*, during self-introduction, it is important to state the exact genealogical relationship between one's clan ancestor and Mubukusu. What seems to be clearly known about Mubukusu is that he had four sons—Maina, Mango, Malaba, and Mungoma. Today, none of these four names occurs as a clan name among the Bukusu people.

Every clan distinguishes itself from other communities based on the same principles. Clan names are patronymic, based on descent from the common ancestor, which links all the members of a clan to each other. The woman in marriage does not lose her own clan identity, for the reason that her marriage is not simply a matter of personal choice. She is a politically placed representative from her clan to another, the patronymically advantageous one to strengthen the Bukusu and Babukusu sphere of influence. The status of the male clan head as a ruler is tacitly assigned to the clan's elder who, by his knowledge and understanding, displays great foresight and maturity in guiding clan matters.

A general condition for obtaining leadership in the clan is advanced age, which is socially marked by the Bukusu institution of circumcision age-sets.[47] The principle of seniority prevails in all social relations among the Bukusu people. That the Bukusu leadership is based on a clan system further reinforces the authority assigned to the wisdom of old age; for example, old age is regarded as a necessary condition for officiating at sacrifices.[48] The Bukusu traditional priest is always an elderly person.

CHAPTER 4

•◆•

WALLED VILLAGES: CLAN STRUCTURE

Among the Bukusu people, the leading elders of a clan are called *bakasa*. Originally, this was the title of the leaders of the old forts (walled villages) in which the Bukusu people lived prior to 1908.[49] The *bakasa* were generally chosen by the community from a ruling age group of that time because of their leadership qualities. These are men who talk gently and wisely and who can influence the people to listen and to return to reason when they quarrel or fight.[50] German anthropologist Günter Wagner says that the native definition of *bakasa* is "the great arbitrator," "the peacemaker," or "the wise man."[51] Skills in arbitration allow a village leader to assert his gentle influence over a cluster of neighboring villages. According to traditional wisdom, rarer skills—such as blacksmithing, telling the future, and circumcising—are a result of spirit possession. Spirit possession is, thus, a double-edged sword, whereby the possession of the individual by the particular wisdom-spirit is also the possession of the wisdom-spirit by the individual himself; the individual fails to accept the rare skill offered by means of the possession at the risk of lasting sickness of spirit. For the Babukusu nation overall, to fail to accept is unthinkable. This assumed societal position of the circumcised according to age creates a stronger framework for social well-being.

The *bakasa* were once responsible for defending the people and fortifying the villages against raiders and invaders, and the *bakasa* supervised clan members in constructing outer stone walls for military defense. Within the wall, the population felt secure from surprise attacks. Life within the fortified villages afforded a high degree of social and political cohesion. According to the Babukusu nation, each fort had its own leader, or *omukasa*, who acted as an arbitrator in the disputes among people of their villages. Here it should be explained that walled villages in those early days could be as large as several miles around. This example describes the walled village of Lumboka, the largest in memory. The *bakasa* were responsible for maintaining law and order and for the unity and continuity of the clan. Today, the Church has taken over the traditional role of the *bakasa*, especially when it comes to ritual.

Today, the Bukusu people talk of an *omukasa* as someone in the highest position who was given a special cloak of monkey skin and an ivory bracelet to wear in formal ceremony. In such a ceremony, the elder was admonished with the following words:

> This bracelet is a sign, which shows that you are now an elder who looks after people. To you, a fully grown up person and a child should be the same. You are now a respectable person. You ought to leave all childish [behavior] now. You ought to be a respectable person who looks after people without discrimination. From now on, you cannot fight with others. You cannot neglect any person, not even a child. The cloak deserves respect. You cannot wear it as an ordinary piece of clothing on just any occasion.[52]

This ceremony is still performed, but it no longer has any connection with political authority at the local level. The position has been relegated to a ceremonial post only.

Age-sets and Warfare

The Babukusu, as the congregation of all Bukusu clans, quite naturally is organized according to age-sets. At age twelve, each male youth enters his age-set group. He will be expected to request his own circumcision within the context of this subdivision. Each age-set derives its name from a historical event that has taken place during that period. It is the prerogative of the presiding elders to name each age-set. This is vaguely similar to the American tendency to give generations names such as "baby boomers," "generation X," and so forth.

It is most likely that the Bukusu people adopted age-sets and male circumcision in 1785 after the Teso nation drove them from the Tororo region, an area that is now part of Uganda. According to the Bukusu legend, the Bang'oma people, the original Kalenjin of Mount Elgon in today's Kenya, received the Bukusu as allies because the Bukusu were willing to go through the Bang'oma initiation rite of male circumcision.

The Babukusu use a revolving sequence of eight name-sets, each of which includes cohorts born within twelve years of each other. The sequence of the twelve-year age-set, "out of eight generations," comes to the sum of ninety-six years. The clan tradition is to use the first name-set, *Kolongolo*; the clan cannot use this title again as long as anyone beyond ninety-six years old is still living. It is when the group has reached the eights age-set that it recycles the names to the first age-set. Therefore, in order to be able to move into the new name-set cycle, traditionally the clan leaders had to ritually remove that elderly person, often by poisoning the person, suffocating him by making him drink blood that clots in the throat, or by sending the person on a journey from which he will not return.

Some years between the age-sets are not accounted for in this process because of unexpected situations, such as war, epidemic, or famine. For example, the age-set between 1934 and 1936 was not named. These were years of famine. The years between 1938 and 1946 were not age-set named because of World War II. And the year 1994 was not acceptable because of the deadly ethnic clashes in Kenya.

It is from these age-sets that all other clan leaders, the *bakasa*, are recruited. The recorded history of the Babukusu age-set scheme goes back only to 1900 for the naming of the first age-set. It was then that the titles of the eight age-set groups were fixed.

Each age-set shared brotherhood (*bakoki*) in common. The table below contains the names and their meanings.

Figure 4.1 The Eight Bukusu Age-sets

Name	Time Period*	Reference To
Kolongolo	1900–1910	The Bukusu community having been displaced at one time, "on account of profound want"
Kipkwamet	1912–1922	The King's African Rifles (KAR) War – At that time, Kenya was a British colony and, therefore, an ally of the British in World War I
Kananach	1924–1934	The first time the Kenya-Uganda railways passed through Bukusuland
Kipnyikeu	1936–1946	"The German war," or World War II
Nyange Lumuli	1948–1958	The time when the first airplane flew over Bukusu airspace
Maina**	1960–1970	African independence from European colonial powers.
Chuma or *Sieng'eniesi*	1972–1982	The lunar eclipse seen in this period
Sawa	1984–1994	The second liberation of Kenya: multiparty system

*Note that the missing year between age-set period represents that time or year set aside for the preparation and installation of the age group entering into warrior-hood—which is to say, the ritual of circumcision.
** This is the age-set to which I belong.

The reader ought to understand how it is for the Bukusu understanding in terms of the need, or lack thereof, for counting time; the Bukusu accounting of time is not the same as the accounting made by cultures that use Gregorian calendar years. Time, for the Bukusu people, is viewed by the event, and the passing of time is marked from event to event in the collective *memory* of the people. Whereas users of the Gregorian calendar might recall what happened last December or in the fall of 1990, the Bukusu might recall what happened right after a period of mourning for a particular leader. It would be good to keep in mind this difference.

Considering the oral tradition background, it should not be surprising that other values besides that of enumeration have been associated with numbers. So, for the Bukusu, the number *one* is not favorable, as it stands alone—not something a tribal lifestyle can easily accept. The number *two* is good, as strength is gained in numbers. *Three* is the very best, as a three-legged stool does serve best on any surface. (And, for us here in this thesis on dialoguing, three serves well as a representative for the notion of the third party.) *Four* is of lesser value to the society, in light of the conceptual advantage of the three-legged stool. Engineers can wax lyrical in agreement with this understanding. *Five* is not a desirable number, as it is really, for the Bukusu, a value extension out of the first four. In other words, if four is a lesser value, then fives is a much lesser value.

Apart from these presages, which happen by chance, people also believe in lucky or unlucky events and objects over which they can gain partial or complete control. Thus, among the Bukusu number *seven* is considered unlucky the same way Europeans consider *thirteen* unlucky number and the Japanese, the numbers *four* and *nine* because of their pronunciation.[53] On the other hand, the Bukusu consider the number *eight* to be a lucky number. If a person has seven children, he or she never admits the fact and prefers to say he or she has six or eight children. Similarly, a person would avoid possessing seven cows, seven goats, or seven objects of any sort. When Bukusu people have to refer to number *seven*, they avoid mentioning the proper numerical and instead say *babandu musafu mubi* (the bad luck number of people).[54]

As for counting people, the feeling is much like that of (1 Chronicles 21:1) which tells us that King David was enticed by Satan to count his men.

Satan knew that if he could get David's focus on the numbers instead of on God, he'd gain access to David's thoughts and trust. The prophet Joab admonishes King David to cease counting his strength in soldiers rather than depending on One—God.

The cultural bias among the Bukusu is to disallow numeration for things odd. They simply won't have anything to do with what wants to stand alone. Thus there are anomalies in trying to represent the Bukusu traditional way of counting. The reader may be experiencing some frustration in trying to understand this system. That's okay. Nevertheless, the dialogue must go on!

Circumcision among the Babukusu occurs biannually (only on the even years). Every male, on reaching puberty, has to undergo the ritual of circumcision. Those who run away are hunted down and forcefully and scornfully circumcised. The members of each age-set go through life together, sharing the same training for warfare, family roles, clan duties, and community obligations. Each age-set, in its turn, comes to power in the community and is referred to as the "warrior set" for its twelve-year term.

In this way, each of the age-set groups comes to experience leadership for their common ethnic identity in rotation. Ethnic identity here refers to a method of orderly endowment for group recognition in leadership. Carolyn Nordstrom, professor of anthropology at Notre Dame University, describes identity as going beyond individual significance, providing a group with a way in which they can be kept together in the face of natural disasters or dangers, the cruelty of fate, and the need for some compensation for what would appear as unjustified suffering by natural circumstances, if not by natural consequences.[55] In addition, age-sets are Bukusu indicators of the past, particularly the traditional past. The Bukusu people recall historic events by reference to the warrior age-set that was in power at the time the events occurred. They were the ones who were in charge and responsible. To that end, such linking of events and warrior age-sets has significant advantages in that it is possible to acquire lists of Bukusu age-sets from large numbers of clan elders in every area, as well as to codify the order in which all of the earliest age-sets were formed.

The Concept of War

Modern warfare is essentially a new phenomenon that has required a revision of the earlier traditional Bukusu life, forcing the people to adapt to the times. The changes are necessary not because of the methods and means of warfare on a single plane but because of the extent of the warfare and the sophisticated technologies used against both soldiers and civilians.

The following virtual model is an example of this complexity. Consider the sophistication of strategies required to play and win in the game of chess. The game requires anticipating all manner of moves by the opponent in advance of a move about to be made against him or her and for several consequent moves in any direction based on the opponent's next move, out to some power beyond the next—all this on a level playing field and in only two dimensions. Add now the notion that some players want to engage in a chess game in which the board is extended into the third dimension. In other words, players would be required to consider all possible moves laterally, vertically, and diagonally in a cubed space in order to play to win. This situation is representative of the phenomenon of modern warfare for the Bukusu.

Time is the only remaining tool that humankind has at its disposal for influencing the future. For this reason, dialogue, which makes maximum use of time, has to take precedence in this world, as it has long done for the Bukusu.

According to the Babukusu, war is retributive action upon another group or people for offenses such as the taking of land, murder, rape, abduction, sorcery accusations, and theft or cattle raiding. The Babukusu people view war as a demonstration of the divine power intervening on their behalf for their survival. Regarding the Bukusu concept of war, Wagner observes, "In prayers, God (*Wele*) is invoked for help and for lending success to an undertaking." While sharpening his sword or spear before going to war, a warrior prays:

I am sharpening the sword,
Wele. If you like me you may give me what you may like.
What shall fall in front of me is what you will give me
If you will not give it to me,
I cannot find it.[56]

Like other traditional peoples, the Babukusu have often resorted to warfare for defense or to gain what they thought was rightfully theirs. Warfare is a special case, because it forces people to choose sides both politically and culturally in soliciting allies. Brian Ferguson and Neil Whitehead wrote the following regarding war: "War, as well as disease, reduces numbers, and so may force previously separate peoples to come together, if only to increase the pool of marriage partners. War forces alliances: deliberate efforts to draw people together and cement their relationships. And war crystallizes oppositions: it separates peoples into clearly identifiable groups. Generally war leads to the differential survival of ethnic formation and political organizations."[57]

War is part and parcel of the political substance of a society. But in Bukusu political organization, war and peace go hand in hand. The *omukasa* can still be called upon as a conciliator, and a more renowned *omukasa* might be called upon to travel many miles from home to lend his weight to a peace settlement. In earlier times, after a settlement had been reached, an animal was sacrificed on the boundary between the two opposing sides, either at a crossroad, or, more commonly, at a nearby river or stream. The warring groups cut the animal in half across the middle, thus separating the forequarters from the hindquarters. The stomach was then extracted and the rumen mixed with blood, into which the warriors of each side dipped leafy branches. Then the warriors sprayed their rivals with the mixture by waving the branches. Sometimes, in this mock fight, local beer was also mixed with the stomach of the animal and sprayed on each other. Afterward, each side roasted its meat separately. A warrior would take a piece of meat, cut it in half with his spear, and offer it to a member of the opposing side from his spear point, and the other would reciprocate in kind. With such a mock fight, the groups reestablished their unity and restored peace with each other. Such demonstrations of cooperation and harmony were, and even now are, certainly essential for any mutual stability and development among this people. For the rest of humankind, even in this modern world of world wars, this is the essence of how people traditionally reestablish peace when the initial impetus to violence is exhausted and what should have been the peaceful resolution of conflict must take place over the wasteland of war.

Among the Babukusu, rituals define relationships between living persons and ancestors and among all living human beings and other perceived spiritual entities. Such relationships are holistic. These people define a certain order without questioning how or why something is done or used in ritual. Anthony Kwame Appiah, professor of African American studies at Harvard, observes, "The ancestors are the sources of tradition, but they are not around to ask."[58] This reiterates the idea that certain meanings and effects of ritual are intrinsic and unique to the ritual form, and further, that ritual is distinct, without alternatives. Among the Bukusu, the concept that the ritual is fixed has been passed down through their own oral transmission; for them, it is paramount that the ritual not be subjected to outside interpretation or influenced by someone's written version of the ritual that is not even in their language.

Ritual is the basic social arbiter in the Bukusu social contract; it includes morality, some concept of the sacred, the notion of the divine, and even the paradigm of creation intrinsic to ritualistic structure. I have not attended a single fund-raiser (*harambee*[59]) or social activity in Africa that did not require, by tradition, the appointment of a leader to preside over it and act as master of ceremonies. This leader conducts the function with some significant ritual opening, libation, and thanksgiving prayer for the good outcome of the event. According to the contemporary Bukusu worldview, some flexibility in modifying absolute traditional form to meet modern situations is acceptable. An easy transition has been made away from traditional, holistic ritual toward the more inclusive, simple courtesies that attend commonplace activities. Thus, the pouring of a libation, despite not having been part of the original ceremony, is not in any way contradictory to the modern Bukusu worldview.

Cultures around the world have evolved their ceremonies and rituals to constitute what the French anthropologist Arnold Van Gennep, in 1935, named "rites of passage"—"those crucial moments when we pass from one state of being to the next."[60] This quote, while specific to an individual, can also apply to the culture of any individual or group. We now turn to the dynamic process of the Babukusu construction of reality.

CHAPTER 5

•◆•

THE RITE OF MALE CIRCUMCISION AND THE ROLE OF COMMUNITY AMONG THE BUKUSU

R ites of passage are processes for crossing from childhood to a next level of maturity. For each individual, this is a perilous passage, and for traditional Babukusu, it has long been accepted that young people need a structured period of growth to guide them. In each of the local, traditional Bukusu communities, rites of passage provide a binding and supportive system that helps young people to transition from childhood to adulthood. In some Bukusu societies today, transitional rites have largely been forgotten or neglected, and this loss has resulted in a renewed desire for the traditional initiation rites. However, the most important rites of passage, including ceremonies relevant to the rite of circumcision, have continued unbroken. Recall here, time in the Bukusu mind is nonlinear and not future oriented. It is reflective of all time past and is entirely relational. All tradition in this way is paramount.

The initiation of circumcision has complex meaning for the Bukusu people. The procession of youth into adulthood is one of the most important moments in the life progression of a male, one that identifies him with the age-set of which he is a member. Moreover, what happens to the single initiate happens corporately to the parents, the relatives, the neighbors, and the spirits of the "living dead" and ancestors beyond memory.

The *living dead* are people who are physically dead but alive in the memory of those who knew them in life. Additionally, the living dead are alive in the world of the spirits. So long as the living dead are remembered, they are in the state of *personal immortality*. This personal immortality is externalized in the physical continuation of the individual through procreation, so that the children bear the traits of their parents or progenitors. From the point of view of the survivors, personal immortality is expressed or externalized in acts like respecting the departed, giving bits of food to them, pouring out libation and carrying out instructions given by the living dead either while that person was alive or when he or she appeared to the survivors in dreams. The appearance of the departed and their recognition by name may continue for up to four generations, so long as someone is alive who once knew the departed personally and by name. When, however, the last person who knew the departed also dies, then the former passes out of the horizon of the *Sasa* period, and in effect, he or she now becomes completely dead as far as family ties are concerned. He or she has sunk into the *Zamani* period.[61]

The circumcision or initiation rite holds profound symbolic meanings that are both instructed and intuited, in addition to offering kinesthetic drama and impact. Through such initiation, youths are introduced ritually to the art of communal living and a lifestyle reflected in the ritual as they withdraw from other people to live in seclusion away from the villages. As initiates, the youths go through a period of withdrawal from home, during which they receive from designated elders instructions meant only for the initiate. This is symbolic of the process of dying—of living in the spirit world and, thus, being reborn. The ritual act of returning to the family symbolizes rebirth, as it emphasizes and dramatizes that the young person is born anew and that his own awareness of self has grown measurably. The initiate is a new person.

After their return from seclusion, these young men are allowed to share full privileges and duties with the adults of the community. They inherit rights and obligations expected of them by their society. This incorporation into adult life, moreover, introduces them to the life of the spirits of the living dead with regard to ancestors, as well as to the lives of those yet to be born in the imminent now. The circumcision rite prepares the young men in matters of their own sexual life, marriage, and procreation and family obligations.

The circumcision initiation often marks the beginning of acquiring new knowledge that is otherwise not accessible.[62] This is a period of awakening to many things—a period of dawning for the young man. He learns to endure hardships, to live with others, and to obey; additionally, he learns the secrets and mysteries of male-female relationships.

In the life cycle of the Bukusu male, circumcision, together with the elaborate initiation rite that surrounds the actual surgical operation, is undoubtedly the most outstanding period.[63]

The circumcision ceremonies have four phases. The first phase consists of preparatory observances by the candidate and leads up to the ceremonial operation. In phase two, the circumcised boys wait in the hut of seclusion while their wounds are healing. The third phase consists of the candidates' separation from home. The boys venture into the bush or mountain, where they are instructed both in the theory and the practical knowledge of manhood. During this phase, they also return home, out of seclusion, for the feast of *khukhwiyalula* (literally "chicken hatching"). The fourth phase consists of the cleansing rite.

Phase I: Preparation of Rituals

Early on any morning except Sundays[64], a candidate is brought to the grave of his grandfather, where the father of the boy slaughters an animal, preferably a bull. In this way, the father contacts the ancestral spirits, making the candidate relaxed, as he believes the ancestors are attentive and approving. The shedding of blood from the animal also makes a bond between the candidate and the ancestors; the bloodshed during the physical operation binds the person to the land and, consequently, to the departed members of his family. In this case, blood symbolically unites the sky and the earth, the living and the dead.[65] Until the individual has gone through the circumcision, he is still an outsider. Once he has shed his blood, he joins the conscious stream of his people. He becomes truly one with them.

Female circumcision (clitoridectomy) is not a Bukusu practice. However, some clans are said to have practiced it. This was the case around Mount Elgon, where the neighboring Kalenjin tribes practice a form of female circumcision. Instead of a formal initiation rite, the Babukusu have a short yet effective ceremony to mark female pubescent changes. The girls undergo a prolonged washing in cold water after their first menstruation. Menstruation is described as an opportunity for women to connect to nature, particularly the moon; to recognize their own divine, life-giving ability; to exercise spiritual powers that are evidently heightened during or before menstruation; and in that way, to virtually experience death and rebirth as it occurs on a monthly basis.

The ritual of washing may also carry with it the deeper religious idea of purification from the condition of unproductive life. It is an opportunity to wash away all past hurts, relationships, and rejections. Some days later, the collective parents of the whole age-set make a big feast, after which the girls may wear full dress. This indicates that they are marriageable. Marriage and procreation are supreme, for matrimony and parenthood are necessary steps in the process of acquiring social status.[66] Should an unmarried woman die, traditionally she will receive no respect in the eyes of the society. Marriage conveys a status that is valid not only in this life but also in the hereafter. Mbiti emphasizes that "to be unmarried is [still] childhood; to be married is maturity and a blessing."[67]

As for the Bukusu man's rite of initiation, the clan elders inspect the entrails of the sacrificial animal, looking for signs by which the elders will guide him as a preventative measure. The elders point their fingers at the different parts of the intestines as they carefully murmur. They do not pronounce their findings immediately, in everybody's presence, but they make a few, rather insignificant remarks, reserving their real knowledge until later, when privately consulted by the father of the boy.

Faith in the divination of the entrails is based on the theory that the ancestral spirits have the power to produce various symptoms in the intestines of domestic animals. The immediate purpose of the inspection of the entrails is not only to learn about the expectations, but also to find out ways of avoiding misfortune and preventing disease.

The outcome of the inspection elicits one of two responses. If the signs are good, one looks into the prospect with confidence and carries on what one has contemplated. If the signs are bad, one goes to the clan diviner for consultation as to the most appropriate steps to be taken to avoid misfortune.

The Candidate at the River

At the grave of the candidate's grandfather, the initiate's body is smeared with the stomach rumen of the sacrificial animal. Henceforth, everything is calculated to infuse bravery in the candidate; the initiate is expected to show courage and is required to display total fortitude when he reaches the part of the circumcision rite when he will be under the knife, betraying no signs of fear; even what might be regarded as involuntary twitches and trembling, such as the blinking of the eyes, are evaluated negatively. The degree of pain is never underplayed; the most commonly used descriptive is *yamemea*, meaning fearsome, harsh, and terrifying.

The ritual party then escorts the candidate to the source of the closest stream of water. Procreative capacity is believed to begin at the source of the river or a natural spring. After the boy has bathed in the river, an adult person specially chosen by the elders for the courage that he displayed when he himself was circumcised covers the body of the candidate from head to toe with thick mud from the spring, which is referred to as *enuma*, "the eye of the river," leaving a free space only around the eyes and the penis. On the head, which has been shaved, he places a lump of clay about four inches high, into which he sticks a long grass called *kwaututu* that waves in the wind and makes the boy resemble a fierce warrior.

The candidate returns home naked to demonstrate that he has no status (liminality) or property of his own and, in brief, nothing that may distinguish him from his fellow neophytes. On the way home, the boy and his party must follow a different route from the one they took when they came to the river, as is the practice of warriors, who thereby mislead their enemies. From this time, the initiate is never allowed to look back. About halfway home, his father, who acts as if he is trying to dissuade the boy from facing a circumciser, meets the son. The father tests the son's courage by telling him to go back to the river, wash off the mud, and return home to his mother. The father gives his son a last chance to change his mind and save the entire clan from the disgrace that would descend upon the clan if he flinched or ran away from the circumciser's knife in the presence of the entire crowd.

Phase II: The Actual Circumcision

A qualified circumciser and his assistant perform the actual cutting of the foreskin. The assistant pulls the skin of the penis forward and the circumciser cuts it away. He goes further and cuts from the penis layer what is believed to later on develop into another top cover for the penis. The circumciser then cuts off a certain muscle, *lurandasi*, on the lower part of the penis. These three cuttings complete the physical circumcision rite. While the initiate is being circumcised, his father stands close by and encourages his son to keep strong and stand still, at the same time admonishing the circumciser to be careful with his knife. The operation is thus as critical a moment for the father and the mother as for their son, the initiate. If the son's behavior is cowardly, the father's shame is so great that he runs away from the crowd and hides in the bush. Later, he will refuse to send food to his son, and their relationship might be seriously damaged for years.

Women and children watch the performance of the operation from a distance, while the boy's mother runs into her hut and clasps the center pole, *enjeko*, with her arms and legs, as this, she believes, will help her son to keep steady. Though the operation is painful, the boy is encouraged to endure it without crying, blinking his eyes, shouting, or showing signs of weakness. There is no anesthetic and no disinfectant. If the boy does show any of these signs of fear, it is believed that his mother will die soon after and no woman will want to marry him.

Immediately after the boy has been circumcised, a girl who is in love with him rushes up from behind him and throws her arms around his hips, thereby claiming him as her future husband. This symbolism of the union to come would have been planned ahead of time. Arranged marriages have been most common in rural Africa, but a gradual change has been taking place, and today more young people are choosing their own partners. This act publicly seals the betrothal. After that, she leaves the ceremony so she will not witness the boy's eventual reaction to the pain of the cuts. The boy is then seated on a special stool and is wrapped in a piece of cloth or blanket. The community dances around him, praising his courage in various songs, shrieking with delight, and offering him gifts in the form of animals and money.

Finally, he is taken to his mother's kitchen, the source of food. Before entering, he is made to walk around the house three times. From this time, for a period of three days, the initiate is not allowed to eat with his hands. A person is chosen to feed him, such as a brother or uncle. If there is no male around to feed him, his mother or some other woman will give him food with a stick so that she does not touch his mouth or any part of his body. This ritual feeding implies that he is still a baby and not yet fully initiated into manhood. Three days after the operation, the circumciser is invited to perform the ritual of washing the initiate's hands. After this, the initiate is allowed to eat with his hands. On that day, the initiate is declared a man.

Phase III: The Seclusion

After healing, initiates go into seclusion, which serves to make them focus on what they are experiencing and doing. They sleep in the sacred grove with a bed of green leaves between them and the ground. With the exception of the elders who have coached them, no one has the right to see them during this period. Their families regularly bring them their meals, but the food is handed over to the senior age-set (the elders who participated in the earlier part of the ceremony), who act as the sole providers by which the initiates may survive.

This seclusion symbolizes the corpse in the tomb, as well as the gestating fetus in the maternal womb. Through this formation comes transformation. The candidates are expected to acquire zeal for the knowledge and wisdom of their clan. They are also encouraged to gain skills of trade, including the making of baskets, huts, and granaries. Another emphasis is on hunting and shooting, using spears, bows, and arrows. The initiates are also trained to defend their homes. Clan elders give sacred and top secret instructions of the clan that the initiate cannot discuss, not even with his parents or spouse. Candidates are also taught how to behave and to show respect for all people in general, especially women.

During the final three months of seclusion, the initiates are joined as a group by the young women, who spend a night with them. But in no case may this brief cohabitation entail sexual relations between the initiates; rather, it constitutes a school of endurance as part of the individual's apprenticeship in the mastery of the body. Parallel to this discipline, the person claims and takes ownership of his physical space, his territory.

Finally, the candidates go to the river, where they are washed. They remove the old clothes and put on new ones. This corresponds to the dressing of the infant when it comes into the world. The initiates are now known as *batembete*, meaning "the new and soft ones." They are now ready to return to their homes, where all their family members, relatives, neighbors, and friends have gathered to receive them and to drink the "beer of coming out" and share a meal together.

Whereas the rites of the first menstrual period are individual in character and take place within the family village, those of circumcision are considered collective, and the focus of the seclusion is communal growth.

Phase IV: The Cleansing Rite

The final phase of the pubescent rites is the young men's reintegration into society with a new status. This process includes some kind of celebratory ceremony publicly acknowledging the changes that have occurred in the young people. It allows for a sense of pride regarding who they have become. Parents also need to be part of the acknowledgment of the young person's new status in the society. Parents encourage the young men to continue living their lives according to their cultural traditions, while at the same time, as today's world mandates, accepting the necessity of considering flexibility.

Having come back from seclusion, the initiates experience the ritual called *sisialukho*, or "the cleansing rite." All the new initiates in the locality have to attend this event. It is an important occasion; all the villagers and even government and Church officials attend to conclude this particular process of initiation. The initiate is no longer a child but an adult ready to assume responsibilities in his community.

Traditionally, there can be no achievement of identity without initiation. According to Bukusu beliefs, without initiation, a man remains a boy, and a woman remains a girl. A Bukusu boy previously could not be considered a man if he did not pass through the customary ritual. The "uncultured" boy was always sidelined and regarded as a coward. However, for most boys today, the reverse is true; go it the traditional way, and they will be called "uncivilized" and "barbaric." There is no more vivid example of the way in which modernity has raided the African cultures than that of changes in attitude toward the Bukusu circumcision rite.

After the celebratory family communal meal that ends seclusion, the elders hand the recent initiates shields, spears, bows, and arrows. Holding these weapons as warriors in front of the community, the initiates receive rules of conduct and clan cultural values from their fathers. The father addresses the son in this manner:

My son, you have left behind your "mother's cloth" (meaning the foreskin), and now you have put on your 'father's cloth' (meaning circumcision). If you come to a house and it is closed, do not open it to enter.[68]

If you see an old man, call him father and an old woman, call her mother, and treat them as you would treat your own mother and father.

If you find him or her carrying grass, help them. If an elderly person calls you "my strength," reply, "Here I am; your strength."

If you meet elderly woman carrying water, firewood, or any other heavy item, help her as you would help your mother, and call her "mother."

Now you are a man. If you see people quarreling tell them, "Do not quarrel," and if you see them hurting each other, stop them.

Now you are a man. No longer ride on a cow or an ox! Do not dance about standing on one leg, because this is childish and a disgrace for a man.

If you see children doing bad things, report them to their parents, but do not punish them yourself.

After the father has completed his exhortations, he hands over the gourd of sour-tasting beer to his son, who takes some sips and then returns the gourd to his father. The son does not say anything in reply to the father's speech. This indicates that he is in agreement with what the father has said to him; he is now ready to share family responsibilities with his father.

Significance of Circumcision

To ask for the meaning of circumcision and the accompanying rites among the Bukusu society would be to misjudge the nature of the issue. Circumcision cannot possibly have only one meaning, but must have many, each of them determined by the point of view from which we consider these rites. First, one must examine the meaning of the actual operation of circumcision. Why do some people consider it desirable or even necessary to remove the foreskin of the penis? Here, one has to distinguish between the original motives, which many generations ago led the Bukusu people to adopt the custom, and the purpose that the operation is intended to accomplish. While originally, circumcision was an indicator of bravery, hence warrior-hood, rituals are a means for society members to communicate values and ways of living, through psychological, social, and symbolic interactions and teaching. In this document, information is largely drawn from the initiation practices of Bukusu people. This ritual is a socially significant act, resulting in the integration of the individual into the community and assurance of acceptance and respect from other community members. Initiation is an important social device in dealing with teenage years; the training and preparation provided at the initiation schools facilitates the shift from childhood behavior to the more complex behavior expected in adulthood.

Next, one must consider the symbolic meaning of the numerous rites and ceremonies and the whole system of thought into which the various ideas may be synthesized. If "religion" is the paradigm by which we define our place in the world, then the ritual is the instrument by which we interrelate and connect with it. This relationship can be defined by its underlying objectives, of which there are two main categories—*unity* and *petition and blessing*. The spiritual ritual requires the use of symbols extensively because of its inherent transcendental and metaphysical nature. Here it is hoped that the reader clearly understands that without this factoring in by some paradigm equal to what the Bukusu people have practiced, there are manifest any number of restless individuals abroad in this world who drift aimlessly through life, growing and proliferating their malaise like proverbial weeds, randomly scattered across the lands, inadvertently putting long-standing cultural values at risk. Thus spiritual ritual requires the use of symbols for maximizing the necessary benefits inherent in the transcendental and metaphysical nature of healthy societies.

Finally, one must turn to what might be called the practical meaning of circumcision—its contribution toward the working and maintenance of a healthy society. This practical meaning, again, will hardly be possible to render by a single formula. Rather, one must carefully analyze all aspects—economic, political, religious, educational, and so forth—that enter into the various phases of the circumcision rite. This functional or practical consideration is of utmost importance. The purpose of the actual operation itself is of little significance to the Bukusu, for whom the operation is only one piece of the whole initiation ceremony.

This brings us to a consideration of the paradoxical character of the Bukusu circumcision ritual. Bukusu circumcision seems designed to produce fierce men but, arguably, fierce men for whom the society today has little use. Ordeals of this kind, linked to warfare, can be seen as a form of training for tough and brave warriors. Dent Ocaya-Lakidi, editor of the *Ugandan Journal*, summarizes the evidence for this association well. About the African societal value of manly excellence, he wrote, "It was strongly connected to warfare and led the Eastern African societies to place undue emphasis on masculinity and manliness, the one to be tested sexually and the other in hot combat."[69] Ultimately, the two tests were one, and taking the Bukusu as an example, Ocaya-Lakidi elaborated, "The length of the initiation rites gave ample opportunity for gauging a man's masculinity, while the supreme pain of circumcision tested his manliness and suitability for warriorhood. That is why becoming a man meant access to physical sex and warriorhood at the same time."[70] Male gender identity linked to circumcision strongly stresses military or warfare. This emphasis is clearly heard in songs that accompany the rites, yet the warfare and raiding patterns formerly associated with circumcision are no longer relevant to the Bukusu people.

Rites and Community

It is necessary to mention several other rites of passage. As has already been indicated, life among the Bukusu people is communal. Particularly, the family and clan are the society to which a person must essentially adhere for survival. The Babukusu have an expression for clan solidarity: "If a child commits nine crimes, it bears a punishment for five." This means that, in the clan system of the Bukusu people, the result of a person's misdeeds is not borne by the person alone but by both the individual and the family or clan so affected. The guilt or pride of one person is the guilt or pride of the collective society. Responsibility rests on the individual, the family, and the clan. The individual can only say, "I am because we are; and since we are, therefore I am."

Further examples of this notion of community are found in the context of the Bukusu celebratory dramas by dance, rhythm, and song, all of which express a way of thinking, feeling, and communicating with one another mutually. In "Person and Community in African Traditional Thought," Ifeanyi Menkiti, a professor of philosophy at Wellesley College in Massachusetts and a published poet, talked about the concept of community in Africa. In contrast to Western mind-set, which focuses on the individual, community is more important and defines a person, he said, pointing to Mbiti's statement, "I am because we are, and since we are, therefore I am." A summary of Menkiti's thoughts on this matter in "Communitarianism in African Thought: Menkiti on Communitarianism" quotes Menkiti thusly: "As far as Africans are concerned, the reality of the communal world takes precedence over the reality of individual life histories. ... Just as the navel points men to umbilical linkage with generations preceding them, so also does language and its associated social rules point them to a mental commonwealth with others whose life histories encompass the past, present, and future."[71]

In commenting on the relationship between the dramatic substance of rituals and ceremonies and the religious power of humans and spirits together at these celebrations, Ogbaa Kalu, associate professor of English at Southern Connecticut University, New Haven, quotes from Chinua Achebe's 1989 novel, *Arrow of God*, "The festivals thus brought gods and men together in one crowd. It was the only assembly in Umuoro [village] in which a man might look on his right and find his neighbor and look to his left and see a god standing there.[72]

The more the community comes together in solidarity, the more power and transcendence it attains, for power flows through relationships; that is the meaning of communal solidarity. Rituals bind a community together. The phase of the pubescent rite of passage that takes place at the river characterizes what Dutch anthropologist Arnold van Gennep called "the liminal phase of rites of passage."[73] Liminality comprises separation, margin, and aggregation. Experiencing the liminal stage, that of being on the threshold of transformation, is frequently compared to death, being in the womb, invisibility, darkness, sexuality, and the wilderness.[74] The liminal phase of the Bukusu pubescent rites of passage refers to the symbolic return to the maternal womb and rebirth.

Perhaps the enduring value of all such sacred rites lies in the way that they afford optimal times for communal togetherness. The collective nature of circumcision ceremonies allows the community to engage in dialogue over divisive issues, providing a common ground for men, women, and children alike. The elemental Bukusu belief system, which is traditional and embraced by people who are willing to share the overlying Babukusu imminent now with things Muslim and Christian, results in the Bukusu practice of and desire for effective dialogue. This point appears logical when considered in light of the Bukusu tradition of peacefully hearing all things brought to the wisdom of the elder men for consensus.

The Bukusu culture is grounded in accommodation; thus the people look for the most virtuous aspects of all that they encounter. That the people are able to bear up under the complex strain of intermingling cultures demonstrates just how highly the Bukusu value the principle of dialogue. The reports of Fred Iklé and William Ury, riding on the shoulders of Martin Buber's philosophy, would persuade the onlooking world of the ultimate ability that these people display and enjoy to maintain their cultural identity while being open to the disparate influences of these religions. The Bukusu demonstrate a grace for keeping peace, even as they seek to protect their own traditional ways. The Bukusu people seem to be able to recognize within these two visiting religions the virtues that are most compatible with their traditional methods of carrying on a peaceful coexistence without a hint of violence.

For Muslims, the virtues of peaceful coexistence are equality, charity, respect, and awareness of the sacredness of human life. For Christians, the terms of Bukusu peaceful coexistence can be equated with the beatitudes, acts of charity, gifts of the Holy Spirit, and so forth.

Part I Notes

1.   The elephant's gestation period is eighteen to twenty-two months, the longest of any land animal.
2.   John Mbiti, *African Religions and Philosophy* (Nairobi: Heinemann, 1990).
3.   The homeland of the Bukusu people is located in western Kenya, north of Lake Victoria, from Kisumu to Webuye going north and south, and from Kapsabet on the east to the Ugandan border on the west. There are also large pockets of Bukusu people in Nairobi and the surrounding areas.
4.   Mohamed Amin, Duncan Willetts, and Brian Tetley, *Spectrum Guide to Kenya* (Nairobi: Camerapix Publishers International, 1989), 161.
5.   George Thomas Kurian, ed., *Encyclopedia of the Third World, fourth edition*, volume III (New York: Facts on File, 1992), 970.
6.   Ibid.
7.   The story of the Maasai people, as well as what is happening in Africa as a whole today, is the result of the last several years, when Europe dominated Africa, first through the slave trade and then via colonialism. If Africans are going to get out of the mess they are in now, the West has a duty to help them.
8.   Africa Guide.com, 1996–2011, http://www.africaguide.com/images/africa_map.gif Map of Africa.
9.   John D. Baines, Victoria Egan, and Graham Bademan, *The Encyclopedia of World Geography: A Country by Country Guide* (Santiago, California: Thunder Bay Press, 2003), 179.
10. The nation's largest ethnic group to which the first president of Kenya, Jomo Kenyatta, belonged, the Kikuyu are Bantu-speaking people.
11. The Bantu are a group of people known more as a language group than as a distinct ethnic group. The Bantu people are characterized by the word "ntu" in their language and have similar social characteristics. These people are divided into three categories: Southern, Eastern and Central; each category has its own language.
12. The Cushite peoples are those who speak languages of the Cushitic cluster in the Afro-Asiatic family. Thus these cultural groups may be of *diverse physical/racial types* and exhibit a variety of physical cultures.

13. The Nilotes live in East Africa and they are believed to have migrated from a place called Bahr-el-ghazel in southern Sudan. They are known as Nilotes because they migrated following the River Nile and its tributaries.

14. Amin, Willetts, and Tetley, *Kenya*, 77.

15. Ibid. Okot p'Bitek, former professor of anthropology at the University of Nairobi, argues, "The term tribe turns out to have no definite meaning, in that it refers to no specific unity in Africa." But this term has come to mean something very different in Africa itself. During the civil war in Nigeria, the *Igbo* [people] were frequently referred to as a tribe, and their struggle to break away from the federation was dubbed tribalism. Corrupt practices by government officers and others, such as giving employment not through merit but by kinship relations, or concentrating public utilities such as hospitals, schools, etc., in one's own home area—practices which have been known throughout history and in all corners of the world—are described as tribalism in Africa. And even the equitable distribution of national wealth, in terms of areas, has been called tribalism. In my opinion, it is misleading and confusing to analyze the social ills of Africa, which are, in any case, universal, in terms of the so-called phenomenon of tribalism. For a clear understanding of Africans' problems, it is suggested that the term *tribe* ought to be dropped from the sociological vocabulary. An even more important reason for dropping the term *tribe* is that it is an insult, generally used to refer to people living in primitive or barbaric conditions. Each time it is used, as in the sentence, "I am a Bukusu by tribe," the implication is that the speaker is a Bukusu who lives in a primitive or barbaric condition. When we read of tribal law, tribal economics, or tribal religion, Western scholars imply that the law, economics, or religions under review are those of primitive or barbaric peoples. See Okot p'Bitek, *African Religions in Western Scholarship* (Kampala: Uganda Literature Bureau, 1990), 13–15.

16. J. Spencer Trimingham, *Islam in East Africa* (Oxford: Clarendon Press, 1964), 19.

17. See Jean-Francois Bayart, *The State in Africa: The Politics of the Belly* (London: Longmann, 1993), 175.

18. Norman Miller and Roger Yeager, *Kenya: The Quest for Prosperity* (San Francisco: Westview Press, 1994), 72.

19. Kenya Government History, May 2007, http://www.worldrover.com/vital/kenya.html.

20. Ibid.

21. Mbiti, *African Religions and Philosophy*, 1.

22. Ibid, 2.

23. Timothy D. Hoare, "Some Basic Concepts in Primal Religion," http://staffjcc. net/thoare/primal.htm.

24. Pierre Erny, *Childhood and Cosmos: The Social Psychology of the Black African Child* (New York: New Perspectives, 1973).

25. Jan J. de Wolf, *Differentiation and Integration in Western Kenya: A Study of Religious Innovation and Social Change Among the Bukusu* (The Hague: Mouton, 1962), 59.

26. The Great Rift Valley is a depression extending more than 4,830 km (more than 3,000 miles) from Syria, in southwestern Asia, to Mozambique, in southeastern Africa. The valley is believed to have been formed by the sinking and tearing apart of the earth's crust along a 50 million-year-old zone of weakness. See James Wood and Alex Guth "East Africa's Great Rift Valley: A Complex Rift System," *Geology.com*, 2000–2011, http://geology.com/articles/east-africa-rift. shtml.

27. Nigel Pavitt, *Kenya: The First Explorers* (New York: St. Matthew's Press, 1989), 121–22, 131. My grandfather was one of the people who escorted Joseph Thompson as he explored the region. It is probable that European penetration into Bukusu land began with Joseph Thompson. He was the first European known to pass through on foot, and was influential in opening up the region to Europeans after his meeting with Chief Mumia at Mumias on December 23, 1883, during his exploratory trip across the present-day Western Province. Afterward, there were bloody skirmishes, mostly between the Bukusu people and the British, which came to be known as the War of Chetambe. Cf. F. E. Makila, *An Outline History of Babukusu* (Nairobi, Kenya: Kenya Literature Bureau, 1978), 229.

28. The word *matatu* refers to taxis that used to cost three ten-cent pieces. Now they cost much more, but the nickname "three-penny taxi" remains. The *matatu* is the equivalent of the *jeepney* in the Philippines.

29. Mount Elgon is an extinct volcano on the Kenya-Uganda border of east Africa. Its crater, from which rise several peaks, is five miles in diameter. The highest point has an elevation of 14,000 feet. See Harman Humphrey, *Men of Masaba* (New York: Viking Press, 1971), 9.

30. Clive Wood, Gordon Boy, and Iain Allan, *Snowcaps on the Equator: The Fabled Mountains of Kenya, Tanzania, Uganda and Zaire* (London: Bodley Head Press, 1988), chapter 3.

31. Miriam Van Heist, *Land Unit Map of Mount Elgon National Park*. IUCN technical report, unpublished.

32. The name *Kalenjin* is a kind of password recently invented that means, "I tell you," for the purpose of self-defense against non-Kalenjin groups. Kalenjin are

made up of the Sebei, Pokot, Nandi, Kipsgis, Markwet, Keiyo, and Tugen. Cf. Walter Goldschmidt, *Culture and Behavior of the Sebei: Study in Continuity and Adaptation* (Berkeley: University of California Press, 1976), 12; Robert B. Edgerton, *The Individual in Cultural Adaptation* (Berkeley: University of California Press, 1971), 81ff.

33. Suzette Herald, *Controlling Anger* (Kampala: Fountain Publishers, 1988), 18.

34. Gideon S. Were, *A History of the Abaluyia of Western Kenya* (Nairobi: East Africa Publishing House, 1967), 108.

35. Makila, *History of Babukusu* , 31. Among other evidence, one European settler, in a recent interview about the Babukusu, authenticates this view that the Babukusu used to be called *kitosh*. Some early travelers, one assumes, came here and asked the *Nandi*: "Who is south of here?" and the *Nandi* replied, "Oh, they are kitosh," which means "enemy."

36. Günter Wagner, *The Bantu of Western Kenya* (London: Oxford University Press, 1970), 393.

37. de Wolf, *Differentiation and Integration*, 1.

38. Amilcar Cabral, "National Liberation and Culture," http://www.panix. com/~lnp3/quotes/amilcar_cabral.htm).http://www.brookes.ac.uk/schools/ apm/publishing/culture/cree.html.

39. Constancio Nakuma, ed., *African Culture as a Culture of Diversity within a Multilingual Society*, http://web.utk.edu/~csms/nak97.html.

40. Ibid.

41. Ibid.

42. Mbiti, *"African Religions and Philosophy,"* 110.

43. David Cohen, ed., *The Circle of Life: Rituals from the Human Family Album* (London: Aquarian Press, 1991), 45.

44. Silikwa is one of the sons of Mubukusu (Babukusu ancestor), who founded settlements in the fertile highlands that were named after him. Silikwa clans include direct descendants of Silikwa, other Bukusu clans that lived in and defended the settlements against Barwa invaders. The Bukusu people absorbed them in past tribal wars.

45. Makila, *History of Babukusu*, 48–49. The fact that he can tickle the sky until it smiles means that he is a rainmaker. On the other hand, the Bukusu people particularly stress this point that they were heroic fighters of Mbayi and Silikwa, who, when their defenses fell, walked away proudly, carrying with them loads of milk gourds and bundles of raffia palms (a symbol of economic wealth).

46. Ibid, 67.

47. Wagner, *The Bantu of Western Kenya*, 373.

48. Ibid, 285.

49. de Wolf, *Differentiation and Integration*, 86.

50. Wagner, *The Bantu of Western Kenya*, 77.

51. Ibid, 81.

52. de Wolf, *Differentiation and Integration*, 130–31.

53. In Japanese, four is pronounced /shi/, which is the same as the Japanese word for "death." Nine is pronounced /ku/, which is the same as the Japanese word for "agony" or "torture." Many hospitals don't have rooms or even floors that include these numbers. The Japanese also dislike Friday the Thirteenth, and there are no seats with the numbers *four*, *nine*, or *thirteen* on passenger planes of the All Nippon Airways.

54. John Osogo, "Superstitions and Taboos Observed among the Luhyia," *Luhyia Culture*, http://www.luhya.net/HTML_files/taboos.html.

55. Carolyn Nordstrom, *A Different Kind of War Story* (Philadelphia: University of Pennsylvania Press, 1997) 189.

56. Wagner, *The Bantu of Western Kenya*, 171.

57. R. Brian Ferguson and Neil Whitehead, eds., *War in the Tribal Zone* (Santa Fe, NM: School of American Research Press, 1992), 14.

58. Kwame Anthony Appiah, *In My Father's House: Africa in the Philosophy of Culture* (New York: Oxford University Press, 1992), 111.

59. *Harambee* is a Kenyan tradition of community self-help events, for example, fundraising or development activities. *Harambee* literally means "all pull together" in Swahili and is also the official motto of Kenya and appears on its coat of arms. *Harambee* events may range from informal affairs lasting a few hours, in which invitations are spread by word of mouth, to formal, multiday events advertised in newspapers. These events have long been important in parts of east Africa, as ways to build and maintain communities. Following Kenya's independence in 1963, the first prime minister, and later first president of Kenya, Jomo Kenyatta adopted *Harambee* as a concept of pulling the country together to build a new nation. He encouraged communities to work together to raise funds for all sorts of local projects, pledging that the government would provide the startup costs. Under this system, wealthy individuals wishing to get into politics could donate large amounts of money to local *harambee* drives, thereby gaining legitimacy; however, such practices were never institutionalized during Kenyatta's presidency.

60. Arnold van Gennep, *The Rites of Passage* (London: Routledge, 1960), 3.

61. Mbiti, *African Religions and Philosophy*, 84.

62. Noel Q. King, *African Cosmos: Introduction to Religion in Africa* (Belmont, California: Wadsworth Publishing Company, 1986), 41–43.

63. Wagner, *The Bantu of Western Kenya*, 134-35.

64. Sunday is a day of prayer; people go to church. More than at any time in the history of Africa, people are now seeking answers to life's struggles, problems, and challenges. Natural and manmade disasters are causing more and more stress in people, and their lives are under intense pressure. Sunday is a day of consolation.

65. In the case of *likuma*, or spilling of blood, such as when a person sheds the blood of another by accident or in a fight, rather than during ceremonial circumcision, the whole community shows concern, and a chicken is ceremoniously sacrificed to appease *bimakombe*, or the spirits of the living dead, who are present on earth and angry at someone shedding another's blood. The victim is not allowed to enter the house until this ceremony is done.

66. Wagner, *The Bantu of Western Kenya*, 379.

67. Mbiti, *"African Religions and Philosophy,"* 141.

68. That is, you may be lured to have sex with the wife. This metaphor is a polite way of saying that it is a serious offense for a man to sleep with another man's wife. The language is polite because the entire community, including the children, is being addressed. The wife is referred to as a closed door.

69. Dent Ocaya-Lakidi, 1979, "Manhood, Warriorhood and Sex in Eastern Africa: Perspectives from the 19th and 20th Centuries," *Journal of Asian and African Studies*, XII: 152.

70. Ibid.

71. Ifeanyi Menkiti in Net Industries, "Communitarianism in African Thought-Menkiti On Communitarianism," http://science.jrank.org/pages/8771/ Communitarianism-in-African-Thought-Menkiti-on-Communitarianism. html#xzz1EwAtIgMB, 1994, 2011.

72. Chinua Achebe, *Arrow of God* (New York: Anchor Books, 1989), 203.

73. Victor Turner, *The Ritual Process: Structure and Anti-Structure* (New York: Aldine de Gruyter Press, 1969), 94.

74. Ibid.

PART II

THE HISTORY OF ISLAM, CHRISTIANITY, AND BUKUSU TRADITIONAL RELIGION

CHAPTER 6

•◆•

ISLAM IN AFRICA

S ubsequent to discussing the dynamics of Babukusu culture and lands, the focus now turns to the account of the encounter between Islam, Christianity, and the Bukusu traditional religion and its culture. Today's Africa is a product of the dialogue process between these three systems. The Bukusu people are heirs to all three of these traditions. Each has provided generations of the Babukusu with guidelines for daily behavior and solutions for life's challenges. All three traditions have also come into conflict with one another in their attempt to direct the lives and culture of the Bukusu people.

Islam is a worldwide faith that has unique aspects in each region or community in which it is practiced. In Bukusuland, Islam takes on the culture of the Bukusu people of western Kenya. One can hardly appreciate "Bukusu Islam" unless special attention is paid to the beliefs and practices of Islam as stipulated by the Holy Qur'an and the teachings of the Prophet Muhammad.

The Arabic word *Islam* means "submission" or "surrender to God," who, in Arabic, is called *Allah*. The word *Islam* derives its meaning from *salaam*, the Arabic word for peace. Thus, a Muslim is anyone who submits or surrenders to the will of Allah, thereby attaining peace of mind and soul, according to Islam.

Islam addresses itself to humanity's most profound nature and considers itself to be an assertion of the universal truth of all religious revelation—Allah's Oneness. The foundation of Islam is the uncompromising unity and Oneness of God, called *tawhid* in Arabic. According to Islam, Allah is beyond distinction and division and has no equal or associate. The Qur'an says this: "Allah is one, the Eternal God. He begot none, nor was he begotten. None is equal to Him" (Qur'an 112:1–4).

For Muslims, Islam is not just a set of beliefs; it is a way of life. Therefore, in order for Muslims to submit themselves to Allah and assert their faith in Islam, they must regularly observe various practices. Each sect and subgroup within Islam adapts these practices to fulfill its own beliefs and needs. Hamid Algar, professor of Islam at the University of California, Berkeley, notes, "The only exception is formed by a small minority of people who imagine that the Qur'an by itself constitutes a sufficient source for the detailed knowledge, understanding, and practice of Islam."[1]

At the core of Islam lies the Qur'an, which Islam professes to be the word of God. The Qur'an is the primary source of Islamic law; sanctity lies in the Muslim consideration of the text as the integral word of God and of Muhammad as the appointed recipient of God's revelation. The Prophet Muhammad is believed to have received the revelations of the Qur'an from God through the Angel Gabriel between AD 610 and AD 632. Until his death, the prophet remained the foremost interpreter of the Qur'an. In the prophet's lifetime, he had companions who he praised for their knowledge of the Qur'an, as well as their ability to interpret it. According to Islam, the prophet heard the words of Allah for the first time and knew their meaning, and his continued inspiration allowed him to state reliably how the Qur'an should be applied to everyday situations. The companions of the prophet wanted to embody the standards of the Qur'an and approximate the ideals of the prophet's lifework that gave rise to the *Sunna* and the hadith.

For twenty-two years, between AD 610 and the time of his death, the Prophet Muhammad received many revelations and said many things that his companions and his disciples wanted to remember and emulate. These words and teachings are found in the hadith. The word literally means "message" or "report." The hadiths are the sayings of the Prophet.[2]

The extra-Qur'anic activity and sayings of Muhammad were collected into a body of tradition called the *Sunna*, which means "example path" or "custom." The *Sunna* contains stories and anecdotes from the prophet's life to illustrate various concepts. "The word *sunna*," notes Algar, "occurs in the Qur'an in a number of different connections which, it must be stressed, do not relate directly to the Sunna of the Prophet."[3] Allah describes himself as having a *sunna*—in other words, an established, unwavering, and consistent mode of conduct for his acts. It is written in the (Qur'an, 33:38), "That [the preceding verse] is the *sunna* [norm] of Allah with respect to those who have gone before; certainly the Command of Allah is a matter of predetermined fixed quality." Later on in the same *sura* (chapter), we read in *aya* (verse) sixty-two, "That is the *sunna* of Allah with respect to those who have gone before and you will not find any variation in the sunna of Allah. The sunna of Allah is thus unchanging, fixed, and consistent."[4]

The Qur'an also ascribes a *sunna* to the preceding prophets. We find an example in (Qur'an, 19:77): "That is the sunna of those whom we have sent before you from among the messengers; certainly you will not find any variation in our sunna." Algar observes, "The word Sunna characterizes both Allah's consistent mode of conduct and the norms observed by the prophets and messengers sent before the Seal of the Messengers."[5]

Another occurrence of the word *sunna* bearing a general sense of the word is found in (Qur'an, 15:13). We read, "The sunna of the ancients has gone before." The context of this verse suggests that, here, *sunna* means something like a warning. Algar explains, "The ancients, in their rejection of guidance, fell victim to the divine norm of retribution, thus furnishing a warning example."[6]

Algar observes:

These occurrences have two features in common. First, sunna is evoked in the context of past events; it is an unchanging norm or pattern of conduct, liable to repetition whenever similar events occur. Second, it relates always to revelation and the sending of the prophets, as well as people's responses to divine guidance and the ensuing consequences ... The word *sunna* also occurs in certain hadith, not always with specific reference to the normative model of the Prophet. In one hadith, for example, the Prophet speaks of *sunnat al-jahiliyya,* the typical mode of conduct followed during the period of ignorance which preceded the coming of the Qur'anic revelation.[7]

Algar points to another hadith, which suggests that, in general, a *sunna* may either be good or bad. "Whosoever establishes a good custom (*sunna*) in Islam, to him shall belong the reward of those who act in accordance with it, without their reward being in any way diminished. Whosoever establishes an evil custom in Islam, the punishment for it and for those who act in accordance with it will be his, without their punishment being in any way diminished."[8]

Often the terms *Sunna* and *hadith* are used interchangeably when they refer to an act or word of Prophet Muhammad. The word *hadith* will be used most often here because of its widespread application in Muslim discussions of *Shar'iah* law. Islamic law is known as *Shar'iah*; in Arabic, *Shar'iah* means "the path to follow, a path well traveled." *Shar'iah* law is a holistic approach to guide individuals in most daily matters. *Shar'iah* is the collective name for all the laws of Islam, including Islam's whole religious and liturgical, ethical, and jurisprudential system.[9] *Shar'iah* controls, rules, and regulates all significant public and private behavior. It provides guidelines and regulations for personal hygiene, diet, sexual conduct, and elements of parenthood. It also prescribes specific rules for prayer, fasting, giving to the poor, and many other religious matters. Where the Qur'an may be seen as the constitution of Islam, the *Shar'iah* is the corpus of laws that explicates it.[10] The *Shar'iah* essentially unites all the diverse communities of Islam because all Islamic groups live by the same *Shar'iah*, but only in principle; there are many differing interpretations of various topics.

The Five Pillars of Islam

The Five Pillars of Islam are core beliefs that shape Muslim thought, deed, and society. A Muslim who fulfills the Five Pillars of Islam, remains in the faith of Islam, and sincerely repents of his sins will make it to *Jannah* (paradise). If he performs the Five Pillars but does not remain in the faith, he will not see paradise.

The Five Pillars of Islam are obligations that every Muslim must follow, thereby upholding the structure of the faith. These are the declaration of one's faith, five daily prayers, fasting, almsgiving, and a one-time pilgrimage to Mecca.

Tash ahhud, or *Shahadah*, means the declaration of faith or belief in the oneness of God and in the finality of the prophethood of Muhammad, through the words, "There is no god but God, and Muhammad is the prophet of God." There is nothing more important than this testimony; it is sufficient for conversion, and it makes a Muslim a Muslim. There are five main elements of Islam that are subsumed under the *Shahadah*—belief in one God who alone is worthy of worship; belief in angels as spiritual beings who do the will of God; belief in sacred books, including the Torah and the Gospels, all of which are considered to be inspired by God; belief in the prophets as examples to follow and as spokesmen of God, going back to Noah, Abraham, Moses, and Jesus, primarily, among others; and belief in the day of judgment and the resurrection.

The *Salat* are prayers said five times each day, spoken just before sunrise, just after noon, at midafternoon, just after sunset, and after nightfall. There are two specific words for prayer—*dua*, which refers to petitions and supplications, and *dhikr*, the word for remembrance used by the Sufi in mystical meditation.

Zakat, or the giving of alms, is mentioned in scripture along with prayer (Qur'an 9:11). Scripture warns against those who amass fortunes and fail to gain from them by assisting others (Qur'an 9:34–35). Building upon a Qur'anic allusion (Qur'an 3:180), *zakat* literally means "purification"; it purifies the giver and what is given.

Sawm, or fasting, is prescribed during the month of Ramadan, which is the ninth month of the Islamic calendar. Prayer and fasting, the second and third pillars, are disciplines found in every religion, and Islam makes a significant place for both of them in the lives of Muslims. Self-purification through fasting is usually done from before sunrise to sunset during each day of Ramadan. In (Sura 2:183–185), the Qur'an explains the rationale for fasting and what is required of the Muslim during this time of self-purification. If the fast adversely affects someone's health, that person is exempted. Pregnant, nursing, and menstruating women are exempted and may compensate for their lost days during other times in the year. Sick people are also exempt.

Hajj is the pilgrimage to Mecca; it is obligatory for those who are able. It is the opportunity to reenact the founding of Islam and renew links with Abraham, Hagar, Ishmael, and Muhammad. Experiencing *hajj* is a return to origins, to roots, and to the prestige of the beginnings. *Hajj* also allows the participant to experience the egalitarian nature and radical unity of Islam. A diverse group of Muslims from around the world performs the same rituals. There is no rank of privilege in this holy place because those there are without rank before God. The *hajj* is also a foretaste of the Day of Judgment, especially as pilgrims stand in pious devotion on the plains of Arafat, near the Mount of Mercy.

Also crucial to the practice of Islam is the commonly misunderstood concept of jihad, which refers to the striving or struggle of Muslims to keep their religion real in their lives and in their societies. Ideally, jihad should be done on four levels—jihad of the tongue, or speaking about one's faith; jihad of the hand, or putting their faith into action by good works; jihad of the heart, or making one's faith real as a spiritual force in their lives; and jihad of the sword, or defending one's faith and lands when one fears it to be under attack.[11] To be forewarned is to be forearmed. The Sufi mystic Al-Ghazali captured the essence of jihad when he said, "The real jihad is the warfare against the passions." In a way, jihad is the Muslim's purest sacrifice to struggle to live a perfect life and completely submit to God.

Another form of jihad is striving to translate the word of God, the Qur'an, into action. If one has experienced God and received guidance from the Qur'an, one struggles to apply that guidance in his or her daily life. So the larger, more prevalent meaning of jihad is the spiritual struggle of the soul. In this case, jihad is always present for the believer, regardless of whether there is an external enemy.

The third level of jihad is popularly known as "holy war." The classic passage is found in the (Qur'an, 2:190): "Fight for the sake of Allah those that fight against you, but be not aggressive. Surely, Allah does not love the aggressors." It is crucial to note that what is condoned is defensive warfare; Islam cannot justify aggressive war. Muhammad and the tradition are also against killing noncombatants; torturing prisoners; and the destruction of crops, animals, and homes. Thus, one should never reduce jihad to violence.[12] The several occasions that would prompt the Muslim to apply jihad in the sense of war are to defend oneself and one's family, country, and religion (Qur'an 4:75); to defend fellow Muslims who are helpless and oppressed (Qur'an 8:72); and to secure religious freedom.

Since the defense of Islam is fighting in the name of Allah, warfare is a sacred duty. If a person is killed in a jihad, he is a martyr, according to the Qur'an. We read, "As for those who are slain in the cause of Allah, He will not allow their works to perish. He will vouchsafe them guidance and ennoble their state; He will admit them to Paradise He has made for them" (Qur'an 47:4–5).

The specific laws that determine a genuine jihad are very similar to the "just war" theory of Christianity. Practically speaking, however, a true jihad is rarely invoked. Certain Muslim factions, in the name of self-interest, engage in political struggle and call it jihad. Only the state, through its leaders—the Caliph or Imam—can authorize a holy war. The Five Pillars of Islam, along with jihad, are the absolute essentials of Islamic practice. Islam makes no distinction between the sacred and the secular; thus Islamic law, or *Shar'iah* law, governs not only religious affairs, but also daily matters, from criminal justice to banking and business ethics. Traditional *Shar'iah* law, for instance, dictates that Muslims should invest only in ventures that hew to Islamic doctrine. Since the Qur'an forbids drinking, investing in a winery is not permitted.

The Divisions of Islam

According to Sunni beliefs, but not to Shi'a beliefs, the Prophet Muhammad, while providing so much for Muslim welfare, left Muslims to determine for themselves how and by whom they would be governed after he was gone. The first divisions within Islam date back to Muhammad's death in AD 632, when his followers debated who would succeed the prophet as their leader. Different factions immediately voiced support for both Abu Bakr and Ali, friends of Muhammad.[13] Ali's supporters maintained that the prophet wanted Ali to be the successor, while Abu Bakr's group was just as certain that Muhammad had not nominated anyone. This difference of opinion led to the initial division of Muslims into two groups, the Sunnis and the Shiites. Today, there are many more sects branching off of these groups and developing independently, but all follow the foundation of Islam. The most prominent sects in Kenya are highlighted here.

The word *Sunni* refers to those who follow the Sunna—the behavior, observances, sayings, and values of Muhammad. According to some sources, they also follow his companions, the first four "rightly guided" caliphs (leaders): Abu Bakr, Umar, Uthman, and Ali. The Sunni sect arrived and took hold in Kenya in the seventh century AD and is currently the dominant group of nearly all native African Muslims.[14]

From the beginning, the basic sources of Islam have been the Qur'an and the Sunna. Muslims have always looked to the Qur'an as their guide and have prayed and fasted and made pilgrimages, as the prophet did. For the details governing their lives, Muslims have relied upon their reason in applying the principles of the Qur'an and the Sunna, and this has been the cause of the different schools of law, the various tendencies, and the sects that are found in Islam. Followers of the Hanafi School of law tend toward rationalism, such as is found among the Mu'tazilities; the Shafi'i school follows the moderate theology of the Ash'arites. The Malikites are predestinationist, and the Hanbalites tend to be literal in their interpretation of theology. These are theological tendencies but not sectarian differences. Egyptian scholars were more accustomed to tolerating differences of opinion, provided these remained within the broad consensus of the Sunna.[15] The history and doctrinal context of Islam shows that belief in one God, one book, and one final prophet has been the basis for a strong, vibrant, monotheistic faith.

Today, one-fifth of the world's population testifies to the dynamism of Islam and to the continued commitment of Muslims to follow "the straight path, the way of God, to whom belongs all that is in the heavens and all that is on earth"(Qur'an 42:52–53). However, Islamic monotheism has not resulted in a monolithic tradition. The unity of Islam, from its early formation to contemporary developments, has encompassed a diversity of interpretations and expressions of faith. Given the long history and immense population of Islam, it comes as no surprise that, over the centuries, various sects, factions, and subgroups have come to interpret their beliefs in Islam differently.

In the ninth and twelfth centuries, the Benaadir coast of Somalia and the Jubba River Valley were major centers of Swahili culture.[16] Jacques Jomier, a French Dominican priest with extensive experience with Islam in many parts of the world, reports, "The Arabs had trade relationships with the east coast of Africa well before Islam. It seems that the Muslim presence began with groups of political refugees and traders who came from the Arabian-Persian gulf. It is to them that the foundation of towns like Mogadishu, Kilwa, Mombasa, Pate and Zanzibar is attributed. In the nineteenth century the Arabs disembarked on the Comoro islands and these Islands continued to be connected with Zanzibar. The Comoro islands and Zanzibar were almost totally Islamized."[17] The resulting people were Islamic, Bantu-speaking fishermen, traders, and woodwork artisans, living in city-states varying from governorships to republics, all with allegiance to the Sultan of Oman and, later, to the Sultan of Zanzibar.

In Kenya, most Sunnis are either *Shafiites*, or followers of the school of law founded by Muhammad Al-Shafi'i (d. AD 820), who came from Saudi Arabia, or *Hanafites*, who follow the Abu Hanifa (d. AD 767) school of law. However, in spite of the many schools of law and theology, the final authority for Sunni Muslims is the interpretation of the Qur'an and the hadith by the *Ulama*. The term *Ulama* refers to a collective body of those knowledgeable in Islamic beliefs or scholars "learned" in Islamic law, the top class of religious officials in Islam. This is in contrast to the Shiites, who rely on their religious leaders, the Imams, for definite guidance.[18]

The main branch of modern Shiism is the *Ithna Ashari*, or "Twelve Imams" Shiism. According to this sect, the line of descent from Ali ended with the twelfth Imam, who is believed to be not dead, but hidden. The notion of the Hidden Imam reinforces loyalty to the house of Ali through the belief that the Twelfth Imam will return one day as the *Mahdi* (the

Expected One). It also strengthens the role of the *ulama*, for during the absence of the Imam, the community is to await his return and be guided by its religious experts.[19]

As the Shiites split from the Sunnis, in turn, other sects diverged from the mainstream Shiite. Apart from the *Ithna Ashari*, the two other major divisions are the *Zaidi* and the *Ismailis*. Sunnis consider the Zaidis to be the most moderate Shiites; they do not reject Abu Bakr or Umar, the first two caliphs. Again, to the outside world, the reasons for the divisions seem obscure. In essence, they reflect the principle of succession, which lies at the heart of Shiite belief. For example, the Zaidis claimed that Zaid ibn Ali, a grandson of Hussein, was the fifth Imam, whereas the majority of the Shiites recognize Muhammad al-Baqir and his son Jafar al-Sadiq as rightful heirs to the Imamate. Unlike other Shiites, who restricted the Imamate to the descendants of Ali by his wife Fatimah, Zaidis believed that any descendant of Ali could become an Imam.

The Ismailis, led by the Aga Khan (the Ismail Imam), are worth mentioning because of their high profile and Khan's forward-looking policies. In particular, his propagation of Islamic architecture has allowed him to lead and draw in Muslims all over the world. The combination of tradition and modernity has generated a global feeling of Muslim pride and identity.[20]

The image of the Ismail today as a prosperous merchant community belies their early revolutionary origins.[21] They constitute part of the Shiite faction. In Kenya, they consist mainly of immigrants and their descendants from India and Pakistan, with very few native African converts. Though small in number, Ismailis, under the direction of their earthly spiritual leader, His Highness the Aga Khan, are financially prosperous and very active in social services, especially in education and health care. The followers are known as Ismailis or Khojas. The full title that they give their community is the Shi'a Imami Ismailia.

Regarding the Ismail establishment in the early nineteenth century, Shirin Walji, a lecturer in the department of history at the University of Nairobi, writes, "From its establishment in the early nineteenth century through to its development in the 1950s, the Ismail community in East

Africa had been heavily dependent on trade. Few Ismailis were able to break out of a *duka* (small retail shop) based economy to establish wholesale houses or develop trading empire, although the *duka* economy did bring prosperity to the Asian Muslim community for many years."[22] At the time, there was an expanding road and railway network; Ismail traders assumed the role of commercial intermediaries in the Bukusu towns of Bungoma, Malikisi, Webuye, Chwele, and Kimilili, where they are still active. Asian Ismail Muslims supplied and imported goods such as beads, wires, salt, sugar, cotton clothing, and blankets to sell to the local population. Simultaneously, these traders began to collect African produce, such as hides and skins, dairy products, and grain, and market them to either the main trading centers or the outside world.

While the Ismailis were engaged in trade, they also moved toward other social and economic goals. One of them was to enhance the quality of education in the community, although Babukusu were excluded out of racial prejudice. The Ismailis also paid a great deal of attention to health matters. The Aga Khan consistently stressed the necessity of maintaining high standards of healthcare. For example, Ismailis and other Asian communities helped to build a number of dispensaries and health care centers for the communities within Kenya. They built large, modern hospitals in Kenya's major cities of Nairobi, Mombasa, and Kisumu. They organized education, from kindergarten through secondary school. The Ismail sect also owns one of Kenya's major newspapers, *The Daily Nation*, founded in 1959 by His Highness the Aga Khan.

The Ismailis in Kenya are organized under three provincial councils. In addition, there is a council for Kenya, and there are executive and supreme councils for Africa, all with offices in Nairobi.

Even today, Ismailis do not mix with local Kenyan population or convert them to Islam. They look upon natives as second-class citizens.[23] Instead, they keep Kenyans as servants in their houses and shops (dukas), and employ Kenyans at poverty wages. Over the years, Ismailis have become an exclusive society within Kenya.[24]

The *Ahmadiyya* sect is the most recently evolved Muslim element in the Bukusu homelands. It was founded by Mirza Ghulam Ahmad

(1835–1908), who was born in Qadian (which is now Indian Punjab).[25] His followers claim that he was the Mahdi, while his denigrators say that he was nothing but a false prophet whose claims thrust him beyond the religious pale.[26] British historian Spencer Trimingham relates that Hamadas do not consider themselves a sect, but rather followers of a contemporary interpretation of Sunni Islam. Most mainstream Muslims, however, consider the followers of Ahmadiyya to be heretics.[27] Their Swahili translation of the Qur'an has caused considerable controversy. They also claim to be a new community, which will not worship "behind" any Imam other than an Ahmadi Imam. In addition, the men will not marry non-Ahmadi women; nor will the women marry non-Ahmadi men.[28]

Ahmadiyya is spreading fast with its energetic spirit of propagation, but the deep impact of its indigenous conversion has yet to be realized. There are very few Ahmadiyya who are born of Bukusu traditional religion; most joined as converts from Christianity. Their unusual attitude isolates them, both socially and religiously.

In recent years, the growing number of new mosques in areas where there were previously no Muslims indicates that there is a fresh movement of proselytizing going on. This is clearly spearheaded by the Ahamadiyya movement, which uses literature to criticize Christianity and to explain the Islamic faith. Through the use of the local and national mass media, as well as via a flood of publications and videocassettes, the events of Islamic life are now transmitted to the remotest areas of Bukusuland. The preaching and literature of the Ahmadiyya provoke discussions and controversy.[29] Neither Sunni nor Shia Islam adherents approve of the Ahamadiyya movement.[30]

The *Shadhiliyya*, alongside the *Qadiriyya*, are influential Islamic brotherhoods in Bukusuland.[31] The Shadhiliyya and Qadiriyya brotherhood in East Africa had developed a type of Sufi-like mysticism, which seeks to preserve the version of Islam transmitted by the Arabs. The main propagator of both groups was a man named Muhammad Ma'ruf (1853–1905).[32] He broke from the *Alawiyya* sect that dominated his community and was initiated into the *Yashrutiyya*, a branch of the Shadhiliyya, by his compatriot, Abd Allah Darwish. Ma'ruf was apparently in conflict with authorities; he traveled to Madagascar and later to Zanzibar to escape the problems. In each place, he worked actively and with considerable success to recruit people to his way, particularly in Zanzibar, where his order came to outshine the Qadiriyya. Like the latter, it spread to the mainland among the non-Arabs, as well as among new converts to Islam. The two orders soon came into conflict over the issue of certain rituals, with the Shadhilis condemning the Qadiriyya practices as being against *Shari'a*.

The protagonists of Sufic asceticism and mysticism, like those of all other divergent sects, trace the development of their movement to Muhammad, the Qur'an, and the hadith. Muhammad was known to have had much respect for Christian ascetics, especially for the legendary monk Bahira; to be sure, the prophet's night journey (*Mir'aj*) had a certain ascetic flavor to it.

A mystical dimension of Islam, Sufism preaches peace, tolerance, and pluralism. Sufis follow a path led by a teacher who acts as the individual's spiritual guide on the journey into the soul. They rely greatly on their knowledge of Arabic to teach and guide the Muslim community. The first and primary function of the Sufi master is what may be called "ego-busting"—that is, to diminish the individual ego in order to establish the supremacy of God.

As with all things Sufic, many layers of meaning lie beneath what can be perceived on the surface. The idea is first to deconstruct and then to construct the seeker of truth before the *tariqah* (the way) can be understood. These esoteric practices allow Sufis to endure hard times, and even times of persecution. One such practice is the ritual of the *dhikr*, which means to remember the name of Allah rhythmically. Each of the ninety-nine names is known to contain a special quality. Pronouncing and repeating the names in a special manner produces a spiritual state in the believer.

The following prayer, as noted by Akbar, sums up the spirit of Sufism. It is from the *Naqshbandi* order, associated with Bahauddin Naqshband, the saint of Bukhara, who lived in the fourteenth century. The universal strands of Islam are clearly visible; it could be the prayer of any religion, anywhere in the world:

> Oh my God, how gentle art thou with him who has transgressed
> against thee: how near art thou to him who seeks thee, how

tender to him who petitions thee, how kindly to him who hopes in thee.

Who is he who asks of thee and thou dost deny him or who sought refuge in thee and thou dost betray him, and drew near to thee and thou dost hold him aloof? And fled unto thee and thou dost repulse him?

The pervasive and tolerant spirit of the Sufis is not surprising when one considers their sources of inspiration. Although the prophet is their ultimate model, other spiritual figures–which include Abraham, Moses, and Jesus also shape them. The well-known Sufi master Junaid of Baghdad articulates this in "The Eight Qualities of the Sufi":

In Sufism, eight qualities must be exercised. *The Sufi has:*
Liberality such as that of Abraham;
Acceptance of his lot, as Ismail accepted;
Patience as possessed by Job;
Capacity to communicate by symbolism, as in the case of Zachariah;
Estrangement from his own people, which was the case with John;
Woolen garb like the shepherd's mantle of Moses;
Journeying, like the traveling of Jesus;
Humility, as Muhammad had humility of spirit.[33]

Where the Sufis diverge most significantly from mainstream Islam is in their belief in the veneration of saints. For example, in Mombasa, Kenya, Sufic processions of chanting and dancing worshipers go to the grave of Shaha Mshaham bin Hisham, who died in 1952 on a cliff on Mombasa Island, facing Kisauni. In the center of the city of Mombasa is the Sheikh Jundan Mosque, containing the Sheikh's grave.[34] Muslims leave offerings and make requests while visiting his grave; his intercession is considered very powerful. Some Muslims reject this notion as idolatry. They believe that one's relationship with God should be direct and not mediated by a third party. Sufism in general has become one of the most controversial subgroups within Islam, because of its unique interpretation of how to practice and believe in Islam.[35]

Sufi mysticism puts music to great use, encouraging music as a way of deepening one's relationship with God and exploring the spiritual world. In one particular ritual, a number of Sufi men form a group that celebrates the *dhikr* (Arabic for the remembrance of Allah), a form of worship that involves chanting the name of God and swaying. According to Sufic thought, the value of listening to religious music is measured by the righteousness of the listener. To sufi mystics, music is existence itself.

Music is also central to the Babukusu lifestyle. Singing and dancing reach deeply into the innermost parts of community life, and many things come to the surface under musical inspiration that otherwise might not be inwardly revealed. For example, while songs and dancing add glee to celebrations, they have also a veiled but significant effect of reforming the hearts and minds of those who have broken norms, conventions, or customs of the Bukusu community. The songs usually are deliberately composed to highlight acts committed and to bring back the offenders. The singing groups, protected by the community's traditions, perform the role of the people's court, to whose verdict the culprits and their relations cannot pretend to be indifferent, and against which they have no appeal.

The Sufi brotherhoods served the diffusion of Islam actively converting people and protecting the newly converted. Initially, this was the case in Bukusuland; but as time passed, the Sufi brotherhood has remained a marginal presence both in Bukusuland and in Kenya as a whole.[36]

Islam on the East Coast of Africa

In contrast to the Muslim conquest of North Africa, east Africa was never subject to a sweeping Muslim takeover. The Muslim influence was based on trade. Islam came to the east African coast in many waves and at different times. There is no specific date, but it is thought that Islam had taken root in east Africa by the eighth century.

Undoubtedly, there was early contact and dialogue between peoples on the east African coast and the peoples of east Arabia, Persia, India, and even China, going back long before the Prophet Muhammad was preaching in the AD 600s. James De Vere Allen, curator of the Lamu Museum, just north of Mombasa, reports that there is also some oral evidence of a pre-Islamic empire, called the Shugwaya Empire, exercising power along the coast.[37] What is clear is that once people arrived, they intermarried with the people of the coast very early on, forming a new kind of coastal society, the Swahili, with their own architecture, style of dressing, and music.

Conversion

Muslim outsiders did not arrive on the coast with the aim of converting people to Islam; they came as slave traders, which meant that they came with force. Not everyone became Muslim. There was a constant movement of slaves and traders coming from inland to the coast. There are few accounts of how these people came to be converted to Islam. On the whole, people converted to Islam only if by doing so they attained some permanent position in coastal society as a leading trader or craftsman or, in the case of women, as a wife or concubine to a rich man. As in North Africa, trade was a powerful strand in the conversion of the people. East Africa offered gold, ivory, and slaves, and later on, very fine woven cotton. In return, traders from the East and Persian Gulf brought textiles, spices, porcelain, and other finished goods.

Islam has been associated with the east coast of what is now called Kenya for over a millennium. Jahann Haafkens, a scholar of Christian-Muslim relations in Africa, declares, "Before the first churches were built in Denmark, there were mosques on the Kenyan coast about 850 A.D."[38] How exactly Islam arrived is subject to conjecture, but evidence of its long tenure in this area is beyond dispute. In the words of Professor Ahmed Idha Salim, a prominent Kenyan Muslim historian:

> Local chronicles speak of Islam as having arrived on the East African coast as early as the days of the second caliph Umar (7th Century A.D.). Certain archeological evidence confirms the existence of a thriving Muslim town in Kenya on the island of Manda during the 10th Century A.D. It is certain that the pre-

Islamic contacts of the coast with Arabia were reinforced during the Islamic era. These contacts led to the rise of many Muslim city states on the coast, whose inhabitants were ethnically mixed from the outset—Arab, African, Shirazi (Persian), Somali, etc. These communities became known as Swahili (a term derived from the generic term *Swahili* (of the coast). Arab geographers and travelers like Al-Masudi and Ibn Battuta wrote about some of those communities and towns in their chronicles.[39]

Scholars think of the east African coast and its interior as separate entities with divergent historical experiences.[40] This is not because there was a lack of contact between the people of the relatively narrow strip along the coast and those in the interior; nor is it because the people living on the coast were different from those of the interior. Rather, it is because the people of the coast were far more influenced by Indian Ocean cultures than were the people of the interior. The east African coast was part of the Indian Ocean world commercially; culturally; socially; and, at times, politically.

Although Islam was present on the east coast of Africa for more than twelve centuries, it did not spread inland for some time. David Sperling, a historian at the University of Nairobi, relates that the influence of Islam in the immediate hinterland and the interior was negligible, hardly extending beyond the outskirts of the coastal towns until the beginning of the nineteenth century.[41] Similarly, Trimingham argues that, "When Islam was confined to the coastal towns, the aspect of acceptance was not in evidence, since its adoption meant the jettisoning of tribal life and assimilation into a new civilization."[42] Another factor that limited the spreading of Islam was the concentration of traders and other agents in coastal towns that had no close ties to the natives of the interior areas.[43]

What initiated the spread of Islam in the nineteenth century among indigenous Kenyans of the coastal hinterland and the interior? The initial answer to this question lies in the nature of the relations between the Muslim inhabitants of the coastal towns and the hinterland natives. There are few documentary sources of early Islam on the east African coast of

Kenya. However, there is one—a journal kept by Acting Lieutenant James Emery of the British Royal Navy during his twenty-three-month residence in Mombasa, from August 1824 to July 1826.[44] Emery observed that, at that time, the community in Mombasa was purely Muslim. He recorded numerous details concerning the relations between the town dwellers of Mombasa and the neighboring hinterland peoples, who were then called the Wanyika (meaning "people of the Nyika"), who are known today as the Mijikenda. Emery writes, "The Mijikenda would capture runaway slaves and be paid to return them; when the occasional dispute arose among the Mijikenda, the Swahili would mediate; … the Mijikenda would be given clothes as presents or be paid their annual payment."[45]

In a general assessment, Emery refers to the Swahili people as being united with the Mijikenda in the "closest alliance."[46] But nowhere does he mention the Mijikenda being Muslims. On this point, Sperling comments, "Mijikenda who accepted Islam were by and large persons who had opted out of their society and been assimilated into town life. There is no evidence that Muslims propagated Islam among the Mijikenda in any way, and there were few adherents of Islam living within Mijikenda society."[47] Relations between the Muslims of Mombasa and the Mijikenda people, living apart, gave little scope for the crossing of Islam into the rural hinterland, where the Mijikenda people continued to follow their own local, indigenous religious beliefs and practices.

Lieutenant Emery's descriptions, however, gives a general idea of the prevailing circumstances and of relations between the Swahili towns and the rural areas. Trading activity dominated these relations and was the main occasion for contacts between Muslims and non-Muslims; however, trade in itself—extensive and regular as it was—did not create conditions conducive to the spread of Islamic influence among the non-Muslim, rurally dwelling people. Sperling argues that to attribute the spread of Islam to trade and traders is correct only in a certain sense. Trade facilitated contacts between Muslims and non-Muslim parties, but any ensuing process of Islamization arose more from the issue of relations between those parties, subject to many and varied circumstances.[48] Trade, however extensive and influential it may have been, could not have promoted the spread of Islam in an atmosphere that lacked mutual respect and dialogue between the parties. Respect for relationships had to come first.

Donal Cruise O'Brien, a professor of politics at the University of London, argues that the Muslims of the Indian Ocean coast failed to bring Islam into the interior of Kenya because the trade routes into the interior were barred by the waterless environment of the Nyika desert and by the hostile nomadic people who lived there.[49] This is a weak case because Muslim traders crossed the two-thousand-mile Sahara desert and spread Islam across West Africa; why then could they not cover the fifty-mile stretch of the Nyika desert?

What was it, then, that delayed Islam from becoming established in the interior of Kenya? Neville Chittick, a British archeologist, gives an elegant summary in response to this question. Chittick replies that the cities of the coast faced the sea, looking out over the great maritime region bordered by the Indian Ocean and its coasts.[50] The maritime orientation of the coastline was advantageous to Islam, as it allowed regular commerce with the holy places of the Arabian Peninsula, thus sustaining the devotional life of the coast. This orientation, however, tended to exclude encounters and regular commerce with those who were perceived as the barbarians of the interior, the *washenzi*, and thus limited the diffusion of the Islamic faith inland.[51] Zanzibar (until 1964 when the Arab sultanate was overthrown) developed the convention that, once born an African, one was "a slave forever, even in the next world." Indeed, the Africans were called *washenzi*—"uncivilized beings of a lower order"—and, on this account, were considered to be deserving of every abuse.

Thus, it was customary to have the wombs of pregnant African women opened so that capricious Arab women could see how babies lay inside of them, even as it was fashionable to have Africans kneel for Arab women to step on their backs as they mounted their mules. In "Arabs Mortal Hatred and Enslavement of the Black Race," Naiwu Osahon reported that a traveler in Sudan observed in 1930, "In the eyes of Arab rulers of Sudan, the black slaves were simply animals given by Allah to make the life of Arabs comfortable."[52]

An additional obstacle responsible for the delay of Islam moving into the interior of Kenya was the economic priority of slave trade. The conversion of the local population to Islam posed an economic problem. There were two options facing the Muslims—to convert the natives of the interior to Islam or to continue enslaving them. A cordial relationship with the interior population would bring an end to the supply of slaves, since Islam prohibited Muslims from enslaving other Muslims.[53] Jeff Haynes, professor of religion at the London Guildhall University, notes, "Islamization in East Africa was a much more patchy process. Islam was, of course, the faith of the region's slavers—Arabs from the Arabian Peninsula—but they were much more concerned with collecting people for export than in spreading a religious message."[54] Haynes continues, "In fact, the Arabs regarded themselves as superior precisely because they were Muslims and their victims were not."[55] In Algeria, even now, Arabs throw stones at black people in markets and other public places even if they happen to be visiting diplomats. It is said that Arabs tend to act as though they are not in Africa. Surprising as this may sound, it is the truth. Once when an innocent abroad was visiting Egypt, he told his Egyptian Arab (Muslim) host to have a taxicab ready for the next morning, as he was going to travel to Kenya. The host responded in disbelief, "So you want to go to Africa to visit? We have no diseases here in Egypt; why are you leaving us?"[56]

In Saudi Arabia, although blacks coming to Mecca on pilgrimage have spent their life's savings to make the journey, they are treated worse than animals.[57] Racism toward black Muslims in Saudi Arabia is so strong it makes one wonder if making the pilgrimage to Mecca is worth it under such conditions. Hundreds of blacks who have lived all their lives in Saudi Arabia are being repatriated to their homelands daily, after suffering the loss of an arm or leg to the legal system for some minor or trumped-up offense and without regard for their well-being or human rights.

Evidently, many Africans claim that Arabs do not consider black Muslims authentic or included by Allah. At best, they tolerate blacks only in their role as ordained slaves, no better than animals to be used as beasts of burden by the "superior Arab race." The rule applies to all blacks, whether Muslims or non-Muslims and whether of Nigerian (Hausa/Fulani or Yoruba), Tanzanian, Ugandan, Malian, or African American extraction.

It was not until the late nineteenth century, when more conventional trade practices finally replaced slavery, that certain ethnic groups in the hinterland and the interior of Kenya—among them the Babukusu—were able to adopt Islam, in part to facilitate trade with the more Islamized coast.[58] It was with the abolition of the slave trade and the establishment of the European colonial rule in the nineteenth century that a great change took place. Islam began to spread rapidly from the coast to the interior peoples and inland trading centers of Tanganyika (Tanzania). On the whole, the spread of Islam into the interior of Kenya was low-key, with not much impact among the local African community. Kenya lacked inland centers, so Islam continued to spread toward western Kenya from Tanzania through Lake Victoria. Chief Mumia of Nabongo accorded the Swahili Muslim traders a warm welcome. During an intertribal war, the Muslims assisted Mumia with advanced firepower to overcome his enemies, the Bukusu. In return, on one Muslim *idd day*, Chief Mumia along with his family and officials of his court, converted to Islam. After that, Islam spread to the surrounding regions of Kakamega, Kisumu, Kisii, and Bungoma. Dr. Ahmed Salim, a prominent Kenyan historian, would have us understand that prior to the building of the Kenya-Uganda railway from Mombasa to Kisumu, the Arab and Swahili traders had already reached the place of the chief in western Kenya, and so the place was named Mumias. This happened between 1870 and 1885.[59] Salim describes the missionary distribution of Islam in Western Kenya as follows: "Sharif Hassan Abdallah from Pangani [Mombasa] was the first to spearhead the trade caravans into Mumias in Western Kenya, the seat of the Wanga tribe, whose paramount, Chief Nabongo Mumia dramatically embraced Islam during one of the *Idd* [Eid] festivals. He then adopted the Muslim name of Muhammad Mumia. Soon many members of his cabinet, his three brothers, Kadima, Mulama, Murunga and others were inspired and accepted Islam as their faith."[60]

This encounter encouraged Sharif Hasan so much that he sent more missionaries to other areas in western Kenya and Uganda as well.[61] In addition, the building of the Kenya-Uganda railway in 1896 brought coastal culture closer to the peoples of the interior. Commercial activities intensified as trade picked up. New job opportunities were created.

Another Muslim scholar, Yusuf A. Nzibo, suggested that the rapid process of the Islamization of the "upcountry people" was distinct from that applied to those in the interior. This rapid spread of Islam was so alarming to the British colonial administrators that the provincial commissioner, C.W. Hobley, issued a circular to all his district commissioners, cautioning them:

> It must be realized that it is not in our interest or in the interest of the people of the Mohammedan faith that the *Sheriah* should spread among the Aboriginal tribes. In fact one may go as far as to say that the policy of the administration should be antipathetic towards Mohammedan propaganda and proselytization.[62]

Trimingham also notes that the moderate diffusion of Islam in western Kenya derives from Islamic nuclei established from Tanzania between 1880 and 1930.[63] These Muslim traders crossed Lake Victoria from Tanganyika into Mumias and eventually arrived in Bukusuland.[64] This was the beginning of what Professor Sperling called "rural Islamization," which marked a significant turning point in the spread of Islam among Bukusu people.

Another Islamic movement came from the Nubia people, who originated in the Sudan and spread to various east African countries due to their involvement with the British Army. Some also stayed when they escaped from slave traders as they were being driven from their homes to the coast. With a history and traditions that scholars can trace to the dawn of civilization, the Nubians first settled along the banks of the Nile from Aswan. Along this great river, they developed one of the oldest and greatest civilizations in Africa. Until they lost their last kingdom (Christian Nubia) only five centuries back, the Nubians remained the main rivals to the other great African civilizations of Egypt.[65] Today, they are still found in urban centers, such as Nairobi, Eldama-Ravine, Bungoma, and Bumbo (Uganda).[66]

Eva Evers Rosander, a research fellow in social anthropology at the Nordic Africa Institute at Upsala, Sweden, describes rural Islam as the contextualized or the "localized form of Islam," which is found particularly in the Sufi context.[67] Rural Islam has also been culturally, as well as religiously, flexible. According to David Sperling, an authority on African cultures, rural Islam originated when the non-Muslim Bukusu people adopted Islam and continued to reside in their rural villages, where traditional Bukusu religious beliefs and behaviors continued to inform their daily lives. For them, this would have been a smooth transition, but the process of mutual assimilation has been hindered by radical Islamists wanting to take root with their own rigid emphasis.[68]

The unique characteristics of Bukusu rural Islam are visible even today, as this facet was not absorbed into Islamic orthodoxy because the Bukusu held out for their traditional cultural values. Such elements were tolerated in existing parallel to the Islamic system of life, although they contributed to the development of new forms of Islam. Belief in spirits is not contrary to Islamic thinking, as in the form of *jinn* and angel spirits. The conflict here concerns certain forms of personal relationship to spirits, especially those reflecting any form of cult that would conflict with the sovereignty of God.

The ancestor cult survives in some form among Bukusu Muslims. For example, propitiation of ancestors on the family graves continues unabated, as Islam, Christianity, and secular civilization have not yet made any significant adverse determination on its practice. The cult survives, since most agriculturalists need to maintain lineage authority over property ownership. The practices of these cults take the form of periodic sacrifices and feasts in memory of the ancestors at the end of a period of mourning, on special occasions when a deceased person has been seen in a dream, or at any critical stage in the life of the clan. These feasts are called *kimisango* or *sadaka*, in which Islamic prayers are introduced. In this way, the appearance of the unity of God is preserved. Practically speaking, ancestors are known to intercede or mediate with God. At the same time, ancestors fulfill exactly the same functions as patrons of traditional feasts, in that they affirm the unity and the solidarity of the family. The Bukusu Muslims, without exception, offer sacrifices at the family graves and ancestral shrines. It is generally believed among the Bukusu people that to disregard or fail to perform this ceremony will make the spirits of the dead come out and cause heightened awareness of the possibility of destruction by means of sickness in the neglectful family. Therefore, among the Bukusu people, exclusive allegiance to either Islam or Christianity as opposed to traditional ways is not allowed to weaken the bonds binding family and clan; and this is why ancestral cult practices persist.

The conversion of individual Muslims or Christians to the other religion is quite frequent. Trimingham asserts that, although the baptism of Muslims is undertaken only with the consent of the father and the uncles, such permission generally is not difficult to obtain. The point is that, in the interior of Kenya, among traditional people—contrary to what prevails in the coastal Swahili sphere—religion is not seen as a divisive element; some families seem to like to have one foot in each of the modern religious spheres.[69]

The extension of British colonial rule into the interior of Kenya at the end of the nineteenth century led to the rapid expansion of Islam, despite hostilities from both Christian missionaries and the colonial administration.[70] Yusuf Nzibo, managing director of the Industrial Development Bank of Kenya, writes, "Many of those that were won over to Islam converted not as a result of the spiritual message of *Allah* preached to them, but because of being impressed by the Islamic style of life and the ties and the security offered by becoming part of the community."[71]

A bond of brotherhood that cut across ethnic lines grew as a result of Islamic festivals and religious activities during the month of Ramadan and the Friday prayers; the feelings of brotherhood and care displayed during these events impressed many of the early Bukusu converts.[72] Trimingham explains, "Islamic civilization was identified with the Arab way of life (*ustaarabu or uungwana*), as opposed to barbarians (*ushenzi*); hence, the domination of a form of Arabism over Bukusu Islam, externally."[73] *Ustaarabu* had to do with honor, dignity, position, rank, respect, reverence, modesty, and courtesy. Bukusu converts to Islam endeavored to follow the Arabs in their customs, not as much due to religious convictions as out of eagerness to attain the *ustaarabu* (sense of being civilized and a good member of the community) or *heshima* (respect) thus acquired. If a person had *heshima*, he or she had a place in the Arab social hierarchy.

Ustaarabu, as defined in the present day, means to have dignity, honor, and respect, as well as knowing how to properly extend courtesy, generosity, and esteem to others. The term was (and still is) found among most Swahili-speaking people on the east African coast. It should be recognized, however, that there are slight differences between regions and times; the meanings of the word are not monolithic. *Ustaarabu* was a critical component of having *uungwana*, meaning, again, civilized, or having a claim to the local culture. It also implies a certain freedom of behavior. Both concepts refer to having a more respected social status. Thus, *ustaarabu* or *heshima* has often been associated with the coastal elite. However, people in the lower classes—even slaves—also strove to have *ustaarabu*.[74] Having a grasp of these social distinctions and the terminology used to describe them is essential to understanding coastal society, especially during the slave trade and after its abolition.

Islam also provided the Bukusu Muslim community with a religion of new social and cultural norms and an attitude of cultural and religious superiority over nonbelievers. The conversion of Bukusu peoples to Islam also involved the adoption of features that served then to differentiate the Muslim from the non-Muslim. The adoption of the material traits of a religious civilization leads to changes in habits and in associated psychological attitudes and is followed by the adoption of the material of purely religious elements. Clothes may not make a man, but they are the first sign of change in his outlook on life. When he adopts the costume of a Muslim and eats like one, he is a Muslim. Bukusu converts who became members of Islam learned the meaning of equality with their non-Bukusu Islamic peers; with such a cordial relationship, trade flourished.

German anthropologist Günter Wagner describes the influence Muslim traders had on the Babukusu around 1930. Chief Sudi of Bukusuland gave permission to Muslims to be butchers in the trading centers. When he did this, there was no other person who could slaughter a cow; if another person were to have done so, the Muslims could not have bought that meat.[75] Wagner continues, "The owners of the cattle, too, did not want other men to slaughter their cattle. If they let another man do so, who was not a Muslim, the owners of the cattle would not make any profit."[76] This tradition continues today. Thus, there was another economic and purely gastronomical attraction to Islam that affected the Babukusu.

Networks of perfectly maintained native highways, which the Babukusu used to trade with neighboring communities, were popular and prosperous during the 1950s. The Babukusu traded hides and skins with the Muslims and in exchange brought home goods, such as clothes, sugar, and salt. Thus, the trading highway linking Lake Victoria and Bukusuland was a vehicle for the spread of Islam.[77] Furthermore, the local chiefs in the area and their agents and intermediaries became partners in the trade opened by Muslim traders. These native traders and chiefs were among the first people to accept the principles of Islam.[78] The acceptance of the new Islamic faith raised the local chief's social prestige.[79] Over time, being a Muslim became an essential condition for cooperation with Muslim traders.

Trade also became an important factor in shaping the development of Babukusu political and economic organizations and trading centers. As trading shifted to town centers, not only did the presence of Muslim traders in the interior increase, but the direction and the focus of trade changed as well. Whereas the town consisted of a single marketplace attracting the surrounding rural peoples without distinction, the town trader viewed the rural interior with interest and sought, above all, to establish contact with those places nearest to the town centers.[80] For example, in the main Babukusu town of Bungoma, Friday was the traditional market day, when people from the rural villages would come to buy and sell their farm produce. At the same time, Friday is an official Muslim day of prayer in the mosque. Selecting Friday as market day became one way of attracting locals who came to the market and getting them to convert to Islam. Non-Muslims in the rural villages surrounding the trading towns became the object of constant and regular visits by proselytizing local Muslim traders and farmers. These interpersonal contacts led to many local Bukusu people being converted to Islam.

Most traders in Bukusuland became Muslim, and, as they were also under the umbrella of the British colonial protection, settled in areas where formerly they could not have lived. Muslim merchants who traded along those routes leading to the interior ensured the circulation of ideas as well as goods.

First and foremost, these ideas were based on Muslim ideals. Thus, many trade routes opened by Muslim merchants, who crisscrossed various parts of western Kenya, were inevitably bound to advance Islam in Bukusuland.

The people who spread Islam in Bukusuland were ordinary men and women, who were not missionaries in the sense of being trained or sent by home communities; but they were missionaries in the sense that, as they traveled, traded, or looked after their homes, they lived their lives as Muslims and encouraged others to join them. Muslims practiced their religion by embracing the motto, "Be cautious of what you do and say; you may be the only Qur'an that your neighbor ever reads."

Another important factor in the expansion of Islam in western Kenya was the growth of the British Army, due to Kenyan membership, during World War I. Many Kenyan coastal people, both Africans and Arabs, were conscripted into the British colonial army. The annual report of the Takaungu subdistrict in Mombasa for 1916–1917, for example, noted that during World War I, all the young and able-bodied members of the local Muslim population were drafted into the Carrier Corps.[81] By the recruitment of these recent converts to Islam, the conversion of many of their comrades in arms took place, thus swelling the ranks of Muslim soldiers in the British forces. Muslims dominated the Kenyan units, called the Kenya African Rifles (K.A.R) in the 1920s.[82] Many of these soldiers became "Agents of Allah" and wasted no time in converting their upcountry colleagues, among them the Babukusu.[83]

Rural Islamization further came about through the veterans of World War I. When these soldiers returned to their ancestral homes after the war, they spread their newfound religion to their friends and relatives.[84] Soldiers, who were engaged in establishing district headquarters and garrisons and in policing the interior, were Muslims and were identified with the new British administration.[85] Using Muslim petty officials, policemen, interpreters, and clerks was less expensive than importing Europeans and less troublesome than employing Asians, due to their political differences. Above all, the British had a great admiration for the machismo and self-respect Islam instilled in people. In each place where Europeans settled, there also arose a realm of Islamic influence.

Islam is an intercultural system that has always sought to expand and embrace all sorts of different peoples. In its response to local geographical, racial, social, and political forces, Islam developed clear regional subcultures; yet all the different regions retained a recognizable Islamic stamp. The nature of the people and their land, culture, and history gave special characteristics to Bukusu rural Islam.

Furthermore, the interaction that took place between Bukusu and non-Bukusu Muslims was dynamic; the influence of Arab Islam and Bukusu culture became reciprocal. Islam dominated the life of prayer and trade, especially in the towns, but Bukusu culture modified the character and the life of the Muslim community in turn. For example, initiation rites continue now among community institutions, thereby preserving Babukusu vitality. However, Islamic elements have taken the place of some traditional lore, and the rites have been modified as a result of Bukusu and Islamic influence. For instance, in the boys' initiation, beer is now acceptable.[86]

Trimingham adds, "Islam knows only the custom of circumcision, a rite of purification, individual in character, yet having considerable social importance in that it opens the way to adult Islamic life. The only people who undergo it in this narrow sense are the Arabs, those assimilated to them, and their immediate families."[87] But for most African Muslims and for the Bukusu people in particular, circumcision is a prelude, which is to be completed through initiation. The period of physical healing is identified with seclusion and training in an initiation school in the bush. This is a period of preparing the youth for adult responsibilities. In Bukusu society, the circumciser is often a traditional elder, but not necessarily a Muslim, and even the period of retreat takes place under the guidance of a Bukusu traditional elder. The Islamic and Bukusu elements have become associated but have not fused. Regarding the rites of circumcision, the Islamic ideal of ritual cleanliness and the European notion of imagined hygiene are easily fitted in with traditional Bukusu life. But above all, there emerges the idea that the boys are no longer just members of the families into which they were born but brothers to one another—alumni of the same graduating class.

Even though Arabization in those early days among the Bukusu people was not coerced, it was carried out in the context of a racially stratified society that deemed the Arab Swahili and Asian Muslim people and their cultures superior and the culture and belief systems of their host, the Babukusu, inferior. Stratification and discrimination remain today and continue to demean the Bukusu people and their beliefs. The Muslims perceive these people of the interior as barbarians or, in Swahili, *shenzi*— that is, uncouth, savage, or pagan, in the Latin sense.

Dean S. Gilliland, professor of African studies at the Fuller Theological Seminary in Pasadena, California, notes that the "attitude of the living toward the spirits of the dead is bound to be an area of conflict when Islam encounters African religion[s]. Yet, the respect that African societies give to their ancestors and to the spirit possession is one of the few universal features of African religions. When these two religious systems meet, the voice of the ancestors seems to have the last word."[88]

Practices, such as spirit possession, have a long history within Bukusu community. Bukusu Muslims continue to rely upon spirit possession, particularly (though not exclusively) for healing purposes, despite social pressure from Arab Swahili Muslims not to engage in this tradition. This is particularly the case during personal crises, such as serious illness. It is common for Bukusu people who have been unable to find any effective treatment for serious illness to seek the therapeutic services of a spirit society or a medium.

This is only one example of the kind of problems that arise when Islam and Bukusu traditional religion coexist within a community. The current cross-cultural relationship between Babukusu and Muslims and their relationships with Christianity will be explained in detail in a later chapter. The following chapter should provide an understanding of the cultural and historical roots that lead to the need for transcultural dialogue in the present.

CHAPTER 7

• ◆ •

THE HISTORY OF CHRISTIANITY IN KENYA IN THE CONTEXT OF THE BUKUSU PEOPLE

Missionary Attempts: The East Coast of Africa

We have discussed the Muslim interface with the east African region and with the Babukusu traditional ways. A second strong transcultural influence on the Babukusu traditions is Christianity.

To appreciate the study of Bukusu Christianity, a brief history of the early Christian influences in east Africa (particularly Kenya) is indispensable. Kenya was one of the first East African countries to see missionaries on its coast in AD 1498, when Portuguese explorer Vasco da Gama arrived with Roman Catholic missionaries at Mombasa and Malindi, on their way to India.[89] The Arab leader permitted da Gama to erect a *padrao* (a large cross monument), thus placing the east coast within the sphere of the Portuguese Conquista. These pillars, which still stand at Malindi and Fort Jesus at Mombasa, are the first signs of the presence of Christianity in east Africa.[90] Although the missionaries did not remain to take up sustained evangelical work, sporadic contact was made with the local population. Still, Kenya was one of the last countries in East Africa to receive missionaries in its interior.

In AD 1500, two years after the arrival of da Gama, a second navigator, named Pedro Alvares Cabral, stopped at Kilwa on his way to India. Cabral had on board eight Franciscan missionaries, eight chaplains, and one vicar (a parish priest). Cabral had been given the royal instruction that these priests should first use their spiritual sword before he thought of using the secular one; but if the "Moors" and the pagans did not accept the Christian faith and refused the offered peace and commerce, he was to wage war against them with fire and sword. One Franciscan duly preached the Gospel (the first recorded sermon in east Africa), but both the ruler of Kilwa and the natives refused the faith, as well as the friendship, of the Portuguese.[91] The Portuguese conquered the island, taking full control in 1505. With the intention of taking control of the lucrative Indian Ocean trade, they built a garrison and established a trading post in Sofala (present-day Beira).[92]

The Visit of Saint Francis Xavier

For nearly one hundred years, the Europeans seemed to forget the east African coast. Recorded history mentions only one event of some importance, in terms of Christianity, in this part of Africa, during this period—the visit of Saint Francis Xavier to Malindi, which he passed on his way to India in 1542. Xavier was highly pleased to see a gilded stone cross on the outskirts of the town, and he commented, "How great is the might of the cross, seen standing lonely and so victorious in the midst of this vast land of the Moors."[93] Both this naive joy and the subsequent dialogue he held with Muslims are revealing of Christian mentality in St. Francis's era. At the same time, John Gray, a British historian in East Africa, related, "A Sheikh told Francis that there were seventeen Mosques at Malindi at the time but only three were in use and these were poorly attended. He asked Xavier whether among Christians religious zeal would be equally low. Francis answered that God could never be pleased by the prayer of the infidels and therefore allowed their piety to go cold. 'I wonder more,' he added, 'that your religion has so long been successful that I wonder at its present decay.'" [94]

Difficulties and Shortcomings

Early Christian missionary conversion attempts in east Africa were usually of short duration. While a few missionaries stayed in the area for longer periods, the lack of a sufficiently strong missionary presence hampered them, and they eventually faded away. The European clergy who could be induced to serve in Africa were mostly of poor quality, and those few who survived the deadly tropical diseases were more active in the slave trade in a desire to make money than in an endeavor to say Mass or carry out any priestly duties.[95]

The next wave of missionaries met with further difficulties came from the local population, whose animosity, suspicion, and mistrust colored their encounters with the missionaries.[96] The Mijikenda people of coastal Kenya, for example—according to Dr. Krapf of the Church Missionary Society (1968)—"never seriously exhort the young to come to school; fearing that the *Ada* (customs) of the *Mijikenda* people will be destroyed and that the young people will conform to the *Ada* of Europeans. They think that *Koma* or spirits of the dead will be angry, and withhold the rain, and send diseases."[97]

Age-based conflict between the youth and the elderly men was often characteristic of village society. With the coming of Christianity and Western education, the elders correctly perceived that the young would gain an independent power base. An Ngoni elder clearly stated, "If we give you [missionaries] our children to teach, your words will steal their hearts; they will grow up cowards, and refuse to fight for us when we are old, and furthermore, they will despise us."[98] Some communities, such as the Mijikenda, responded to the situation of religious pluralism with sheer agnosticism. Dr. Krapf reported, "The chief of Kambe [near Mombasa] said openly, 'There is no God since he is not to be seen.'"[99]

Others, like the war leader of the Ngoni people of Malawi, expounded a kind of relativism, suggesting that each people has its own path to God, appropriate to its own culture. As the Ngoni chief explained, "The Foundation of our kingdom is the spear and the shield. God has given you [Europeans] the Book and cloth and has given us [the Ngoni] the shield and the spear, and each must live in his own way."[100] And so the Ngoni chief resisted the European presence and the spread of Christianity in his area.

The Bukusu people argued that Christianity undermined the sacred offices of traditional elders, such as rainmakers, medicine men and women, the blacksmiths, soothsayers, circumcisers, priests, and diviners, who are religious traditional specialists. Yet, surprisingly, diviners and their children were among the first converts to Christianity. John Kapuye, the first Anglican convert in Mashonaland (Zimbabwe), was a son of a famous diviner.[101] Elizabeth Isichei, an African Christian historian, argues, "One could not succeed in this field without considerable insight into human nature and social change, and diviners were sometimes among the first to perceive the crucial importance of Western education and literacy. Some diviners were alienated from their own arts when divination failed."[102] The only choice, as the diviners saw it, was to throw in their lot with the Christians.

Such a religiously and culturally mixed climate posed serious obstacles to the advancement of Christianity on the east coast of Africa, however, the complete withdrawal of the missionary work around 1800 was not entirely due to the African social climate; nor was it due to the priorities of the Portuguese slave trade. One cause might have been the waning of religious fervor of the laity in the Catholic Church in Europe, largely as a result of the advent of the Age of Reason leading to the French Revolution and to the backlash of the ego-driven Napoleonic wars. In this way, the French Revolution did undermine the work of Christian evangelization out of Europe. We might say that, when a culture becomes sick, it will have to experience a natural cathartic consequence. In other words, it will perforce simply throw up. The French Revolution and its effects can be seen as an example of this phenomenon.

Early Converts to Christianity

At first, Christian converts were drawn from those for whom the traditional indigenous world offered little solace. For example, the first Church Missionary Society convert in Kenya, Mrenge of Rabai, was disabled, and the first Christians in the Usambara Mountains (in Tanzania) were lepers or mothers of twins. The first ordained Moravian pastor in Nyasa Province of Malawi was a former slave.[103] In Bukusuland, the first Christians were needy widowed women who settled on the mission compound. In the beginning, only the less fortunate were allowed by their local communities to join Christianity, where they could find economic assistance.

Forced into a different cultural experience of the world, villagers may have found that Christianity provided a wider and more helpful perspective on life than their local religions, which were generally centered on ancestral veneration. Some traditional religions were spread over large regions, but it was true that, as one elder put it, "There was no *special* religion in the area between *Masai* and *Makonde*."[104] Political institutions were fermenting, and many new states were created. In this situation, some new communities chose to follow missionary leaders, who in effect became chiefs, beginning circa AD 1900.

Christianity and Education

Nineteenth century leaders in Kenya were enthusiastic advocates of technical education, but it gradually became clear, in the colonial context, that artisans were less esteemed and rewarded than were teachers or clerks. From this realization sprang the demand for literacy education, which missionaries and administrators tended to deplore, offering only with caution. The following examples reveal the enthusiasm and appreciation that young people had for literacy education. P. Walakira, a government economist, relates the story of an African third-grade teacher who told his pupils in the classroom, "Less study, much work, less pay. Much study, less work, more pay."[105] This became a popular slogan and motivation with which African children and their parents increasingly agreed. Ngugi wa Thiong'o, a Kenyan scholar of literature, narrates that the Kikuyu children, in promoting education, sang:

Father, mother
Provide me with pen and slate
I want to learn
Land is gone
Cattle and sheep are not there
Not there any more
What's left?
Learning, learning.[106]

In this context, being literate is synonymous with being a Christian. It is said of Edward Lwaijumba of Kabale (Uganda) that he "read and was baptized."[107] Many who were drawn to the schools by the desire for education or because of the schools' sheer novelty later became convinced and fervent Christians.

Another person who became a Christian through education is Filipo Njau, a *Chagga* from Kilimanjaro. Njau went to school because he had small prospects of an inheritance from his parents or clan. He relates, "Many boys came to instruction to learn to read and write things to their advantage. Then behold! In the midst of their craving to read and write, the word of God in their reading books overwhelmed them ... they became Christians, saved by Jesus, children of God. So it was with me."[108] Young people were drawn to school by the charm and power of the written word and often became Christians without much conscious choice. As one put it, "I wanted to become a Christian, just because everybody in the village was becoming a Christian."[109]

Kenya Inland Missions: Christianity's Second Trial

The first phase of the history of Christianity in the interior of Kenya began in the nineteenth century with the arrival of the first missionaries from Europe. The story of Christian evangelization is equally Catholic and Protestant, and among Protestants, equally the story of liberal Christians and evangelicals. Similarly, it is equally the story of men and women. The Protestant missionaries took with them their wives, who were usually eager to share their domestic skills with their African acquaintances. Moreover, they enjoyed the assistance of young lady volunteers. The Catholic missionaries, from the beginning of their missionary endeavors in Kenya, sought the cooperation of the Brothers' and Sisters' congregations of European missionaries.

For the sake of convenience, we may divide the modern Kenyan Christian churches into three main groups—Protestant, Roman Catholic, and African Independent Churches (AICs).[110] Along with these groups, the Quakers, or Friends, is a significant group among the people of western Kenya and especially in the Bukusu community.[111]

The Protestant Churches in Kenya

In a significant article comparing the democratization processes of Zambia and Kenya, Michael Bratton, professor of comparative politics, public administration, and African politics, compares what he calls the "lead institutions" in the two countries—the trade unions and the churches. In describing Kenya, Bratton writes, "The Protestant faiths are joined, along with numerous independent African churches, in a countrywide umbrella body known as the National Council of Churches of Kenya (NCCK), and it [gradually confusing politics with faith] proceeds to portray the church in Kenya [as] an informal, extra parliamentary opposition to the Moi regime."[112]

Protestants in Kenya were converted by Protestant missionaries and retained significant identification with European and American Protestant churches. These churches tend to stress the authority of the Bible and the need for a personal relationship with Jesus Christ as one's personal savior. African Protestant churches range from churches of the Anglican community, which has much in common with the Roman Catholic community, to the Pentecostal mission churches under African leadership.

The Pioneering Work of Krapf and Rebmann, 1844–1874

The modern missionary enterprise in Kenya began almost as an accident. Johann Ludwig Krapf and Johann Rebmann, both Swiss German recruits from Basel Seminary, played an important role in the early history of Christianity in Kenya. Dr. Krapf began his missionary career in Ethiopia in 1837. When the government forbade him to do his work in Ethiopia, he shifted his efforts to Mombasa in 1844. In his missionary strategy, he dreamed of a chain of Protestant mission stations stretching across Africa.

Krapf and Rebmann established the first Christian mission at Rabai near Mombasa in 1846, among the Giriama people.[113] One Sunday, Rebmann and Krapf invited the local population to the first service at the new church they had built. Only a few people came, and when the service was over, the two missionaries rushed to the entrance of the church to hear the people's reactions. What they heard was far from enthusiastic. When asked whether they would come again on the following Sunday, the native people said no. When asked why not, they answered that they were accustomed to worshiping in another way. An animal should have been slaughtered; there should have been food and plenty to drink. There should have been drumming, singing, and dancing.

Rebmann and Krapf told the people that they were speaking like that because they were sinners. When the missionaries explained the notion of sin, the Warabai (the local people of Rabai) asked them who had been slandering them. The missionaries replied that God had sent His only Son so they might know that God loved them. Surely they could understand this love of a God, who had "given them their lives, their children, the sun and the moon, the rain and the harvest, and even their beer."[114] The concept of what worship looked like—including animal slaughter food and drink, and music—were deeply rooted in the African consciousness, and the missionaries had to go back to the deep origin of these roots if they were to convince the Africans of anything. They were not going to make progress if they addressed only superficial behaviors.

Slowly, the insistent rhetoric of the missionaries did produce converts, but the missionaries' failure to respect local cultures limited the Christian religions to growing only shallow roots. Having made that strong comparison of sudden outside influence versus long-standing tradition, there is a reason Christianity did not take, and still has not taken, root to the depth that it might have. The bottom line is that missionaries have tried to grow the Gospel on alien, multiple foundations of Western and modernist cultures, and these have failed to consider the fertile soil of the African cultures. "We no longer want you (missionaries) to come and teach us the Bible" is the frequent cry; "we want you to come and read the Bible together with us."

A New Kind of Christianity

When Pope John Paul II visited Kenya in 1985 for the 43rd International Eucharistic Congress, almost one hundred fifty years after the first missionaries arrived, he had a very different experience of the Church's local relevance. During Mass, parishioners brought live animals, fruits, beer, and honey to the altar as offerings. Two goats were tied to the altar;

they bleated all through the Mass. Drums were played, and people danced, and the whole congregation took part; even the security team put down their rifles and joined others in a meal. Partly as a result of this kind of cultural immersion, Christianity in Africa flourished through the joint efforts of overseas missionaries and the Kenyan Christians. Additionally, Christian missionary schools have been the nurseries of Christian growth and membership retention.

Understand, however, that the spread of Christianity in Kenya during the last one hundred fifty years is far more the story of Kenyan Christians spreading the Gospel than it is the story of only European or American Christians spreading the Gospel.[115] Unfortunately, African Christians rarely went on record with their stories, while European and American missionaries regularly sent letters to their relatives, mission boards, and financial supporters in Europe and America. Evidently, people came to know far more about European and American missionaries than they did about the African catechists and evangelists, whose role in spreading Christianity all over Africa was far more significant.

The most effective Christian mission activity began in Kenya's rural hinterland when its interior was opened to rail travel between Mombasa and Uganda at the end of the nineteenth century. Since those early days, the railway has helped to spread pastoral activity.

Many churches were founded in the 1920s and 1930s, especially in areas where Babukusu, Kikuyu, and Luo peoples predominated. Most churches tended to be ethnically homogenous, since colonial authorities maintained a policy of allocating a mission to a particular territory. Although this practice has changed with increasing communication and mobility, traces of it are still visible today. The first missionaries to be allocated to work among the Gusii people of western Kenya were the Seventh Day Adventists (SDA) and the Mill Hill Fathers (Roman Catholic Society), whose respective followers sometimes resorted to violent confrontation over land and members.[116] The natives came to internalize these conflicts, which they had played no part in creating, as will be discussed shortly.

John Baur, a Catholic priest and professor of Church history at Saint Thomas Aquinas Seminary in Nairobi, writes, "In 1895, after the creation of the Uganda Protectorate, the remaining area between Uganda and Mombasa was, without further ado, also taken under Queen Victoria's protective wings."[117] This area was called the British East Africa Protectorate until it became the Kenya Colony in 1920. Thus, the missionaries came to the interior of Kenya with the colonial settlers. They were allocated large portions of land, like the European settlers, and so, in the opinion of the people, the missionaries were indistinguishable from the colonizers. Baur continues, "Out of the twelve original mission societies spreading over Kenya, nine were Protestant. Unlike Tanzania and Uganda, Kenya appeared throughout its colonial history as an essentially Protestant country, and the heritage of the Reformation still today shapes its face in a remarkable way."[118]

The leading mission society in the early days of Kenya's missionary experience was the Anglican Church Missionary Society. In 1885, the Anglicans modified Dr. Krapf's ideal of the chain of mission stations across Kenya to Uganda. In 1888, the Anglicans were in the land of the Akamba people, where they significantly called their station Mlango (Gate). In 1900, the Anglicans built their Nairobi headquarters at Kabete and manned it with the famous Leakey family. One of the world's most productive groups of paleoanthropologists, the Leakey family has, over the span of seventy years, made major discoveries proving that humankind originated in Africa and that human ancestors were much older than scientific researchers previously believed.[119] The next step in the chain took them, in 1906, from Uganda to Maseno in western Kenya, which became the Protestant center of higher learning in western Kenya.

Although Kenya was the first east African country to see missionaries on its coast, it was the last one to receive them in its interior.[120] According to historians, there was no proper trade route across Kenya until the Kenya-Uganda railway was built; this railroad reached Nairobi in 1899 and Kisumu on Lake Victoria in 1901. William Anderson, a British historian, exclaimed, "On this new highway, at once a flood of missions poured into the Kenya highlands and the Nyanza area (western Kenya), unheard of in an African church, except in Zimbabwe." The coast was almost forgotten; the Galla people, once highly coveted as Christian converts, were left to the Muslims, and the Giriama people, to their traditions, while the Wataita complained in vain that the missionaries neglected them.[121]

The Roman Catholic Church

In Kenya, the Roman Catholic Church was founded by missionary orders of men and women who came from Europe and America in 1889.[122] The Catholics have, by and large, retained the distinctive elements of Roman Catholic tradition regarding the unity and authority of the Church. Participation in the sacrament of the Eucharist is as essential to the Kenyan Roman Catholic Church as it is to the worldwide Roman Catholic Church; it is the central act Catholics hold as signifying membership in the body of Christ. In addition to providing a spiritual influence, the mission stations served the people in practical ways that affected the culture. Where a mission was opened, things would begin to hum; lights went on, classes started, and wonderful medicine began to run its magic course. The Christian mission stations remained forever the focal points of local technical progress.

In describing the first Catholic missionaries into the interior, Baur wrote, "The [Roman] Catholic evangelization of inland Kenya was shared among three societies: the Holy Ghost Fathers from Ireland, advancing from the coast of Mombasa towards Kikuyuland; the Mill Hill Missionaries from England, expanding from Uganda to Western Kenya; and the Consolata Fathers from Italy, settling among the Kikuyu people around Mt. Kenya."[123]

The Holy Ghost Fathers

In 1899, the Holy Ghost Fathers were among the first to arrive in Nairobi. Their interest was not in the nascent town but in Kenya's largest ethnic group, the Agikuyu. From the leading chief, they received a plot in the uninhabited land between the Agikuyu and the Maasai, where they built Saint Austin's, the Catholic mother church of Nairobi. This missionary congregation, which originated in France, then migrated to Ireland, where it became famous for its pioneering work in coffee growing. Its efforts in the realm of evangelizing were directed toward Kiambu on the outskirts of Nairobi. However, planting coffee seedlings proved much easier than planting seedlings of faith. The major obstacle was the land issue that has been a running sore between Europeans and black communities in Kenya. Even in 2010, this conflict is a matter of great divisiveness.

The Mill Hill Missionaries

The Baganda, the Bukusu's western neighbors, were the first to welcome the "White Fathers," or the French Catholic priests, to Uganda. To show that their religion was not just a French religion, the White Fathers invited English-speaking priests to join them. They were called the Mill Hill Missionaries of Saint Joseph.

The first group of Mill Hill Missionaries followed their leader, Bishop Hanlon, the new bishop of the upper Nile, across the country in 1895.[124] The Mill Hill fathers arrived in western Kenya as soon as the railway had reached Kisumu, on Lake Victoria. We shall pick up the story of the Mill Hill fathers when we discuss the beginning of the Roman Catholic Church in Bukusuland.

The Consolata Fathers

The Consolata Missionaries took over Nyeri, the area around Mt. Kenya. Baur notes that their missionary method, from the beginning, was unique. First, great importance was placed on daily visits to the villages. Though the missionaries encountered some language difficulties, things improved greatly after they had trained some African catechists to accompany them and serve as translators. Second, the mission's dispensary offered free medical services. For this purpose, the Cottolengo Sisters were sent and later replaced by the Consolata Sisters. The third priority was given to schools; the local language, Kikuyu, served as the medium of instruction.[125]

AICs: African-based Versions of Christianity

The acronym AIC has stood for different things—African Independent Churches, African Instituted Churches, African Initiated Churches, and/ or African Indigenous Churches. The word "independent" signals that their origin or organization is autonomous in nature (unaffiliated, self-reliant, and free). Whatever the acronym may stand for, it reflects a genre of a great variety of African expressions of the Christian faith.

African Independent Churches (AICs), depending on who is describing them, were initiated by Africans and typically grew out of the Protestant mission context. Often frustrated with the Western missionaries, AICs have gone their own way and function without reference to overseas churches. AICs range from independent versions of Western Protestant churches to highly syncretistic Christian versions of traditional African religions, which may use Christian language in reference to God but have no real role for Jesus Christ.

First, AICs vary greatly. Even the initials *AIC* as the designation of a genre of African expressions of Christian faith are themselves understood in different ways. African *Independent* Churches are those that are independent in their origin and organization, though since the historic churches missionaries founded in Africa are at least juridically independent from their mother churches, this description is somewhat confusing. African *Instituted* Churches are those that came into being by the initiative of Africans.[126]

Second, while mainline churches emphasize Christology, AICs make the Holy Spirit the focus of belief and practice. While they firmly believe in the person of Jesus Christ, AICs appear more comfortable with the Holy Spirit, who seems more relatable, especially since Christ has ascended into heaven.[127]

Third, AICs represent a radically biblical movement. Taking off from the Protestant claim that the Bible is an open book subject to individual interpretation, the AICs have seen the Bible as a source to legitimate a wide variety of basic Christian patterns, often with special relevance to local conditions or special appeal to local people. Arguably, AICs represent a renewal movement, particularly in terms of effective evangelism and greater ability to communicate the Gospel to Africans than that of mainline Christian churches.[128]

The Quakers

Quakers believe that our own experience guides us toward God and toward God's will. Scriptures and the wisdom of others can help us, but God's spirit speaks to each of us, and it is our task to try to hear and understand it. Quakers try very hard to listen to their consciences, regarding messages from that realm as one way the Spirit speaks to us. The official title of the Quaker movement is the Religious Society of Friends, and Quakers are often referred to as "Friends." There are about twenty-eight thousand members of the Society in Britain but many more in America, Africa, and other parts of the world.[129]

The presence of early American missionaries in Kenya was altogether out of proportion to the political interest of the United States in Kenya at the time. The work of the Quakers, as well as of their Catholic colleagues, disproves the fashionable accusation that missionaries came as stooges of the colonial government. Some preachers came from typical American backgrounds. The Quakers settled down at Kaimosi, in western Kenya, in 1902.[130] Their official name was the Friends African Industrial Mission, and they were commonly known as the Friends.

The Kaimosi mission played an important role in the development of education, teachers' training, hospital work, and printing and industrial initiatives. The Quaker Rural Service Program did much in the fields of agriculture, nutrition, literacy, and family planning. They radiated a strong identity, stressing the spirit so much that baptism in water was not practiced. The Quakers called their community gatherings "meetings," rather than Masses or Services. The Quaker religion spread very quickly, and in 1914, it entered Bukusuland.[131] The first Quaker mission stations were at Lugulu and Kamusinga in Bukusu country. David Barrett, an anthropologist among the nomadic Turkana people of Kenya, reports, "Kenya has the largest 'Yearly Meeting' of Quakers in the world, outside the United States."[132]

The Friends Church was strongly in favor of development activities. Sometimes, however, some felt the urge to invest more heavily in evangelism. Thus, the 1927 Roho Revival in the Anglican Church affected the Friends church, and many of Anglican Church members joined the new Roho churches around Alfayo Odongo Mango.

Politically, too, the Friends were quite active. The Quakers organized the first Luhyia political association, with the Northwestern Kenya Central Association, in 1932.[133]

Growth and the Methods of Christian Evangelization in Western Kenya

The Mill Hill Missionaries Reach Western Kenya

After following Bishop Hanlon across the country, the Society of Saint Joseph (usually called the Mill Hill Fathers and Brothers) arrived in western Kenya as soon as the Kenya-Uganda railway reached Kisumu, in 1901.[134] They found little opportunity for evangelization in the isolated town of Kisumu, and in 1906, they moved on to Ojolla, into the heartland of the Luo people. Simultaneously, two stations were erected among the Abaluyia—one at Mumias, the ancient capital, and the other at Kakamega, the British headquarters of Western Province. The Bukusu people who chose to become Catholic had to trek a long way to Mumias, where they received catechetical lessons, until a Catholic mission was founded in 1931 in the Bukusu homeland, at Kibabii.

In the beginning, the Mill Hill Missionaries did not have a clearly defined method of evangelizing, though generally speaking, they used the school method, which seems to have been forced upon them by the competing Anglicans. In the recent past, when people spoke of missions, they usually had in mind the mission schools. For many, the schools were the most important institutions. A historian could well use schools as the barometer of Kenya's development. However, some of the Mill Hill priests—those with strong individual characters—invented their own methods of evangelization. Father Nicholas Stam, who was also known as the "apostle to the Bukusu people," was one who came up with his own method. Between 1895 and 1908, "Father Stam selected six newly baptized lectors and sent them out to start catechumanates, in which they had to teach prayers and the words of the catechism to the new readers."[135] Members of the following generation of baptized Bukusu were directed to do a year's teaching of religion, in what Father Stam referred to as "a token of gratitude to God for the grace of baptism."[136] These directives made for a very quick spread of Catholicism, despite determined opposition from the local chiefs. The native chiefs were hardly friendly to the missionaries in those days, despite the fact that, from very early on, these same chiefs had entrusted their sons to the missionaries for education.[137] The chiefs evidently resented the power of the priests, and that resentment spilled over onto the catechists and the head Christian leaders. In *The Way the Catholic Church Started in Western Kenya*, Hans Burgman, a Mill Hill Missionary from the Netherlands, argues that most of the chiefs were not really traditional leaders of the people:[138] Because the British colonizers appointed them, they had to assert their positions.[139]

In the midst of all this, a strong Catholic Church was shaping up. The flock grew in numbers and strength. Upon examination, it becomes clear that this growth was attributable largely to Father Stam himself and to the way he lived with his people. His favorite pastoral practice was simply to endure with the people in their times of trouble. When floods were high, he was there with his canoe. When famine was killing his catechists, he was right there feeding them. When Christians were fined and harassed by the colonial chiefs, Father Stam went and lived with them, in rough conditions. When catechists were put in prison for teaching Christianity, he went to their rescue, got them out, and stayed with them for some weeks until conditions improved. Baur claims that the response of the Luhyia community to Christianity was the most positive in Kenya, not only in terms of Catholics but also of Protestants.

Another Mill Hill missionary, Father Bouma, lived between 1908 and 1915 at Aluor, the mother church of the Luo people. He aimed his literacy efforts at the grassroots level and printed a leaflet with twelve rules of etiquette for his Christians. The people loved to read them so much that, a few years later, he gave the people fifty-one rules of etiquette, putting them together in an eight-page booklet called *KIKI* (don't). The booklet opens with these lines: "What does KIKI teach you? KIKI teaches you what things you should not do. So many things are forbidden. For example, do not give somebody something with your left hand; if you give somebody something, give with the right hand."[140] Father Bouma gave this direction because, culturally, the left hand is considered weak. Like in many international cultures, the local culture forbade using the left hand for anything of significance, such as eating, handling money, waving, shaking, or in any interactions with other people. The left hand is reserved for cleaning one's private parts and, therefore, considered dirty. He drew the rules from the taboos of the local people.

Like so many of the early missionaries, Father Bouma was an ardent traveler. He crisscrossed Luoland in patriarchal style, seated on a mule, carrying an elder's walking stick with a cross affixed to the top. Where he put his stick in the ground, there his tent had to be put up. He would chat with the elders from the area, and at the end of the day, he told them a few words about Jesus Christ. If the people wanted to know more about Christ, they would have to give him one of their boys, who would be instructed to deliver the whole message. At the end of the safari, he would ride back into the mission at the head of a long line of happy boys. At the Aluor Catholic mission, he gave them trousers and instructed them for three years. After that, they would be sent back to their own areas as catechists.[141]

Between 1908 and 1915, Father Witlox at Kakamega worked most successfully with outdoor instruction on Sundays, during which he included question-and-answer opportunities and settled disputes. All this was attractively framed within traditional songs and dances. His approach was a resounding success because of its apostolic medium, which took into account the context in which the people lived.

Not all of the missionary colleagues were enthusiastic. They argued that they had come to drive out the devil from this dark corner of Luhyia land and that one of the devil's favorite hiding places was in the dance. After all, in Europe, dancing was considered bad, even though the movements were decorous, restrained, and boring. But the *Isukha* women wiggling their hips, swinging their bottoms, and making their breasts tremble—surely this was immorality in its most blatant form! Therefore, Father Witlox's method was not taken over by other missionaries. Witlox did not intend to export the method either; he was happy enough to see his own people happy. Years later, his friend, Father Stam of Mumias, wrote, "Father Witlox had little thought that these dances would become the curse of the country … [or that they would lead] to a good deal of immorality."[142]

The people disagreed with Father Stam's verdict that Father Witlox's methods were harmful, and, today, one is inclined to agree with the people. Today, the Kenyan Christian church is referred to as a "dancing church," which affirms Father Witlox's method of evangelization.

Christianity Moves into Bukusuland

In the early years of the Catholic expansion in Bukusuland, the Church encountered the institution of the council of elders, called the *baraza*.[143] Here, local people, together with their leaders (*bakasa*), met to engage in dialogue, at least once weekly. The *baraza* played an important role in the community. In the *baraza*, doctors addressed people regarding public health issues, the agricultural officers spoke about better farming, and so on. The Catholic Church adapted the same method of the *baraza* under prominent Christian laity, who were answerable to the Mumias Catholic mission. In practice, the *baraza* were much more self-governing than consultative bodies. They diminished in importance as the mission stations multiplied.

The area north of Mumias, reaching into the foothills of Mount Elgon, had always attracted travelers and missionaries. In 1931, at Kibabii, the first Catholic mission in Bukusuland became an independent mission station with two resident priests. The establishment of many Roman Catholic schools followed. In 1935, another mission station, called Kiminini, was established at Elgon Club in the White Highlands to serve the natives who worked for the European settlers. A third new station was opened at Misikhu in 1951, and in the early sixties, there was a station at Sirisia, on the slopes of Mount Elgon.

During this time, the Catholic priests appeared to have worked more through the catechists they appointed than through representative councils of laypeople, although the latter existed on paper.[144] The priest visited every outstation within the parish at least once a month to hear confessions and to celebrate the Mass. On Sundays, in the absence of the priest, catechists led prayer services for the people in the outstations. Normally, the people who wanted to join the church attended the services, and there were occasions when catechumens were helped by the catechist to memorize set prayers, rather than listen to him preach. At times, a xeroxed text taken from the New Testament was read, together with a short explanation.

Priests, Catechists, and Religion

The work of extending the faith into the rural villages of Bukusuland began as soon as the first Catholic Church was established at Kibabii, in

1931. The Mill Hill Fathers and Brothers soon introduced education in Church-sponsored primary, middle, and secondary schools. When the Catholic sisters arrived, clinics and hospitals became popular centers, especially for the Bukusu rural population.

The catechists, together with the schoolteachers, as well as leading elders of Bukusu rural villages, were the backbone of the Catholic Church, even in the face of the lack of cultural conversion on the part of the missionaries. Chosen from among the noble and well-respected families within the community, catechists constituted a vital link between the missionaries and the local people and made Christianity, to some extent local and authentically Bukusu. The catechists had the advantage of knowing the local language and of a natural respect for the customs of the people. They also became examples to their compatriots, and they took over the responsibilities of teaching and looking after the mission stations when the missionaries went back to Europe on holiday. The candidates for baptism looked upon their catechists as protectors; the schoolchildren saw the catechists as their proper teachers of religion; and penitent sinners found in them mighty advocates. There was even a time in Bukusuland when the priests used catechists as interpreters during confessions. Even though the Mill Hill fathers were eager to learn the local language, they found these confessional interpreters very useful because the common people often trembled with fear when they approached a priest.

Christianity through Education

Here we describe the religious innovation among the Bukusu people and deal with another type of formal organization foreign to the Bukusu people, namely, the various Christian denominations or churches, each of which wanted to convert the Babukusu to their specific creed through education.

Historically, the Christian missions have played a leading part in the development of education in Bukusuland and in Kenya as a whole. In fact, it would be no exaggeration to say that the educational system in Kenya/Bukusuland was solely a creation of the Christian missions. This is not to ignore the informal education in traditional Bukusu society or Islamic learning, especially on the coast. However, formal education, in the modern sense, and the schools in which it is given, owe their origin to the Christian missions. De Wolf argues, "The [British] administration was interested in 'bureaucratic power'; the missions were interested in 'influence,' in order to persuade the Bukusu people to lead their lives according to Christian principles as they interpreted them."[145] The missionaries hoped to achieve this aim through control over the system of education.

During the colonial period, the government was slow to get involved in education. Even as late as 1949, when the Beecher Report (*African Education in Kenya*) was written, the churches still bore the burden of supporting and staffing most of the schools in the country, and in return, it was through the schools that they gained converts. Thus, the participation of the churches in education at the primary and secondary level was and is exercised now mainly through church sponsorship, which involves the responsibility for maintaining the religious traditions of the school. The meaning of sponsorship is further clarified by a ministerial circular that clarifies that some approved syllabi will include teaching that is closely connected to the pastoral aspects of religion.

The traditional belief system has proved to be the essential starting point for beginning to integrate Christian and Muslim religious views. It is as if a comprehension of the traditional belief system, not the least of which is the Bukusu excellence in applied dialogue, is the pre-catechetical necessity to understand the mutual relatedness of the traditional system with the other two religions.

The colonial government was happy to leave the education of the Kenyan people to the missionaries, since the government did not have the funds or personnel to train people for the development of the colonial economy. A. B. K. Kazozi, a historian at Makerere University, explains that the British government "was happy when Christian missions offered education as part of their evangelization process. Education was not only a means controlled by missionaries to produce the type of citizens they desired, but also a powerful vehicle of recruitment among the elite."[146]

Many Bukusu people were more interested in the means that the missionaries employed than in the missionaries' goals. A Western education became a necessary qualification for anyone who wanted to take advantage of new opportunities that the new society was able to offer. Thus, as soon as one had achieved such a qualification, he or she could discard Christianity.[147] Since the churches tried to expand as fast as possible, inhabitants were given leading positions in formal organizations that were set up to further this expansion. And since schools had to be licensed by the local chiefs and their councils, it became important to get the people to make decisions in favor of their own denominations.

European education became one of the key elements in the new political arena and the interplay between convert, missionary, and colonial government. Colonization led to a great demand for education and to the proliferation of schools. The Protestants had stressed literacy, education, and reading the Bible from the beginning of their missions, but the advent of colonial power meant that literacy gained social, political, and economic, not merely religious, importance. The Protestant and Catholic missionaries virtually monopolized the schools in Bukusuland, which in turn became a major conduit for new mission converts. These new converts, however, did not usually stay in school. They fanned out across Kenya in search of work, and in the process converted others, sometimes in astonishing mass movements. The new generation of educated Christians was quite different from the first generation of converts, which consisted largely of social outcasts finding safe refuge in mission villages.

There were many different Christian denominations at work in Bukusuland in the early twentieth century. The Anglican Church Missionary Society and the Catholic Mill Hill Mission in Kenya were natural extensions of their work in Uganda, which had captured the imagination of imperialists and missionaries alike so early.[148] Naturally, the Catholics and Protestants competed against each other, with the intention of expanding as quickly as possible. From the beginning, Catholics and Protestants believed that the very real threat was Islam, which had become the acceptable religion among the neighboring Wanga chiefs and headmen, who were used extensively in the colonial administration of Bukusuland as chiefs and security men. On the other hand, both Protestants and Catholics thought that Christianity as practiced by the other denomination was almost as bad as Islam.[149]

The construction of the railway line from Mombasa to Kisumu attracted various North American missions, including the Quakers, the Church of God, and the Pentecostal Assemblies of God.[150] The Pentecostal Assemblies of God work very much alone and consider any type of formal leadership unnecessary, since the Holy Spirit leads the church.[151] In their preaching, members always argued that membership in a particular denomination could not save anyone. The Pentecostals are notable for the extent to which women play leading roles in pastoral and evangelical activities, as well as in higher education. Women are pastors and teachers. Harvey Cox, an American theologian, writes about the Pentecostal use of drums and African instruments, as well as ancestral veneration, in worship, in opposition to the standard European expressions of Christianity.[152] Drumming and dancing are rather unrestrained during services, and faith healing and prophesying attract much curiosity from the nonreligious.

Jan de Wolf relates how the Bukusu people came to be divided along religious lines. In 1909, the Kakamega District was divided into locations with officially authorized chiefs. Chief Murunga of Wanga, a Muslim and a non-Bukusu, was sent to rule over the northern Bukusu. He reserved his area for the Protestants, while Chief Sudi, who ruled over the southern Bukusu, though not a Catholic at the time, wanted his area for the Catholics only. This marked the split of a once-united Bukusu community into two warring groups, Protestant and Catholic. Pascal Nabwana, a head Christian who championed the advance of Catholicism in the Protestant area, expressed sorrow at this division. His own argument was that it was wrong that the Bukusu community should be divided along these religious lines, which would confirm the arbitrarily drawn boundaries between the Bukusu locations, north and south.[153] After all, in Limuru (near Nairobi), where Nabwana had worked for a timber company and on the European farms, people from different religious persuasions lived peacefully under one roof. "Why should this be impossible at home?"[154] Nabwana questioned. Yet the Protestants, whose stronghold was the northern Bukusu, did not acquiesce. A Quaker account from 1926 reports:

The Catholics tried to enter the district and start at six places. Some boys came to blows with them. Native Council decided to grant only one school. Our teachers hold a place of influence and respect on these Councils.[155]

The Kibabii Catholic Diary of 1926 notes, "The border schools [north Bukusu] work but give a lot of quarrels and 'fighting.'" In 1929 the Quakers also tried to establish territory, according to the Diary:

In April a lot of fighting put up by Americans. Thirty of them came down to Mahero's [south Bukusu] and settled there and built their school. Chief Sudi burnt it down. In 1928 assistant Chief Waluchio of [north Bukusu] arrested Pascal Nabwana and his friend Gaitano because they kept open two unlicensed schools. They were brought before chief Murunga who sentenced them to six months' imprisonment. But the priest could appeal to the DC [district commissioner].[156]

In a letter dated 1932, a Kibabii Catholic priest wrote:

The *baraza* of north Bukusu consists of the greater deal of followers of Mr. Ford's mission [head of the Quakers]. Continually they are exercising their secular power to prevent us [Catholics] from teaching in north Bukusu … continually they get hold of our readers and beat them up.[157]

In response to both warring communities, the district commissioner gave an independent assessment of the situation, in a summary of events between 1929 and 1935:

South Bukusu has always been a RC [Roman Catholic] stronghold. Traditional elders bowed to the inevitable, but tried hard to allow one religion only and Quakers were consistently kept out. This again could not last and broke down again in 1934. In Kimilili [north Bukusu] Catholics had as hard a time in establishing themselves as the Protestants had in south Bukusu. But friction is now less. Catholics frequently complain of obstruction but on the whole they get on well together.[158]

The expansion of churches among the Bukusu people depended on the level of activity of the teachers, who gained various advantages in their jobs. They received a modest income in cash, and a teacher would often combine teaching with being a part-time secretary for the local headman in the reserves, or teachers became clerks on European farms and ran part-time evening classes for the African employees.

Chief Murunga of north Bukusu, though a Muslim, was impressed by the advantages that chiefs in Buganda had gained from cooperation with the missions. He wanted his subjects to wear clothes, go to school, and learn handcrafts. Equally important must have been the attraction of a new religion after the troubles of World War I. Learning to read and write helped the young men (only young men could attend school) to qualify for employment with the missions as teachers.

The Bukusu Union

In an effort to unify the confluent religions for the betterment of all, Paschal Nabwana, head Christian of the Catholic mission in north Bukusu in 1935 started the Bukusu Union as the Bukusu Education Society. Another person who played a role in this form of dialogue was Henry Kerre, a Catholic and the son of Chief Sudi of south Bukusu. From north Bukusu came Daniel Simiyu, a Quaker. From the same area came Musa Mbuto of Lugulu, also a Quaker. As de Wolf notes, there was no precedent elsewhere in the district for people of different denominations coming together.[159] Nabwana and his fellow Catholics simply took the missionaries' argument against denominational segregation to its logical conclusion—desegregation came quietly to Bukusuland.

The dialogue Anglicans, Catholics, Quakers, Muslims, and traditional believers achieved was remarkable, in light of the competition between Catholics and Protestants during the previous decade. At the first meeting, the group was able to come to four important decisions, with integration of the Bukusu people as the main theme. They decided that the three

Christian denominations—Catholics, Anglicans, and Quakers—and the Muslims should be brought together by introducing a system whereby pupils of different backgrounds would be able to associate in games and education with one another; [160] that all missionary boundaries should be abolished, as the Bukusu people had had no say in this issue; that there should be a single leader through whom they could communicate with the government (there and then it was agreed that Chief Sudi should be this person); and that contributions of money should be made toward the building of more schools without thinking in terms of religion, as well as for the establishment of a Bukusu football (soccer) team. Funds were actually used to assist in the building of schools at Kibabii (Catholic), Butonge (Anglican), and Chwele and Lugulu (Quaker).[161]

Much writing on Christianity in Africa, my own included, has been shaped by a reaction against a tradition of missionary biography wherein the foreign Christian is the heroic actor and the Bukusu Christians merely the backdrop for his or her good report. Often, the natives are depicted initially as savage and degenerate to highlight the beneficial impact of Christianity brought by the missionaries.

The refutation of this distorted lens, which Nigerian historians Ajayi and Ayandele have pioneered, has emphasized both the role of Africans themselves in the spread of Christianity and the favorable dialoguing that has led to mutual acceptance of all religions practiced there.[162] However, one cannot do justice to African encounters with Christianity without some understanding of those who were bringing it. Christianity has never existed in an abstract form; it is always incarnated in a particular milieu. The age, nationality, gender, church affiliation, and theological bent of the missionaries had a decisive impact on the message Christianity would impart.

The churches in Bukusu homelands played a dual role in the dynamic of social change among the Bukusu people. The churches brought people together in a formal organization that transcended the traditional limits of effective social interaction, but they isolated members from neighbors and kinsmen, with whom they could no longer share common concerns. Those interested in formally organized religion and the culture it espoused, which diminished the importance of multiplex ties, were often better placed to see opportunities for advancement in a wider society, which seemed irrelevant to other people. Such opportunities, the result of church affiliation, contrasted directly with traditional ways of gaining prestige. The economic differentiation resulting from some taking advantage of the new opportunities led to even greater isolation.

CHAPTER 8

• ◆ •

THE HISTORY OF BUKUSU TRADITIONAL RELIGION

Traditionally, the Bukusu have expressed their communication relationship with the visible and the invisible through myth, folklore, proverbs, and sayings. The oral traditions of a people are vehicles for capturing a culture, tradition, religion, spirituality, and social behavior. Dominique Zahan, professor of anthropology at the University of Paris V, Sorbonne, notes, "Spirituality is found principally in the mystical emotion provided by African people's [beliefs], and can also be seen in the meanings they give to the dialogue between humanity and the invisible [world]."[163] Geoffrey Parrinder, professor of the comparative study of religions at the University of London, concurs with Zahan when he asserts, "The unity of African spiritual concepts can be perceived in the attitude which the individual may adopt toward the world and the invisible."[164] Paraphrasing a biblical verse, Parrinder writes, "Man beneath the sky lives on the land, not in a void but as a sovereign vital force. He has no doubt that he was made to have dominion over every living thing that moves upon the earth. It is his duty to 'be fruitful, and multiply, and replenish the earth, and subdue it.' On the other hand he knows that he is not able to do these things by himself, and he seeks the help of every available power, spirits and gods 'that share this earth with man as with their friend."[165]

As for the substance of religion, according to Parrinder, it is polarized in four directions—"the earth below, the sky and the Supreme being above, the ancestors on one side, and the deities and natural forces on the other."[166] But humanity is at the center of the universe. Babukusu spiritual life is based on this vision of one's position and the role that one plays in relation to the universe. Zahan observes, "The idea of finality outside of man is foreign to African spirituality. Man was not made for God or for the universe; he exists for himself and carries within himself the justification of his existence and of his religious and moral perfection. It is not to please God or out of love for God that the African prays, implores or makes sacrifices, but rather to become himself and to realize the order in which he finds himself implicated."[167] The sky and the divinity are thought of only insofar as they represent something about the African people, who constitute the keystone of the Bukusu religious structure. In order to understand the history of Babukusu traditional religion and its social implication, this study analyzes the Bukusu's origin myth and meaning, as well as their folklore and religious cosmology.

Babukusu Oral Tradition
According to their myths, passed down through oral history, the Bukusu people are said to have originated in Egypt. They came up the river Nile to *Esamoya* (Uganda) and then moved into *Mbayi* and *Sirikwa* (Uganda), where they found suitable soil for settlement, and lived there before moving on into *Namarare* in Bughishu and *Solokho* and then into *Ebwayi*, south *Teso*, near Tororo, Uganda. They later migrated into Bukusu, where they are found today. According to Bukusu historian Makila, two factors must have forced *Mubukusu* (Bukusu ancestor) and his followers to leave *Misri* (Egypt). First, the weather changed so drastically that dry spells began to occur quite frequently. Animals died of starvation and dehydration due to the scarcity of water, and the standard of agriculture declined considerably.

Secondly, there appeared a strange race of people (Arabs) in the neighborhood, who terrorized Bukusu herdsmen from time to time, kidnapping their women and children and stealing their animals. As time went by, conditions deteriorated and were particularly worsened by the second factor.[168]

Most Bukusu people continue retelling their ancestral stories of migration, although, considering the limits of human memory, not in great detail. However, a handful of elders, traditional Bukusu historians, and the "comforters" (*baseni be kumuse*) are able to give a detailed outline of Babukusu origin and migration.[169] A small number of Bukusu scholars have also committed some information to writing.

The Babukusu categorically admit that whenever they tell the story of their migration, they do not mean to imply that one hundred percent of their people moved together at once. The fact that has to be recognized by historians, and that is sometimes made clear among the Babukusu through oral tradition, is that in every corner of the world, communities of different ethnic backgrounds have coexisted side by side and have even intermingled with and influenced each other. When migration movements occurred, there were several ways in which each group of people tended to lose its own members to other groups.

The passing on of Bukusu myths and other cultural stories is the duty of grandparents. Around age eight or nine, children are sent to live with their grandparents, who pass on to them the knowledge of the clan. The following narrative is what I remember being taught by my grandmother at age eight.

This is the story of Mango, the first elder, who killed the monstrous snake called *eyabebe* and restored the circumcision rite, which has continued until today.

A long time ago (yabao khaale)—no one knows how long—a small, wandering group of people came from Egypt to settle in the shadows of Mount Masaba (or Elgon, as it is commonly known today). The journey was slow; each bit of distance was a matter of burning the land clean, of sowing and reaping millet, of making grass-thatched houses, of birth and death. But by the time Bukusu people reached Mount Elgon, they numbered enough to be called Babukusu nation.

The Babukusu lived at a place called *Mwia'ala* for a very long time. During this period, war, weariness, and constant migrations caused them to neglect the circumcision practice. Bwayo of the Bakhurarwa clan had a son called Mango.

Mango Mukhurarwa was a very brave and resolute young man, and his popularity won him leadership over the majority of the clans that lived at Mwia'ala. Mango desired a certain *Sabaot* (a beautiful woman from across the valley in *Sabaot* land). The girl's parents told Mango that to marry a *Sabaot* girl, he'd have to be circumcised. And to be circumcised he must kill an *eyabebe* (python) that has been terrorizing our community.

The serpent was unleashing untold mischief in the community, swallowing animals and people alive. Mango, a great hunter and determined man, sharpened his *machete*. He smeared his body with mud to hide his human odor and waited for the python in its cave.

In the evening, the python returned home, coiled itself comfortably to take a nap, its head facing outside the cave. Skillfully, Mango took his *machete* and slashed the serpent's head off with a swift and deadly stroke. The python was dead.

Mango's bravery won the hearts of the *Sabaots*, and that very day, under the fierce tropical sun, he was circumcised as the overjoyed *Sabaots* ululated and sang songs of praise.

The mark of circumcision served as a constant reminder of Mango's bravery, and from then on, the Babukusu have possessed the gift of circumcision, and they have carried on with that custom diligently for decades.

These are not historical narratives in the ordinary sense. These stories have no dates, no orderly procession of events, and no real beginning or end. Rather, they are a meaty, succulent stew of myths, proverbs, legends, fables, jokes, and cautionary tales told by a people about themselves through generations. Some of the Babukusu stories may surely be exaggerated; some may never have happened. But this is not important, for what is captured in their stories is the essence of a people, called the Babukusu, who are alive and who continue living their myth day in and day out. A person who would understand the nature of religion must start with its story. A religion is a story of relationships. Herald Scheub, professor of African languages and literature at the University of Wisconsin-Madison, describes myth thusly:

> [Myth is] a story that contains within it the deepest held beliefs, the hopes and fears, dreams and nightmares of a people. If a storyteller is the guardian, the repository, of the past, he is also its interpreter, always in the process of revising history, recasting our notions of origins, and so it is that, within the context created by the storyteller, the past and the present are constantly in a process of becoming. The world of the storyteller is a churning cauldron of images that, worked into form, becomes a momentary means of establishing union between the present living generation and all generations that have preceded it.[170]

Scheub continues, "Nor are the stories that comprise the myths of a people merely fable, explanatory tales, children's versions of complex adult themes." Rather, Scheub declares:

> In a rich and enormously complex way, story is a religious system of a people. It is not a means to understanding, not a path to God; rather, it is the means whereby humans, as members of audiences, move to oneness with God. That is the effect of myth, and that is why we humans will not let stories go. They are our means of communing with our deepest beliefs. So myth is not simply the story behind the ritual, myth is the ritual, the essence of religious faith. The fantasy elements, the "irrational" elements, of myth are

at the center of an artistic activity that has the effect of joining the emotions of the audience—for story is always and primarily, if not exclusively, a process of feeling—to the images of the past, those images conjuring up the emotions and then joining them to the past. The enormously complex performances, aspects of storytelling, the art of the storyteller, are the key to understanding the meaning of myth.[171]

The sanctity of mythmaking is that it is a place where all members of the community come into focus, and this is what has to be comprehended if we are to understand the force of a story, in terms of its relevance as a religious belief. In this capacity, the audience, by means of its emotional contribution, expands and, therefore, redefines the term *audience*, as it is not merely a group of spectators. Those watching are an integral part of the performance. The Bukusu people express their cosmology with their myths, which are not merely projections into a vacuum but conditioned responses to the real world that penetrate unconditioned reality to reveal a deeper truth.

Human Beings: Center of the Universe

As the creator of the universe, God is outside and beyond it; at the same time, since God is also its sustainer and upholder, He is very close to the universe. Although in African creation myths, human beings put themselves at the center of the universe, they are not the masters of the universe; they are only the center, the friend, the beneficiary, the steward, sustained by nature. For that reason, humanity has to live in harmony with the universe, obeying the laws of nature and its moral and mystical order. Nature, as God's "creature" is alive, and deserves protection. Destroying nature is equivalent to destroying life, and it offends God; protection and proper use of nature is synonymous with respect for God.

At the heart of Bukusu traditional religion is the belief that the purpose and the meaning of any particular object in the universe is determined by its relationship to human beings. This idea is engraved in the following Bukusu creation myth:

In the beginning, God [Wele] created the sun, and Wele wondered for whom the sunshine would shine? So Wele made the first man called Mwambu. Since Mwambu would talk and see, he needed someone to talk to. Then, Wele made the first woman, whose name was Sela. Mwambu and Sela wanted something to drink, so, Wele made water fall from heaven, which filled up the holes and valleys to make lakes and rivers. Wele instructed Mwambu and Sela about the flesh they could eat. Some animals were allowed for food; others were prohibited.

In the creation story of the Babukusu, humanity is at the center of experience, and everything else is seen in relation to the human point of view. For everything that was created, there was a human-related reason. Robert B. Fisher, professor of theology at Xavier University in New Orleans, confirms, "Every other creature exists for the community of humans … the content of the dance, the drumming, the myth, the folktale, the proverb, and other rituals and artifacts revolve around human being in community, whether family, lineage, village, clan, or ethnic group, living or dead."[172]

Bukusu Cultural Phenomena
All cultures are naturally inclined to change and, at the same time, to resist change. In any situation, there are active processes operating that encourage acceptance of new ideas and things, while there are others that encourage changeless stability. Within a society, processes leading to change include adaptation through the fascination with novelty and loss of culture. I have seen that some Bukusu people defend culture by acting as if culture is a fixed entity that must never be changed. There are some who hold that a traditional society determines its own creative potential, while modern society is determined by the creative activity that pushes an envelope of possibilities. European and American thinkers of the Enlightenment, such as Johann Herder, German philosopher and theologian (1744–1803), formulated theories of history in which peoples were viewed as advancing through several stages, starting with nature and primitivism and progressing until they reached the height of advanced,

modern civilization.[173] Europeans sought their own primitive origins through studies of language, folklore, and archeology, as well as history. Through ethnography and the study of comparative religions, they also explored the people they had colonized, using them as examples of earlier stages of cultural development.

Building on this information, I attempt to unpack the term *culture* in the context of the Bukusu people and their surroundings. Take, for instance, as Zahan relates, that water often dictates the orientation of habitations; water always conditions human existence wherever the scarcity of it, or lateness of rains, endangers the means of subsistence. Water is the harbor of life. One can, therefore understand, the great role played by the personage commonly called the "rainmaker," who is in contact with the earth and who is no less than an intelligent master of elements. Zahan insists "From this point of view, the individual does not constitute a closed system in opposition to the outside world. On the contrary, the individual enters into the surrounding environment, which in turn penetrates him. Between the two realities there exists a constant communication, a sort of osmotic exchange, owing to which humanity is found permanently listening, so to speak, to the pulse of the world with her surroundings."[174]

The idea is that the environment dictates the sort of cultural constraint each community has. The term *culture* here contains two key elements. The first element of culture is the shared response of a group of people to the challenges of their habitat. For example, the surroundings or environment may constitute a river that challenges the community's happiness. The river gives good fish, but it will not readily give fish to the people; it holds water for agriculture, but that is not so easy to transport; it can enable you to travel, but it can also bring invaders. The river can give life by offering water to the thirsty and bring death by malaria.

The second element of culture responds to the challenges raised by the answers that people work out in the face of ecological problems, which take the shape of tools, artifacts, systems, and achievements. These things become the cultural surroundings of a people, presenting new challenges to which they must respond. Thus, culture moves, and the possibilities of development are infinite.

In the Bukusu homelands, people coped with the age-old circumstances of migration, climate, and geography, the availability of food, human relations, and group security. This was a productive, successful culture, assigning a fair share of life's burdens and rewards to every type of person in the community, emphasizing the simple, common enjoyment of life, and discouraging excess. They knew that the struggle to survive was only part of life, not all of it.

Avenues of Dialogue

Anyone interested in the history and culture of the Bukusu people, Makila, a leading Bukusu historian and scholar, stresses, must understand the importance of experiential learning when studying religion. Makila suggests four steps such a person should take in order to avoid the risk of oversimplification. First, he says, "A researcher should, without any pre-arrangement, attend funeral gatherings held in honor of deceased distinguished Bukusu personages and listen to spontaneous utterances of *Baseni be-kumuse* (public comforters), whose public function is to communicate to the audience certain important facts of life in Bukusu society that have been handed down from generation to generation through the medium of oral traditions and myth."[175]

In this case, *kumuse* is a public forum that is inclusive and does not make distinctions on the basis of age, sex, or other factors. *Kumuse* provides an occasion for public therapy. Hence, the ritual performer is referred to as *omukambisi*, comforter or counselor. The "comforter" is called in to speak to and comfort the people when they assemble after a funeral to distribute the property of the deceased; to decide who should inherit the widow(s); and to settle claims, debts, and disputes.

The death of each clansman marks a critical occasion for the preservation of peace within and between the clans, as such a death invariably leads to accusations of witchcraft or sorcery as the cause of death. It is, then, the responsibility of a comforter to forestall the effect of such accusations by pointing out that all peoples are born into this world to die and that people should not harbor grievances and accuse one another of sorcery, as such an attitude will merely increase the sorrow that has overcome them.

Killing someone intentionally, or even accidentally, is the worst crime one can commit in Bukusuland. Once you have murdered someone, it is your immediate duty to report the case to your clan elder, whose role is to reconcile the people and end the conflict immediately. To carry out the reconciliation for murder, both parties must be present. The killer comes out and owns up to his or her mistakes, asking for forgiveness and giving compensation; this allows the family of the deceased to live in peace. As for the killer, the situation pinches his or her ears, meaning the killer will never live it down. This practice demonstrates that the Bukusu value life—this is why the deceased's clan does not seek revenge. It is also a lesson for the killer to value life and never kill again. The comforter usually concludes his speech with a review of the great deeds of the clan and with exhortations to live up to that ancient tradition to dismiss petty quarrels and to enter into dialogue for the sake of peace.

Equally important at this ceremony is a clan leader, or *omukasa*, a symbol of unity. The clan leader is expected to speak for unity when legal disputes are discussed before Bukusu elders. The degree to which the *omukasa* succeeds in such efforts determines his recognition as a leader.

Secondly, Makila recommends that a researcher should interview clan elders individually and then follow up with interviews in informal *barazas*, or open meetings for group discussions. Thirdly, the researcher should approach literate elders or individual clansmen for free opinions, provided that what he or she hears is relevant. Finally, one should compare and contrast one's research collections with existing published and unpublished records. This form of approach leads to the researcher's understandings of the religious beliefs.[176]

Bukusu Religious Beliefs

In many respects, what makes a society cohesive is the relative centrality of its religion. Religion expresses and determines what people consider being reality—how something came to be, how it is structured, and how people need to behave. One common form of behavior in societies with centrally relevant religiosity is that which is ritualistic because, in religious rituals, the community commitment to a shared reality is expressed and reinforced. In a positive sense, religion highlights and sanctifies. In a negative sense, it restricts. Where there are reverence and ritual, there is also taboo.

To followers of the various religions of the world, each believer's own religious tenets does not appear as a myth of creation but as the truth regarding ultimate reality. Traditionally, the Babukusu had a conceptualization of a high God, the creator of the world, and of human beings, that was comparable to the Biblical God or the Qur'anic Allah, whom they call *Wele Khakaba* (God the giver). Along with this high God, Babukusu tradition includes a number of minor spirit beings who are God's associates. Günter Wagner asserts, "Although Christian influence started among the Bukusu people at a much later date than among other Luhyia communities, it seems that the Babukusu traditional concept of the Supreme Being has not only been better preserved, but that the concept of God was much more fully developed than among other surrounding neighbors."[177] The foremost quality ascribed to Wele is that of the creator of the world and of humankind. God's role as a creator becomes evident from the elevated formula by which He is addressed in prayer:

Wele ewe wakhung'ona khukende khusialo siowo
Wele, you who made us [so that] we may walk on your earth

Wang'ona chikhafu ne bibindu bilimo
You who made the cattle and the things which are on it

Following this invocation, the actual prayer request is evoked before all in attendance. It is also said that, when Wele had created both the world and the people on it, He said to himself:

Ese nang'ona babandu
Niye nganile akhula
Ne niye ndobile afwa.

It is I who made the people;
Whom I like I will to grow
and whom I refuse he (shall) die.[178]

Therefore, Wele, having created human beings, is also thought to have retained control over their welfare.

Traditional Bukusu religious beliefs are in harmony with the prevailing Abaluhyia and generally Bantu idea that the spirits of the dead have a continuing influence over the fortunes of the living. A crucial aspect of the relationship, which the Bukusu people believe exists between the living and the dead, is the distinction they make between the recently deceased relatives, or *bimakombe*, and the ancestral spirits, or *kimisambwa*. The living dead (*bimakombe*) live in the now, or *sasa* period, while the ancestors (*kimisambwa*) live in the past, or *zamani* period.[179] It is of paramount importance to secure and maintain the support of *kimisambwa*.[180] This support is gained through rites of prayer, which are most commonly held at Bukusu homestead ancestral shrine (*namwima*).[181] Bukusu folktales give instances of specific phenomena and types of behavior that are good or bad and then offer particular explanations as to why. Babukusu also support the traditional assumption that the ancestral spirits are the only generalized source of power. If the ancestral spirits, *kimisambwa*, are indifferent or angry toward someone, that person will not receive blessings. Man-eating giants (*kamanani*), not ancestors, are the superhuman agents of evil in Bukusu myths. Wild animals, enemy tribes, and those phenomena traditionally considered bringing ritual danger (*luswa*) and the actions of sorcery are commonly cited as other agents of danger.[182]

Owing to the antisocial nature of witchcraft, the real or alleged activities of the witches (*balosi*, plural) are always carried out in secrecy. No person would ever publicly admit to being a witch (*omulosi*, singular), and to call someone by this name is one of the most terrible insults one can level against another. The person thus insulted would not rest content until he or she had vindicated him or herself by swearing an oath or by submitting, together with the accuser, to an ordeal. Witches are regarded as inherently bad. Witches are believed simply to enjoy using their marginal powers to make people barren or to make them sicken and die. The witches get their evil nature either from having a "disposition of blood" present in their family or from having acquired such a disposition intentionally, through learning.

There are also diviners (*baliuli*), or sorcerers, among the Bukusu who are not witches. They use their supernatural powers primarily to protect their families and clients from the medicine and spells of witches and enemy sorcerers.[183] Sorcerers are believed to turn their art against other people mainly for two reasons. The first reason is jealousy over another's wealth, health, or good luck. Jealousy, however, is also believed to characterize witches. Any known sorcerer who seems, by character, to be especially prone to jealousy may be suspected of being a witch.

The second common cause of a sorcerer's negative influence is that of exercising vengeful anger beyond that which would be considered justifiable. A sorcerer may hold something against someone whom he or she suspects of having harmed a member of his or her family. No one among the Bukusu people, young or old, is believed to become seriously ill or die simply because of an accident or because of natural death. At every death and serious illness, a human agent is suspected, unless there is clear evidence before the death or the onset of illness that the person has fallen into a state of ritual impurity (*khukwa luswa*); that he or she has violated an oath, for which the consequence always is illness, if not death; or, that he or she was possessed of an evil spirit (*simakombe*), which was conjured to attend with evil in mind.

Running counter to this traditional thinking, today the Babukusu readily accept the modern medical explanations of doctors and dispensary nurses as to the causes of illness—for example, that the mosquito is responsible for malaria. Bukusu thinking about the reasons for disease and death, however, still remains unchanged. No one among the Bukusu people ever denied that the strike of a poisonous snake was the direct cause of the victim's death. But a Bukusu person is not satisfied with this level of explanation. The issues become: Why did the snake get in the way of the man to strike him? Why did the malaria-infected mosquito bite that baby? Now that modern drugs can cure many diseases, with relative ease, there has been a change for most people—they no longer try to figure out who or what was deliberately responsible; they simply take the medical cure. In the case of diseases that modern medicine can cure only through extended treatment, however, most Bukusu people still seek the services of the traditional diviner and the sorcerer.

The Ancestors as Bukusu Elders

In Bukusu culture, ancestors beyond remembrance by name have mystical powers and authority. Theirs is a functional role in the world of the living, or what Mbiti terms *collective immortality*, specifically in the life of their living kinsmen; indeed, Bukusu kin groups are often described as communities of both the living and the dead. The relation of the ancestors to their living kinsmen has been described as ambivalent—either punitive or benevolent—and sometimes, quite unpredictable. In general, ancestral benevolence is maximized through propitiation and sacrifice. Neglect of the ancestors is believed to bring about punishment. Ancestors are intimately involved with the welfare of their kin group, but they are not linked in the same way to every member of that group. Such relationships are structured through the elders of the kin group, and the elders' authority is related to their close link to the ancestors. In a sense, the elders are the representatives of the ancestors and act as the mediators between them and the community. The Bukusu emphasis is clearly not on how the dead live but on the manner in which they affect the living. Different ancestors are recognized as relevant to different structural contexts (for example, in groups of different genealogical levels); not all, but only certain dead with particular structural positions, are venerated as ancestors. The dead members of the lineage are collectively appealed to in times of crisis and more regularly on such occasions as the marriages of women of the lineage; the breaking of sexual taboos, such as incest; and the coming out or initiation rites for the youth.

It should be noted that Bukusu people believe today, as formerly, that there are those among the elders who, above all others, have the authority to preserve the well-being of the living. But they who consolidate also can kill. The death of an elder does not belie this notion; rather, in the eyes of the Bukusu people, it reaffirms this idea by suggesting that the remaining elders are as powerful as or more so than the one who has just died. An elder is not usually taught most of the important rituals until he or she has reached middle age. It is believed that some of the most powerful and dangerous methods of sorcery may make their practitioners permanently sterile. Thus, these medicines are almost exclusively the tools of the very old, as they have passed child-bearing age.

Care of the shrine is the responsibility of the homestead elder. Only the man who has reached the age of the elders can keep such a shrine, which is set up for him in his own homestead by his clan elders; a man is obligated to call in a senior member of his clan to preside at all ceremonies held at his homestead shrine, until he himself has become a senior elder.

In times of offerings and sacrifice, it is common for a presiding elder or priest first to beseech and praise one or two of his deceased family members, usually mentioning them by name. Then he implores the ancestors for help. The ritual elder assumes that the way to get the attention and help of the ancestors is by first remembering and praising the recently deceased members of the family (Mbiti's the "living dead").[184] The living dead, flattered by being remembered and praised, may then be moved to solicit help of the ancestors on behalf of the living descendants. The Bukusu people view a personal connection as most helpful in dealing with the supernatural, just as they do relative to the living.

Western Interpretations of Bukusu Witchcraft and Sorcery Beliefs

Witchcraft for the Bukusu is neither "black" nor "white." Witchcraft is a belief that respects Mother Nature, and she is neither completely positive nor completely negative; the same holds true for witches. Western skepticism toward witchcraft and sorcery beliefs prompts the question of why witchcraft should even exist.[185] Several responses to this question have been proposed, foundational to many of which is the functionalist approach first applied to witchcraft beliefs by Kluckholhn and Clyde Kay Maben, American anthropologists at Harvard. Their work remains influential, despite unease about the meaningful exaggerations of a system of witch beliefs.[186] Lucy Mair, professor of anthropology at Makerere University, Uganda, suggests that, in the absence of scientific knowledge, witchcraft beliefs are needed to somehow explain suffering, and particularly unjust suffering, the responsibility for which cannot be referred back to the victim.[187]

Mair's approach requires expertise. First, it assumes that witchcraft as a reason for suffering will disappear in the face of scientific reason, which has not been the case, since traditional and scientific approaches operate on different levels. Secondly, the scientific approach fails to show why, in so many societies throughout the world, witchcraft explains misfortune. Witchcraft is applied only to those matters that cannot be explained through natural causes. Rather, the witchcraft is used to explain misfortunes in socially relevant terms—that is, the question of why a certain disaster happened in certain temporal and spatial relations, given the social circumstance in which it was embedded. Witchcraft tries to explain the peculiarity associated with certain misfortunes, consequences that cannot be accounted for by resorting to natural and perceivable causes alone. For instance, say a hut collapses and people who were under it were killed. A Bukusu knows very well that the hut collapsed because ants had been gnawing away at the straws and that people were under the hut because it was a hot day. But the Bukusu asks: Why is it that these two events happened concurrently to kill people who were in the hut? This is the kind of question that must be answered by witchcraft. And insofar as this involves attributing the act of "bewitching" to someone who would be perceived as causing the misfortunes, this attribution is always socially relevant. There must have been social reasons for such misfortunes.

Moral and Religious Approaches to Witchcraft

Although they are frequently criticized, witchcraft and sorcery beliefs are understood as a means by which the Babukusu affirm and enforce their moral code. In this respect, they operate in a number of ways. First, the image of the witch represents the values of society by offering the contrast of amoral, antisocial behavior, particularly incest and the destruction of one's own kin, but also of lesser antisocial traits, such as solitariness, selfishness, and rudeness.

For one to avoid the allegation of witchcraft, it is advisable to cultivate constructive relationships with the community, and the Bukusu people give specific instructions to their children with this danger in mind. The behavior of the Babukusu may be motivated by fear of being accused of sorcery. This fear requires that they conform to accepted standards of social behavior, such as friendliness, good manners, hospitality, and generosity. A person who is habitually rude, who builds his or her house in the bush far away from other people, and who neither invites others to dine with him or her nor accepts invitations from neighbors to share their food and drink is likely, sooner or later, to be accused of sorcery by someone whom he or she has offended. Children are not to be gloomy, proud, unpopular, or isolated, and they must show sympathy to a bereaved neighbor.

Fear of evoking attack by exciting the hostility of a witch or a sorcerer may also exert pressure to conform to moral norms. For example, a prosperous person is well-advised to be generous and to avoid giving offense through his or her arrogance or meanness. In addition, every prudent Bukusu seeks to have and to retain good relationships with his or her neighbors. The Bukusu people attach a high value to good neighborly relations, especially since to make oneself despicable leads to accusations of sorcery.

Witchcraft beliefs can also be interpreted from the perspective of religious thought. Zahan shows the religious significance of some of the motifs of witchcraft or sorcery, such as the association of the witch with night, in that "the actions of the witch are the result of knowledge so profound that it escapes the ordinary methods of investigation."[188] Zahan seeks to demonstrate that sorcery and witchcraft beliefs are understandable only within the total structure of a people's religious thought, of which, in terms of the Bukusu, they are an integral part.

Having discussed some of the complexities of Babukusu culture and its historical interactions with the religions with which it is intertwined, the discussion now moves on to an analysis of appropriate means by which to better integrate traditional and mainstream belief practices.

Part II Notes

1. Hamid Algar, *The Sunna: Its Obligatory and Exemplary Aspects* (Oneonta, NY: Islamic Publications International, 2000), 3.
2. The word *Sunna*, spelled with a capital *S*, refers to the path and example of the prophet, consisting of all that he said, did, approved of, or condemned. *Sunna* (with a lowercase *s* or as the plural *sunan*) refers to the pattern of Allah in ordering creation or any part or aspect of it, usually referred to as "cosmic laws."
3. Algar, *The Sunna*, 4.
4. Ibid, 4–5.
5. Ibid, 5.
6. Ibid.
7. Ibid, 6.
8. Ibid.
9. Ira G. Zepp, Jr., *A Muslim Primer* (Westminster, Maryland: Wakefield Editions, 1992), 58.
10. Daniel Pipes, *In the Path of God: Islam and Political Power* (New York: Basic Books, 1996), 36.
11. David A. Kerr, "Questions and Answers about Islam," in Zepp, *A Muslim Primer*, 132.
12. Hammaduh Abdalati, *Islam in Focus* (Delhi: Crescent Publishing Company, 1988), 146. It is unfortunate that Islam has been stereotyped as the "religion of the sword." The historical reality is that the expansion of Islam was usually achieved by persuasion and not by military power. In any case, Islam cannot be forced on anyone; if profession of the Shahadah is forced on someone, it is not true Islam. "There is no constraint in religion," says the Qur'an. Fazlur Rahman wrote, "What was spread by the sword was not the religion of Islam, but the political domain of Islam so that Islam could work to produce the order on the earth that the Qur'an seeks." Fazlur Rahman, *Major Themes of the Qur'an* (Minneapolis: Bibliotheca Islamica, 1989), 63.
13. Other candidates were first put forward.
14. On the worldwide scale, the Sunni are the most dominant sect of Islam, comprising about 85 percent of all who call themselves Muslims today. See

Caesar E. Farah, *Islam* (New York: Barron's Educational Series, Inc., 1968), 174.

15. Mervyn Hiskett, *The Course of Islam in Africa* (Edinburgh: Edinburgh University Press, 1994), 58.

16. Orville Boyd Jenkins, "People Profile: The Swahili People," in *Thoughts and Resources on Culture, Language, Communication, and* Worldview, 1996, 2008, http://strategyleader.org/profiles/swahili.html.

17. Jacques Jomier, *How to Understand Islam* (New York: Crossroad, 1991), 33.

18. John L. Esposito, *Islam: The Straight Path* (New York: Oxford University Press, 1988), 45.

19. Akbar S. Ahmed, *Discovering Islam: Making Sense of Muslim History and Society*, (London: Routledge, 1988) 53.

20. Akbar S. Ahmed, *Living Islam: From Samarkand to Stornoway*, (London: BBC Books Ltd., 1993), 54.

21. See Bernard Lewis, *The Origins of Ismailism* (Cambridge: Cambridge University Press, 1940), 10–20.

22. Shirin R. Walji, "Ismailis in Kenya: Some Perspectives on Continuity and Change," in *Islam in Kenya*, ed. Muhammad Bakari and Saad Yahya (Nairobi: Mewa Publications, 1995), 3.

23. Bayart, *State in Africa*, 146.

24. Hannah W. Kinoti, "Religious Fragmentation in Kenya," in *Proselytization and Communal Self-determination in Africa*, eds. Abdullahi Ahmed An-Na'im (Maryknoll New York: Orbis Books, 1999), 282.

25. Jeff Haynes, *Religion and Politics in Africa* (Nairobi: Zed Books, 1996), 192.

26. The Mahdi is a hidden Imam who will destroy the kingdom of evil and establish a reign of justice on earth. See Emmanuel Sivan, *Radical Islam* (London: University Press, 1990) 193. "Hidden" only in Shia belief, in Sunni belief the Mahdi is yet to be born.

27. Haynes, *Religion and Politics*, 192.

28. Trimingham, *Islam in East Africa* 111.

29. Ibid, 110.

30. Bukusu people are well aware of the presence of Ahmadiyya in their villages because of their attacks and misrepresentation of both Sunni Islam and Christianity. Their main approach is through the medium of Swahili and English, since these languages can be used over the whole area, but they also make use of *Lubukusu*, the indigenous language, as a means of communication.

31. Trimingham, *Islam in East Africa*, 97. It is difficult to estimate the influence of the sects among the Swahili people. What is clear is that they affect only a small proportion of the population directly. Their popularity varies and is certainly

declining, in favor of new forms of association. In east Africa as a whole, the Qadiriyya is the strongest of the tariqah, but each coastal center varies. There is a considerable rivalry between them, based chiefly on the personalities of the leaders.

32. Ahmed b. Abd al-Rahaman Alawi, *Manaqib al-Sayyid Muhammad b. Ahmad b. Abi Bakr al-Shadhili al-Yashruti* (Cairo: Mustafa al-Babi al-Halabi, 1934; Martin, 1976), 152–58. Also see Nehemia Levtzion and Randall L. Pouwels, *The History of Islam in Africa* (Athens, OH: Ohio University Press, 2000), 455.

33. Akbar S. Ahmed, *Living Islam* (London: BBC Books Ltd., 1993), 55.

34. Shah Idries, *The Way of the Sufi* (London: Arkana/Penguin, 1990), 246.

35. James D. Holway, "Islam in Kenya and Relations with the Churches," in *Kenya Churches Handbook*, eds. David B. Barrett, George K. Mambo, Janice McLaughlin, and Malcolm J. McVeigh (Kisumu, Kenya: Evangelical Publishing House, 1973), 297.

36. Donal B. Cruise O'Brien, "The Muslim Predicament in Kenya," in *Religion and Politics in East Africa*, eds. Holger Bernt Hansen and Michael Twaddle (Nairobi: E.A.E.P., 1995), 203.

37. James De Vere Allen, *Swahili Origins* (Ohio: Ohio University Press, 1993), 259.

38. J. Haafkens, "Christian-Muslim Relations in Africa: A Pan-African View," in *Islam in Africa: Perspectives for Christian-Muslim Relations*, H. S. Wilson, ed. (Geneva: Print shop of Ecumenical Center, 1995), 12.

39. Walji, "Ismailis in Kenya," ix.

40. The "hinterland "of Kenya is that area between the interior and the coast. It tends to be a farming area bordered by the Nyika Plateau desert to the west and the coastal region, which is also called "the ten mile strip."

41. C. David Sperling, "The Coastal Hinterland and Interior of East Africa," In *The History of Islam in Africa*, eds. Nehemiah Levtzion and L. Randall Pouwels (Athens, Ohio: Ohio University Press, 2000), 273.

42. Trimingham, *Islam in East Africa*, 59.

43. Ibid, 57.

44. Sperling, "Coastal Hinterland," 275.

45. James Emery, "Short Account of Mombasa and the Neighboring Coast of Africa," *Journal of the Royal Geographical Society* (1833), 283.

46. Ibid.

47. Sperling, "Coastal Hinterland," 274.

48. Ibid. See also Donal B. Cruise O'Brien, "Coping with Christians: The Muslim Predicament in Kenya," in *Religion and Politics in East Africa*, eds. Holder Bernt Hansen and Michael Twaddle (London: James Curry, 1995), 201–2.

49. Ibid, 202.

50. Neville Chittick, *KILWA: An Islamic Trading City on the East African Coast*, vol.1, (History and Archeology) (Nairobi: British Institute in Eastern Africa, 1974), 245.

51. Randall L. Pouwels, *Horn and Crescent: Cultural Change and Traditional Islam* (Cambridge: Cambridge University Press, 1987), 24.

52. Naiwu Osahon, "Arabs Mortal Hatred and Enslavement of the Black Race," *The Nigerian Voice* (2009), http://www.thenigerianvoice.com/nvnewsp/10876/1/pagenum3/arabs-mortal-hatred-and-enslavement-of-the-black-r.html.

53. This is the corruption of Islam, since the central task for every Muslim is to spread Allah's message through the Qur'an. Islam has a religious message to all humanity. "We have sent you forth to all mankind" (see Qur'an 34:38). Abu Hurairah relates what the prophet said regarding enslavement: "A Muslim is the brother of a Muslim. He should not cheat him, nor tell him a lie, nor humiliate him. Everything of a Muslim is forbidden to a Muslim; his property and his blood. Righteousness is a quality of the heart. It is enough evil for a person to look down upon his brother Muslim (Tirmidhi)." From Muhammad Zafrulla Khan, *Gardens of the Righteous* (New York: Olive Branch Press, 1975), 59, 236–37.

54. Haynes, *Religion and Politics*, 28.

55. Ibid.

56. Naiwu Osahon, "Arabs in Africa," *Edofolks.com*, 2009, http://www.edofolks.com/html/arabs_in_africa.htm.

57. Ibid.

58. Haynes, *Religion and Politics*, 28.

59. Ahmed Salim Said, "An Outline History of Islam in Nyanza Province," in *Islam in Kenya*, 21. Mumias is close to Bukusuland. Murunga, a non-Bukusu, became the chief of Kimilili in North Bukusu.

60. Salim Said, "Islam in Nyanza Province," 21.

61. Salim describes his dispatching missionaries to Bukusuland and other parts of Western Kenya. Maalim Gaziti was sent to preach in Shieywe (now Kakamega in Western Province); Maalim Mwinyi Akida Jeshi went to teach in Kisumu (in Nyanza Province); Maalim Masangeni went to Kisii (Nyanza Province); Maalim Mvuta was sent to Lumbwa (now Kipkelion in Rift Valley); and Sharif Abbakar went to teach in Bungoma (in Bukusuland).

62. Yusuf A. Nzibo, "Islamization In the interior of Kenya: A General Overview," in *Islam in Kenya*, 40.

63. Trimingham, *Islam in East Africa*, 56.

64. Sperling, "Coastal Hinterland," 274.

65. Tariq, "Who Are the Nubians," *Afraka.com*, http://www.afraka.com/showthread.php?208-Who-Are-the-Nubians, last accessed March 2011.

66. Orville Boyd Jenkins, "The Nubi of Kenya and Uganda," in *Thoughts and Resources on Culture, Language, Communication and Worldview*, 1996, 2000, 2006, 2008: http://orvillejenkins.com/profiles/nubi.html.

67. Eva Evers Rosander, "The Islamization of 'Tradition' and 'Modernity,'" *African Islam and Islam in Africa*, David Westlund and Eva Evers Rosander, eds. (Athens, Ohio: Ohio University Press, 1996), 1.

68. Sperling, "The Beginning and Growth of Rural Islam," in *The History of Islam in Africa*, 281.

69. Trimingham, *Islam in East Africa*, 178–79.

70. Nzibo, "Islamization in the Interior of Kenya," 40.

71. Ibid.

72. Ibid.

73. Trimingham, *Islam in East Africa*, 59.

74. See Elisabeth McMahon, "'A Solitary Tree Builds Not': Heshima, Community, and Shifting Identity in Post-emancipation Pemba Island," *International Journal of African Historical Studies* 39 (2) (2006), 197–219.

75. Wagner, *The Bantu of Western Kenya*, 164.

76. Ibid.

77. French political scientist Jean-Francois Bayart explains that trade routes were difficult and hazardous. But whatever difficulties it posed to the circulation of men and goods, Bukusuland did not prevent all movement; nor did the dispersion of its population inhibit trade.

78. Trimingham, *Islam in East Africa*, 59.

79. de Wolf, a Dutch sociologist, writes of a chief who was attracted to Islamic culture and benefited from the Muslim traders in Western Kenya: "The walled village of the Wanga chief of Mumia in Mumias had always been friendly with Muslim traders and he eventually became a Muslim himself. He had also tried to ingratiate himself with white explorers and company of officials who passed through his country .... In 1894, some of the soldiers who lived at the fort of Mumias had sold their guns to the Bukusu, who lived to the north of Nzoia River. A patrol was sent out to try to recover the arms but was exterminated." See de Wolf, *Differentiation and Integration*, 133–34.

80. Sperling, *Coastal Hinterland*, 283.

81. Nzibo, "Islamization in the Interior of Kenya," 49.

82. Ibid.

83. Col. R. Wilkinson, commanding officer of Northern Bridge of Kenya African Rifles in 1933, wrote, "We take a great number of Akamba, Nandi, and

Kavirondo [Bukusu]. When they come to us, the biggest proportion are pagans, but it is the fashion I think, to take on a religion, and the tendency is, as far as I can see, in the K.A.R. to embrace the Mohammedan religion. We do not have many Christians, except in the 4th Battalion in Uganda." See Yusuf A. Nzibo, "Islam and the King's African Rifles," in *Islam in Kenya*, 49.

84. For example, during World War I, my grandfather went to Burma to fight for the British. While in Burma, he converted to Islam and returned home a devout Muslim; however, on his return, his conversion to Islam made it difficult for him to enter into his native community life as fully as before. Consequently, he was forced to adapt to a more rural Islamic life.

85. Trimingham observes that all the auxiliaries of the European penetration, pacification, and government—guides, interpreters, soldiers, and servants— were Muslims. See Trimingham, *Islam in East Africa*, 57.

86. Beer: Islam allows Muslims to eat everything that is good for the health. It restricts certain items, such as alcohol (*khamr*) or pork.

87. Trimingham, *Islam in East Africa*, 129.

88. Dean S. Gilliland, *African Religion Meets Islam* (New York: University Press of America, 1986), 104 (in reference to "functioning through control and mediation"). What is meant by control is the calling of the living dead, revealing the truth, special power for special acts, moving about at night. What is meant by mediation is sleeping on the graves, which opens up communication; healing only comes through the ancestors; laws concerning ancestors must be kept to promote health in the community.

89. John S. Mbiti, "A History of the Kenya Churches," in *Kenya Churches Handbook*, ed. D. B. Barrett (Kisumu, Kenya: Evangel Publishing House, 1973), 29.

90. John Baur, *2000 Years of Christianity in Africa* (Nairobi: Daughters of St. Paul-Africa, 1994), 87. The Portuguese built Fort Jesus, located on the edge of a coral ridge overlooking the entrance to the old port of Mombasa in 1593 to protect their trade route to India and their interests in East Africa. Throughout its tumultuous history, the Fort changed hands no less than nine times between the Portuguese and Omani Arabs. See Ali Abu-Bakr, ed., *National Museums of Kenya-Fort Jesus Museum*, March 22, 2001, http://www.Museums.or.ke/regftjes.html.

91. Ibid, 87.

92. Utalii Travel and Safari, http://www.utalii.com/Off_the_normal_path/kilwaruins.htm.

93. Ibid, 87–88.

94. John Gray, *Early Portuguese Missionaries in East Africa* (London: Macmillian, 1958), 11.

95. C. Boxer, *The Portuguese Seaborne Empire, 1415–1825* (London: Hutchinson, 1969), 7–8.

96. Gwyn Prins, a British anthropologist who wrote about colonial experience in western Zambia, reported, "On one occasion when Francois Coillard, a Protestant Frenchman, employee of the *Societe des Missions Evangeliques de Paris*, was preaching at a Sunday service, an elderly man began to recite the Lozi creation myth at the top of his voice. This sort of behavior by an elder was a clear indication that the local community of the Lozi people did not approve of Christian teaching in their land." Gwyn Prins, *The Hidden Hippopotamus. Reappraisal in African History: The Early Colonial Experience in Western Zambia*, (Cambridge: Cambridge University Press, 1980), xvi and 319.

97. J. L. Krapf, *Travels, Researches and Missionary Labors*, 2nd ed. (London: Cass, 1968), 190.

98. Margaret Read, "The Ngoni and Western Education," in *Colonialism in Africa 1870–1960: III Profiles of Change: African Society and Colonial Rule*, ed. V. Turner (Cambridge University Press, 1971), 355.

99. Krapf, *Travels*, 140.

100. The Ngoni war leader, Ngonomo, quoted in Read, "The Ngoni," 355.

101. J. Farrant, *Mashonaland Martyr Benard Mizeki and the Pioneer Church* (Cape Town: Oxford University Press, 1966), 127.

102. Elizabeth Isichei, *A History of Christianity in Africa* (Grand Rapids, Michigan: Africa World Press, 1995), 134.

103. Ibid.

104. Kolumba Msigala, quoted in T. Ranger, "Missionary Adaptation of African Religious Institutions: The Maasai Case," in *The Historical Study of African Religion*, T. Ranger and I. Kimambo, eds. (London: Heinemann, 1972), 223.

105. P. Walakira, "Part of the establishment: Catholicism in Uganda," in *African Reactions to Missionary Education*, ed. E. Bernard (New York: Teachers College Press, 1975), 149.

106. Ngugi wa Thiong'o, *The River Between* (London: Heinemann, 1975), 93.

107. A baptismal song for a Haya king, quoted in L. Stevens, "Religious Change in a Haya Village, Tanzania," *Journal of Religion in Africa*, (1991), 4.

108. Filip Njau, "Aus meinem Leben," quoted in J. Iliffe, *A Modern History of Tanganyika* (Cambridge: Cambridge University Press, 1979), 222–25.

109. G. S. Haule, "The Entrepreneur," in *Modern Tanzania*, ed. J. Iliffe (Dar es Salaam: Historical Association of Tanzania, 1973), 159.

110. Many of Africa's new religious movements, which arose between the 1920s and the present time, started as religions of the oppressed and later became movements of protest, opportunity, and mobility. Their protest has often been

expressed as a challenge to the authority and liturgy of mission churches. An example is *Dini ya Musambwa* (DYM), the "religion of traditional customs," which was founded among the Bukusu people by Elijah Masinde's people in the 1940s. Masinde's followers were active in opposing the colonial government, and he was imprisoned on several occasions. DYM was founded as a conscious return to the old ways: God called Elijah in a vision at night. God informed him that everyone in this world belongs to me [God], even the polygamist belongs to me; "God told me to leave friends (the American Quaker Mission) and follow the religion of my ancestors." Though the sect may have formed in protest to mainstream religious infrastructure, it is so full of Christian elements that it could well be called a church in the usual sense, and it was originally called *Dini ya Israel.* The holy place for his religion is the lake high on Mount Elgon, which DYM's followers call Zion. They wear a cross on their uniforms and claim that the trinity was foreshadowed in traditional Bukusu thought. The first Bukusu progenitors, according to their beliefs, were Mary and Joseph, and ancestors and angels were seen as members of one family of spiritual beings. Members of the church pray, "Oh God the father, forgive us and feel pity for us. The foreigners brought the new missions which made us leave our traditional customs which are now lost. We are asking you to bless and give us freedom." What is explicit is the sense of loss—the loss of land, the loss of the adventure and celebration of the cattle raids that marked the young men's entry to adult life, and the loss of the unquestioned respect enjoyed by the old. See Isichei, *Christianity in Africa*, 257.

111. The Religious Society of Friends (the Quakers) is an alternative Christianity that emphasizes the personal experience of God in one's life. Quakers understand the necessity of listening to God before working in the world. They affirm the equality of all people before God regardless of race, station in life, or gender, and this belief leads them into a range of social concerns. As self-described "Children of Light," they find recourse to violence intolerable. Quaker thought is both mystical (waiting upon God) and prophetic (speaking truth to power). Friends believe that God's revelation is still continuing—that God is not absent or unknowable, but that we can find God ourselves and establish a living relationship with him, thus being able to live in the world free from the burden and guilt of sin. The search for a closer relationship with God is the way. A logical process of thought does not attain religious knowledge; like the appreciation of beauty, religious knowledge is achieved through experience and feeling. Quakers maintain that the teaching of Jesus is a practical method for the guidance of the world today; that religion is concerned with the whole of life; and that, beyond a certain point, definition becomes a limitation. See

Hans Weening, ed., *World Quaker Website*, 1995, http://www.quaker.org/fwcc/ EMES/booklet.html#1.

112. Michael Bratton, "Civil Society and Political Transitions in Africa," in *Civil Society and the State in Africa*, eds. John W. Harberson, Donald Rothchild, and Naomi Chazan (Boulder, Co: Lynne Rienne, 1994), 66–67.

113. Baur, *2000 Years*, 224.

114. Joseph G. Donders, *Non-Bourgeois Theology* (New York: Orbis Books, 1985), 2.

115. Mbiti, *Religions and Philosophy*, 232.

116. Audrey Wipper, *Rural Rebels: A Study of Two Protest Movements in Kenya* (Nairobi: Oxford University Press, 1977), 31–32.

117. Baur, *2000 Years of Christianity in Africa*, 257.

118. Ibid, 255.

119. Richard Robinson, "Leakey Family," *Biology Reference*, http://www. biologyreference.com/La-Ma/Leakey-Family.html.

120. Baur, *2000 Years of Christianity in Africa*, 257.

121. Ibid.

122. Ibid.

123. Ibid.

124. Hans Burgman, *The Way the Catholic Church Started in Western Kenya* (Nairobi: Mission Book Service, 1990), 7.

125. John Baur, *The Catholic Church in Kenya: A Centenary History* (Nairobi: Saint Paul's Publications-Africa, 1990), 68–74.

126. John S. Pobee, "African Instituted (Independent) Churches," from the revised edition of the *Dictionary of the Ecumenical* Movement, World Council of Churches and the Wm. Eerdmans, 2002, World Council of Churches, 2011, http://www.oikoumene.org/en/member-churches/church-families/african-instituted-churches/dictionary-of-the-ecumenical-movement-african-instituted-independent-churches.html.

127. Stanlas Ndambuki, "The Missionary Factor in the Africa Inland Church Kenya: The Life, Work and Relevance of Peter Mualuko" (2001). ResearchKenya.org, http://www.researchkenya.org/?ID=9687&search=Africa+Inland+Church%2 C+Kenya.

128. Ibid.

129. King's Lynn Quakers, http://www.kingslynnquakers.co.uk/whoarequakers. html.

130. David B. Barrett, ed., *World Christian Encyclopedia: A Comparative Survey of Churches and Religions in the Modern World, AD 1900-2000* (Nairobi: Oxford University Press, 1982), 436.

131. Wagner, *The Bantu of Western Kenya*, 38.

132. Barrett, *World Christian Encyclopedia*, 436.

133. Burgman, *Catholic Church Started in Western Kenya*, 290.

134. Baur, *2000 Years of Christianity in Africa*, 254.

135. Burgman, *Catholic Church Started in Western* Kenya, 97.

136. Ibid, 98.

137. Ibid, 99.

138. This is true with some notable exceptions, such as Chief Sudi of south Bukusu, who was a local man, not one of the Mumias stooges, and whose authority among the people was great. Chief Sudi's name is forever linked to the church among the Babukusu; he gave them land for the mission of Kibabii. By June 1918, Sudi had helped to build a large church at Kibabii, with a sleeping room for a visiting priest. He is indeed linked to the Christians of all Kenya, for he gave them his son, Maurice Otunga, who became the first Kenyan bishop, archbishop, and cardinal of Nairobi. See Burgman, *Catholic Church Started in Western Kenya*, 110.

139. Ibid, 99.

140. Ibid, 67.

141. Ibid.

142. Ibid, 69.

143. I use the term *baraza* to refer to public assemblies.

144. de Wolf, *Differentiation and Integration*, 114.

145. Ibid, 159.

146. A. B. K. Kazozi, "Christian-Muslim Inputs into Public Policy Formation in Kenya, Tanzania & Uganda," in *Religion and Politics in East Africa*, eds. Holger Bernt Hansen and Michael Twaddle (Nairobi: E.A.E.P, 1995), 223.

147. Ibid.

148. de Wolf, *Differentiation and Integration* , 162.

149. Mbiti, *African Religions and* Philosophy, 232.

150. Burgman, *Catholic Church Started in Western Kenya*, 289.

151. de Wolf, *Differentiation and Integration*, 115.

152. Harvey Cox, *Fire from Heaven: The Rise of Pentecostal Spirituality and the Reshaping of Religion in the Twenty-First Century* (London: Cassel, 1996), 246.

153. de Wolf, *Differentiation and Integration*, 164.

154. Ibid.

155. Jan de Wolf, "A Quaker Account from 1926 Reports," quoted in *Differentiation and Integration in Western Kenya*: A Study of Religious Innovation and Social Change among the Bukusu, (The Hague: Mouton, 1977), 164.

156. Ibid, 165.
157. Ibid, 164.
158. Ibid, 165.
159. Ibid, 178.
160. Ibid.
161. Ibid.
162. J. F. A. Ajayi, *Christian Missions in Nigeria 1841–1891* (London: Longman, 1965), 28–35; and E. Ayandele, *The Missionary Impact on Modern Nigeria 1842–1914* (London: Longman, 1966), 56.
163. Dominique Zahan, *The Religion, Spirituality, and Thought of Traditional Africa* (Chicago: University of Chicago Press, 1979), 1.
164. Geoffrey Parrinder, *African Traditional Religion* (London: Hutchinson's University Library, 1962), 25.
165. Ibid.
166. Ibid.
167. Zahan, *Religion, Spirituality, and Thought*, 5.
168. Makila, *History of Babukusu*, 135.
169. The *Omuseni we kumuse*, whom Wagner refers to as a public comforter, is usually selected from particular clans. His major role is to address the public on the occasion of the third day after the burial *mulufu* of a reputable elder. He is expected to be conversant with the history of the people and adept in the skills of conciliation. See Wagner, *The Bantu*, 485 and Makila, *History of Babukusu*, 94.
170. Harold Scheub, *A Dictionary of African Mythology* (New York: Oxford University Press, 2000), xvi.
171. Ibid.
172. Ibid.
173. Ibid.
174. Zahan, *Religion, Spirituality, and Thought*, 9.
175. The comforters are elected to their offices on the basis of four qualifications. First, a promising candidate must be a member of one of the clans that practice this art (in other words, the art of comforting the public); second, he must be married, with a male child as his firstborn; third, he must display a brilliant memory; and fourth, he needs to have a magnetic personality. The third qualification is important because, in terms of traditional education, *baseni be kumuse* are looked upon as "educated elite." They are official rememberers, whose memory is often prodigious, repeating historical events from generation to generation. Their services are called upon in times of great sorrow (for example, following the demise of a beloved leader), when it is thought that

people need solace and reassurance. Their speeches are tailored to appeal to the sense of reason and unity. They recapitulate good qualities of national culture, deeds of certain national and clan ancestors, national and clan lineage, and important events and places in the community's migration movements and, ultimately, draw up parallels of national ethics. Counterparts who normally sit in the front row of the audience are entitled to point out errors and suggest corrections in the comforter's speeches. See Makila, *History of Babukusu*, 116–17.

176. Ibid.

177. Wagner, *The Bantu of Western Kenya*, 168.

178. Ibid, 168–69.

179. *Sasa* covers the now period. It is a sense of immediacy, nearness, and nowness; it is also a period of immediate concern for the people, since that is where or when they physically exist. *Zamani* is the ocean of time, in which everything becomes absorbed or housed in timeless reality. All the myths, the wisdom of the ancestors, and the traditions of the people are held there. *Zamani* is the final resting place of time, the period of termination. See Mbiti, *African Religions and Philosophy*, 23.

180. *Kimisambwa*: When a person falls sick, healing diviners and medicine men and women usually try to establish clan peculiarities as the first step in the healing process. They do so by tracing the *kumusambwa* (spirit) back to the clan or cluster affiliation. See Makila, *History of Babukusu*, 97.

181. *Namwima:* a sacred hut for the ancestral spirits that is erected in the courtyard. Apart from being a place for offering sacrifices, a namwima is also used as a sacred place from which members of the family feed the spirits of the living dead and ancestors daily.

182. *Luswa*: ritual impurity of human beings. Examples include an infant cutting its upper teeth first, a beard growing on a woman's chin, and a man having sexual intercourse with a cow or a sheep. If a woman climbs upon the roof of a hut, it will be interpreted as the desire to kill her husband and so forth.

183. Wagner, *The Bantu of Western Kenya*, 258.

184. Mbiti, *Religions and Philosophy*, 83.

185. Lucy Mair, *Witchcraft* (London: World University Library, 1969), chapter one.

186. Max Marwick, *Witchcraft and Sorcery* (Harmondsworth: Penguin Books, 1982), 232.

187. Mair, *Witchcraft*, 9.

188. Zahan, *Religion, Spirituality, and Thought*, 93.

PART III

STRATEGIES FOR DIALOGUE IN
BUBER, IKLÉ, AND URY

CHAPTER 9

• ◆ •

UNDERSTANDING THROUGH MEANING

Overall, dialogue is not mere discussion. Dialogue shares its root meaning with "percussion" and "concussion," both of which involve breaking things up. Nor is dialogue a debate. This form of conversation contains an implicit tendency to point toward a goal, to hammer out an agreement, or to try to solve a problem or have one's opinion win through, and good dialogue results in a win-win situation.

Effective dialogue, however, is characterized as resulting from those skills proven to achieve mutual understanding, trust, and respect. Skilled dialogue allows participants to communicate at the level necessary to ensure all parties are satisfied with the outcome. It does, by and large, yield the desired results and benefits. Success in essential skills here does yield the desired benefits and results, by and large.

Here is a proven dialogue skills approach—a field-tested model for respectful, reciprocal, and responsive interactions that honor cultural beliefs and values. Among those communities participants jointly want to serve, they should improve "right relatedness." Right relatedness refers to the way in which God intended us to relate to one another according to the second commandment—that we must love our neighbors.[1] Dialoguing for mutual understanding in light of cultural diversities is more appropriate between nations than between individuals. Ideally, each nation appreciates being part of such a dialogue. All participants learn to exercise their cultural competency and work through any challenges they may face with others. When two (or more) parties sit down at a negotiating table, it is expected that everyone will be committed to the process of dialogue.

David Bohm, University of London professor, traces the roots of dialogue to the Greek *dia* and *logos*, which mean "through meaning." Dialogue is the heart and soul of mentoring. Through it, a unified understanding emerges, common ground is developed, and creative and generative concepts come to life. In short, discovery and learning take place in mentoring relationships through dialogue.[2] The picture or image that this word (*dia-logos*) suggests is that of a stream of meaning flowing among, through, and between people. Effective dialogue moves beyond the individual's understanding, to make the explicit implicit and build collective meaning for community. In a dialogue, writes Bohm, "Nobody is trying to win. The paradigm of a winning and a losing side is obsolete; the essence of what is now agreed on in view of dialogue is the idea of mutually assured benefit or mutually assured destruction: we are all winners or losers."[3] Everyone wins if anyone wins. While the goal of debate is winning, the goal of dialogue is learning.

People everywhere need strategies for dialogue, particularly when communicating one-on-one about divisive topics such as religion, as well as in daily life with family members. Moreover, communication is even more difficult in small groups than it is between two individuals. In a group of thirty or forty or more, many find it very hard to communicate unless there is a set purpose, agenda, and leader. People will have different assumptions and opinions.

Assumptions are beliefs or ideas that we hold to be true—often with little or no evidence required. We make assumptions every day of our lives. For example, as a driver on the highway, I assume that other drivers will obey traffic signals; thus, when I go through an intersection on a green light, I assume that the cross traffic will stop at its red light. Of course, such assumptions can turn into presumptions. Generally speaking, most drivers do obey traffic signals, and therefore, we do proceed through intersections on green lights, assuming that the other drivers will comply with the law.

A person's understanding of the meaning of life or of his or her own self-interest, national interest, or religious interest are all deeply ingrained. People make assumptions about politics, economics, culture, or religion and about what they think an individual should be or do in this life. When their beliefs (assumptions) are challenged, they will resist, defending their opinions with a firm emotional conviction. We all can assume that things are true, even when we have no evidence to back up our notions. We must learn to be patient with one another in polite conversation, and even more so in serious dialogue.

Given that assumptions are subjective, we must be aware of our own and others' mind-sets as we come to the negotiating table. We must understand why people believe what they believe. Contrary views of others that challenge our childhood assumptions do prompt us to be more aware of our limits and better able to define what we think we "know." For example, during a visit from a sick patient, a doctor might formulate one or more assumptions before choosing which procedure she will employ. The doctor will order tests and perhaps seek a second opinion from another qualified person. She is curious and searching; she is open to more information and willing to set aside her first impression. If another diagnosis or procedure is called for, she would be expected to try another procedure. That doctor should welcome the additional information so that she can best pass on her findings to others. So it is with dialogue: It must reflect the thought process that confirms or denies the first impression.[4] We must identify our hidden assumptions; if none exist our argument is valid, but if our argument is not valid, we need to carefully explore adding additional premises to the argument.[5] Understanding this relative complexity going in should produce sensitivity in both the individuals and the groups participating, as well as regarding the subject of dialogue and its scope.

Bohm points out that it is important to understand that a person's opinions are the result of past experiences that others, including teachers, parents, family associations, authors, and other influences, have imposed.[6] Assumptions are a function of a person's "intelligence" according to standardized tests. A person may then identify with those conditionings and react accordingly, maybe even violently. In the process of dialogue, this is not acceptable. Bohm concludes that input tends to be experienced as truth, even though it may reflect only one's own assumptions that developed as a result of one's background. When such a person gets defensive, he will not have productive dialogue with anyone.

The Cry of the Tiny Ant

Expressing our desires, feelings, thoughts, and opinions clearly and effectively is only half of the communication process needed for effective interpersonal dialogue. The other half is the ability to listen and understand what others communicate to us. When a person decides to communicate with another person, he does so to fulfill a need. The person wants something, feels discomfort, and/or has feelings or thoughts about something. In deciding to communicate, the person selects the method or code that he believes will deliver the message to the other person most effectively. The code used to send the message can be either verbal or nonverbal. When the other person receives the implicit message, that person goes through the process of internalizing it into some understanding and meaning. Effective communication exists between two people when the receiver interprets and understands the sender's message in the same way that the sender intended it. How can we determine whether this is the case? The receiver must restate the message received to the sender for some level of acceptance, or there must be further dialogue on the issue addressed.

Personal opinions and assumptions that Muslim, Christian, and Bukusu believers hold about themselves and each other become practical challenges, if not barriers, for dialoguing common ground. Howard Thurman, former Dean of the Chapel at Boston University, confirms, "We are one at any level."[7] Speaking of his work in promoting interreligious fellowship, Thurman noted:

> Man builds his little shelter, he raises his little wall, builds his little altar, worships his little God, organizes the resources of his little life to defend his little barrier, and he can't do it! What we are committed to here, and what many other people in other places are committed to, is very simple—that it is possible to develop a

religious fellowship that is creative in character and so convincing in quality that it inspires the mind to multiply experiences of unity—which experiences of unity become over and over and over again more compelling than the concepts, the ways of life, the seeds and the creeds that separate humanity. We believe that in the presence of God with His dream of order, there is neither male nor female, white nor black, Gentile nor Jew, Protestant nor Catholic, Hindu, Buddhist, nor Moslem, but a human spirit stripped to the literal substance of itself.[8]

Thurman understood the need of all human beings to proclaim the uniqueness of their own experience and to build protective walls around their community until they feel secure in their identity. However, he warned, "Community cannot feed for long on itself; it can only flourish where always the boundaries are giving way to the coming of others from beyond them. We belong to [one another], and if we shut ourselves away we diminish ourselves."[9] Thurman adds that there is something so private and personal about an act of thought that the individual may very easily seem to be a private island on a boundless human sea. To experience oneself is to enter into a solitary world that is one's unique possession and that can never be completely and utterly shared. Here is the paradox. A human being is always threatened in his or her very being by a sense of isolation, by feeling cut off from his or her fellows. Yet, people can never separate themselves from their fellows, for mutual interdependence is characteristic of all of life.[10]

The need to care, and, the need to be cared for, is another expression of the same basic idea of "the common ground of this, our collective humanity." Thurman notes that whenever the individual is cut off from the private and personal nourishment, from dialoguing with other individuals or from certain individuals, the result is "a wasting away," a starvation, a failure to acknowledge that part of one's life needing to be vitalized and nourished.[11] On that note, Thurman maintains that we ought to be feeding on each other on an emotional level. Where this nourishment is not available, the collective human spirit and the collective human body tend to sicken and die. The human spirit cannot abide the enforced loneliness of isolation. This is not an overstatement. The purpose of all of the arrangements and conventions that make up the formal and informal agreements under which people live in society is for the nourishment of one another with one another.[12] As with any river, it may twist and turn, fall back on itself and start again, stumble over an infinite series of hindering rocks, but at last "the river" must answer the call to "the sea."

While leading a student "Pilgrimage of Friendship" trip to India, Thurman and his wife, along with the Sue Bailey, had a meeting with Mahatma Gandhi that gave focus to a growing passion in Thurman's ministry. He envisioned an interracial church in the days when most blacks were excluded from white churches. When Thurman asked Gandhi, "What is the greatest enemy that Jesus Christ has in India?" Gandhi responded, "Christianity." Thurman resolved to remain within his Christian tradition, but to work at overcoming the divisive influences within race and religion that split so much of society.[13]

In contrast to our time, we have the profound wisdom of the spiritual masters, some of the teachers, past and present, who keep reminding us that there *is* more to life, advocating the highest order of dialogue—unceasing prayer. Henri Nouwen, the renowned Catholic priest and theologian, focuses on the spiritual life as it relates to the experiencing of ourselves. He observes, "The movement from hostility to understanding of the other cannot be thought of without a constant inner connection with the movement away from sheer aloneness to a fulsome acceptance of the other. As long as we are simply lonely, we know not how to be hospitable as persons, we singly cannot create relative space. However, our personal need to still our inner cravings that loneliness has us cling in a dependence on others instead of cheerfully creating space for them."[14]

According to the thinking of Bishop Fulton Sheen, Nouwen would allow that sickness can be adjusted with medication but loneliness has no cure standing alone. It requires the sharing of relative space.

Again, Bohm wisely suggests that to come to common ground, we need to adopt three attitudes. The first is the willingness to suspend old assumptions; often, people are unaware that old assumptions, which they hide from themselves, are getting in the way of a mutual understanding with others. Secondly, we must be aware that every person has his or her own experiences and will bring these experiences into related conversations. Finally, we must consider that each person is looking at life from his or her own perspective. Bohm also recommends that we listen and speak without judgment! This is a real challenge. People must learn to judge and to evaluate with equanimity in order to make decisions that are acceptable to everyone involved. We, as humans, make thousands of decisions every day. It is this inner dialogue that forms a person: "I like this, but I don't like that."; "This is good, and that is bad." "This is right, and that is wrong." Each person has a personal store of experiences against which to measure the apparent good. In open dialogue with others, listening is the key to the practical challenge of sharing relative space. An Igbo tribal saying from Nigeria suggests, "Drop the ear on the ground and hear the cry of the tiny ant." "Hearing the cry of the tiny ant" refers to the recognition in this native culture of the necessity of open dialogue.

This Igbo saying is about the actual phenomenon that one can hear even the tiny ants working in concert beneath the ground, inhaling and exhaling in unison. Why this is so can only be the subject of speculation, but the fact is, people have heard the ants, and this phenomenon has a place in the Igbo understanding of the way things are. The ants share a relative space. They work together, relying on team spirit for their survival. What, for humans then, is comparable in terms of sharing relative space in ideal relatedness? Human diversities in the kaleidoscope of this world's peoples must have such a harmonic potency as these ants. For humankind, it appears now that this is the dialogic model—a lesson the Igbo learn from the ants—for sharing relative space. Additionally, it may be said that the ants are using their exhaling rhythm as the Bukusu have used drumming and that the cry of the ants is comparable to the idea of "drumming up dialogue."

Brenda Ueland, an American journalist, observes, "Listening is not merely an auditory act. It is not solely the process of interpretation. In a world that gives privileges to the visual, the complexities of listening have been neglected. Collecting people's stories of hardship and tragedy is dependent on 'listening well.' But the value of listening extends beyond this."[15] Roland Barthes, a French social critic, holds that, as a creative force, true listening goes far beyond the mere hearing of words; it is the sophisticated deciphering of discursive meaning. Barthes explains, "To listen is to adopt an attitude of decoding what is obscure, blurred, or mute, in order to make available to consciousness 'the underside' of meaning."[16] Listening, then, is a textured and nuanced activity and one that requires our full attention.

In true dialogue, all parties should understand that they are equal partners. There should be no inferior or superior participants; all must be valued equally and held to the same standards and expectations. In other words, individuals are asked to be equally committed to dialogue, even as they may think of themselves all as "experts" in their own life experiences. There is no place in authentic dialogue for authority or hierarchy. What is required is mutual trust and openness. Dialogue is a living process of releasing—of letting go and understanding others in order to be serviceably present in the moment and of speaking only from the heart.

The next chapter provides an overview of the dialogue process as described by Martin Buber, along with his rationale for using it. Buber holds that there is an authentic way or a deeper way of rightly relating to the world. His *I–Thou* encounter and his *I–It* dialogue are the terms that have become part of the vocabulary of engagement among individuals of goodwill. In this place, individuals come together and encounter one another on the highest and the deepest levels.

CHAPTER 10

•◆•

MARTIN BUBER'S PHILOSOPHY OF DIALOGUE

As Martin Buber's philosophical ideas on dialogue are a foundation for my understanding of interfaith relations and strategies that can enhance cross-cultural relations, we will take a brief look at Martin Buber's philosophical ideas for dialogue as found in three of his books—*I and Thou* (1923), *Between Man and Man* (1965), and *The Knowledge of Man* (1966). All three touch on *I-It* and *I-Thou* relationships with monologic and dialogic meanings. From Buber's concept of community emerges his concept of dialogue and, more specifically, his position on political dialogue. As a Jewish philosopher, Buber is best known for his treatment of *I* and *Thou* dialogue. He has proposed a paradigm, described below, in which there are two types of interpersonal relationships.

I–It Relations

The objectification and the control of nature and people characterize the *I-It* relationship. The *I* in this relationship seeks to acquire and possess as much as it can; it perceives itself as being a separate individual who is set above objects of its perception.[17]

Buber did not consider the world of the *I-It* relationship to be intrinsically evil. He observed that we all live in this world. We all relate to that which is outside of us, and even to ourselves, as objects. We cannot live unless, to some extent, we manipulate nature to meet our basic needs. The problem has to do with proportion. If we allow the *I-It* way of viewing the world to dominate our thinking, feeling, and actions, we will be spiritually emaciated and pauperized and live lives of quiet or obvious desperation. This *I* pays a price for such selfishness and its will to dominate because it becomes isolated and alienated from the source of life—God's presence as manifest in others. There is in humanity a natural inclination to objectify life—to treat life and all its parts as something to be examined, understood, used, or controlled. For a child, this seems to be a natural way to relate to the world. Buber describes the operation of this early experience of objectifying the world: "I perceive something. I am sensible of something. I feel something. I think something .... This and the like establish the realm of *It*."[18]

People objectify life for many practical reasons. In the outside world, Buber points out, all sorts of aims are pursued, in the course of which a person works, negotiates, and preaches. The pursuit of these goals creates a tolerably well-ordered and, to some extent, harmonious structure, in which, with the manifold help of people's brains and hands, the process of affairs is fulfilled.[19] In the inner realm of feelings and thoughts, fantasies and beliefs, "the spectrum of emotions dances before the interested glance. Here a man's liking and hate and pleasure are indulged, and his pain, if it is not too severe. Here he is at home, and stretches himself out in his rocking-chair."[20]

An *I-It* relationship comprises the normal everyday interaction between human beings and the things surrounding them. Human beings can also regard their fellow men and women in terms of *I-It* relationships. According to Buber, people do this most of the time. They view the other from a distance, like a thing, a part of the environment, something forged into causality and usefulness.

Buber's thoughts about the dialogic relationship between human beings and nature are quite compatible with the Babukusu worldview. Bukusu traditional religion teaches that nature is a friend of human beings and vice versa. If this relationship is disturbed, it is humankind that suffers most. The central search in Bukusu tradition is for wholeness of being and harmony with the powers of nature. The following scene illustrates Buber's idea of the *I-It* relationship for those who regard other human beings as objects of their personal experience.

A small boy was kicking a doll. A casual observer did not see that it was a doll. It seemed to be only a piece of dark wood. A small girl was trying to get the doll from the boy. She was shouting, "Don't kick her! It is my doll. It is Lucy; it is my Lucy!" The boy kept on kicking the doll, shouting, "It is not Lucy; it is only a thing!" He kicked and kicked.[21] In this case, the boy maintained an *I-It* relationship with a piece of wood, while the girl expressed an *I-Thou* relationship with a beloved doll.

The dynamics of such subjective emotional relegation of people to objects can be found in one of the most horrible episodes in Africa's struggle for independence, between 1959 and 1960. During this period, so many people were tortured, maimed, and killed that some doctors, psychologists, and psychiatrists started to wonder how such inhuman behavior was possible.[22] Researchers found that a specific precursory action always preceded the torture of one human being by another. Before the police, the soldiers, or the public started to kick and beat someone, something else happened first—they had to declare their victim to be nonhuman, to be merely an object. They shouted, "Vermin!" or "Insect!" Then they were able to kill or crush the devalued "object" under their feet.

I witnessed just such an incident. A man lay on his face on a street in Nairobi, surrounded by a mob. Some policemen were guarding him. Under his neck there was a caption on a piece of paper stating that he was a thief. The police had come just in time to save him from being beaten to death by an angry mob. The police, however, had not come in time to prevent the crowd from cutting off one of his fingers.

It is about these types of events that Buber is writing when he refers to objectifying people and treating them as things or *its*. Buber notes, "If I face a human being as my *Thou*, and say the primary word *I-Thou* to him or her, he or she is not a thing among things, and does not consist of things."[23] Here he implies that reducing others to the state of things or commodities leads to disaster in terms of human right relatedness.

I-Thou Relations

Radically different from *I-It* relationships are *I-Thou* relationships. This is the condition in which people come together and encounter one another on the highest level humanly possible. Buber writes that this is the relationship "where the dialogue is fulfilled in its being between partners who have turned to one another in truth, who express themselves without reserve and are free of the desire of semblance, [whereupon] there is brought into being a memorable common faithfulness which is to be found nowhere else."[24] Characteristic of the *I-Thou* relationship, according to Buber, is that it is only within the human experience of truth and faithfulness that real dialogue may occur. Buber contends that *I-Thou* relationships occur when all else is no longer of consequence; when all preconceptions, all assumptions, all mind-sets, and all opinions are given up; and when one fully engages the other and carries on a mutual, all-confirming relationship.

Buber argues for an ethic that requires us to refrain from "using" other people and from considering them objects of our own personal aggrandizement.[25] Instead, Buber suggests that we must consider everything around us as "speaking to us" and requiring a complementary response. When we regard another as *Thou*, we share a mystery—the mystery of being totally present in our response to the other individual and, thus, engaging that person on the level of spirit. A person becomes a related person (as opposed to an alienated individual) when he or she enters into relations with the others where needs, desires, and beliefs are rightly expressed, with or without the spoken word.

Buber affirms that to enter into an *I-Thou* relationship is to perceive reality from a new and higher vantage point. Through my relationship in which I give of myself dialogically, I turn my being toward the center of reality—where I well might approach the face of God, as surely must be manifest in the other. Through authentic relationships with our fellow men and women, we come to know the eternal *Thou*—God.

The difference between *I-It* and *I-Thou* relationships does not lie in the nature of the object to which one relates. Not every relation between persons is an *I-Thou* one; nor is every relation with an animal or a thing an *I-It*. The difference is in the relationship itself. An *I-Thou* relationship is one of openness, presence, and rightly owed mutuality.

Examples from Bukusu Life to Match Buber's Philosophy

Community morals govern the welfare of the whole Bukusu society. Whatever is regarded as strengthening the community is viewed as good and right, and whatever is regarded as weakening the community is to be avoided. Taboos are instituted to protect the community from anything less than right relatedness. Breaking taboos is considered a violation of morals within the community. For example, to deny hospitality, even to strangers, is not encouraged. Ultimately, no one comes as a stranger because God is in everyone. According to Bukusu belief, God appears in the mandated preferential treatment of all. This includes widows, orphans, the disabled, strangers, or those who are at any societal disadvantage. People must honor, respect, welcome, and help strangers and must never mistreat them.

Respect and reverence for creation are inherent in respecting God as the creator, for God expresses Himself through creation. The value derived from this view is that people must honor and respect the earth and all that is upon the earth because all is of God and God is in everything. This value is expressed in several ways. Children are to be honored and respected because children are the people's greatest wealth and greatest gift from God. To explain this point further, Laurenti Magesa, a Tanzanian and one of Africa's best-known Catholic theologians, notes, "The ancestors are directly interested in and concerned about the birth of a new baby into their community, their clan. It is important to note that in birth, in most cases, it is an ancestor's vital force that returns to earth in the person named."[26] Moreover, children are the seal of marriage. Among the Bukusu people, once a marriage has produced children, it is very rare to see it broken up, since nobody wishes to part with his or her children.

To emphasize the connectedness between humanity and creation, and to ward off the chaos that might ensue if this bond is not respected, Bukusu traditional religion erects a system of ritual prohibitions or taboos that refer to certain animals or particular modes of behavior. In all cases, the common idea is to evade dangers of a magical nature that would threaten the community if the prohibition were disregarded. Taboos have great moral authority to direct a community's behavior and that of its individual members. The Bukusu experience the system of taboos in daily life and pass it on from one generation to the next. The origin of taboos may be obscure or unknown, but that is not important. What is relevant is that their purpose is to preserve harmony and to keep chaos at bay.[27]

Among the taboos the Bukusu people observe, there is a prohibitions against killing certain birds, animals and plants. These include the cobra, the python (*ebaka*), and other large snakes (but not small ones), as well as certain small birds that build their nests under the eaves of the living hut.[28] It is believed that if one kills a python, even in self-defense, one will subsequently suffer from impotence and be unable to beget any children, even if many years have passed between the act of killing the snake and his or her marriage.

Babukusu people also avoid killing frogs. When a big frog happens to stay near a homestead, the people build a small shrine (*namwima*) under the eaves of the hut for the frog. If the frog occasionally stays in this little hut or returns to it, this is thought to bring good luck to the homestead.[29]

Large fig trees (*kumukhuyu*) and other shady trees with a big crown and rich foliage are considered to be the occasional abodes and meeting places of the ancestral spirits and, therefore, must not be cut down.

Four Elements of Dialogue

There are four elements that comprise *I-Thou* relationships, as Buber understands them: presence, mutuality, inclusion, and confirmation.

Presence

Presence is a highly important element of the *I-Thou* relationship. According to Buber, presence refers to being fully present—not thinking about the past or the future or being mentally/spiritually truncated as a result of being caught within one's inner workings or off in a fantasy somewhere else. Buber compares this experience of being present and meeting someone

with openness to the potential of an *I-Thou* relationship: ⸢
exists and becomes as what is over against him, always sim
and each thing simply as being … nothing is present for
one thing, but it implicates the whole world. Measure and ⸢
disappeared; it lies with yourself how much of the immeasurable becomes
reality for you. These meetings are not organized to make the world, but
each is a sign of the world order. They are not linked with one another, but
each assures you of your solidarity with the world."[30]

Thus for Buber, "real life" is lived only when the *Thou* is available and
present. Buber continues, "The real filled present happens only in so far
as actual availability and relation exist. The present arises only by virtue
of the *Thou* becoming present."[31] It is here in the *I-Thou* relationship that
"the cradle of real life" is found.[32]

Mutuality

"Mutuality" is the availability of each party in a transaction. Buber proposes
that *I-Thou* relations require both parties to be involved in a mutual and
confirming dialogue. In his words, "Mutuality takes place when the *Thou*
meet me, but I am [also] obliged to step into direct relation with it. Hence,
the relation means being chosen and choosing."[33] *I-Thou* communication
is mutually engaging. Buber writes, "Between you and it, there is mutual
giving; you say *Thou* to it and give yourself to it, it says *Thou* to you and
gives itself to you."[34] According to Buber, the motto of life is give and take;
everyone must be a giver and a receiver. In this way, "My *Thou* affect[s] me,
as I affect it."[35] Buber means that, in such relations, there is not one person
giving and the other receiving but, rather, two people sharing as equals in
a reciprocal encounter that affects both people and makes them partners
in the moment of meeting.

Inclusion

Inclusion is the acceptance of all people regardless of their differences. It
is an attitude and an approach that seeks to ensure that every person can
participate meaningfully in all aspects of life. Inclusion refers to what
occurs when the reality of one person is given full importance by the

ıer person and vice versa. Buber explains inclusion thusly: "[It] is the extension of one's own concreteness, the fulfillment of the actual situation of life, the complete presence of the reality in which one participates. Its elements are, first, a relation, no matter what kind, between two persons, second, an event experienced by them in common, in which at least one of them actively participates, and, third, the fact that this one person, without forfeiting anything of the felt reality of his activity, at the same time lives through the common event from the standpoint of the other.[36]

Thus, moments of sincere *I-Thou* interaction are full of mutual importance. Each values the other. Each becomes the other's partner in what Buber calls a "bipolar situation."[37]

Confirmation

There is a yearning within each person to be accepted and affirmed, to be respected for what he or she is and for what he or she can be. There is a need within each person to share this way of being with others. Buber calls this sharing *confirmation*.[38] Each person waits to be honored by the other. "The human person needs confirmation secretly and bashfully he watches for a Yes which allows him to be and which can come to him only from one human to another. It is from one man to another that the heavenly bread of self-being is being passed."[39]

In an *I-Thou* relationship, one person meets another in a spirit of reverence and respect. Each honors the other, in spite of differences that may exist. In such a relationship, each person affirms the other's reality but does not necessarily agree with him or her.[40] Buber explains what he means by this sort of confirmation:

> I become aware of him, aware that he is different, essentially different from myself, in the definite, unique way, which is peculiar to him, and I accept whom I thus see, so that in full earnestness I can direct what I say to him as the person he is. Perhaps from time to time I must offer strict opposition to his view about the subject of our conversation. But I accept this person, the personal bearer of a conviction, in his definite being out of which his conviction has

grown. … I *affirm* the person I struggle with: I struggle with him as his partner, I *confirm* him who is opposed to me as him who is over against me. … If I thus give to the other who confronts me his legitimate standing as a man with whom I am ready to enter into dialogue, then I may trust him and suppose him to be also ready to deal with me as his partner.[41]

To confirm the other person is to hold each person as precious, even when standing against the other and disagreeing with something another is sharing. Such a confirmation does not equal approval, Buber explains, "but no matter in what I am against the other, by accepting him as my partner in meaningful dialogue I have confirmed him as a person."[42]

When a person is validated, he or she may feel willing to share important feelings, thoughts, hopes, and fears that he or she might otherwise hold back in self-protection. Further, when one confirms another's point of view, both can approach the edge of the predictable and walk along what Buber calls the "narrow ridge of uncertainty."

When a person enters into an *I-Thou* relationship, he or she gives up the certainty of personal agendas, roles, and programmed conversation. Instead, direct relation that is mutually inclusive and fully present occurs. Both *I* and *Thou* are confirmed as they make the journey forward into the unknown together.

Forms of Dialogue

Authentic dialogue is in contrast with assorted and positive technical dialogues or unilateral monologues. Buber explains: "There is technical dialogue, which is prompted solely by the need of immediate objective understanding. And there can be parallel conversations disguised as dialogue, in which two or more men, meeting in space, speak each with himself in strangely tortuous and circuitous ways and yet imagine they have escaped the torment of being thrown back on their own resources."[43] Buber adds eloquently, "Being, lived in dialogue, even in extreme dereliction … elicits a sense of reciprocity; being, lived in monologue, will not, even in the tenderest intimacy, grope out over the outlines of the self."[44]

Monologue Disguised as Dialogue

Monologue, a distorted form of dialogue, is the most often-experienced form of conversation. Words are said, but there is little or no depth of connection. Time and again, people become involved in conversations that Buber describes as having "the appearance but not the essence of dialogue."[45] This kind of parallel conversation dialogue can be described as two people talking *at* each other rather than *with* each other. Monologue under the pretense of dialogue happens when two or more persons speak, each wanting his or her argument or thoughts to prevail. Furthermore, according to Buber, often "the thoughts expressed [are] so pointed that they may strike home in the sharpest way, without consideration for the other person."[46] In this type of conversation, people talk to confirm their own points of view.

Nothing is as harmful to relationships as when one party or the other enters a dialogue prepared with an answer—unwilling to listen to the other, he or she is simply waiting to pounce and delineate the drawbacks of whatever new idea the other person offers. Buber calls this "speechifying," adding that, in such a monologue, people do not speak to one another, "but each although turned to the other, really speak to a fictitious court of appeal whose life consists of nothing but listening to him."[47] This is an area in which one aims at parading the image he possesses rather than the essence he has.[48]

In "being" present to "whoever," explains Buber, people communicate themselves to one another as who they are. The one who lives from his being looks at the other just as one looks at someone with whom he has one-on-one personal dealings.[49] Buber suggests that there are two different ways of interacting with others: The first proceeds from what one really is, and the other from what one wishes to seem.[50] In any meaningful relationship, there is always an interaction between monologue and dialogue.

There are three forms of dialogue, according to Buber—technical dialogue, one-sided dialogue, and genuine dialogue. Buber considers many kinds of interactions that one might imagine to be dialogue as self-disclosing disguised as dialogue. Genuine dialogue takes place—whether verbal or nonverbal—when each of the participants is fully present with the other(s) involved in the dialogue and intends to establish a living, mutual relationship.[51]

Technical Dialogue

Technical dialogue is driven by the need to understand something, by an objective exchange of material fact, not to engage the soul.[52] In other words, technical dialogue refers to the dialogue that is prompted solely by the need for objective understanding.[53] An example among the Babukusu people is realized in the consultation of the oracle in the case of illness. The diviner asks his male client, who has arrived with the sick man's wife, "What kind of trouble do you have?" The go-between replies, "This woman has come here because her husband is very sick; she came so that you may divine for her (*omulakule*); she came in order to learn what it is that made her husband ill." The diviner responds, "Yes, we shall try, we shall see whether the ancestral spirits wish that he may recover." Then he fetches his basket in which he keeps the pebbles and the hide he uses for divining. Then he begins to speak: "I may see, I may see, whether it is the ancestral spirits or perhaps the 'grain picker.'"[54] Perhaps it was his father who, after his death, wished that the patient should brew beer for him; if now he brews the 'beer of death' then the spirit of his father will rejoice." After he has spoken thus, he lets the pebbles drop on the hide; when one of them falls down away from the others, he says, "Yes indeed, the pebble has said so." In this case, then, the spirit of the sick man's deceased father has been detected as the agent responsible for his illness.

One-sided Dialogue

One-sided dialogue is the dialogue in which one of the parties experiences the "normative limitation of mutuality." By this Buber refers to those relationships, most often helping relationships, wherein one person focuses energies on another but not vice versa. One person is inclusive and confirming of the other but does not need or want the same care and concern in return. This is often the case between priest and parishioner, teacher and student, counselor and client, or doctor and patient. The parties do not expect a complete mutuality of interaction due to the nature of the relationship.[55] An example of one-sided dialogue can be found in the following Bukusu riddle, commonly told to the community by a distinguished clan elder at a meeting. Telling the riddle helps the community to learn the art of listening; it provokes their thinking and helps them to absorb the message the story entails before they continue on with the agenda of the day.

> Three people were crossing the river. The first person saw the water, walked through it, and crossed. The second one saw the water and did not walk through, but crossed. The third person did not see the water and did not walk through the water, but crossed.

To solve the riddle, one must determine who the three people were. The people are left on their own to think of possible answers before the elder tells them the answer.

The riddle is about a Bukusu pregnant mother with one child on her back. The pregnant mother saw the water, walked through it, and crossed. The child on her back saw the water but did not walk through and crossed. The third one is the baby in the womb; the baby did not see the water, did not walk through the water, but crossed. This riddle speaks volumes about children's dependence on their mother. It defines and situates dependence within the fundamental categories of Bukusu human behavior. The riddle persuasively demonstrates that dependence on each other is the key to understanding people, whether singly or in groups, as well as to understanding cultural works, ideas, morality, and even politics.

When we examine the question of who is dependent, the truth of the matter is that everyone is dependent—everyone, in his or her own way and to varying degrees, is dependent on one or several objects in a manner that is dynamic and variable according to the circumstances. The portrait of the dependent person sketched here could, after being judiciously retouched to suit the particular case, be that of anyone. The dependent person is still one of the most common and most indisputable images of universal humanity. Dependence is often the same image seen under different light, for if people frequently dominate one another, they at least as frequently have need of one another.[56] Albert Memmi, professor of sociology at the University of Paris, asserts, "Dependence isn't an illness. If it were, everyone would be sick."[57]

Genuine Dialogue

Communication occurs continually throughout our lives. As the saying goes, "One cannot *not* communicate." Therefore, if we are constantly communicating, it is important that the exchange represent our ideals and values in order to display us as we truly are. We need to eliminate all blockages to effective dialogue and keep communication open. The most important human connection that can be made, according to Buber's model, is that of genuine dialogue. Genuine dialogue refers to speech from certainty to certainty and also from one openhearted person to another openhearted person.[58] In genuine dialogue, one does not try to convince others of his or her point of view. There is no emphasis on winning but, rather, on learning, collaboration, and the synthesis of points of view. Dialogue is an element of life that is extremely important to Buber. For Buber, dialogue has to do with the way we respond to actual situations. Hence, we are called to seek self-responsibility instead of self-realization—in short, response. In genuine dialogue, the speed of the interactions is slower than that at which most groups converse. This slowing down is achieved because the group employs deeper levels of listening and reaction.

The genuine dialogue that Buber is talking about is not a casual conversation over a cup of coffee or a heated negotiation to solve a labor dispute. Buber is describing a meeting not only of minds but also of wills, of that which resides at the core of one's being. The meeting involved in genuine dialogue is rare and is, in a real sense, a meeting of souls. The primary sentiments expressed in the *I-Thou* interaction can be spoken only with the whole being. For dialogue to be alive, each party involved must turn toward the other party (ies). In my experience, such honest interaction is not found by contrasting, but by grace. According to Buber, in a very real sense, we are called to manifest revealing conversations of spirited transparency rather than forcing the other person to keep looking for it.

Genuine dialogue cannot be arranged beforehand; it will come forth in open spontaneity and candor. In other words, nothing can be pre-heard, as attempting to understand before really listening will result in an understanding that is sadly limited or veiled. Genuine dialogue seems to be rare and not always pointedly practical. Its course is of the spirit. Some discuss what they have to say only when they receive the call of the spirit.[59]

Community Relations

Community Is Primal

Community relations refer to the various methods that groups use to establish and maintain a mutually beneficial relationship with the communities in which they operate. In Buber's words, "Man has always had his experiences as *I*, his experiences with others, and with himself; but it is as *We*, ever again as *We*, that he has constructed and developed a world after his experiences."[60] Commentators with diverse sets of interests often speak about the need for humans to experience a sense of community. But what is this thing called community, and how is it relevant to cross-cultural relations?

A sense of community stems from a sense of belonging to some group more inclusively than to biological family. It is an acknowledgment and a welcoming of relationship modeled more in the way of one's interactions with those "other" than one's kin. This sense of community is experienced only consequent to our relationships with others. Hence, community is ultimately a systemic property—so much so, that the system in question comes to be referred to as just that.

From this perspective, we must recognize that, while communities must involve groups of beings, not all groups are communities. The key element that transforms a group into a community, at least in the sense of human communities, appears to be the sharing of experience. For example, I feel that I am an integral part of a group, that I somehow belong, when I can laugh, cry, sing, tell stories, and break bread with those in the group—when I can rejoice in their happiness and suffer their pain. Buber affirms, "Where there is no sharing there is no reality. Where there is self-appropriation there is no reality. The more direct the contact with the *Thou*, the fuller is the sharing."[61] Members of a community do things in a rhythm and harmony; that is how bonds of relationships are forged. The dynamics of shared activities can be varied in nature and may include shared labor or collaboration in order to complete a large or complex task; shared play, such as engaging in dance, song, competitive games, and the like; shared learning, which involves coming to see the world *I* in the same terms as others see it; and shared worship, acknowledging together one's place in still more encompassing wholes.

To the extent that we engage in these shared activities at all today, we tend to do so with different groups of people. We may worship with one group, work with another, and play with yet a fourth group. In traditional Bukusu culture, the four forms of shared activity listed above would blend as a single body harmoniously, and hence, would not be engaged in with different groups. Consequently, people in such a culture are embedded in a seamless fabric of community, or authentic community, according to Buber.[62]

A neighborhood may or may not experience a sense of shared community. For most of the people in "modern societies," it does not. We no longer work side by side with our neighbors. We seldom spend any significant portion of our leisure time actively engaged in doing things with our neighbors. While some of what we learn may be done in the presence of our neighbors, education is pursued in an environment that most often promotes competition at the expense of cooperation. And it is doubtful that we worship, if we worship at all, with our neighbors.

It is important to experience genuine community dialogue, because out of sharing flows caring, real caring about others, not the reverse substitute of institutional caring for others. Members of immersed communities can have true caring for one another. They are present to ease suffering and pain, even to mourn the dead for the nourishment of the living. It is for this reason that so many voices call for the development of a sense of community. In spite of our glorification of individualism, all people want to feel that they belong, that they are embedded in a network of people who genuinely care about them. The followers of Jim Jones and David

Koresh, the members of street gangs, Nazi skinhead hate groups, and street children of Nairobi are but particular manifestations of the desperate searching that has resulted from the loss of an authentic community in human cultures.

Buber's starting point is a strong and unmistakably communitarian position. Relationships, not individualities, are his central theme. Writing in *I and Thou*, Buber puts it explicitly, succinctly, and unmistakably: "In the beginning is the relation."[63] This statement evokes the first line of the book of Genesis: "In the beginning God created the heavens and the earth." Jonathan Sacks, the chief rabbi of Britain, points out that the first time doing good in the eye of the Lord is mentioned in the Bible (Genesis 2:18) (which contains frequent admonitions to do no wrong) is when mention is made that it is not good for man to be alone.[64] Sacks also observes that Adam, which means "earthling" in Hebrew, is not named man (*ish* in Hebrew) until God sets him in a relationship by creating woman.[65] Returning to Buber, truest personhood is born out of right relationships, formed within human beings, as one interdependent whole; this is because the "I am" requires a *Thou* to "become"—that is, as myself sets apart the other, becoming I, I say *Thou*. "All actual life is encounter,"[66] Buber says, giving each his or her just due.

From a Buberian point of view, a personalistic orientation misses the crucial point of existence. As Buber puts it, "Man becomes an *I* only through a recognized *Thou*."[67] Indeed, Buber writes that true *I*'s, true persons, emerge through the *I-Thou* relationship: "Persons [appear] by entering into relation to other persons."[68] According to Buber, there is no separate person prior to or outside of relationship, which requires at least one other.[69]

For Buber, relationships (extending to community) are not merely or mainly a matter of choice, contracts, or exchange, but rather are a primary element of natural consequence in history and culture. Buber emphasizes the importance of communities by which people may come to understand their membership not as a result of a loose and free agreement with others, but as their destiny and as a vital, intended-by-design dynamic.[70] Again, Buber writes:

It was shown how fundamentally important it is to know in every moment of thought this as well—that the one who thinks is bound, in different degrees of substantiality but never purely functionally, to a spatial realm, to a historical hour, to the genus man, to a people, a companionship in convictions. This entanglement in a manifold *We*, when known in an actual way, wards off the temptation of the thought of sovereignty: man is placed in a narrow creaturely position. But he is enabled to recognize that this is his genuine width; for being bound means being bound up in relation.[71]

Indeed, one cannot stress enough that, for Buber, the centrality and precedent of relationship over individuality is not merely historical, sequential, or causal, but also evolutionarily existential. It is not as if relationships merely precede the formation of the individual—for instance, in the way infants may first feel themselves to be part of a mother-child whole and then gradually come to a glowing sense of self apart, or the way members of preliterate ethnic groups become aware of their individuality when under the influence of a foreign culture. The individual person is not merely formed, but is dynamic and gains awareness as a participant in the seeking of ideal relationships throughout life.

Genuine Community

Genuine community is a critically important part of any assembly, a place where one can know and be known, love and be loved, serve and be served, celebrate and be celebrated. Buber sets forth his concept of community as a third alternative to the primitive individualism and collectivism found in most primitive groups of early man. He writes, "In individualism the person ... is attacked by the ravages of the fictitious, however much he thinks, or strives to think, that he is asserting himself as a person in being. In collectivism the person surrenders himself when he renounces the directness of personal decision and responsibility. In both cases the person is incapable of breaking through to the other: there is genuine relation only between genuine persons.[72]

Buber's alternative, which he refers to as real community or genuine community, is not a compromise, consolidation, or creative synthesis of individualism and collectivism but rather a distinctly different third type of community.[73] His paradigm of genuine community is based on frequent dialogic meeting of a group's members: "It is rooted in one being turning to another as another, as this particular other being, in order to communicate with it in a sphere which is common to them but which reaches out beyond the special sphere of each. I call this sphere ... the sphere of "between." Though being realized in very different degrees, it is a primal category of human reality. This is where the third alternative must begin.[74]

Buber proposes that there are two essential components of a genuine community, "a living center," and "mutual relations." He claims, "The true community does not arise through people having feelings for one another (though indeed not without it), but through, first, their taking their stand in living mutual relationship with a living Center, and, second, their being in living mutual relation with one another."[75] It is in this binding together of people united by a focus on a living center and a dialogically relational life, that real community exists. Buber puts this in his somewhat poetic form in suggesting, "Only so long as they exist, does there arise and exist, round about the invisible altar, a human cosmos [a community] with bounds and form, grasped with the spirit out of the universal stuff of the aeon, a world that is house and home, a dwelling for man in the universe."[76]

Buber's concept of a living center can be misinterpreted if it is thought to refer merely to the *raison d'être* of the group. Each group obviously has a reason for being; however, Buber adds that for there to be *genuine* inspirited community, that reason must be rooted in dialogic interactions that are not only manifest between people, but also "transparent into the divine."[77] Buber defines this living center as "the central presence of the *Thou*, or rather, more truly stated, by the central [eternal] *Thou* that has been received in the present."[78] Thus, for Buber, the eternal *Thou* is the living center, which is present when people work toward a goal with an attitude of mutual presence, inclusion, and confirmation, amounting to a right relatedness that sustains mutual "Thou-ness" intentionality.

Buber goes further to propose that a genuine community is vital and full of life when it is founded on the dialogic principle of people addressing each other as *I* and *Thou*.[79] In such a community, Buber wrote in *I and Thou*, people are "no longer side by side but as one in a thousand of persons. And this multitude, though it also moves toward one goal, yet experiences everywhere a turning to, a dynamic facing of, the other, a flowing from *I* to *Thou*."[80] Such a dialogic community consecrates and tests people by necessitating that they intentionally treat each other as *Thous* with openness and honesty with each other, affirming and confirming of one another. Buber thus believes that rightly dialogic communities arise from, and reflect "the heart of the world."[81]

When people meet in such a dialogic ideal *I-Thou* fashion, they experience what Buber calls "the essential *We*." By this he means a group of independent persons who are willing and capable of "holding place with the *We* of an ontic directness which is the decisive presupposition of the *I-Thou* relation."[82] Buber warns, however, that dialogic community cannot be forced or demanded. It can arise only when people meet openheartedly and open-mindedly. "This is how it must take place," he explains. "Only when the individual knows the other in all his otherness as himself, as man, and from there breaks through to the other, has he broken through his solitude in a strict and transforming meeting."[83] This meeting of persons is the miracle gift of the moment, and this moment is not cast in the fabric of "time" as we experience time. This encounter happens and then passes without enough time to take root for further development in an ineffable moment of recognition; one can't describe having achieved real dialogue—when you have it, you know it. In memory, we can treasure moments of *I-Thou* encounter, which is not static. And yet, according to Buber, even that brief moment of "dialogue" matters—for it is one filled with a significant meeting of open and unveiled spirit.

Buber gives examples of such meetings occurring when, "in the deadly crush of an air-raid shelter the glances of … strangers suddenly meet for a second in astonishing and unrelated mutuality; when the All Clear sounds it recedes in the awareness; and yet it did happen, in a realm which existed only for that misty opening of moment." He also gives the example of a darkened opera house, when such a sensation of unity can occur within the audience "who do not know one another, and who are listening and will hear the same purity with the same intensity to the music of a 'Mozart' a relating which is scarcely perceptible and yet is one of pure elemental dialogue shared from beyond, and which has long vanished when the lights blaze up again."[84] Buber also writes of crises and emergencies when people pull together as one and treat each other as equals, in spite of their differences.[85]

An essential point that Buber makes, however, is that such genuine community is not a permanent condition, one that a group can form, claim, and hold onto. Rather, real community exists only as long as people recognize this potential in the *I-Thou* relationship in each other dialogically. Real community "does not exhibit a smooth continuity, but is ever and again re-constituted in accordance with men's meetings with one another."[86] In other words, real community happens only in inexplicable moments and then slips away into mere social conversation, waiting fertilely for the next dialogic moment to arise. This is what Buber means when he writes, "Community is where a sound I-Thou is."[87]

There are certain groups, however, in which the likelihood that dialogic relations will arise and continue is greater. Writing in 1947 after the experience of World War II, Buber gives examples of two groups in which a sense of community is more likely to arise: "In revolutionary groups, we find a *We* most readily among those whose members make it their labor among the people to awaken and teach quietly and slowly; in religious groups we find among those who strive for an unemphatic and sacrificial realization of faith in life." Buber also warns, "It is enough to prevent the *We* arising, or being preserved, if a single man is accepted, who is greedy of power and uses others as means to his own end, or who craves for importance and makes a show of himself."[88]

Almost any group of people who are dedicated to the betterment of each other and life itself can become a dialogic community where people meet and address each other as *Thous* rather than as *Its*. A family, a group of coworkers, a gathering of friends, even a community meeting or a discussion group can lead to the building of a dialogic-enhanced community, which can grow to become more habitually and intentionally meaningful.

However, as Buber notes, it is rare for sudden conglomerates of people to become genuine dialogic communities. "The essential *We* has hitherto been all too little recognized, both in history and in the present, because it is rare," Buber notes, "because group formations have hitherto been considered mostly in respect of their energies and effects and not their inner structure—though the direction of the energy and the nature of the effects ... depend most closely on the inner structure."[89] This being so, Buber clearly distinguishes between two meanings of the principle of the inner experience—experience directed inward and experience directed to the outside world. You go out, but when you meet God, you go inward. It is remarkable how pervasive this split is, although Buber speaks of the "ontology of the between," the living Center. Buber explains, "It is when these two realities are united as one people that life takes on its inspirited fullness of meaning. It is then that human life is shaped into a fullness of ultimate reality, and even though human life neither can nor ought to overcome the connection with *It*, it is so one in relation that that ideal wins in it a shining streaming constancy: the moments of supreme meeting are then not flashes in the darkness but like the rising moon [effulgent] in a clear starlit night.[90]

A Philosophy of Negotiability as It May Be Applied to Political Realities

Martin Buber affirms that, in the long view, the essential hope of history depends upon a genuine community of the human race.[91] He recognizes that the social and the political implications of his own thought are profound; and while courageous in expressing himself, he was viewed by many of his peers as being of questionable significance. For example, he looked to some form of reconciliation with the Germans earlier than many Jews and Israelis. He also argued that Israel should not be an exclusively Jewish state but, rather, that Jewish and Palestinian factions should equally share state power. Buber even looked to the time when the nation-state might be obsolete. He saw political activity as a means of transforming the relationships within these two communities. He believed that activism was not just a case of working for justice and economic advancement; it was also a way of bringing about spiritual transformation. He sought to create a dialogical community, a third way to resolve the tensions between individualism and collectivism, wherein community attempts to reconcile between right-wing and left-wing conflicts.

The quality of life in a community or in a society depends on the extent to which *I-Thou* relations exist. Buber puts it this way: "A dialogue between man and man allows a common discourse to develop and crystallize and it is this that is essential for holding a society together and sustaining cultural creativity."[92] Thus, he emphasizes the fact that an individual is related to his or her world by telling us that "community is where community happens."[93] In a world where people are searching for a sense of community in their lives, it seems to Buber that we must begin with the concrete—with a real community of people connected to us in space and time—and then expand the bounds of our definition of inclusiveness. Buber suggests that the interests of a community's survival override an individual's interests or rights. Indeed, for him, it is the community that determines for individuals the range of their liberties, which are enjoyed only in the context of the community's vision of the purposed world. Here, Buber affirms that no one human lives for himself or herself, as appears to be the case made by philosophic individualism in the West. At its extreme, the Western form of community is a threat to the freedom of the individual. Ideally, it would seem that, instead of community swallowing up the individual, the gifts of the many individuals are allowed to come together to create the living, human community that satisfies the aspirations of each. Thus we encounter the necessity for ongoing dialogue.

Despite this emphasis on the group, Buber would add that at the heart of any such community are special people—"the builders." In stressing the components of community, he notes, "The community is built up out of living mutual relation, but the builder is the living effective Center."[94] These builders tend to live the dialogical life with all who are alive to the clustered human dynamics, reinforcing a sense of animate community.

On this point of mutuality, Buber concludes, "If communal life were parceled out into independent realms, one of which is the 'spiritual life,' this would certainly not be done; that would only mean to give up once and for all to tyranny the provinces that are sunk in the world of *It,* and to rob the spirit completely of reality."[95] Moreover, given true relationship with God, we do become true; "we" become the truest of true, never more to drop back into being institutionalized. Buber concludes that institutionalized religion does become a barrier, while true prayer is One-to-one.[96] While in the world of persons, the *It* has a legitimate, and indeed, an essential role; God is pure *Thou.* Buber would agree that, by the very nature of the eternal *Thou,* one cannot be reduced to an *It.*[97]

Buber and Culture

It can be said that all cultural narratives have a starting point that is particularly revealing. Many religious accounts start with a generic notion of a god as one who is revealed through Moses; Jesus; Muhammad; or in the case of Bukusu traditional religion, the ancestor *Mubukusu.* If one accepts the notion of one's God as the one true reality, the rest of the narrative will follow cohesively. Buber observes:

> Every great culture … rests on an original relational incident, on a response to the *Thou* made at its source, on an act of being made by the spirit. This act, strengthened by the similarly directed power of succeeding generations, creates in the spirit a special conception of the cosmos; only through this act is a cosmos, an apprehended world, a world that is homely and house like, man's dwelling in the world, made possible again and again. Only now can man, confident in his soul, build again and again, in a special conception of space, dwellings for God and dwellings for men, and fill swaying time with new hymns and songs, and shape the very community of men. But he is free and consequently creative only so long as he possesses, in action and suffering in his own life, that act of being—so long as he himself enters into relation. If a culture ceases to be centered in the living and continually renewed relational event, then it hardens into the world of *It,* which the glowing deeds of solitary spirits only spasmodically break through.[98]

For Buber, an essential element of personhood is dependent on the intensity of maintaining this mutual relationship in the community. For example, one may appreciate the importance of initiation and rites of passage in the growth and development of a person among the Bukusu community. Through these rites of passage, an individual learns about and experiences the channels of relationship in order to become a more responsible and respected community member. One is human because of others; one lives with and for others. This is expressed in the Bukusu and African saying, "I am because we are; and since we are, therefore I am."[99] The basic orientation for existence in an African mind-set is that life cannot exist in terms of an isolated individualism. Rather, the individual is experienced as part of a whole community and cultural group. The existence of the individual is the existence of the community. Although the individual may physically die, this does not relinquish his or her social, legal existence; the *we* continues to exist for the *I*. This continuity is of great psychological value. It provides a deep sense of security in the otherwise insecure world in which the Bukusu people live. Viewed in this light, the elaborate Bukusu kinship system seems to act as an insurance policy, covering both the physical and the metaphysical dimensions of human life.

According to the Bukusu worldview, an individual owes his or her existence to others, including those of past generations, those not yet born, and his or her present contemporaries. Thus for individuals and the community, social life is a type of dialectic process. The *I* is simply a part of the whole. Additionally, in Bukusu beliefs, the community makes, creates, or produces the individual, for the individual depends on the community. Only in terms of other people does the individual become conscious of his being, duties, privileges, and responsibilities toward himself and toward other people. "I am because of you." Whatever happens to the individual happens to the whole community, and whatever happens to the whole community happens to the individuals in it.

Buber and the Politics of Dialogue

For Buber, politics is an essential dimension of the life of dialogue and one's service to God. How so? Politics, he affirms, is neither extraneous to the life of the spirit nor simply an unavoidable task occasionally imposed by the exigencies of history. He argues, "In the ultimate matrix of interpersonal and everyday life, politics provides the necessary test and gives concrete reality to religious and ethical teachings."[100] Here, Martin Buber states the utility of wholeness for the art of dialogue. Communitarians stress that the commonly posited opposition between private and public sectors, or the market and the state, ignores the important role that society plays in people's lives and, further, that social norms are important as a source of social order in their own right and as the foundations of laws that the community members truly heed. Buber basically shares this position. Buber views the state as appropriately stepping in, but only when the society can no longer carry the load.

People living together at a given time and in a given space are only, to a certain degree, capable of their own free will, of living together rightly, of maintaining a right order and conducting their common concerns accordingly. The line that, at any time, limits this capacity forms the basis of the state at that time; in other words, the degree of incapacity for a voluntary right order determines the degree of legitimate compulsion.[101]

At the same time, Buber is aware that, to keep the state at bay, people need a vibrant communal life, one that is mindful of the dangerous potential of the state to become oppressive if communal life wanes. In this context, Buber introduces the important communitarian concept of responsibility.[102] This concept strongly implies that serious effort must be made toward all right relatedness.

So long as society is richly structured, so long as it is built up of manifold communities and communal units, all strong in vitality, the state is a wall narrowing one's outlook and restricting one's step; but within this wall, a spontaneous communal unit could flourish and grow. However, to the extent that the structure grows impoverished, the wall becomes a prison.[103]

Why Buber Is Important

Buber's analysis and explication of the complexities of interpersonal dialogue is extremely useful in the context of leaders meeting one-on-one. He suggests that dialogue exists when people within a group address each other as important equals. Following this logic, one can assert that the same reality would be true between groups. One could not suggest that groups in general could be dialogic but, rather—to be true to Buber's logic—that a specific group could interact dialogically with another specific group of people in any meeting. In other words, to project Buber's concept into group interaction, one cannot generalize but must speak in specifics.

Buber contends that dialogic relations between contending factions are not usually long-term but are momentary and transitory. He encourages dialogue between people and groups. People must be aware that there are likely to be far more moments of monologue than of dialogue in any series of interactions but that those moments can provide a fertile soil for dialogic meetings and, therefore, must be appreciated for the potential they hold.

Buber's dialogic philosophy encourages inclusion and confirmation, which imply an appreciation and respect for the other party's worldview while maintaining one's own. Applied to intergroup or interreligious relations, Buber's model suggests that religious or cultural groups with significantly different beliefs and traditions can relate respectfully and meaningfully without having to demand agreement or assimilation over accommodation.

CHAPTER 11

•◆•

FRED IKLÉ'S STRATEGIES FOR INTERGROUP NEGOTIATION

This chapter moves beyond Buber's emphasis on individual and community dialogue to a consideration of Fred Charles Iklé's perspectives on the breakdown and rebuilding of intergroup relations, especially as they pertain to religious, cultural, and national groups. Formal negotiation is, for Iklé, what dialogue is for Buber.

The Need to Negotiate for Dialogue

To set a context for the relevance and applicability of Iklé's ideas to the cultural confluence in Bukusuland, we'll look at several current real-life examples; these examples will give us a glimpse into the sort of challenges that people of good faith seeking dialogue and negotiation might face. In Africa, as elsewhere, conflicts have arisen due to economic, political, cultural, and religious factors. Typically, people use religion to justify discord, although, in fact, religion intensifies it and, thus, can foster divisions and fan the fires of conflict. For example, some Muslim groups believe that the Kenyan government and business communities have deliberately interfered with the progress of economic development in predominantly Muslim areas. They also believe that a nation's business community, as dominated by the Christian population in the "up-country" areas, deliberately allocate to non-Muslims most of the jobs created in predominantly Muslim regions. Consequently, Muslims have increasingly perceived themselves to be treated as second-class citizens in a predominantly Christian country. Such perceptions and actions have weakened reasonable religious tolerance among peoples.

A few instances of violence have erupted between adherents of different religious groups in Kenya. For example, some Muslims threw stones and attacked Catholic worshipers stopping in front of the mosque. Muslim worshipers were inside and believed that the Christians were mocking them. In the resulting confrontation, even the local bishop was hurt. Providentially, however, members of the two faiths came together to resolve the misunderstandings and make amends a few days later.

On another occasion, some Muslim worshipers fought over lands surrounding their mosque with some local developers in a residential neighborhood, resulting in the deaths of four innocent residents and injuries to numerous others. Originally a land conflict, this could have become a religious conflict. A mosque, a learning center, a Christian church, and one business were burned down. It took riot police to restore calm.

According to Iklé's words, in cases like these, Buber's approach to dialogue would likely not have been sufficient to resolve the differences that escalated to violence.

Iklé's understanding is that negotiation in itself represents an approach to interaction that takes over when a sense of unity in a shared community breaks down. When Buber's inclusivity and confirmation break down or are not enough, Iklé's approach to negotiation becomes highly valuable for restoring dialogue. Like Buber's approach, Iklé's is based on mutual respect, but it includes an element of power and force, by imposition of agreed-upon boundaries and agreed-upon responses to differences through genuine *I-Thou* dialogue. Iklé's position is essentially that two conflicting parties should be able to find mutual, acceptable understanding, taking into account the eventual risk of untoward responses and the natural consequences of not reaching an understanding; failing to do so, the discussion may escalate into verbal assaults and resentment. In the worst cases, it may lead to hostility or even war. It is important that conflicts be resolved as soon as possible. This approach could be useful to cross-cultural relations in Bukusuland.

Iklé's Central Thesis

In his 1964 book *How Nations Negotiate*, Iklé argues that historians, foreign affairs experts, and military strategists have devoted far more thought to the questions of how and why wars begin than to questions concerning how to end them and what to do about postwar conditions. This imbalance in attitudes toward wars detrimentally affects how political leaders and military planners make decisions about war and peace.

Iklé points out that, once incursions start, dynamics are unleashed that make bringing the relationship among factions into balance difficult. Overt violence transforms the future, moves boundaries, topples governments, and expands or breaks up empires, leaving scars of death and destruction. Such violence has lasting consequences. People have difficulty coping with such heightened animosities.

To counter this problem, Iklé suggests that overt violence must be addressed nation-to-nation. He looks at war as an unconventional means of conflict resolution. He believes that wars are more easily started than stopped. Therefore, he provides a diplomatic perspective on how people can bring wars to an end. Essentially, Iklé's position is that we need to apply restraint to both the means and the ends of lawless violence in order to stop armed hostilities. He argues that historians, students of military strategy, and experts on foreign affairs have tended to neglect this question, focusing rather on how wars begin. The way in which such an aggression is brought to an end has the most decisive long-term impact on the people of the enmeshed countries.

The Value of Iklé's Approach

Invited negotiators who are from the same culture approach a discourse with shared sympathetic values and understanding. Their common institutional ideology becomes the backdrop against which optimal deals and decisions may result and disputes are resolved. On the other hand, when negotiators are from different cultures, each must seek quite different approaches to his or her focused interaction, including the economic interests, legal precedents, and political and social realities of the group he or she is representing.

In today's global environment, negotiators must understand these dynamic cultural differences. Adeptness in the fundamentals of negotiation gives a decided advantage at the bargaining table, allowing the parties to focus on finding solutions when negotiating across boundaries of national, ethnic, and religious cultures. Perspectives that are focused on everyone involved provide understanding in the moment and should be the rule for negotiators who deal with disputes and help craft decisions that bridge cultural differences. This can be applicable to negotiations among diverse groups and nations and, for our purposes here, among Muslim, Christian, and, traditional Bukusu people.

According to Iklé, conflict is a perception of opposing interests involving scarce resources, goals, or procedures.[104] For example, in a 1992 US-Chinese joint venture, the Chinese wanted access to American state-of-the-art cartoon technology, and the United States wanted to protect its intellectual capital while gaining access to the vast Chinese marketplace. In negotiating the joint-venture agreement, a transfer of technology was agreed to in principle, but once the venture began, the Chinese negotiators became dissatisfied. Iklé used this example to point out that conflict, even when associated with strong negative emotions, is not always a bad phase for negotiating groups. It exposes the important differences that are calling for acknowledgment, respect, and response. He suggests, for example, that conflict in the workplace is a natural result of transition and growth. However, when conflicted people lack avenues to negotiation, the efforts become misunderstandings with prejudices, and animosity, which in turn may lead to further conflict.

For Iklé, the avoidance of conflict shows that restraint applied to both the means and ends of warfare is essential to reaching a successful outcome in regard to war. Secondly, a nation's Armed Forces ought not to be committed to combat without clear rules of engagement, whether for defeating the enemy or for expelling the aggressors and restoring the peace. A third lesson is that a nation's military forces should not be sent into combat merely for the purpose of demonstrating resolve and commitment. Such a "demonstration strategy," notes Iklé, is no substitute for a clearly constituted military strategy designed to defeat the enemy's spirit.[105] Iklé continues, "The fourth lesson tells us that [a country such as] the United States should not enter a war based on a strategy of inflicting 'punishment' on the enemy by bombing or shelling targets whose destruction will not serve to defeat the enemy's forces militarily."[106] What happens to a people when the landscapes of people's lives—personal, social, and cultural—are destroyed, when the maps of meaning that order people's lives are blown apart? They may refuse to comply and instead seek revenge. Or, when what they believe makes them human—home, family, and tradition—has been wrenched from their grasp, they may escape war and flee to another country and a lifestyle far different from anything they have known before. Those who have been mutilated may only be able to fight for survival and end up seething with impotent bitterness. Thus, destruction based on a strategy of inflicting punishment on the enemy population is a strategy Iklé warns against. To examine the question of how to resolve disputes successfully across cultures rather than between ruling governments, it is first useful to look at how conflicts arise.

When Conflicts Arise

"Conflict termination" is the process leading to the resolution of a conflict and the reestablishment of mutual acceptance of interests and objectives to ensure minimally short-term conditions. The issue of conflict termination is clouded by interpretations of the terms used to discuss conflict dynamics. Iklé defines conflict as a clash of political, ideological, economic, or religious interests between groups.[107]

Clear objectives for conflict termination are important, but it is also important to know what the end should look like because the end result will affect the means used in implementing the peace. The end state is defined as a clear and doable description of the conditions that, when achieved, will satisfy the mutually adjusted objectives.[108] The end state is assumed to be one in which there is potential for ongoing peace and mutual acceptance.

Iklé's practical approach to negotiation of conflicts is based on strategies of intergroup dialogue. He suggests that, to avoid or to resolve conflicts, the terms and ground rules must be clarified in advance. We will examine these ground rules, but it is first useful to understand Iklé's vocabulary of conflict. There are signals, Iklé points out, that indicate that conflict is arising and that the negotiation of differences is called for. These signs of surfacing disputes include warnings, threats, commitments, and inducements. The following explains each of these in the context of Babukusu and Kenyan cultures.

The Difference between Warnings and Threats

Warnings and threats may sound similar at first, but Iklé points out that they represent significantly different processes. Iklé notes, "Warnings and threats thus belong to the same category, but they differ from one another."[109] They are similar in that, in both, the aggressor tries to dissuade an opponent from making a certain move or to maintain the status quo by persuading the opponent to comply with a demand. The difference between a warning and a threat, as Iklé conceives it, is that warnings are tough talk about how the relationship will suffer if positive actions are not pursued, whereas threats are previews of forceful actions about to be taken.[110] There are times, however, when Iklé uses these words almost interchangeably, as the concepts become more complex and the distinctions blurred. We will look at each of these concepts independently.

Warning Signals

Iklé defines warning signals as hints from one party of an impending conflict for the suspected purpose of changing the other party's expectations and, consequently, influencing the latter's choices.[111] He explains that, by restating the suspected proposal in one's own words for clarification, one keeps this point of the issue under discussion. This means that the party that warns is indicating the natural or relational consequence likely to follow from the other's veiled actions not seen as being in the spirit of the intended dialogue. For example, at one time, the International Monetary Fund and World Bank institutions lent money to countries that were in deep economic trouble under the condition that the countries show transparency of accounting and accountability for resource allocation.[112] However, these countries did indulge in corruption by mismanagement, and so they were warned and directed to change their modus operandi and abide by the original agreement—or consequences would be that future funds would not be forthcoming.

Warnings of Exclusion

A specific type of warning Iklé identifies is that of exclusion, meaning that a group warns an opponent against unacceptable behaviors under threat of exclusion from participation in economic or political decision-making organizations. Examples of political exclusion can be seen in the recent treatments of Libya, Iraq, and Cuba by Western powers.

According to Iklé, if a party that is reluctant or indifferent toward rightly related dialogic suggestion, that party is susceptible to being rejected. He indicates that the initiator of a different interpretation will want to have the essential parties in agreement. One has to be careful, lest his or her effort to win over reluctant participants jeopardize his or her own basic goals. The parties that are included may refuse to accept the proposal.

Iklé suggests that warnings of exclusion can be ineffective in certain cases when the intervention appears meaningless, especially if it stops the participation of what those who propose it would add—as might be the case, for example, when those who would be excluded have the support of people in the upper levels of the organization who could veto the exclusion. Circumstances under which the opponent may choose noncompliance, even at the risk of being excluded from the presiding organization's benefit exist. These include situations in which the opponent expects that absorbing the predicted losses will be less costly than meeting the costs of the demands, in which the opponent decides that these losses will be less harmful than the damage done to its reputation by giving in, or in which the opponent does not believe that the threat will be carried out or that predictable consequences will follow.

In Kenya's Bukusuland, there are numerous examples of exclusionary warnings. Christian missionaries, for example, expect their adherents to be monogamous. These missionaries turn a blind eye to the cruelty and injustice involved in disrupting polygynous unions that are deeply rooted in the Bukusu social fabric. Bukusu chiefs cement good relations with subject tribal communities by virtue of the institution of polygynous marriage. One might allow that great value is placed on children by these marriages (and these are "marriages"). Moreover, the contributions made by the numerous wives in village farming guarantee more prosperity; these overwhelmingly provide strong motives for polygamy.[113]

In comparison, for Christians, monogamy is part and parcel of the Word of God "Good News,"[114] particularly with the indissolubility of marriage in the Catholic Church. Polygyny is seen by Christians as a sign of refusing to truly convert to the Christian faith. Those who would marry more than one wife are excluded from fellowship of "church"—especially in terms of the Roman Catholic rite. This becomes a problem in the Bukusu traditional way of life, in which polygyny is practiced, and the refusal of Christian burial rites causes families great anguish. Bukusu Roman Catholics have been led to believe that they will go to hell if they are refused burial rites by the church authority. For these believers, this is a denial of a main source of Bukusu faith—unity and strength. A great number of these Bukusu Christians presently are excluded, not only from burial, but also from participating in all the sacraments. This is a standing and unresolved problem to this very day. As a consequence of ongoing exclusionary warnings, many people have quit the Catholic Church and gone to the Protestant church or converted to Islam.[115]

On the other hand, one of the Christian groups that responded seriously to the Bukusu dilemma over tribal tradition is the African Israel Church Nineveh (AICN). Gerald B. Brown, a British scholar of religion, writes, "The problem of polygyny was solved by allowing men who were polygynous when they joined the church to continue so, but by forbidding it to others; and an important place was provided for women who, in this church, outnumber men by two to one."[116] The rise of a number of local independent churches such as the AICN has resulted in the movement of many Catholics and Protestants to the AICN. This shift has posed a real threat to the traditional Christian denominations with long histories in Africa.

A similar incident concerned the followers of *Dini ya Musambwa* (religion of veneration of ancestral ways). Bukusu traditional religion, being one of these, was founded by Elijah Masinde with the Bukusu people of western Kenya in the 1940s.[117] Masinde's followers were active in opposing the colonial government, and he was imprisoned on several occasions for his political statements against the government. *Dini ya Musambwa*, in its day, was a mix of Christianity and African traditional religions. It is a fading religious phenomenon now, but such religious syncretism can take place when foreign beliefs are introduced to an indigenous belief system and the teachings are blended. The new, heterogeneous religion has taken a shape of its own. *Dini ya Musambwa* was first founded as a conscious effort to return to the traditional ways of the larger Babukusu traditions that once would say, "Everyone in this world belongs to me [God]; even the polygamist belongs to me." Here, God told Masinde to quit the Friends (the American Quaker mission) and return to the religion of his ancestors. The sacred center of this religion was a lake high up on Mount Elgon, which Masinde's followers called *Zaioni*. The members were to wear a cross on their uniforms, and Masinde claimed that the Trinity was foreshadowed in traditional Bukusu thought. It follows, then, that the first Babukusu progenitors being Mary and Joseph, the ancestors and angels were to be seen as members of one family of spiritual beings. The members of the church were to pray this prayer:

> Oh God the Father, forgive us and feel pity for us. The foreigners brought the new missions which made us leave our traditional customs which are now lost. We are asking you to bless us and give us freedom.[118]

Implied in this prayer is an expression of a sense of loss; this evokes the loss of the Bukusu's God-given land to the Europeans, the loss of freedom of movement and speech, the loss of the celebration of traditional dances, and the loss of the unquestioned respect enjoyed by the old. These losses meant that their traditional religion was altogether compromised.

The *Dini ya Musambwa* often emphasized secret knowledge. This was the lure that drew the novice through one secret initiation into another for his cultural and spiritual ascent. The secret was often trivial, but its possession was believed to be a real source of power. Furthermore, Masinde claimed that his prophecies had come true because, at the time, (1963) Kenya had won independence. He argued that the education in schools was not relevant to African needs and that the real knowledge to invent things had been held back from the African peoples. He asserted that, in school, one would not even be taught how to make a simple thing like an insignificant needle. Elijah also told his adherents not to wear European clothing or visit hospitals run by Europeans. Many people were encouraged to stop sending their children to school. Consequently, *Dini ya Musambwa*, as a religious movement, was proscribed by the independent government of Kenya in 1968.

Threats of exclusion are sometimes effective, but they can also elicit unexpected or harshly painful results. For example, back in 1947, a crowd of *Dini ya Musambwa* advanced on the police station at Malakisi in Bungoma District and had to be repulsed with gunfire. Eleven *Dini ya Musambwa* followers died. The adherents had been duped into believing that bullets would turn into drops of water. They had only "heard" how, at Kibabii Catholic Mission—one of the priests having fired one shot—the *Dini ya Musambwa* had not been driven away and no one suffered a bullet wound.[119]

Threats

Threats are not the same as mere warnings, from Iklé's perspective, in that threats give notice of the potential for future use of force that may be deadly. In a threat, the threatening party gives advance notice of intent to cause the opponent to reconsider or suffer serious consequences. In a threat, both the prediction of the loss and the willingness to cause the loss are made explicit, and thus the threats become an ultimatum. Iklé asserts that, once a threat has been made, it *must* be carried out if an opponent does not desist. Otherwise, the threatening party will not be believed in the future.

An example of the importance and the impact of threats can be seen in the case of Alexander Muge, a Kenyan Anglican Bishop of the Diocese of Eldoret, who was an outspoken critic of government corruption and the assassinations of dissident politicians. In 1989, Minister of Labor Peter Okondo threatened Muge with death. Because the bishop did not cease making his public pronouncements, followers of Okondo killed him. British historian David Throup explains:

> Immediately after Okondo's incautious threat, Bishop Muge had issued a press statement on Monday, August 13, 1990—the same day that Assistant Minister Pancras Otwani was warning bishops not to "preach politics" in his constituency—declaring that Okondo's remarks heralded a plot to kill the church leader in order to silence his accusations against senior politicians and civil servants. The bishop asserted that he would visit Busia, where he was prepared to die at the hands of the minister's gang, youth members of a political party KANU (Kenya African National Union), and had warned that he might meet a fate similar to that of murdered Foreign Minister Robert Ouko, who was rumored to have been murdered by cabinet colleagues who feared his investigations into government corruption. The Eldoret bishop concluded by prophetically forewarning his ministerial critic: "Let Okondo know that my innocent blood will haunt him forever and he will not be in peace, for God does not approve murder."[120]

In September of that year, Muge ignored the warnings of the district commissioner and visited West Pokot lands. He visited Busia in western Kenya the next day, where he received a warm public welcome. After conducting a massive open-air service outside Saint Stephen church in Busia, which attracted street traders and local workers, the bishop left in a four-car convoy, taking an indirect route back to Eldoret that skirted Kisumu before joining the Webuye-Eldoret road. A few miles from town, Muge's car was involved in an "accident" in which a truck crashed head-on into the driver's side of the bishop's vehicle, dragging it one hundred feet and crushing the bishop behind the steering wheel in the mangled wreck. Although his three passengers survived, Bishop Muge died on the roadside. Kenya was plunged into crisis, as suspicion of murder fell upon

Minister of Labor Okondo and Bishop Muge's other critics among the political elite.[121]

Instilling Fear

Iklé observes that in slow-moving negotiations, "there are pressures of a different kind that can be generated to make the opponent anxious for a quick settlement."[122] One technique is to cause the opponent to fear that the proponent's terms, far from moving closer to the opponent's wishes, might actually harden or become worse. One's opponent must get the idea that he or she would miss a golden opportunity should he or she fail to accept the proponent's offer. Iklé cites an example from the Korean truce talks, in which continued American casualties from Chinese attacks and the uncertain fate of American prisoners induced the UN negotiators to accept the communists' terms on many issues. Often one side suffers far more from the postponement of an agreement than the other side. Such an asymmetry is one of the most cogent factors in pushing the side that is in a hurry toward its minimum position.[123]

In the history of Kenya, there are many cases of political leadership instilling fear in people. Frightening rhetorical speeches became warnings that reinforced the message that citizens must choose between the status quo and chaos. According to Professor Angelique Haugerud, editor of *American Ethnologist*, in a gathering that occurred in 1979, a Kenyan cabinet minister (CM) addressed a rural meeting at which he was a guest of honor. The gathering occurred just a few months after the overthrow of Dictator Idi Amin in the neighboring Uganda.

CM: "Would you like this country to be like that of Amin?"

Crowd: "No!"

CM: "You wouldn't want that? In order that we stay in peace, ruling ourselves here in Kenya, there is one big secret. Do you want to hear that secret?" (Slowly) "It is to obey! People fear Amin's place; they have guns. Is that a good place?"

Crowd: "No!"

The cabinet minister then described how people in Uganda were pushed into a type of dump truck that carries sand, then put into a helicopter and transported with their hands tied, and then dropped from the door of the helicopter into Lake Victoria. He asked the crowd, "Would you want leadership like that?" Of course the crowd responded, "No!" The cabinet minister concluded by saying, "Then let us obey our government."[124]

In an effort to marginalize or silence opposition parties, Kenyan officials still use rhetoric that invokes images of political disorder in neighboring nations to persuade. Uganda, Somalia, Sudan, Liberia, Ethiopia, and the Democratic Republic of the Congo have all provided convenient examples of the dangers of letting political conflict and dissent run amok.[125] Between 1990 and 1991, terrifying portraits of chaos and violence were featured in some Kenyan authorities' exhortations to allow them to ignore multiparty advocates. When President Moi criticized those behind Kenya's violent social protests in July 1990, he invoked images of chaos and described multiparty advocates as "selfish troublemakers" out to destabilize the country.[126] Drawing parallels between Eastern Europe and Kenya, Moi warned that "Eastern Europe is in chaos" and that having multiple political parties in Kenya would only encourage similar ethnic divisions and instability.[127] Ironically, in 1992, many citizens believed the ruling party itself was instigating ethnic violence in an attempt to discredit opposition. Also in the early 1990s, some government supporters appeared to advocate violence against political dissidents, publicly urging the citizens to cut off the fingers of multiparty advocates and to arm themselves with *rungu* (knobbed sticks) and spears to crush opponents of one-party rule.[128]

Assertions about the destructive consequences of multiparty politics were not a new rhetorical theme in the 1990s. In 1979, an election year in which Kenya was still a one-party state, officials emphasized that bloodshed would inevitably follow if there were to be multiparty politics. According to Haugerud, the cabinet minister spoke thus to the crowd in the name of KANU:

"The ruling party KANU has led Kenya for more than sixteen years now. There are many different parties in far off nations such as Ghana, Nigeria, and Egypt ... and in all, no one leads more than two, three, or four years before it collapses, and by the time it collapses people wash themselves in blood, but has KANU done that?"

The crowd replied, "No!"

The speaker, a cabinet minister addressing a KANU rally in Bukusuland some months before an election, repeated the question, "Has KANU ever done that?"

Again, the crowd replied, "No!"

The cabinet minister then referred to the difficult struggle for independence, and to Jomo Kenyatta's admonition (after he was released from detention) to forgive those who did us wrong so that we can work with them. The cabinet minister went on to list the fruits of independence, such as the building of many secondary schools in the district. Here again, after describing the effort to bring secondary education to the people, the minister elicited replies from the audience. Claiming development rather than politics as the meeting's focus was an attempt to discourage or undermine in advance explicitly critical or politically incendiary words a rival might utter. [129]

Along with all such examples of deliberately instilling fear in the citizens, the one-party state may affirm itself as an iconic presence that sets limits on tolerable behavior. All this is also the Kenyan experience. Through fear, citizens are cowed into accepting the political machinations imposed by those in power. The cost of submission in this dynamic is serious, ranging from unwonted patronage to unwonted surveillances, harassment, imprisonments, and even deaths.

Bluffs

A bluff, as opposed to a threat, is "a failure on one's part to inflict the predicted damage upon the opponent."[130] Iklé points out that a claim is determined to be a bluff "only after it has been challenged by the opponent's noncompliance."[131] In other words, a threat becomes exposed as toothless only after the opponent will not accede to the proponent's demands.[132]

Exuberant showmanship (or bluffing), thus far, is an enduring element in Kenyan political life. Back in the 1800s, a European traveler recorded the scene his group witnessed at a Kikuyu assembly. "The speeches were screamed out rather than spoken, the meaning being emphasized with a club until the club was reduced to splinters. The bearing of the speakers was aggressive and insolent."[133] Europeans traveling through Kenya were so disconcerted by such incidents that they were unable to be sure whether they were genuinely threatened or merely being intimidated by the huffing and puffing of "tribal" leaders trying to impress them.

A century later and on a more peaceful occasion, an anthropologist joined some two hundred people sitting on a grassy clearing on Mt. Kenya's foothills. On this sunny day in March 1979, just months after the inauguration of President Moi, the anthropologist reported hearing a politician tell his people, "Not long ago, before we had our new president, there were many things that were spoiling citizens here. There used to be a lot of drunkenness, bribery and corruption. People have spoiled the footsteps, fallen away from the path they should have followed."[134] Another Kenyan leader also asserted, "Now, however, Kenya is a nation on the move, on the run toward rapid development." [135] He warned the crowd that those who could not keep up with the new president's rapid changes would be left behind in a ditch.[136] Another orator at that rally implied that a great change had already occurred; gone were the days when the citizen must "cook tea" (pay a bribe) in return for routine government service. This speaker contended that no longer would officers at the Land Registry delay farmers by demanding "tea," repeatedly putting off those who sought assistance to settle boundary disputes.

Here was the public face of a fresh national political culture—a new tradition of disservice in the making. However, the various politicians presented conflicting images that shifted at their convenience. Every new head of state pledged to end past evils, simultaneously assuring citizens he would follow the footsteps of his eminent predecessor Jomo Kenyatta, who, in fact was well known for his corruption.[137] Such speeches by politicians sound hopeful and determined. Their words are meant to inspire; but they have all been bluffs, and the local people knew it.

For the Bukusu people, such bluffing became something of a diversion. They turned out for rallies called by the visiting politicians merely for the entertainment but not to be fooled. They called it a "free movie." They laughed and joked and then went home.

Commitments

Iklé defines diplomatic commitment (no bluff) as an effort to convince one's opponent that one will maintain "one's current position."[138] A commitment suggests to the opponent that the proponent's intentions are inflexible as stated and will not change as long as the commitment cannot be revealed as a lie. In addition, is a forewarning that, should the unacceptable action be taken, there will be consequences, at least until new agreements or commitments to negotiation have been established.[139] Implementing such consequences would constitute wasted time.

Unwillingness to Change one's Terms

Your opponent may realize, however, that you would still prefer agreement if you had to lower your terms. You must, therefore, employ other techniques to demonstrate to your opponent that your terms are unlikely to soften. A useful device, Iklé explains, is to maintain a commitment not to change you terms or "a commitment not to accept the opponent's demands."[140] This means that apart from convincing one's opponent that one's terms are firm, one must make an effort to dissuade the opponent from further bargaining by making a postponement of the agreement seem dangerous to the opponent's interests. In an acute crisis, the danger of postponing a settlement is a particularly compelling reason for accepting the offered terms.[141] Iklé cites as an example the USSR's leader Khrushchev sudden acquiescence to John F. Kennedy in October of 1962. The withdrawal of Soviet missiles from Cuba was largely motivated by the fear of sudden American action. Iklé is pointing out that delay or refusal would have put Khruschev in a worse position.[142] In addition, it seemed wiser to Khrushchev to drop his counterdemands for a withdrawal of American missiles from Turkey than to face the risks of further escalation in Cuba. Thus, a commitment not to change one's terms or a commitment not to accept the opponent's demands is a useful device, but only when one has the obvious moral and logistic advantage.

Inducement

Inducement is another negotiation strategy. According to Iklé, "Inducement is a style in which the opponent must be made to believe that the estimated consequences of final non-agreement are worse for the other than for the proponent of the agreement."[143] This means that while one is engaged in the process of bargaining, the negotiator must induce the opponent to prefer agreement to non-agreement and persuade the other to desist from further arguing his position.[144] In the law of contracts, the inducement is a pledge or promise that causes an individual to enter into a particular set of agreed-upon conditions.

As long as the opponent continues to reject terms of agreement, the proponent must press to make the opponent acquiesce to the terms. While one is engaged in such bargaining, the proponent has to make the other prefer the proposed agreement in lieu of further delay.

To make the terms more attractive, the proponent first wants to offer concessions, giving the impression of a win-win situation. To do this, the proponent will look for areas in which his and the opponent's viewpoints are not at odds. The following is an example of how the underprivileged people of Kenya have been exploited through such methods since the colonial era.

The British colonial administrators experimented with some devious devices for inducing public acceptance of taxation. Their argument went like this: How do you make the Bukusu people work for the English when the Bukusu would prefer to remain on their own undersized farms? Tax them! But tax them for what? The people could be taxed for having a head (a poll tax) or for having a home (a hut tax). Both of these taxes were instituted, and Kenyan citizens were required to pay in a currency that the English had minted. The English summoned the people, saying, "Come and take the money. You can earn what you need by working for the English. Then you can pay the money due in taxes."[145] Thus, taxes were used to indirectly induce the Bukusu people to labor for the English settlers.[146]

This clever ploy continues even now in postcolonial Kenya. This same inducement is worked on the people of Bukusuland being, who are being prevented from adequately feeding their families. The current Kenyan government has induced the Bukusu to pull out their millet crops, their food, and instead plant sugar cane and tobacco, cash crops to support the government. Propaganda dispersed via radio, television, and government agents justified these changes. These state-mandated changes, however, run counter to the Bukusu culture. According to Bukusu custom, God told them to dig up the land and cultivate millet. Millet meant life for the Bukusu; their food, their beer, and their trade wealth all came from millet. Tradition forbade pulling it up. The Bukusu families were culturally crushed by the government requirements to produce other crops for export, but the government insisted, in the name of national development. The Bukusu have yet to get anything in return. Bukusu families are crushed now by requirements. Moreover, any payment they get for these crops is two to three years late, and the prices are lower than the market price. The remaining profits find their way to the personal accounts of corrupt government officials.

Deliberate Deadline and Threats of Rupture

Another strategy recommended by Iklé is to set or emphasize a deadline for talks to end. Iklé writes, "The opponent might be induced to accept the available terms by the prospect that negotiations will end at a certain date regardless of whether or not an agreement has been reached."[147] This prospect could arise either because external circumstances have created a deadline or because the proponent deliberately created an arbitrary deadline or issued a threat of rupture.

Threats of rupture and deliberate deadlines are double-edged swords. The opponent can turn it against the proponent if the proponent is convinced that the opponent is bluffing. It is also possible that the opponent will let the deadline approach closer and closer, gambling that the proponent's negotiator will make concessions. Or, the opponent might risk letting the deadline go by, expecting the negotiations to resume. Here is an example of what Iklé means:

After the 1946 Paris Peace Conference, the final decisions on the peace treaties were made at a Council of Foreign Ministers meeting in New York. Soviet Foreign Minister Yvachelsav Molotov refused to accept most recommendations of the peace conference. Secretary of State Byrnes warned him, "It is with the greatest reluctance, therefore, that I have come to the conclusion we will not be able to agree upon the treaties. Having become reconciled to this, I think we should agree to disagree." Molotov was impressed by the risk of rupture when Byrnes stood by his warning, and a few days later, he gave in, accepting almost all the Paris recommendations.[148]

Iklé affirms that the "threat of rupture" can be highly effective, as the negotiator with the upper hand is in the process of departing in such a way that there would be no excuse at all for staying unless the opponent were to call the proponent back, ready to offer a concession.[149] For example, in the Catholic Church, priests from Africa are often sent to the United States for graduate study. Their home bishop and his diocese normally would not provide any financial support. Rather, their bishop would expect the priests to solicit "mission appeals," in which American parishes send substantial monies to Africa—yet the priests in America must, by necessity, find their own income to pay all expenses. Paradox arises when, at the bishop's sole discretion, a priest may be called back to the home diocese, regardless of any other consideration. Bishops without due circumspection may arbitrarily set a deadline that may cause a priest great distress over the premature termination of his studies. Such deadlines are known to have prompted priests to resign from their vows. For an African diocese, then, to lose its American spokesperson is to lose its "cash cow"—all of this would seem either the result of the bishop's parochial concerns or evidence of his need to demonstrate ecclesiastical power. Juxtaposed with the threat of rupture and the setting of deliberate deadlines is the strategy of influencing the force of public opinion.

The Consequences of the Court of Public Opinion

Iklé suggests that an important function of negotiation is to use moral standards to impress on the opponent the sense that any proposal must conform to those standards and that no more concessions might be considered. He writes, "A commitment may actually be reinforced by the act of explaining it in a public conference, because the [opposing] negotiator will be afraid of 'public criticisms' if he makes a concession after having argued that his proposal was vital."[150] One has to know that the domestic opinion argument is effective only if it conveys the message that people who can influence broader policy also hold their own domestic views. The case of Kenya's S. M. Otieno, whose death led to conflict when two parties claimed the opposing right to bury him, provides an example of the concern regarding the importance of one's domestic constituency. His case has been widely interpreted as little more than a rich cultural debate about personal and legal identity arising from the context of state manipulation of the judiciary and the violation of civil rights. The basic facts are these: A sophisticated Kikuyu widow was suing the kinsmen of her deceased Luo husband for the right to bury his body. His kinsmen contended that she had no such right—that they, not she, were the next of kin and that they alone could legitimately bury him. The husband had been a prominent lawyer in Nairobi. The wife, who came from a politically prominent Kikuyu family, was a well-known leader in her own right, having been active in the National Council of the Women of Kenya. But more important than her public life was the fact that she was the mother of nine of her husband's children. Wamboi (the widow's given name) and her husband were Christians first and had, in many respects, adopted a Westernized, modern, urban style of life. Otieno had not written a will; nor had he left any instructions regarding burial. The court excluded all suggestions of what he might have wished to do. The court also decided that statutes regarding marriage and succession that might have been construed as favorable to the widow had no relevance and that there was no common-law rule on the topic. Thus, by slippery process of elimination, the court had decided that customary law, as the only remaining residual category, defined the question the court had left to them. For the question remained:

Did the Luo customary laws truly govern this case? Disagreements were left unresolved. The case went on to the court of appeals, where it was ordered that the man's clansmen in Nyalgunga, a village in clan territory, by custom, be left to bury S. M. Otieno.[151]

By this account, the Otieno case became the object of public commentary all over Kenya. The case was about the opposition between African beliefs and modern secular practices; it was about the resentments of rural Kenyans toward the minority rich and Europeanized urban populations.[152] In this story, the courts did not listen to the modern form of a court of law; instead, it listened more to the traditional opinions of the Luo people, who jammed the court to influence the case. In the end, the court decided for the tribal viewpoint. This is a typical example of the use of a domestic opinion argument, which can be effective only if it conveys the idea that the domestic views are most firmly held by people who desire to influence policy as well as the legal process, in this case, allowing ethnic traditions to win. In truth, this case was heard around the world, with the result that the split in the case is indicative of that in the world at large. Populations that are not "native" to the lands they occupy have lost their sense of place. Virtually all populations that still maintain the importance of place did side with the Kenyan court's considered and considerate decision.

Iklé would suggest a number of basic approaches that ought to be used purposively in negotiation. Warnings and threats, particularly warnings of exclusion that instill fear, can be useful. The use of bluffs may fool an opponent, and stated, firm intent may also convince an opponent of the negotiating party's true resolve. These inducements may lead to success in negotiation, leading to application of deadlines and threats of rupture, with the realization that there is always the impact of the court of public opinion.

Conflict Negotiation: Rules of Accommodation and Suggested Practical Behaviors

Iklé's approach to conflict resolution is centered on his ground rules for negotiation. These ground rules are crucial to Iklé's theory because, in them, he provides negotiators with practical guidelines on how conflicts may be resolved. His ground rules offer concrete advice for negotiating across cultures and provide criteria for distinguishing the good from the bad.

It is conflict that causes and invites negotiation. Negotiation is the process in which explicit proposals are put forward, ostensibly for the purpose of reaching agreement on an exchange or on the realization of a common interest, where conflicting interests are present. Negotiation is "a process of conferring among two or more interdependent parties to arrive at an agreement about some matter over which they are in conflict."[153] Hence, it is important to know that, without conflict, there is nothing to negotiate.[154]

Iklé's theory allows there are three ways of dealing with conflict—domination, compromise, and integration. With domination, only one side gets what it wants; with compromise, neither side gets what it wants; with integration, we find a way by which both sides may get satisfaction.

All humans naturally experience conflict, make and reject claims, and try to resolve disputes. There is no culture that is immune to conflict. Iklé notes that the ways in which people deal with conflict vary inexorably within cultures, based on why claims are made and rejected, how claims are made and rejected, and how claims may be made. Variety may also be seen in methods of resolving disputes and what might prompt people to seek resolution.

Iklé would want people to follow his recommendations for negotiation. Violation of rules would seem invariably to compromise right relationship, at least temporarily; therefore they must be scrupulously but flexibly honored. He suggests that the ground rules for negotiation are as follows: (A) One must avoid ambiguous lies. (B) One must not issue explicit threats. (C) One must not blatantly violate agreements in principle. (D) One must not deliberately subvert mutual understandings.

Along with these ground rules, there are practical behaviors that Iklé believes cannot be violated without causing erosion of a right relationship. He identifies practical behavior as meeting on neutral grounds, adhering to the agreed-upon agenda, keeping discourse in common, avoiding rudeness, maintaining flexibility, reciprocating concessions, easing the way for the other to save face, negotiating for the interests of the entire community, and never killing the negotiator (not only physically but also virtually).[155]

Avoid Lies

Trust is one of the most important elements of a good working relationship between entities. Nothing can be as disappointing as learning that there is a lack of credibility and trust among the parties that you believed were committed to productive negotiations. There is no point in attempting to come to an agreement if the people involved cannot trust each other. The assumption will grow that the dishonest party will not keep the commitments of the pact. Thus, the first standard of behavior for successful negotiation that Iklé notes is that the parties must avoid lies and keep explicit promises.[156]

One way to handle disagreements without creating the perceived need to lie is for an agreement to be made that intentionally uses ambiguous terms that mean different things to each of the parties.[157] Iklé calls this equivocality.[158] Equivocal language is used to cover up unresolved disagreement on issues that must be included yet can be delayed for later settlement. An equivocal agreement is one that has sections or elements of negotiations that are deliberately and mutually left ambiguous. We can see an example by examining the negotiations of a local trade union. For over twenty years, management has allowed Local 10 members of the Nairobi Factory Union to swap shifts on holidays, even though this is not mentioned in the written contract. Given that the owner did not object to this practice when bargaining and given how long and consistently this practice has been in place, acceptance of the continuation of the practice is implied. Furthermore, almost all contracts contain general or ambiguous language. Rather than hammer out specifics at the bargaining table, negotiators rely on implied agreements to fill gaps and clarify meanings.

Do Not Issue Explicit Threats

In constructive, intercultural dialogue, all parties should refrain from making threats. Threats are strong, clear statements of danger. Iklé suggests that threats should be used sparingly and only when the party making the threats is prepared to act on them.[159] Those who make threats that they do not intend to carry out lose their credibility. Their threats are not believed and will be unlikely to generate a successful outcome in negotiations. On the other hand, those who are known to follow through on their threats retain their credibility. However, when threats are made, people tend to become defensive and abandon a spirit of mutual negotiation.

An example of an explicit threat is Imam Khomeini's fateful *fatwa* (formal legal opinion) condemning Salman Rushdie for his novel *The Satanic Verses* in 1988. In Iran—as indeed in most parts of Muslim world—Rushdie's novel was seen as a deliberate attempt to humiliate and ridicule the most revered figures in Islam. It is important to remember that laws of blasphemy bind all Muslims in Islamic states. In Pakistan and Iran, it is illegal and considered blasphemous to mock the Qur'an or the prophet. The point here is not that Muslims respect the Qur'an and the prophet because of injunctions in their constitution but, rather, that the constitution reflects the wishes of Muslims by embodying this public demand. In countries that are overwhelmingly Muslim, no one would think of insulting the prophet or the Qur'an. Thus Muslims responded in anger to this book, which they perceived as being exactly such an insult. Explicit threats were made by the Islamic Foundation in Iran, and bounty money was offered to anyone who would carry out the death sentence on Rushdie.[160] As Rushdie still lives, Islamic justice has not been satisfied.

Honor Agreements in Principle

An agreement in principle is "an exchange of conditional promises, by which each party declares that it will act in a certain way on condition that the other parties act in accordance with their promises."[161] These promises are significant to the process, since both parties have an interest in living up to them. As long as an agreement is honored, both parties are likely to work to do their part.

In close-knit cultures, the desire to maintain goodwill is an exceedingly important motive for keeping agreements. This is often the case among the Bukusu people. Bride wealth negotiations are the responsibility of the fathers of the couple; they are assisted in such negotiations by relatives and friends. Traditionally, an exchange of some number of cattle must be agreed upon. This ends up being about fourteen or fifteen cows and three goats, except in the case of divorcées or of women who have borne children out of wedlock. In these cases, fewer cows are given. The agreement concerning the payment of these animals constitutes the legal bond of marriage, although very often, the couple will have lived together already for some time. If the woman is pregnant, parents usually wait to conclude the arrangements of the bride wealth until a time after the child is born. Additionally, not all the animals must be transferred at once. A first payment may consist of the goats and four or five cows, followed by the rest of the cattle over a period of years. Only wealthy people who desire a wedding in a church or in the district commissioner's office will pay the entire bride wealth before the celebration of the wedding may be held.[162]

The son-in-law is required to give a raincoat, a blanket, and some cash to his father-in-law. Lately, fathers-in-law have tried to get as much as one year's earnings from the daughter's husband—particularly if the woman enjoys regular income as, for example, a teacher or a nurse. Negotiations over this amount start after the number of animals has already been agreed upon. All such negotiation seldom comes to final conclusion. The matter is left to the father-in-law and his son-in-law, but in most cases no end is reached.[163] In this cultural tradition it can be seen, then, that the essence of a marriage agreement is implicit, even as negotiable elements are ongoing.

Work for Mutual Understanding

It is here that mutual understanding is called for, to achieve the goal of reaching an integrative decision. "Mutual understandings," Iklé suggests, "must not be deliberately misconstrued later on."[164] In mutual understanding, one does not seek to impose a solution but, rather, to help the other party to make the choice that is best for both the opponent and the proponent. In short, the local culture is used to educate and to unite to achieve a peaceful existence without discord.

Regarding mutual understanding, in Islamic thought, the Prophet Muhammad used a bold family metaphor to convey his view of the close relationship and mutual understanding among all prophetic religions: "I am the nearest of kin to Jesus, son of Mary, in this world and the next. The prophets are brothers, sons of one father by co-wives. Their mothers are different but their religion is one."[165] Furthermore, the Qur'an gives this instruction to Muhammad: "Say: We believe in God and the revelation given to us, and to Abraham, Ismail, Isaac, Jacob and the tribes; we believe in what was given to Moses, Jesus, and to all other prophets from the Lord. We make no distinction among them, and we commit ourselves to God" (Qur'an 2:136).

In the Christian context, Jesus emphasized a similar message of inclusiveness. When his disciples asked him to denounce a healer who did not belong to their group, Jesus replied, "Do not stop him ... for whoever is not against us is for us" (Mark 9:39–40). As long as people are being helpful, they should be treated with mutual understanding and respect.

Recognize the Benefit of Soft Rules

Along with these four ground rules for negotiation are "soft rules" that cannot be violated repeatedly without eroding congenial or friendly relationship. Iklé asserts that soft rules are those "rules of accommodation [that] are observed even between bitter enemies. If this is the case for both sides, the prerequisite common interest for negotiation exists."[166] Therefore, given a common interest in an agreement, both sides must also have an interest in methods that can help in facilitating agreement. This explains the tacit or explicit understandings between bitter antagonists on rules to facilitate the negotiating process. These include saving face, never killing a negotiator, meeting on neutral grounds, and adhering to an agreed-upon agenda.

Allow for Saving Face?

Allowing for saving face refers to helping to maintain good self-images all around. Often in a negotiation, people will continue to hold out not because the proposal on the table is inherently wrong but simply because they want to avoid the feeling or appearance that they backed down to the other side. Similarly, people won't admit that they are wrong because they don't want their error known. Consider, for example, that you've just discovered a serious error in a report you wrote, a report that is now on the desks of senior management, who will in turn be using it to deliver presentations to dozens of clients. How do you negotiate your way through this without losing face? It's at moments like these that people believe their reputations—their images or very beings—are under threat. People strive to maintain a positive image in the eyes and minds of those they deal with at work and socially. Doing so is vital. Thus, people often maintain a righteous stance simply to avoid losing face.

To allow people to save face, it is important that opponents be left to make concessions gracefully. A simple change in wording or an exchange of concessions will help negotiators maintain a positive image, even when they are actually giving in substantially. Negotiation expert Iklé recommends that negotiators "go slow to go fast." By moving slowly, negotiators can trade minor concessions and can focus more on what they have gained than on what they might have lost. Superior power is useless, cautions Iklé, if it drives your opponent into a corner and makes him resist you with all his might.

Leaving the opponent a way out is a time-honored precept. One aspect of this principle is that of not gloating or bragging over successes as a result of the other's mistake. Gloating makes the other side look and feel inadequate, which could precipitate his or her withdrawing cooperation in subsequent issues.

Iklé asserts, "The opponent's domestic difficulties should not be exploited in public; debts of gratitude should be honored."[167] Assisting all parties in maintaining a good public self-image is paramount to successful negotiations. In societies like that of the Bukusu culture, the issue of saving face looms large. Outward appearances are as important as substance. "Make your harvest look big," runs a popular Bukusu saying, "lest your enemies rejoice." The Bukusu people also hold that it is better to starve and have others think you are satisfied than to reveal a weakness.

The Bukusu circumcision ritual puts the self-preservation basis of saving face into context. The circumcision ritual is almost as critical a moment for the father as for the son. When a boy is being circumcised, his father stands close by and encourages his son to keep outwardly steady while at the same time admonishing the traditional circumciser to be careful with his knife.[168] If the son's behavior is other than brave, the father's shame would be so great that he would leave the crowd and hide in the bush. If the circumciser's work is not quick and clean, the boy will show signs of fear and pain, and again, the father will be shamed.

In a negotiation, the proponent needs to be sensitive to the changing needs and concerns of the opponent. The proponent needs to be prepared to adjust the negotiations so that the opponent does not experience unnecessary private or public humiliation. For example, when a Roman Catholic bishop in Africa censures a priest for misbehaving, it is wise to make the admonitions in private, and in such a way that the priest is not made to feel embarrassed in front of his flock. Rather, the priest must feel supported, encouraged, and redirected. Bad publicity about someone that arises due to intercultural conflict may affect that person's reputation within his or her own culture.

Never, Ever Kill the Messenger

When you kill a messenger, you deliver a message of your own. Metaphorically killing virtual messengers has such predictable results that you have to question any report you receive—good news or bad. In other words, such behavior drives truth underground. The most elementary rule of accommodation, writes Iklé, is that "the opponent's representatives should not be physically harmed."[169] The sending of the messenger, who has come from a neighboring community that may consist of a rebellious clan or a feuding rival, might be said to mark the beginning of negotiation. In spite of repeated violations of this principle in antiquity, the immunity of the messenger largely has been regarded with kindness and respect. This principle has been firmly established and gradually extended into the modern code of diplomatic immunities.[170] It allows representatives of foreign governments to work and operate under the laws of their home country while abroad.

In his book *A Grain of Wheat*, Kenyan novelist Ngugi wa Thiong'o associates the messenger with the voice that says, "We are only voices sent to you from the party."[171] The messenger is only a voice of the authority that sends him or her. A Bukusu proverb says, "The carrier of a secret message is not told its meaning." A messenger cannot be held accountable for the message. Never, ever, kill the messenger.

Meet on Neutral Grounds

In keeping with long-established customs, Iklé argues that "meeting on 'neutral ground' serves to avoid disputes about the status of the negotiating parties."[172] The site of a meeting is a critical issue if one is involved in high-visibility negotiations between parties. The choice of location can have widespread political implications for the public. Avoiding disputes about status permits the parties to concentrate their negotiations on those issues for which the meeting presumably was convened. Appearances can have political ramifications linked to the negotiating environment. Opposing leaders must maintain an image of power at home.

The rule about the neutral meeting ground, however, is often compromised due to unavoidable circumstances. The head of a smaller community usually is the one who must travel to the capital of the larger state when negotiations are called for.

In rural Africa, neutral meeting grounds are usually located in the traditional sacred places. They are communally owned. Some of the sacred places for convening community meetings are near the river, under a large fig tree, near the mountain, and at the community sacrificial shrine. These places are singled out as the common grounds for meetings, regardless of whether they generally are used by Bukusu Muslims, Christians, or traditional believers. This is the case with the *Kaaba* and the Plain of Arafat, which are common ground for all Muslim peoples in the world, regardless of whether they are art of the major Sunni or Shiite groups.[173]

Adhere to an Agreed-upon Agenda

Bilateral agreement on an agenda has two implications, according to Iklé. It means that prior to a conference, the parties, by way of their envoys, agree on the subject they will be discussing. The mutual consent to an official title for a conference can imply an agreement to discuss certain topics. The agreed-upon agenda then constitutes a procedural agreement regarding the sequence in which the subjects will be addressed.[174] These processes do affect the outcome of negotiations. The subjects discussed determine the issues that are to be settled, and the particular sequence in which separate issues are negotiated may favor one side to the disadvantage of the other.

Keep Discourse Reasonable

Iklé points out, "Discourse ought to be reasonable in the sense that questions are answered, arguments are to the point, facts are not grossly distorted, repetition is minimized and technical discussions are kept on the factual level."[175] The language used by the negotiating parties ought to reflect a respect and consideration for both sides.

An example of this approach can be seen in the art of discourse among the Babukusu, which involves negotiations that are formal to an extent that might seem overdone to an outsider. For example, much time is spent on the usual greetings—trivial questions about weather, the condition of one's home, and the road just traveled are mainstays. Such questions may seem unnecessary. But the greetings, including handshakes and the holding of both hands, along with more minute courtesies such as offering a drink of water, known to the Bukusu as "tired water," are considered essential. Negotiations open with speeches, including preliminary comments made by elders who set the mood and tone of the talks with a proverb or two before the work of negotiation commences. For example, an elder might say, "Do not roast baobab kernels and leave those who have teeth chewing."[176] This means that one must not cause quarrels among other people by telling tales, gossiping, or spreading propaganda. Then another elder might stand up to say, "That which has passed away is not sickness; let us cure what is here and that which is yet to come,"[177] meaning that the discourse of negotiation should focus on the problems that confront them where they are and in the moment, so as to safeguard against failed dialogue. Still another elder may come with a reminder: "Do not forget what it is to be a sailor because of being a captain yourself."[178] In saying this, the elder statesman will be trying to get across the message that participation in conflict negotiation is a concern for all and that those involved must not ignore anyone in the negotiating process.

Finally, the head elder may conclude this introductory phase of the process with a gentle warning to everyone within the *baraza* about the abject seriousness of the proceedings, with his words reminding them that "when you play with a lion, do not put your hand in its mouth; that would be going too far."[179] In saying this, the elder would be reminding all the parties that they should direct their attention toward the spectrum of community-perceived needs and not toward the individual. Thus, the meetings begin with traditional statements from the accumulated wisdom of the ancestors; with these statements and sentiments, the *baraza* may begin.

Avoid Rudeness and Overt Emotion

Disputes engage people's emotions. Sometimes disputants can get so angry, hurt, or frustrated that they fail to control their emotions. What follows is a strategy for disputants to overcome emotions in negotiations. It is unwise to make concessions to the other in response to an emotional outburst. According to Iklé, crying or other emotional displays in a negotiation can be distracting. The crying person seems to demand a sympathetic response from the listener, and the crying indicates to those present that, for a moment, that person is incapable of handling the situation. Crying also annoys and angers people who are already primed to be defensive, and it may be construed as attempted manipulation. This behavior represents, in fact, a self-defeating loss of face among any who value his or her own dignity.

To explain the importance of avoiding emotionalism and rudeness, Iklé cites Harold Nicolson, an English biographer, historian, and diplomat. In his enumeration of the qualities of the "ideal diplomat," Nicolson includes the quality of remaining calm. He maintains, "Not only must the negotiator avoid displaying irritation when confronted by the stupidity, dishonesty, brutality, or conceit of those with whom it is his or her unpleasant duty to negotiate; but one must eschew all personal animosities, or personal predilections, all enthusiasms, prejudices, vanities, exaggerations, dramatizations and moral indignation."[180]

Although most Western diplomats do not practice Nicolson's concept of calm absolutely, they tend to observe the rule that strong emotions should rarely be displayed. Iklé recommends that one should address his or her opponent respectfully and avoid interrupting his or her opponent.[181] Among rightly related communities, any breach of such rules of dialogue etiquette could serve to break down the relationship.

Consider this example: War is not primarily about adult male soldiers doing battle. Combatants and noncombatants cannot be cast into labeled categories; nor can lines between them be clearly distinguished. Children and adults, women and men fight and die—some in uniform and some as civilians in wars they neither started nor support. The battle fields become home to rogues and thieves, as well as to the honorable, to the old and young, the rich and poor, the political and apolitical. All the different people forge a reality of war and peace. All their stories are woven together in the web of daily life on the front lines.

The recognition that no one voice is more important than another is significant to Iklé. The experiences of the village woman who has just suffered an attack are as relevant to understanding war as the voices of the soldiers who carried out the attack. The ordeals of a five-year-old child in a battle zone are as real to the child as policy proclamations to the political elite. The "jackal" who sells information to grieving families concerning the whereabouts of their kidnapped kin and the soldier who protects a village from attack and then loots it for himself are contradictions as painful to the people in war zones as are the opposing military factions.[182] The point is that to understand the processes of conflict and peace negotiation is to give a hearing to all of these interconnected voices. Many people go through life keeping their beliefs largely to themselves for one reason or another; yet given the right chance to speak, even the quietest will come forward to be heard.

Maintain Flexibility

In spite of his emphasis on hard and soft rules, Iklé maintains that flexibility is another one of the conditions for effective politeness when dealing with negotiations. In the West, observes Iklé, the rule that one should be flexible in negotiations presumes a moral value. The question of whether it is not advisable to be flexible at every turn is resolved by his conviction that it would be both improper and disruptive not to be truly flexible.[183] All must be heard. In other words, one must continue to recognize that each person's need to be heard is as valid as everyone else's.

Ideally, flexibility means being able to respond skillfully to opportunity in the moment in which it is presented. If your initial approach isn't working, Iklé suggests, you might try another. Life's problems and the problems of negotiation are ever challenges that need to be overcome in the moment of need. Iklé suggests that the community might show flexibility by formulating its position in a further flexible fashion, offering the opponent several specific alternatives, expressing willingness to consider any alternatives proposed by the opponent in return, and being willing to change position with the next response.[184]

There is an even greater degree of flexibility to be considered. A community might not only keep its position changeable, showing open-mindedness toward the opponent's proposals, but it might abandon having a position at all.[185]

Flexibility is at the heart of closing a deal in a way that satisfies each side and that is workable in the real world. One must be flexible in a negotiation in order to fit one's goals and needs with the goals and needs of the other party.

Iklé asserts that a good negotiator should also be flexible—not by being without a firm position but by utilizing both firm and flexible proposals. The negotiator should be tactically flexible by discriminating between occasions when it pays to adhere to rules of accommodation and when it does not. He or she must distinguish between situations where it would be disastrous to make a threat and those where it is essential to threaten or even to bluff. The negotiator must know when to humor the personal quirks of the opponent and when to ignore them. He or she must be willing to disregard propaganda losses at one time and to negotiate merely for propaganda at another time. Good negotiators must be prepared to follow domestic opinion at home as well as to encourage a new consensus, both in their government and in their country.[186]

Reciprocate Concessions

Iklé's theory of effective negotiation combines the virtue of flexibility with the norm of reciprocity; Iklé observes that a standard recommendation for facilitating agreement is "making concessions."[187] It is more important to negotiate well by reciprocating concessions than to maintain what is perceived to be the "rightful" negotiating position. Not to indulge in reciprocations, Iklé argues, might be regarded by others as unfair.[188] For example, regarding the rule of Islam on the "excellence of fair dealing," Abu Hurairah in hadith relates that a man came to the Holy Prophet and was harsh in demanding repayment of his loan. The companions were about to take hold of this man when the Holy Prophet said, "Leave him alone, for one to whom an obligation is due is entitled to make a demand." He added, "Give him a camel of the same age as the camel that is due to him." He was told that only a better camel than the one due to the creditor was available. The Holy Prophet said, "Give him the better one, for the best of you are those who discharge their obligations best."[189] This means that negotiating hard for one's interests does not mean being closed to the other side's point of view. On the contrary, one can hardly expect the other side to listen to his or her interests and discuss the options he or she suggests if one doesn't take the other side's interests into account and show him or herself to be open to suggestions. Successful negotiation requires being both firm and open.

Make Use of the Community Spirit

The notion of community spirit is important to Iklé's perspective. He suggests that negotiators are wise to focus on common interests rather than on trade-offs between conflicting interests, in order to maximize the advantages of joint undertakings rather than to gauge separate gains and losses with each other. The community generates particular social practices in its culture—manners, food, language, and so forth. The Prophet Muhammad's hadith (sayings) encourage the *ummah* (or community of believers) to greet one another warmly, to avoid gossip and slander, to call on those who are sick, and to join funeral processions. It teaches children to respect their parents and parents to give love and affection to their children. The *ummah* encourages social activity, a sense of belonging, and a sense of place. It allows ideas to be carried across national borders and can generate emotions wherever Muslims live. It is also the notion of the *ummah* that triggers a deep response when

Muslims see or hear scenes of other Muslims being denied their rights or being brutally suppressed for voicing their faith.

Iklé maintains that the life of a community depends on everyone looking upon and treating community matters as matters of joint responsibility.[190] A negotiating style in the community spirit is necessary, but is not a sufficient condition for the successful integration of independent nations. Other conditions must be met, such as the formation of interest groups that invariably cut across national boundaries, the absence of strongly conflicting objectives, and the existence of specific functions that are important to certain members of the community and can be relegated to the universal good. If one remains standing apart, having a common external enemy also encourages integration across national boundaries.[191] Each partner's active interest in negotiating by reciprocation should help preserve community spirit over all, which in turn permits negotiators to dispense with some of the more rigid rules of accommodation they formerly found necessary between less friendly nations.

How Parties Come Together

Iklé notes that the coming together of the parties is an integral aspect of negotiating. As he puts it, "It is an essential feature of negotiation that the process of finding out the opponent's terms is also part of the process of inducing the opponent to soften his or her terms."[192]

The Ways of Advancing Agreements

Indeed, proposals play a key role in the process through which negotiating parties reach resolution. Iklé echoes that, yes, sometimes the whole of the negotiation includes simply the confrontation, revisions, and final acceptances of proposals at the conference table. In "Tools of Statecraft: Diplomacy and War, Angelo Codevilla sums up Iklé's philosophy well. "The essence of Iklé's teaching," he writes, "is that the negotiator's primordial job is to judge correctly whether the other side is negotiating for "available terms" or is waging war through diplomatic means and, hence, to choose whether to negotiate for agreement, walk away, or treat the diplomatic table as a battlefield."[193]

As opposing parties bring their positions into agreement, they will want to adapt their earlier expectations to a single agreed-upon set of terms. Such integrity has to be the visible manifestation of mutual agreement. Trust is maintained in the minds of the signatories and, thereby, in the inner councils of communities. Of this concern, Iklé warns, "The terms of agreement are reached through a contest of wills, wits, and interests, much of which remains concealed from the opponent."[194] All through this process, the parties continually have to revise their expectations and shift their evaluations, measuring gains and losses. As long as they seek agreement, the parties continually weigh the choice between accepting the available terms and continuing the bargaining.[195]

When the terms of agreement have been settled, they become a legally binding document for settling differences between two parties. As such, the legalities must be drawn up by a competent person in conformity with applicable laws.

Conclusion

Iklé's process of conflict resolution has the objective of achieving mutual understanding between opposing groups. He points to ground rules that can serve as guidelines for negotiating differences. He presents an approach for reaching compromises and final agreement.

It is useful to keep in mind that Iklé designed his perspective to be applicable to nations seeking to avoid war and its consequences. This perspective has a theoretical base; it relates to conditions that go beyond the typical state of affairs that had been experienced among Bukusu peoples of different cultural backgrounds and religious beliefs.

In comparing the two thinkers we have examined thus far, we see that Buber's theory of dialogue is directed primarily toward individuals, while Iklé's theory is directed primarily toward nations. The theory of William Ury is more pointedly rooted in culturally diverse worldviews held in common universally. It is designed to be used by groups of any size or context. As such, it represents a very useful point of conflict resolution for any study of this nature. With this in mind, we now delve into this anthropologist's theory.

CHAPTER 12

•◆•

WILLIAM L. URY'S TECHNIQUES
FOR NEGOTIATING DIALOGUE

A s an anthropologist, William Ury addresses what he considers one of the most endangered species on the planet—human beings. The danger, he explains, "comes not from the outside world, but from the inside—from the human habit of falling into destructive, often deadly conflict whenever a serious difference arises between two people, two groups, or two nations."[196] Ury's main concern is how people can get along, despite their deep differences. Before exploring Ury's theories, a brief introduction to the person and his works is in order here. This will give the reader a sense of why this man is so central to the thesis of the rest of this book.

Ury's Place in History
William Langer Ury is one of the world's leading negotiation specialists. He was born on September 12, 1953, in Harvey, Illinois, and was raised in California and Switzerland.[197] He attended Yale University for his BA (magna cum laude, 1975) and continued his studies at Harvard University, receiving his MA (1977) and his PhD (1982) in the field of cultural anthropology. His doctoral dissertation was called *Talk Out or Walk Out: The Role and Control of Conflict in a Kentucky Coalmine.*

Ury was an assistant professor at Harvard Business School from 1982 to 1984. He cofounded Harvard's Program on Negotiation in 1984 and, as of 2011, continues to direct its worldwide negotiation network. Presently he serves as advisor to the International Negotiation Network for the Carter Center at Emory University. Ury served as director of the Harvard Nuclear Negotiation Project at Harvard Law School from 1980 to the present and has served as consultant to the White House on establishing nuclear risk reduction centers in Washington and Moscow. Ury has taught negotiation to corporate executives, labor leaders, and government officials around the world. President Jimmy Carter honored Ury's work by affirming the positions he expressed in one of his books: "All too often, our nation and others seek to impose solutions with military attacks or punitive sanctions against innocent people. Ury's book *Getting to Peace* shows us a better way."[198]

As one of the world's leading negotiation specialists, Ury has also served as a third-party negotiator in disputes ranging from family feuds in California to wildcat strikes in Kentucky coal mines and from corporate turf battles to ethnic wars in the former Yugoslavia. Ury has also negotiated Muslim-Christian disputes in the Balkans and Israeli-Palestinian conflicts in the Middle East. He has worked on the problem of how to prevent nuclear war, both as a researcher and as a consultant to the White House Crisis Management Center.[199]

Of special interest to this study is that Ury has lived and conducted research among the nomadic Bushmen of the Kalahari Desert. The lifestyles and life challenges of Bushmen of South Africa, Botswana, and Namibia are similar but not identical to those of the Bukusu people of western Kenya in many ways. They each live with an intimate closeness to the land from which they have wrested their livelihood. The fertile ground for each gave birth to the many myths and tales they love to tell as they sit around campfires. But the Bushmen and the Babukusu are most similar in their relationships to the animals in the wild; they consider them to be their brothers and sisters.[200] Similarly, as their simple lives are confronted by modern realities and cross-cultural influences, these people face similar social and cultural challenges. Thus, Ury's remarks that pertain to the

Bushmen hold a special meaning in their potential for application to the Bukusu people. Three of Ury's books, *Getting to Peace* (1999), *Getting Past No* (1991), and *Getting to Yes* (1991) represent the best of his thought thus far, and they pertain directly to the difficulties of the confluent cultures in Bukusuland today.

Ury's central thesis holds, to use his words, that it takes two sides to fight but a third side to step in and stop a conflict from getting out of hand. Having distilled the lessons of his two decades of experience in dealing with family struggles, labor strikes, and wars, Ury presents a strategy for defusing instances that could escalate that is altogether useful for the specific understanding of conflict resolution between confluent cultures, as in Kenya, and for the specific negotiation needs of the Bukusu people and perhaps for the world at large. We now examine the several principles Ury discovered for recognizing interdependence and the need for cooperation.

Whether young or old, rich or poor, African or Arab, we all have need for relationships, as they are necessary for quality of life. It is through our best relationships with others that we may freely work, play, and celebrate life; when we are earning a living, building a family, and coping with life's problems, our relationships make our lives worth living. Ury declares that now more than ever, "People need to learn how to cooperate." He explains, "For centuries, humans have relied on top-down [authoritative] decision-making to get things done."[201] But we know the times are changing, and the old hierarchies are declining. "The father, the boss, the chief, the king cannot give orders anymore. Increasingly, we cannot compel others to do what we want; we depend more and more on their voluntary cooperation."[202] People have little choice but to learn how to make their decisions cooperatively and to negotiate differences to some satisfactory resolution. We live in a global economy, a global village, and are more interdependent today as a result of globalization.[203] Because of these interdependences, cooperative negotiations are necessary. They are aspects of the ways in which peoples may accomplish the transactions on which communal entities and organizations are coming to depend, even as they exercise no direct control in the agreements. They cannot impose a decision; more often the interdependent parties are compelled to negotiate.[204]

Thus we see the progression of the thinking of Buber, for whom dialogue at its depth consists of an *I-Thou* relationship to that of Iklé, who suggests that strategies and tactics of negotiation must be addressed with the same precision that has heretofore been developed in the service of the science of war. We have gone from individual relationships to relationships between groups. Next we will examine the ideas of Ury, who explored ways to reduce conflict between entire cultures.

In the corporate world, Ury points out, "Work is increasingly carried out by task forces; business is carried out through joint ventures; and strategic alliances, and growth is achieved through mergers and acquisitions." Ury goes on to paint the picture more clearly: Every time we enter a hospital, our health depends on effective cooperation between nurses and doctors. When their conflicts turn destructive, patient care suffers and people die. Similarly, the health of our families, our businesses, our societies, and our natural environment depends on intricate webs of cooperation among individuals, organizations, and nations, which all too often are disrupted by quarreling and violence.[205]

This level of cooperation is advisable now for all African traditional life. Already, community cooperation is a fundamental condition of Bukusu life, as it should be for all humans. Kenyan scholar John Mbiti observes, "To be human is to belong to the whole community, and to do so involves participating in the beliefs, ceremonies, rituals and festivals of that community. A person cannot detach himself from the religion of his group, for to do so is to be severed from his roots, his foundation, his context of security, his kinships and the entire group of those who make him aware of his own existence. To be without one of these corporate elements is to be out of the whole picture."[206]

How Community Cooperation Works in the Bukusu Life

Cooperative negotiations can be seen in various forms in Bukusu daily life. The chief commodities exchanged on an economic trade basis are objects produced by local artisans, who exchange their practical or artistic products for chickens, goats, and cattle. In the past, iron hoes formed part of the traditional bride wealth (cattle constitutes bride wealth even today) and functioned to some extent as currency. The Bukusu once would exchange elephant ivory for manual tools made by their neighboring blacksmiths, the Samia. This exchange required the Bukusu people to negotiate with their Samia neighbors for the desired goods. These negotiations were based on constructive relationships of trust. As they were comfortable mutually calling each other "customer," friendships flourished and conflict was avoided. Short of that, there would be an element of conflict in the offing.

Every person who enters a business is also someone's customer. Even though the person may not purchase something today, he or she may purchase something tomorrow. What a salesperson needs is some better way of understanding who the customer really is. One way of getting to that point is by determining appropriate steps for the buying and selling process. This process is contingent on prior customer relationships remembered. Any customer coming to you for services or goods is given every courtesy. This generally works in every situation.

Negotiation as a Constant Reality

Negotiation, after all, is only the process of back-and-forth communication for agreement with others when some of our interests are shared with others. For Ury, negotiation does not refer only to the settling of disputes while sitting across a table dialoguing for agreements. Ury suggests that it is also the informal activity between persons, as even during informal activities interactions consist of individuals wanting to exchange something with other individuals. People do negotiate every day of their lives; in fact, a great deal of time is spent in reaching agreement with others. Whether as a contract, a family quarrel, or a peace settlement among nations, people routinely engage in what Ury defines as positional bargaining. In this dynamic, each side takes a position and argues for it but then may make concessions to reach a compromise. A practical example of this phenomenon in Bukusuland is the haggling that is culturally the norm between Bukusu farmers and the East Indian Muslim shopkeepers. One such conversation might go like this:

Customer: How much do you want for this hoe?

Shopkeeper: That is a good strong hoe, isn't it? It was made in London. I guess I could let it go for eighty shillings.

Customer: Oh no, come on, it's secondhand. I will give you twenty.

Shopkeeper: Really! I might consider a serious offer, but twenty shillings certainly isn't serious.

Customer: Well, maybe I could go to thirty shillings, but I would never pay anything like eighty. Quote me a realistic price.

Shopkeeper: You drive a hard bargain, sir. How about sixty shillings cash right now?

Customer: Thirty-five.

Shopkeeper: It cost me a great deal more than that. Make me a serious offer.

Customer: Forty shillings. That is the highest I will go.

Shopkeeper: Have you noticed the quality of that hoe? In two weeks a hoe like that will fetch twice what you might pay today.

The conversation goes on until a mutually beneficial compromise is reached.

In the process, a relationship is growing between the two individuals. In every exchange of trade, this interaction, in some form, takes place. Ideally, this should be as true in the home as it is in the marketplace.

Ury would have us think of a typical day over breakfast. He gives the following examples:

You get into an argument with your spouse about buying a new car. You think it's time, but your spouse says, "Don't be ridiculous! You know we can't afford it right now." You arrive at work for a morning meeting with your boss. You present a carefully prepared proposal for a new project, but your boss interrupts you after a minute and says: "We already tried that method and it didn't work. Next item." During your lunch hour you try to return a defective toaster-oven, but the salesperson refuses to refund your money because you don't have the sales slip: "It's store policy." In the afternoon you bring an already-agreed-upon contract to a client for his signature. You have trumpeted the deal to your associates and made the necessary arrangements with manufacturing. But your client tells you: "I'm sorry. My boss refuses to okay the purchase unless you give us a fifteen percent discount." In the evening you need to return some phone calls, but [your thirteen-year-old ties up the line]. Exasperated, you say, "Get off the phone." The teenager shouts down the hall, "Why don't you get me my own phone line? All my friends have them!"[207]

Bargaining continues endlessly, according to Ury. Perhaps people will reach agreement, and perhaps not. Each person faces tough negotiations with "an irritable spouse, a domineering boss, a rigid salesperson, a tricky customer, or an impossible teenager."[208] Therefore, it is not surprising that under stress, people often end up expressing anger and irritation. When this is the case, Ury points out, "Negotiation can bog down or break down, consuming our time, keeping us awake at night, and giving us ulcers."[209] With this comment, Ury initiates another element of his perspective, that on the "culture of conflict."

The Culture of Conflict
Ury reports that some people consider conflict to be innate to human nature. Looking at the world caught in strikes, lawsuits, and political battles, the conventional picture of human beings as naturally prone to violence is understandable.[210] The expressed wish to end war—whether in Bosnia or Rwanda, Ireland or Afghanistan—is often deflected by the refrain that we humans have been aggressive for centuries.[211] This implies, as Ury puts it, that the combatants would "go on fighting for centuries and therefore we bystanders could not really do anything to change the pattern."[212] Fatalism paralyzes our will to act. But what are the consequences of fatalism? The belief is that "what will be will be," the idea here being that since all past, present, and future events have already been determined by God or another all-powerful force, we are helpless to change anything. In religion, this view may be called predestination; it holds that whether our souls go

to heaven or hell is determined before we are born and is independent of our good deeds. Our present challenge is to defy this fatalistic culture of conflict in favor of all right relatedness within our families, our workplaces, our communities, and our world. According to Ury, that which "prevents people from getting to peace, perhaps more than anything else, is the lack of an alternative to force when conflict turns serious."[213] Ury calls for cultures to resolve even the most serious disputes on the basis of mutual interest and coexistence, not by force and bullying. Ury further suggests that rather than eliminating differences, our challenge must be to make the world safe for our kaleidoscope of differences.[214]

Ury is convinced that "most of the time, most people get along."[215] Regardless of differing temperaments, habits, and communication styles, families can manage to live together in peace and harmony. Even if they disagree on basic values, neighbors may succeed in living side by side. Peace is the norm for harmonious human coexistence.

Seeing human life as peaceful conflict resolution interrupted by periods of strife, rather than the other way around, transforms the challenge from the negative one of ending war to the positive one of extending the peace.[216] Peace has always been among humanity's highest values—for some, it is the supreme value. Consider the following sayings—ideas that are echoed in different forms worldwide: "Peace at any price." "The most disadvantageous peace is better than the most just war." "Peace is more important than all justice." "I prefer the most unjust peace to the justest war that was ever waged." "There never was a good war or a bad peace." Yet, we agree little on what peace is. All these are only samples of the attitude that would condemn conflict.

Conflict Resolution as Three-sided

Conflict generally is thought of as being two-sided—as being between husband and wife, union and employees, Arabs and Israelis, Muslim and Christians.[217] A polemic is used to define sides and set the good against the bad or the righteous against evil. In such instances, the suggestion that a third party become involved is not considered helpful but, rather, as the potential for someone to meddle in someone else's business. But when conflict threatens harmony for one or more groups, third-party intervention surely must be welcomed.

People tend to forget what the simplest societies on earth have long known—that every conflict is actually three-sided.[218] How so? Note the use of the word "actually" and how it conveys the sense that only the two in conflict are perfectly able to resolve the issue. As the issue is bigger than even the two, resolution is beyond them. The actuality is stretched by necessity to virtuality, that being of a level of expertise needed to bring resolution from the beyond. What is beyond? It must be that dimension that the two parties in contention must realize is ultimately best for all right relatedness. That is the importance of rising out of mere actualities into the vitality of ideal relationship: Hence, we see the importance of ever seeking the ideal third one.

No dispute takes place in a vacuum. There are always others around—relatives, neighbors, allies, neutrals, friends, or onlookers. Every conflict occurs within community, and it makes sense to have another intercede to keep conflict from getting out of hand. Here, Ury brings in his notion of the third side.[219]

The third side is the surrounding community or someone from it who serves as "container" for any escalating conflict. In the absence of that container, a serious conflict between two parties all too easily turns into destructive strife. Through the influence of the container, however, conflict can gradually be transformed from destructive confrontation into cooperation.[220]

In other words, third-side negotiators are "people from the community using a certain kind of peer-power from a certain perspective of common ground supporting a certain process of dialogue and nonviolence—and aiming for a certain product—a 'triple win.'"[221] The third side that Ury describes arises from the "vital relationships linking each member and every other member of the community."[222] To explain this idea, Ury suggests, "A simple experiment will reveal, in its most elementary form, the influence of the third side. Introduce a neutral third person into any argument between two people. Even if the third person does not talk, the parties' tone will usually begin to moderate and their behavior will be more controlled. If the third person commands special respect, the effect will become even more pronounced."[223]

Ury claims to have grasped his vision of the third-side phenomenon of negotiation as a nonviolent alternative to force while on a research visit to a group of Bushmen in early 1989.[224] The nomadic Bushmen live deep in the Kalahari Desert, and are traditional hunters and gatherers. Living in small groups of about twenty-five, embedded in larger networks of about five hundred, they are relatively egalitarian and have no formal leaders.[225] They are perfectly capable of violence; each man carries a hunting bow and arrows coated with a poison deadly to humans. In this context, they manage to control themselves, avoiding conflicts.

Ury describes the secret of the Bushmen system for managing conflicts as being based on "the vigilant, active, and constructive involvement of the surrounding members of the community."[226] Explaining the process by which the Bushmen defuse disputes, he writes: "All the friends and relatives are approached in a dispute and asked to have a calming word with the disputants."[227] This process continues until the entire community is involved. Each community member has a chance to contribute to the resolution. This open and inclusive process may take days, lasting until the dispute is quite literally talked out. The community members work hard to discover what social rules have been broken to produce such discord and do what needs to be done to restore social harmony. [228]

Among the Bushmen, decisions are reached by common consent. If tempers rise suddenly and violence threatens, the community is quick to make a reasoned response. Ury noted on his visit, "People collect the poisoned arrows and hide them far away in the bush. Others try to separate the antagonists. And the [dialogue] continues."[229] He adds that the Bushmen simply will not rest until the dispute is fully settled.

Similar to the conflict resolution pattern of the Bushmen, the moral reasoning determination of traditional Bukusu people becomes clear to outsiders through the cultural imperative they follow—the inclusion of others in problem solving. To the Bukusu, excluding others is an act of destruction. Exclusion does not serve to cement the bonding that is morally necessary to form and maintain the community. Nothing that weakens community bonds or in any way helps to abet such weakening can be accepted as morally wholesome. The use of third-party negotiations is, therefore, an essential part of the social fabric of the Babukusu.

In the context of traditional Bukusu peoples, the often-used third side is known as *wamuuanda*, or the "go-between." An example of such negotiating can be seen in Bukusu courtship and betrothal rituals. After the suitor family has ascertained the girl's willingness to marry the proposed groom, and after the man's father has promised to provide him with the cattle needed for the marriage, an emissary acting as a go-between is sent to put the proposal before the parents of the girl. The "third-sider" here is always a woman, usually the suitor's mother or aunt. She starts off to the home of the girl's parents early in the morning to be certain of finding the girl's parents still at home and without any other visitors. After the customary salutation, she sits down near the door in the front partition of the hut and puts forward her proposal in metaphorical language, saying, "I have come about the handle of a hoe." The parents know that the messenger has not actually come to borrow the handle of a hoe but is there to make a marriage proposal. If they are quite willing to give their consent, pride and modesty require that they should not agree immediately but pretend to have no hoe handle. The suitor's representative, however, insists that she knows they have a handle and a very good handle. If the parents of the girl are willing to allow the marriage, they finally give in and say, "Indeed, we may see, perhaps the handle of the hoe may be here." No further details are brought up on this occasion, but the visitor is offered food and a chicken to take home with her in appreciation.

If the family of the girl refuses to give her away, they will continue to claim that they have no handle of a hoe and finally will change the subject to something else. If their refusal does not appear to be final, the inquiring mother comes back after a few weeks and may even try to pursue the matter a third time.

Ury's concept of the third side can also be seen in the following traditional story of *Maina*, a famous Bukusu elder and ruler, that also demonstrates the importance of inclusion of others as third parties to conflict resolution. The story goes that one day, Maina beat the war drum and summoned all the villagers and elders of the neighboring peoples to come to his home. The people turned up in great numbers, some of them under the impression that the ruler was preparing for an imminent battle with the enemy. When all the people and the elders had gathered around, Maina addressed the crowd in these words: "My cherished elders, my own son has dressed in my cloak; just now he is in that house." Maina was referring to his son who was having an affair with one of his younger wives. The son's action was a very undignified act in the eyes of the Bukusu people. Maina was seeking the elders of the Bukusu and the neighboring communities to assist in resolving this problem. The first response, issued by an elder from the Bamasaba people, came: "The young man should be killed." The second elder, who came from the community of the Barwa people, declared, "The young man should be killed." The third elder, from the Teso people, responded differently than the first two elders did. "The young man should not be killed," he said, "because a woman is like a flowing river" (meaning a woman by her nature is fickle in her marital loyalties, so the woman is to ever to blame and not the son). The elders representing the Babukusu spoke as one voice: "When a person grows old, he should let his sons make children with his young wives. All we can say is that the ceremony of *siluukhi* (ablution) must be performed to cleanse the youth so that Maina can pardon his son for even such abhorrent behavior."[230]

The Third Side Is Us

Third parties are used in many cultures to facilitate the resolution of differences or overt acts. Those involved in such matters do not always have the option of choosing whether to consider a third party. "The job of getting to peace is too important to be relegated only to a special ambassador," claims Ury. The task cannot be assigned solely to extraordinary leaders, such as Nelson Mandela or Kofi Annan, or solely to civil or religious authorities.[231] As simple societies such as the Bukusu have long recognized, it is everyone's responsibility to prevent harmful conflict. Every person in a community has to help resolve disputes. The way the Bukusu people express this truth is the common saying, "Friends for life don't let friends fight."

Ury contends, "We may not think of ourselves as third parties—in fact, we generally don't. Yet each of us has the opportunity to serve as a third party in the conflicts around us."[232] As a people, we constitute family, friends, colleagues, neighbors, onlookers, and witnesses. Each of us at one time or another will have some opportunity to mediate a dispute by taking the third side. Thus, the third side is, in reality, no one but us. What may be missing as an alternative to force and domination has to come from us.

The Strategies and Roles of the Third Side

If the third side is the most sensible alternative to force in conflict, how do people come to realize their opportunities to prevent destructive conflict and violence? And what can people do practically to facilitate settlements by negotiation?

Ury points out three major opportunities, or strategies, for channeling conflict resolutions toward constructive change. These are (1) prevention, or to prevent destructive conflicts from emerging by addressing tensions before any would lead to conflict; (2) mutual determination to resolve overt conflicts as they appear; and (3) mutual determination to contain any escalating power struggles that would forestall resolution. These three strategies lead to the motto of the third side: "Contain if necessary, resolve if possible, best of all prevent."[233] Thus, what is not prevented is resolved by the process of dialogue, and what is not resolved is contained.[234] By this means, the dialogue is permitted to progress.

The following paragraphs review each of these three strategic opportunities for handling conflict. In addition, there are various roles that can be recognized or mobilized within each of these strategies. We can bring these roles and their long-standing tradition in Bukusu life into focus.

Strategy One: Prevent Conflict

"An ounce of prevention is worth a pound of cure," says the old proverb. According to Ury, prevention is the best intervention. He argues, "When people are able to meet their basic needs, thanks to the Providers among us; when people have skills for handling their everyday tensions, thanks to the Teachers; and when people know, understand, and trust one another, thanks to the Bridge-Builders, destructive conflict diminishes in quantity and intensity. Latent conflict may not become overt and people may not even think of it as conflict. What does become overt, the parties can often handle by themselves.[235]

Ury claimed that the greatest lesson that his father taught him and a Bushman elder told him was to "never cause a problem, so that it won't have to be settled. Try to live in harmony."[236] Using an interdisciplinary approach, Ury borrows medical language to explain his point. "We are learning in our modern societies that prevention is better than cure when it comes to fighting disease. The best way to deal with heart attacks, for example, better than the most sophisticated bypass operations, is to prevent them through good nutrition, regular exercise, and medication. As the Bushmen demonstrate, the efficacy of prevention holds true in the arena of destructive conflict, too."[237]

Prevention, as depicted by Ury, means "addressing the root causes of conflict and laying down the foundation for the cooperative management of differences."[238] Prevention of conflict calls for restraint from overt hostility. The best means of prevention, Ury contends, is to meet a person's or a group's basic needs, enable the development of needed skills, and encourage the maintenance of good relationships.

Basic needs are the essentials of life, without which there is no survival. These include food, health care, and shelter. Conflicts usually arise when basic needs are frustrated or go unmet, asserts Ury. This helps to explain why the Bushmen go to such lengths to share food and other resources.[239] Ury narrates that the Bushmen hunters, arriving in the village with a large, freshly killed antelope or eland, divide the animal in successive waves of gifts to kin and friends, at least sixty-three times before it is even cooked, after which the meat is distributed widely yet again, with the beneficial effect that no identifiable need goes unmet.[240]

The Babukusu have similar social practices in which ritual killings are performed for the avowed purpose of pleasing and appeasing the spirits of the dead, both the recently passed (the living dead) and those from time long past (the ancestor spirits). The Bukusu people have a custom in which wealthy members of the community will fulfill their moral obligation to the community by slaughtering an animal and distributing the meat to various clansmen and kinsmen. The Babukusu call this *ekhafu eye lulwasako*, meaning "the animal of splitting." The slaughtered animal is split up among a large number of people. This ritual killing is not merely a voluntary act of individual generosity; rather, any person whose herd of cattle is flourishing is under the moral obligation to slaughter an animal of splitting.[241] The clansmen and other kinsmen who have been invited to fetch their portion of meat sit around the slaughtered animal. As soon as the animal is slaughtered, its blood is drawn and given to every member of the community, including children, to drink.[242] While the animal is being skinned, a debate begins as to who gets what. Someone claims each part of the animal. If the people begin to quarrel over their respective shares, which is always the case, the donor of the animal will reprimand them and even send them away, threatening to cancel the distribution. Later, after their arguments have been sorted out, the disputants are free to come and get their traditional shares.

The rules for distribution of the meat are clearly laid down. The donor of the animal keeps a very small amount of meat for himself and his family. The whole share goes to those for whom the animal was slaughtered. In other words, the meat has to be distributed to the community, rather than preserved for the immediate family. The distribution is as follows: The donor's elder brother receives a hind leg, as well as some ribs and the hide. The other brothers receive slightly smaller shares and paternal cousins still less. As a rule, the head is given to the donor's aunt (the father's sister or *senge*), while the uncle (the mother's brother, *khocha*) gets part of the feet or sometimes the second head if two animals have been slaughtered. Other extended family members and in-laws, as well as some distant clansmen, also receive a share; the range of the people varies in relation to the number of animals slaughtered. This is a symbol of community, solidarity, and good relationship. The maintenance of good order is stressed during this moment of the "blood pact."[243]

The distribution of the meat is also extended to the old and the influential men of neighboring clans as the representatives of their respective groups.

By accepting the meat sent to them, these men assume the obligation of reciprocating the gift when they slaughter their "animal of splitting" for their own clansmen.[244]

For the Babukusu, refusal to share one's "animal of splitting" is wrong. Self-centeredness is an act of destruction, because it does not serve to cement the bond that is required to form and maintain community.[245] The unity of the community is a paramount good; the opposite constitutes paramount destruction.

In addition to the concept of frustrated needs, Ury addresses the issue of insufficient skills for handling the tasks of life, especially the task of avoiding or resolving conflicts. He believes, "Tensions over conflicting needs can easily escalate when people lack proper skills or attitudes to defuse them."[246]

To explain his point, once again Ury applies strategies and techniques of the Bushmen. The Bushmen carefully teach their children to control their tempers and refrain from violence. Children learn to tolerate and respect others and to avoid giving offense. They are also taught to share what they have with their peers. Ury depicts an incident of sharing: "When two girls were quarreling over the blanket, Purana, an elder I interviewed, explained how he told the one with a blanket that 'she is very lucky that Bise [the good God] gave it to her and, to show her happiness, she should share the blanket with her friend.' He was teaching these young girls how to find ways in which both win.[247]

Children learn how to resolve differences from their parents, family, and community. Ury notes, "Children learn mainly from what adults do. The adults place great value in talking as a way to handle the problems; indeed, the Bushmen call themselves 'the people who talk too much.' Go into the Bushmen camp and you will hear the steady stream of chatter and joking. The sounds of the human voice seem to rise from the very desert, from the early hours of the morning to the late hours of the evening."[248]

The nonstop chatter lets people know how everyone is feeling and whether any friction needs to be resolved or any problem hashed out. Among these people, listening is the overriding metaphor. Listeners continually respond to people's stories, myths, sayings, and proverbs, often echoing what they hear. In effect, Ury observes, "They are practicing what modern psychologists call 'active listening,' a technique used to defuse negative emotions. Humor and fits of laughter punctuate the talk. People continually express and release their emotions, thus preventing tensions from building."[249]

Possessing negotiating skills without having good relationships with others is futile. As Ury explains, "Relationships receive most attention in the adjudication of what is good and bad, what is desirable and undesirable in life." He adds, "Good relationships are the solution to preventing conflicts. A web of emotional and economic ties among the Bushmen fosters mutual understanding, trust, and clear communication. Through constant visits and the exchange of gifts, they nurture their relationships in other [groups of people] as well as their own."[250] A *Kung* Bushman described the gift-giving custom: "Hxaro is when I take a thing of value and I give it to you. Later, much later, when you find some good thing, you give it back to me. When I will find something good, I will give it to you, and so we will pass the years together."[251] Thus, relationship is closely connected to community values. The community values of the Bushmen are inclusive. Whether people are members of the immediate family or the extended family, close friends, or only visitors, everyone participates in the close community relationships and friendships.[252]

One of the best ways to acknowledge the other side in a conflict, and to build a good working relationship with that person or group is to meet informally. Informal meetings allow people opportunities to talk about hobbies, families, or whatever their interests are. They also provide time for small talk before the negotiation session begins. "Little gestures of good will can go a long way," notes Ury.[253]

Roles for Preventing Conflict

Writing about strategies for preventing conflict, Ury proposes that there are several roles that are typical in most societies and can have significant influence in averting aggressions or hostilities. The three main preventative roles of the third side are those of provider, teacher, and bridge-builder. Ury describes these roles for preventing conflict in the following diagram:

Why Conflict Escalates		Ways to Prevent Conflict
Frustrated needs	→	1. The Provider
Poor skills	→	2. The Teacher
Weak relationships	→	3. The Bridge-Builder

The Provider

A provider enables people to meet their own mutual needs. Each human being wants to feel well, safe, respected, and free. "Third-Siders," as Ury calls them, must see to it that three needs—prevention, resolution, or containment—are met in order to evade destructive conflict.[254] To convey the concept of the provider, Ury tries to reduce all images of the provider to that of the mother or father. Any disruption or neglect for these advocates will lead to conflict or destruction. Conflicts often take on destructive dimensions after a long time of dormancy. It is only when such conflicts have reached unmanageable proportions that they become the subject of serious attention. Ury observes, "Whatever the surface issues in a dispute, the underlying cause usually lies in the deprivation of basic human needs like love and respect. Frustrations lead people to bully others, to use violence, and grab someone else's things." Ury describes his point using this analogy: "If disputes resemble the matches that light the fire, the frustration of needs is like the flammable tinder."[255] It takes just a spark! Sharing a meal is a central value in Bukusuland and a significant way in which disputes are discouraged before they arise. The majority of young people and middle-aged adults share three or four of their five daily meals with outsiders, usually close neighbors, and will directly return the hospitality in the same manner, so that the man who first eats at his neighbor's house, half an hour later shares the food that his wife has cooked with the same neighbors, engaging in "the principle of reciprocity." The rule of reciprocation states that humans have an inherent desire to return favors. Sometimes the men of two or three neighboring houses ask their wives to bring the food regularly to one place where they like to sit and talk. Similarly, co-wives or women neighbors informally drop in at each other's houses to borrow salt or fire and take the opportunity to ask what each is cooking for the evening meal.[256] If these women happen to be preparing different dishes, they may invite one another to share the meal. Children also eat at the homesteads of their playmates or at those of their paternal and maternal uncles. Willingness to share food with friends and neighbors is looked upon as one of the greatest Bukusu social values.[257]

Providers may not necessarily be able to address the needs of others directly, but they may enable people to meet their own needs. Ury explains, "Each of us can open doors to resources that others can use to help themselves."[258] For example, for the Bushmen and Babukusu, enabling their neighbors to meet their basic needs makes common sense.

The Teacher

"Give a man a fish, and you feed him for a day. Teach a man to fish, and you feed him for a lifetime," goes the ancient wisdom. Thus, teaching right relationship and conflict-prevention habits is in the best interest of the community and the individual. Ury considers this second role of the third party important to the prevention of conflicts, noting, "The goal of teaching is to help create a culture of collaboration and constructive conflict, as genuine co-culture."[259] The teacher gives people the skills they need to handle differences and disagreements. Ury points out that the first step for a teacher is "to teach that violence solves nothing."[260] Ury provides an example from the Bushmen, who carefully teach their children about the enormous cost of initiating violence, about the pain it causes, and about the risks it poses to the entire community.[261] Members of the community help to teach the way of nonviolence through the practice of tolerance.

Ury believes, "The alternative to violence must be tolerance." Tolerance does not mean agreeing with the other or remaining indifferent in the face of injustice but, rather, "showing respect for the essential humanity in every person."[262] In the hadith, Abu Hurairah relates that the Holy Prophet Muhammad said, "The strong one is not he who knocks out others in wrestling; the strong one is the one who keeps control over himself when he is roused."[263] Tolerance is an alternative to the conviction that one's beliefs and methods are the only correct perspective or position. Tolerance is based not on indifference or self-righteousness but on respect for the other.

According to the Qur'an, no religious group can presume that Allah has made it His exclusive elected. The Qur'an asserts, "Let the scriptural people know that they have no control over the grace of God; that grace is in His hands alone, and that He grants it to whomever He wills. God's grace is infinite."[264] According to Fazlur Rahman, probably the most learned of the major Muslim thinkers in the second half of the twentieth century, statements in the Qur'an are "absolutely unequivocal that no community may lay claims to be uniquely guided and elected."[265] Muslims are instructed in their holiest scripture to be very tolerant of people of other faiths.[266]

Many participants in the Judeo-Christian traditions have often willfully disregarded the inclusivity theme. The prophet Amos declared in his day that Israel's covenantal relationship with God does not suggest that that nation has immutable divine protection from heathen invaders.[267] As God's spokesperson, Amos proclaimed, "People of Israel, I think as much of the Ethiopians as I do of you. I brought the Philistines from *Crete* and the Syrians from *Kir*, even as I brought you out of Egypt."[268] Amos was bold to claim that God's care extended to Africans as well as Asians, and even to the migrations of Israel's enemies. God's universal sovereignty is affirmed in the whole of Hebrew tradition, in a poem about an ideal metropolis, personified as Mother Zion. Discounting special election of one people, (Psalm 87) envisions the "City of God" as having international progeny:

Of Zion it will be said,
All nations belong there.
The God above all gods will strengthen her.[269]

Among those who belong, the psalmist includes peoples of different colors and cultures. The register of Zion's children encompasses Israel's prominent pagan foes—the Egyptians, Babylonians, and Philistines. Conversion to the psalmist's religion is not a condition for being among those who sing and dance in Zion. Judaism's religious and cultural bias for the tolerance of all others is an important tenet of the faith. It must follow, then, that religious tolerance is central to the Christian tradition too.

Jesus advocated the good works as a test of inspired prophetic pronouncements: "By their fruits you shall know them" (Matthew 7:20). Jesus also said, "But to you who are listening, I say, Love your enemies, do good to those who hate you, bless those who curse you, pray for those who ill-use you. To him who strikes you on the cheek offer the other cheek also" (Luke 6:27–28). The Christian ethic is positive, not negative. It does not consist of not doing things but of doing them in real time. Jesus gave his followers the golden rule that bids its members to do to others as they would have done to themselves. The children of Abraham should go beyond asserting that Moses, or Jesus, or Muhammad is the greatest and let the impact of each be the standard for judgment.[270]

The Bridge Builder

The idea of "bridge building" reflects an enormous platform for conflict resolutions; it prevents communities from becoming further divided. Ury explains that giving people a forum in which to speak their minds gives them the opportunity to air the historical and current trends that are presently preventing people from communicating with each other. For example, you might successfully negotiate a time-out, offering a bully an alternative path to violence and, thus, a means to coexist peacefully with the party who otherwise might have been the recipient of the violence. Instead of starting from where one is, one starts from where the other person is—and is guided by that understanding toward reconciliation.[271]

In his writing about bridge building, Ury makes some important comments regarding dialogue being essential to bridge building. The aim of dialogue is not to convert others or to reach agreement in issues but, rather, to promote mutual understanding and build relationships that can prevent escalation into violence.[272] Engaging in dialogue provides a safe environment in which people can openly share differences. In doing so, the dialoguers might discover underlying commonalities that might retard or even avert a conflict's escalation into overt violence. While it may seem obvious to outsiders, the parties involved in dialoging or negotiating can be amazed that their enemies are quite as human as themselves.[273] They find themselves on that proverbial level playing field where the mountains are brought low and the road is level.

Simultaneously, Ury perceives dialogue as the most strenuous psychological work one can do. He acknowledges, "It requires listening to a point of view that you absolutely don't want to hear and that makes you angry."[274] It is not pleasant to listen to painful experiences that people have gone through. They may talk about wounds of the past, their suffering and anguish, or a frustrated need for respect and autonomy. Dialogue is demanding! It is much easier to fight the stranger, especially from a place of emotional, if not physical, distance. But it takes courage to face the pain of human contentions and be able to dialogue in a subservient fashion, even about things that really matter.[275] Despite the awkwardness and frustration of such encounters, dialogue, in the end, has the power to change those who willingly come to the table. Will, after all, is more than reflex action. It is an acceptance from the source of the harmony of all right relatedness.

Such dialoguing might well take place every day over the normal interactions of life. Ury holds that by "acting as third parties, even if we say very little, we can foster dialogue by bringing the parties together in a comfortable and neutral place."[276] Neutral places such as counselors' offices, conference rooms, or a friends' living rooms can serve as a secure setting in which the bridge builder can work to bring people together as rightly related again.

The bridge builder, teacher, and provider are useful roles for the resolving and prevention of further conflict. However, there may be times when people in such roles are not present or when their skills or input are not sufficient to promote harmony through cooperation. When this is the case, conflict may surface, and third-side negotiators need to shift direction and focus their efforts on resolving the issue in a timely manner.

Strategy Two: Resolve Conflict

If one is unable to circumvent conflict, the next best alternative Ury proposes is to move on and seek to resolve it. If one cannot prevent a conflict, tensions can escalate, and hostility and power struggles can arise. When this is the case, the third party needs to address that conflict directly, rather than allowing it to fester or escalate. A sure sign of pending conflict, according to Ury, is "finger-pointing, personal animosity; tit-for-tat retaliation."[277] Animosity and finger-pointing are, according to a traditional Bukusu saying, "*Ekhima ekhukhoma kamania.*" This phrase means, "The ape does not see its own backside; rather, he sees his companion's backside." This speaks to the hazard of pointing a finger at another's mistake while not seeing one's own foibles.[278] I have witnessed no end of finger-pointing on television, in newspapers, and on the Internet in the context of economic crisis and corruption in Africa. I have seen the "experts" blame the leaders, the members of Parliament, the bankers, the consumers, the economists, the rich, and all the rest of the "experts." Strangely enough, I have seen no one pointing a finger of responsibility toward himself or herself! Wouldn't it be refreshing to hear at least one person confess publicly that one of the main reasons Kenya (and all of Africa) is in trouble is because "certain people, like myself, have failed to act responsibly. I was really wrong on this one."

Blaming and seeking revenge were addressed in the Greek classics, such as Homer's *Odyssey* and Aeschylus'*Agamemnon* and, more importantly, in the *Lex Talionis* or "law of the talon" (Deuteronomy cf.19:21), which may be thought of as the law of tit-for-tat. This law appears in the earliest known code of laws, the Code of Hammurabi: "If any harm follows, then you shall give 'life for life,' 'eye for eye,' 'tooth for tooth,' 'hand for hand,' 'foot for foot,' 'burn for burn,' 'wound for wound,' 'stripe for stripe.'"[279]

This law became part and parcel of the ethic of the Hebrew Scriptures and is phrased identically to the Hammurabi Code in Exodus; it also appears in the laws of other cultures.[280] The eye-for-an-eye mandate, when it comes to overt conflict, means that the perpetrator shall suffer equal punishment to that inflicted on the victim. In this legalistic framework, retaliation and restitution are linked. Restitution is positive because it gives back to the victim what was taken away. Retaliation is also positive because it strips the perpetrator, at least symbolically, of whatever power or respect he or she gained at the victim's expense. In addition, compensation is not merely quantitative but also qualitative, and the penalty is thought to fit not only the amount, but also the kind of damage done.[281]

Nonetheless, eye-for-an-eye justice is not the sole perspective reflected in the Jewish tradition. For example, in (Leviticus 19:18), the law is expanded to include the admonition; "You shall not take vengeance or bear any grudge against the sons of your own people." In (Proverbs 25:21), it is written, "If your enemy is hungry, give him bread to eat; and if he is thirsty, give him water to drink." In these statements, an ethic of revenge is replaced by an ethic of mercy.[282]

Ury reports that the Holy Qur'an also speaks to concerns regarding blaming and revenge. While the Qur'an acknowledges the law that demands "an eye for an eye, a tooth for a tooth, and a wound for a wound," (Qur'an 5:45) it also encourages pardoning as an act of charity.[283] For example, Allah said, "Those who suppress their anger and forgive people … Allah loves as benevolent" (Qur'an 3:135). We also read, "The wronged one who endures with fortitude and forgives, indeed achieves a matter of high resolve" (Qur'an 42:44).[284]

This approach to justice with mercy and compassion is also found in the Christian tradition. Jesus teaches about forgiveness in (Matthew 6:14–15): "If you forgive others their transgressions, your heavenly Father will forgive you. But if you do not forgive others, neither will your Father forgive your transgressions."[285] This perspective can also be found in Paul's writings, in which he proclaims, "Bless those who persecute you; bless and do not curse them … Do not repay anyone evil for evil … No, if your enemies are hungry, feed them; if they are thirsty, give them something to drink; for by doing this you will heap burning coals on their heads. Do not be overcome by evil, but overcome evil with good" (Romans 12).

To avoid vengeful responses to conflict, Ury proposes four roles that can enable conflict resolution. As mediators, we can help reconcile the parties' interests; as arbiters, we can determine rights; as equalizers, we can help balance the power between the opposing sides; and as healers, we can help repair injured relationships. Ury formulates these roles in the following diagram:

WHY CONFLICT ESCALATES		WAYS TO RESOLVE CONFLICT
Conflicting interests	→	4. The Mediator
Disputed rights	→	5. The Arbiter
Unequal power	→	6. The Equalizer
The injured relationships	→	7. The Healer

Let it be noted that these four in application may be hard to separate out from the full spectrum of the process. The natural flow from one to the next may be indefinable even as the whole comes together mysteriously. No one by mere reasoning will be able to say how it came out in good will.

The Mediator

The mediator is one who helps the conflicting parties embrace agreement, if possible. A mediator does not decide the case. If the conflicting parties fail to reach agreement, the case goes to a judge.[286] However, the strength of the mediator must lie in avoiding taking sides. In the process, Ury explains, "The mediator does not seek to determine who is right and who is wrong, but rather tries to get to the core of the dispute and resolve it. The core matter is [that] each side's interests are met; their needs, concerns, desires, fears and aspirations."[287] A mediator has a responsibility to assist the two opposing sides to uncover and unite the interests underlying those positions.[288] To do that, the mediator needs to find ways to get both parties to sit down together to discuss their concerns.[289] The aim is to make sure that all unresolved conflicts are taken care of by engaging the disputing parties in genuine dialogue.[290]

There is no point in having a discourse that lacks honesty and meaningful communication between parties. Ury points out that one of the mediator's key functions is "to help each side to understand what the other is really saying or asking for."[291] The mediator has to maintain clear channels of communication by encouraging the mutual understanding that the solution has to come from the parties themselves, even though there may be moments when the mediator will have to suggest options, especially if the communication seems to be breaking down.

The goal of the negotiation is to reach a mutually satisfactory agreement. I have seen disputes between major shopkeepers in Nairobi and the street vendors along the street corners that often escalate into bitter fights with city police. The shopkeepers claim that street vendors affect their businesses. The city police usually send the street vendors away, but as soon as the police disappear, the vendors return to continue their selling. However, from time to time, the city police fear that the confrontations with the street vendors may escalate and that the vendors might want to attack the police in the night. In one case, the deadlock was broken by the city council's propping up of each side's interests. The shop owners feared the vendors would scare away customers and therefore hurt business. The negotiation brought about the setting up of proper kiosks or booths, which, in fact, did boost the vendors' business. In return, the vendors then promised to keep the streets clean. Having begun as adversaries, the parties ended up as partners—thanks to mediation.

The Arbiter

Ury describes the arbiter's as a "familiar role, embodied in the judge in the courtroom or the arbitrator in a work setting."[292] More informally, Ury notes, the arbiter is the teacher resolving a dispute between two quarreling students, the parent ruling on a matter involving two children, or the manager determining an issue between two employees. We are all potential arbiters.

The third side can usefully play the role of arbiter. Whereas a mediator can only suggest a solution, an arbiter can decide. This is a private, rights-based, adjudicative procedure. The arbiter's goal is not just to determine who is right and who is wrong but to repair the harm done to victims and to the community and to forgive the offenders by accepting them back into the community. Each side must guard against finger-pointing.

Pointing fingers inflames conflict. "The role of the arbiter," Ury notes, "is to encourage a negotiated settlement whenever possible and appropriate."[293] Ury explains how arbiters should operate. Leaders can urge disputing employees who come to them for assistance to first try to resolve the matter themselves. Similarly, a judge can take disputants into chambers and instruct them to go back to mediation before involving the court. A parent might tell two children quarreling over a piece of cake, "Okay Johnny, you cut the cake, and Mary, you get the first pick."[294] In such a way, an arbiter best serves peaceful resolution.

The Equalizer

The mediator-arbiter sometimes will do well to act more as an equalizer. Ury makes the following comment about the role of equalizer being the democratizing power. "Every conflict," Ury observes, "takes place within the larger context of power. Imbalance of power often leads to abuse and injustice. The strong refuse to negotiate with the weak or to submit their dispute to mediation or arbitration—why should they, they think, when they can win? This is where the Equalizer has a contribution to make."[295]

There is an old Sufi story. A master and his followers came upon a village in which the local residents were engaged in a skirmish with government soldiers. "Master," said one of the devotees, "shouldn't we help out here?" "Oh, yes!" said the master. "But tell us, Master, which side should we help?" The master smiled. "Both," he said.

A similar story tells of a medieval Chinese leader named Mu Tzu, a great general who is remembered for great skill in intervention. When two neighboring warlords would be about to do battle, Mu Tzu would ask each if he might help them work out their differences. If either side refused his assistance, they would learn that Mu Tzu intended to ally his own private army with that of the other side, thus bringing the matter to a standstill. Then Mu Tzu would again ask if it was time to work out a peaceful resolution.[296]

This equalizing strategy may be seen in Bukusu mutual pursuit of peace. If the eldest son in the family has reached marriageable status and his father has died, he is obliged to take the place of the father as a trustee for his younger brothers. It is his duty then to assist his younger brothers in turn, assembling their bride wealth. It is also his duty to collect bride wealth when his sisters are married. Thus, the elder son acts as an economic equalizer, and by doing so, prevents, early on, conflicts that might occur as a result of inequality in family contributions. The equalizer must be capable of empowering the weak and unrepresented so that there can be a mutually satisfactory understanding.[297] Equalizers assist the weaker party by bringing their stronger counterparts to amelioration.

The Healer

For the Bukusu people the *mganga*, or village healer, is believed to have the power to heal those who are physically ill, suffering misfortune, or spiritually weak. To become an *mganga*, a person must offer evidence that he or she is guided by a healing spirit. Often this is the spirit of an ancestor who had been a healer and wishes to continue his or her work through the living descendant. By legend, a child is chosen by the *simakombe*, or the spirit of the living dead, and taught the ancient and mystical healing arts.

The Bukusu people say, "It is not illnesses that are healed, but people." The repairing of injured relationships is one of Ury's central concerns. He is convinced that "a conflict cannot be considered fully resolved until the injured relationships have been healed." Ury asserts, "Each of us has a chance to heal the feuds in our families, in our workplaces, and in our communities."[298] An example of healing in the family is drawn from the story that follows.

There was a little girl whose parents had a miserable marriage and so divorced, having nothing in common, save affection with the child. One day, as the girl was playing in the street, a bus knocked her down and she was seriously injured. When she was taken to the hospital, the doctors examined her but found her to be beyond human aid. Hastily summoned to the hospital, her parents heard the sad news and stood silently, one on either side of the bed, looking down helplessly at the little girl. As they stood there, the child's eyes suddenly opened and, seeing her parents, she tried to smile. Then, drawing one arm from under the blanket, she held it out in the direction of her father. "Daddy," she said, "give me your hand." Turning to her mother, she stretched out her other arm. "Mommy," she said, "give me your hand." Then with a final effort of her ebbing strength, she drew them close together.[299] Why would this be a lesson for us all?

James S. Hewett's example supports Ury's premise that each of us has a chance to heal the feuds in our communities. To our surprise, the conversation in the above story takes a healing turn; for certain, the little girl spoke from her heart. All in hearing should attribute the good coming out of it to the presence of the little girl, who reminded her parents of the importance of getting along. In the end, she wordlessly proposed that her parents reunite. Similarly, like this little girl, anyone might fulfill the role of healer.

Naturally, when attempting to heal wounds and to avoid the danger of conflict recurring, one has to create a climate conducive to health. To do so, Ury suggests using containment as an alternative tool for fostering protection. The next section serves to outline the nature of containment.

Strategy Three: Contain Conflict

Many people still believe that force is the only way to resolve serious conflicts, and that short-term dialogue for prevention and resolution might well not stop escalation.[300] The final challenge for the third side, Ury says, is "whether, in these circumstances, it can contain the power struggle so that the parties may be brought back to the negotiating table."[301] Conflict can be contained by integrating the three successive and increasingly interventional roles—witness, referee, and peacekeeper—as in the diagram below:

WHY CONFLICT ESCALATES		WAYS TO CONTAIN CONFLICT
No attention	→	8. The Witness
No limitation	→	9. The Referee
No protection	→	10. The Peacekeeper

Witness

To witness is a strategy through which people readily acknowledge conflict escalation. Ury writes of the "power of ordinary community members who, by paying attention to escalation, are capable of containing violence."[302] For instance, by paying attention to proximal escalation to famine, the community might want to develop strategies early on for coping with it. The following poem by Adelaide B. Vawter about famine in Africa captures the momentum of Ury's idea of what it is to witness.

"Famine"

Skin drawn taut as a drum
Across his swollen belly
Child, when did you last eat?

Eyes staring blankly
With unremembered pain
Child, when did you last hope?

Arms and legs like matchsticks
So fragile they would break
Child, when did you last move?

Throat parched, cracked lips
Covered with flies
Child, when did you last laugh?

Your name is victim
Thousands of innocent victims
World, when will you ever care?[303]

Through careful attention, one can detect warning signals, which, if acted on early enough, can save lives.[304] Ury argues, "Early warning signals appear most clearly to those of us immediately around the disputants."[305] Ury responds to what a Semai tribesman told him concerning community environment: "We know everyone intimately; we know everyone's personality. We can tell when they are angry and when trouble is brewing."[306] In this context, Ury suggests three practical steps he believes can be used to contain conflict:

(1) vigilant patrolling of the neighborhood
(2) speaking out whenever we sense something going wrong in the village
(3) giving the alarm (for the Bukusu, the alarm is given through the talking drum)

Ury proposes that, as witnesses, we need not limit ourselves to watching; more actively, we must go on patrol.[307] For example, in an African village, people know each other well. If something of an unbecoming nature happens, any member of the community should be concerned enough to report the matter to the elders or to the police. The heart of the matter is to watch out for each other and help each other. Reporting crimes is the right thing to do.[308]

Witnesses must not limit themselves to watching and patrolling; they can speak up to deflect wrongdoing. Witnesses must speak to the parties caught in destructive behavior as soon as they see it. In addition to the individual, social entities such as government or religious leaders or an entire community must be seen to stand up and say, "Look, the community is telling you that the violence has to stop. If it doesn't, the whole system here is going to work around you for the good of all."

In explaining the role of a witness, Ury asserts that the witness sounds the alarm to call the attention of any other third-siders to align with each other and intervene as mediators and peacekeepers to augment the witnessing.[309] As an example, Ury notes that the incidence of street violence is low in Japan because citizens participate as witnesses, reporting matters to the authorities from within the neighborhood.[310] Among the Bukusu people, sounding the drums, whistles, or bullhorns are means of calling people to witness within a homestead, village, or town. When sounded, these instruments alert the villagers to get ready to turn out for the alarm whatever the cause of the alarm, be it theft, cattle raiding, or the danger of fire or flood.

The media also plays a great role in sounding the alarm of public concern or governmental action, even on a worldwide scale. This is true in Kenya as well. During ethnic clashes in Kenya between 1991 and 1994, the media played an enormous role in alerting people about when and how to escape from war-torn areas. Similarly, media are often used to alert the people when fierce animals, such as lions and elephants, are on the loose.

The Referee

While the role of the referee is to set limits on disputation, Ury is convinced that "some fighting can be salutary."[311] He suggests, "In democratic politics, fair fighting can ensure that injustices are addressed, abuses stopped, and excesses kept in check."[312] When there is rioting in the streets of

Nairobi, students can be part of a sympathetic coalition with striking workers against injustices caused by the corrupt regime. They can be observed attempting to rein in the oppressive government. Thus, those demonstrations can serve the function of bringing suppressed problems into the open. Let it be understood that the government in power gives no deference to a student status in such demonstrations. The force of that presiding law will have no consideration. The students will suffer under the gun with all others.

Referees can change the way people come up against authority, replacing more destructive weapons and methods with substantially less destructive ones. Ury contends that conscientious parents and teachers exemplify good referees who must set limits. He further suggests that for children, "Pillows are okay but fists are not."[313]

Certainly, Bishop Desmond Tutu and other leaders attempted to function as referees during the dismantling of apartheid in South Africa in the 1980s. In traditional Bukusu life, it is the elders who must play the role of referees for clan or family disputes, as do priests for parishioner or community conflicts; and it is the mullahs who serve in disputes for mosque and their community issues.

The Peacekeeper

Peacekeeping is a community function that anyone (anyone!) may be called upon to serve when community rules break down and a dispute escalates. The community ought to employ forceful measures minimally to avoid harmful conflict in problem-solving.[314] The United Nations Peacekeeping Forces have filled this role in many countries over more than a half century. In that time, they have helped inter- and intramural parties who need help waging peace, breaking the syndrome of conflict. Peacekeepers' primary responsibilities are to monitor ceasefires, separate the rivals, and serve to resolve or mediate hostile issues within the community. Normally, UN peacekeepers are equipped with light firepower and have strict instructions to not fire until they are threatened personally and only as a last result. However, sometimes for a community, there may be a need to employ force to protect the innocent by force of peacekeeping interdiction.

No matter how strong the aggressor may be, the peacekeeper as the third side must appear stronger.[315] Recall here the strategy of General Mu Tzu: His power as the third side was used, and can be used, by anyone to overcome the aggressor. On this note, Ury concludes, "The aggression will be stopped by the armed will of a united world community."[316]

Ury provides an example of an extreme case of peace enforcement that occurred among the Bushmen. A Bushman who was psychotic killed two people and threatened to kill more; after exhausting all other remedies, the community finally ran him down and killed him. All the men and women stabbed his body with spears in a traditional fashion, so that all shared responsibility for killing him.[317]

In Bukusuland, one cannot think of the police as peacekeepers. The police are thought of as enemies of the people because they are corrupt. From the perspective of most Kenyans, the police advance themselves by cheating and lying. In so doing, they make a fortune through bribes. The Kenyans' true peacekeepers are the elders of the villages and the religious leaders of the mosques and churches. These are the ones who more often are willing to come between disputants, using their influence to encourage peaceful resolution.

Conclusion

The value of Ury's writings about conflict resolution in terms of its application in Kenya is quite high, as Kenyans can apply his philosophies to the practical matters of homestead and village life. Ury writes with an understanding of African realities. Further, his emphasis on the role that any one community member may play in stemming, redirecting, or containing conflict is compelling. Moreover, he acknowledges the powerful force that he sees in the Bukusu tradition in the form of the community elders and holds this dynamic up as an example to the world community.

The following section presents traditional Bukusu patterns of communication through dialogue in which the ideas of Buber, Iklé, and Ury can be seen, with special focus on the family, the clan, and the entire community.

Part III Notes

1. "Then one of the scribes came, and having heard them reasoning together, perceiving that he had answered them well, asked Jesus, 'Which is the first commandment of all?' Jesus answered him, 'The first of all the commandments is: 'Hear, O Israel, the Lord our God, the Lord is one. And you shall love the Lord your God with all your heart, with all your soul, with all your mind, and with all your strength.' This is the first commandment. And the second, like it, is this: 'You shall love your neighbor as yourself.' There is no other commandment greater than these" (Deuteronomy 6:4, 5; Leviticus 19:18). The first great commandment teaches us to love God with all our heart and soul, mind, and strength. And the second defines the relationships we should have with one another. We must love our neighbor as ourselves. The central pillar of life—the central place in our hearts—is God, and our relationship to one another naturally follows and falls into place given this centrality of love of God. It sets us into *right-relatedness*. This—love—is God's will and God's nature.

2. David Bohm, *On Dialogue*, Lee Nichol, ed. (London: Rutledge, 1998), 6.

3. Bohm, *On Dialogue.*

4. Ibid, 9.

5. Joe Lau and Jonathan Chan, Critical Thinking Web, "Identifying Hidden Assumptions," *Argument Analysis*, http://philosophy.hku.hk/think/arg/hidden. php.

6. Ibid.

7. Haward, Thurman, *The Search for Common Ground* (Richmond, Indiana: Friends United Press, 1986), xi. In my opinion, these passages of Thurman's are so important that they bear rereading over and over again in contemplation. Dr. Martin Luther King knew the man as his teacher and held him in highest esteem.

8. Ibid.

9. Ibid, xi.

10. Ibid, 2–3.

11. Ibid, 3.

12. Ibid.

13. Jean Burden, "Howard Thurman," *Chicken Bones: A Journal for Literary and Artistic African-American Themes*, from *The Atlantic Monthly* (1953), http://www.nathanielturner.com/howardthurman.htm.

14. Henri J. M. Nouwen, *Reaching Out* (New York: Doubleday, 1975), 101. When we feel lonely, we have such a need to be liked and loved that we are hypersensitive to the many signals in our environment and easily become hostile toward anyone whom we perceive as rejecting us.

15. Brenda Ueland, "Tell Me More," *Utne Reader* (November/December, 1992), 104–109.

16. Roland Barthes, *The Responsibility of Forms*, Richard Haward, trans., (New York: Hill and Wang, 1985), 249. Barthes further explains, "First of all, whereas for centuries listening could be confined as an intentional act of audition (to listen is to want to hear, in all conscience), today it is granted the power (and virtually the function) of playing over unknown spaces: listening includes in its field not only the unconscious in the topical sense of the term, but also, so to speak, in its lay forms: the implicit, the indirect, the supplementary, the delayed: listening grants access to all forms of over determination, of super-imposition" (258).

17. Martin Buber, *A Land of Two Peoples: Martin Buber on Jews and Arabs*, ed. Paul R. Mendes-Flohr, (Oxford: Oxford University Press, 1994), 3.

18. Martin Buber, *I and Thou*, A new translation with a prologue "I and You" and notes by Walter Kaufman. (New York: Charles Scribner's Sons, 1970), 4.

19. Ibid, 30.

20. Ibid, 43. Buber adds a warning, "The separated *I-It* of [outside] institutions is an animated clod without soul, and the separated *I* of [inner] feelings an easily fluttering soul-bird." He adds, "Feelings … and institutions are necessary; but put together they do not create human life: this is done by the third, the central presence of the *Thou*" (44, 46).

21. In other cases, an apparently insignificant object seems so important to certain dependents that it does not seem to matter who procures the object for them. There is, as everyone knows, a sort of camaraderie among smokers; a smoker will accept a cigarette even from an enemy, and offer tobacco even to someone he or she hates. One doesn't care at all about the background of the supplier; it is the supply that counts. See Albert Memmi, *Dependence* (Boston, MA: Beacon Press, 1979), 12–13.

22. Joseph G. Donders, *Praying and Preaching the Sunday Gospel* (Maryknoll, NY: Orbis Books, 1990), 21.

23. Buber, *I and Thou*, 8.

24. Martin Buber, *The Knowledge of Man,* Ronald Gregor Smith, ed., (San Francisco: Harper and Row Publishers, 1966), 86.

25. Buber, *I and Thou,* 21. In the context of traditional Africa, people do not perceive themselves as surrounded only by things; rather, the metaphysical world is loaded with beings. The whole of reality is of primary concern. Nature is not objectified as in science; orientation toward totality is reflected in the intense feeling of the community. See Jacob K. Olupona, ed., *African Traditional Religions in Contemporary Society* (St. Paul, Minnesota: Paragon House, 1991), 40–41.

26. Laurenti Magesa, *African Religion: The Moral Traditions of Abundant Life* (Maryknoll, New York: Orbis Books, 1997), 91.

27. Geoffrey Parrinder, professor of the comparative study of religions at the University of London, echoes this in writing: "Taboos exist to make sure that the moral structure of the universe remains undisturbed for the good of humanity." See Geoffrey Parrinder, *West African Religion: A Study of the Beliefs and Practices of Akan, Ewe, Yoruba, Igbo and Kindred Peoples* (London: Epworth Press, 1961), 172–75.

28. The name *ebaka* refers to any large, poisonous snake.

29. In explanation of this peculiar attitude toward frogs, the Bukusu people have the following story. One day in the distant past, a woman took a basketful of millet to the market to barter it for some meat. When she received the meat, a small piece was added to the big chunk as *nyongesa*. (It is a common practice among the Bukusu people when making a purchase to get a small amount over and above the quantity that the customer can claim. Nowadays this extra bit, *nyongesa*, is also referred to as *baksheesh*). Then she went home, and on her way back met with a big frog called *Namakanda*. Namakanda begged the woman for the small piece of meat that she had been given as *nyongesa*. Being kindhearted, the woman gave the meat to the frog. When she came home, the husband asked her for *nyongesa*, saying that he wanted to roast it for himself. When his wife told him that she had given it to a frog she had met by the roadside, her husband at first disbelieved her and then became angry and scolded her for her foolishness. He took a club and asked his wife to lead him to the place where she had seen the frog. When they arrived, Namakanda was still, there and the woman asked her, "Did I not give you a piece of meat?" The frog merely replied, "ee" (meaning yes). Then the wife stood aside, and the husband quarreled with the frog. "Why did you ask my wife to give you the meat?" he demanded. The frog just listened and the man went on, "Was it my millet for which the meat was bought or yours?" The frog replied, "It was the millet from your garden." The man went on scolding, "Did I dig the garden for myself or for you?" Then he took his club and poked the frog under its legs where its soft spots are. Namakanda did not reply and the man went on beating

it severely until it was nearly dead. Then Namakanda said, "I am dying now because you have beaten me, but from now on, the people shall all die from the illness of the chest." According to some people, Namakanda was the wife of the Bukusu ancestor, *Mubukusu*. Since that time, the Bukusu people have given the highest respect to frogs.

30. Buber, *I and Thou*, 32.
31. Ibid,12.
32. Ibid, 9.
33. Ibid, 11, 76.
34. Ibid, 32.
35. Ibid, 15.
36. Buber, *Between Man and Man*, 97.
37. By this he means that "in order that this effect upon him may be a unified and significant one, he must also live this situation, again and again, in all its moments not merely from his own end but also from that of his partner."
38. Buber, *Knowledge of Man*, 68.
39. Ibid, 71.
40. It is this position of respectful disagreement that, in part, sets Buber apart from the renowned psychologist Carl Rogers. See Buber, *Knowledge of Man*, 166–84.
41. Ibid, 79–80.
42. Ibid, 61–62.
43. Ibid, 19.
44. Ibid.
45. Ibid, 20.
46. Ibid, 19.
47. Ibid, 78.
48. Buber supports this claim by asserting that, where the dialogue is fulfilled in its being between partners who have turned to one another in truth, who express themselves without reserve and are free of the desire for semblance, memorable, common fruitfulness that is to be found nowhere else is brought into being.
49. Buber, *Knowledge of Man*, 76.
50. Ibid, 75–76.
51. Ibid, 19.
52. Ibid.
53. Ibid.
54. During the oracular consultation, the alleged cause of the trouble is frequently alluded to by a circumlocution so as not to arouse its anger. "Grain picker," stands here for chicken.

55. Buber notes this pattern, affirming, "Every *I-Thou* relationship, within a relation which is specified as purposive working of one part upon the other, persists in virtue of a mutuality which is forbidden to be full" (Buber, *I and Thou*, 134). Buber again points to the limits of such a relationship in writing: "As soon as the relation has been worked or has been permeated with a means, the *Thou* becomes an object among objects." (Buber, 17).

56. Is there anyone who has never seen a panic-stricken child, lost among the crowd in a department store, crying for his or her mama and no one else, refusing to be consoled by anything—kind words, candy, toys—and whose despair miraculously vanishes as soon as "Mama" appears? Is there anyone who does not know a married person who gets "worried to death" when his or her spouse is the least bit late and whose anxiety disappears abruptly when the absent partner returns, if it doesn't change to sudden anger? In the marital relationship, as in the parental, the mere presence of the other person can be protection against distress.

57. Memmi, *Dependence*, 158.

58. Buber, *Between Man and Man*, 7.

59. Ibid, 87.

60. Ibid, 107.

61. Buber, *I and Thou*, 63.

62. Bernard Susser, *Existence and Utopia: The Social and Political Thought of Martin Buber* (Rutherford, NJ: Fairleigh Dickinson University Press, 1981), 14.

63. Buber, *I and Thou*, 69. Note the use of *is*, not *was*; Buber used the verb in its present tense, not its past tense. He wrote that relation "*is* in the beginning and is now, not *was*, in some time past.

64. Jonathan Sacks, *Community of Faith* (London: Peter Halban Publishers, 1995).

65. Ibid.

66. Buber, *I and Thou*, 62.

67. Ibid, 80.

68. Ibid, 112.

69. In these words, Husserl says that man's essence is not to be found in isolated individuals, for a human being's bonds with his generation and his society are of his essence; we must, therefore, know what these bonds really mean if we want to know the essence of man. See Martin Buber, *Between Man and Man*, *with an afterward by the author on* "The History of Dialogical Principle," trans. Ronald Gregor Smith (London: Routledge & Kegan Paul, 1947; Macmillan, 1965), 160.

70. Buber, *Between Man and Man* 157.

71. Ibid, 80.
72. Ibid, 202. Buber makes a similar point when he writes, "The fundamental fact of human existence is neither the individual as such nor the aggregate as such. Each, considered by itself, is a mighty abstraction. The individual is a fact of existence in so far as he steps into a living relation with other individuals. The aggregate is a fact of existence in so far as it is built up of living units of relation. The fundamental fact of human existence is man with man" (Buber, *Between Man and Man*, 202–203). Buber makes a poignant comment as he expands on this point. He writes, "For the typical man of today, the flight from responsible personal existence has been singularly polarized. Since he is not willing to answer for the genuineness of his existence, he flees either into the general collective which takes from him his responsibility or into the attitude of a self who has to account to no one but himself, and finds the great general indulgence in the security of being identical with the self of being. Even if this attitude is turned into deepened contemplation of existing being, it remains a flight from the leaping fire. The clearest mark of this kind of man is that he cannot really listen to the voice of another; in all his hearing, as in all his seeing, he mixes observation. The other is not the man over and against him whose claim stands over against his own in equal right; the other is only his object. But he who existentially knows no *Thou* will never succeed in knowing a *We*" (Buber, *Knowledge of Man*, 108).
73. Buber also uses the terms aggregate, collective common life, group, social, and genuine community to refer to a collective group of people coming together for some specific or random cause but without encountering each other in dialogic ways. He writes of such groups as "a bundling together: individuals packed together, armed and equipped in common, with only as much life from man to man as will inflame the marching step" (Buber, *Between Man and Man*, 31).
74. Ibid, 203.
75. Ibid, 45.
76. Ibid, 115.
77. Buber makes this point in writing, "The real essence of community is undoubtedly to be found in the—manifest or hidden—fact that it has a center. The real origin of community is undoubtedly only to be understood by the fact that its members have a common relationship to the center superior to all other relations: the circle is drawn from the radii, not from the points of the periphery. And undoubtedly the primal reality of the center cannot be known if it is not known as transparent into the divine. But the more earthly, the more creaturely, the more bound a character the circle takes, so much the truer, the more transparent it is." See Martin Buber, "Comments on the Idea

of Community," in Martin Buber, *A Believing Humanism: My Testament, 1902-1965*. Translated and with an Introduction and Explanatory Comments by Maurice Friedman (New York: Simon and Schuster, 1967), 89.

78. Ibid, 46. Buber adds, "The bright building of community, to which there is an escape even from the dungeon of 'social life,' is the achievement of the same power that works in the relation between man and God ... for it is the universal relation into which all streams pour, yet without exhausting their waters. Who wishes to make division and define boundaries between sea and streams? There we find only the one flow from *I* to *Thou*, unending, the one boundless flow of the real life" (Buber, *I and Thou*, 107).

79. Buber explains, "The person who is the object of my mere solicitude is not a Thou but a *He* or a *She*. The nameless, faceless crowd in which I am entangled is not a We but the 'one' [or the 'group']. But as there is a *Thou* so there is a *We*" (Buber, *Between Man and Man*, 175).

80. Buber, 31. Buber also writes, "[The] structures of man's communal life draw their living quality from the riches of the power to enter into relation, which penetrates their various parts, and obtain their bodily form from the binding up of this power in the spirit" (Buber, *I and Thou*, 49).

81. Ibid, 31–32.

82. Buber reinforces this point in claiming that "only men who are capable of truly saying *Thou* to one another can truly say *We* with one another," (Ibid, 175–76.)

83. Ibid, 201–202.

84. Ibid,176. In these examples, Buber was writing about the meeting of two people; however, they were applied here in relation to groups of people, as the point Buber was making has equal relevance to this context.

85. Buber explains, "Beside the constant forms of the essential *We* there are also transient forms, which nevertheless merit attention. Among those is to be reckoned, for example, the closer union, which is formed for a few days among the genuine disciples and fellow-workers of a movement when an important leader dies. All impediments and difficulties between them are set aside, and a strange fruitfulness, or at all events incandescence, of their life with one another is established. Another transient form is seen when in face of a catastrophe which appears inevitable the really heroic element of a community gathers together within itself, withdraws from all idle talk and fuss, but in it each is open to the others and they anticipate, in a brief common life, the binding power of a common death." It is at moments such as these, according to Buber, that "in truth 'deep calls to deep,' it becomes unmistakably clear that it is not the wand of the individual or of the social, but of a third which draws the

circle round the happening. On the far side of the subjective, on this side of the objective, on the narrow ridge, where *I* and *Thou* meet, there is the realm of the 'between'" (Ibid, 176, 204).

86. Ibid, 204.
87. Ibid, 31.
88. Ibid, 176.
89. Ibid.
90. Buber, 114–15.
91. Martin Buber, "Idea of Community," 87.
92. Martin Buber, *On Inter-subjectivity and Cultural Creativity Heritage of Sociology*, S. N. Eisenstadt, ed., (Chicago: University of Chicago Press, 1992), 11.
93. Buber, *Between Man and Man*, 31.
94. Buber, *I and Thou*, 45.
95. Ibid,50.
96. Ibid, 62, 167.
97. Ibid, 161.
98. Ibid, 54.
99. Mbiti, *African religions and Philosophy*, 144.
100. Buber, *Land of Two Peoples*, 25.
101. Susser, *Existence and Utopia* 47.
102. Buber, *Between Man and Man*, 80–82.
103. Susser, *Existence and Utopia*, 27.
104. Charles F. Iklé, *How Nations Negotiate*, (New York: Harper & Row, 1987), 2.
105. Charles F. Iklé, *Every War Must End*, (New York: Columbia University, 1991), x.
106. Ibid.
107. Ibid.
108. Ibid, 14.
109. Iklé, *How Nations Negotiate*, 62.
110. Ibid, 62.
111. Ibid.
112. Negotiators willing to apply moral imagination can sometimes generate strategies that may actually stymie an unscrupulous opponent. Like the Wicked Witch of the West in *The Wizard of Oz* who could not stand water, corruption cannot sustain itself in the spotlight of publicity. Corruption thrives in environments in which information is controlled, and it withers in the light of public scrutiny. As part of its response to the Asian financial crisis, the International Monetary Fund pressed countries to publish more financial information, which is now available on its website (located at http://www.imf.org). In Indonesia in 1999, the fact that the government was unable or unwilling to prosecute corruption

did not stop the Indonesian Bank Restructuring Agency from resorting to a strategy of shaming. It began publishing the names of the country's one hundred worst debtors in the local newspapers. See Jeanne M. Brett, *Negotiating Globally* (San Francisco: Jossey-Bass, 2001), 198.

113. In the nineteenth century, converted Ababukusu people grappled in various ways with the relationship between their new Christian faith, their cultural inheritance, and the needs and obligations of their immediate environment. One of the most enduring and complicated problem was plural marriage. Some new converts renounced all their wives but one. However, for many Ababukusu, this was impossible. The Yoruba people of Nigeria experienced a similar condition. In the words of a certain elder, "I have long renounced idolatry ... here are my two wives; from this I have got children, but she is poor; that one has no child, but she finds my daily bread. I have also suffered from a long sickness which has thus disabled me."A Yoruba clergyman, Emmanuel Moses Lijadu, told him to choose between children and bread. He died before he decided. See Isichei, *Christianity in Africa*, 159.

114. God is love. He created us to be loved, and out of His love can we love ourselves and love other people. Salvation is not just about going to heaven; salvation is about being made whole in your spirit, soul, and body. When we believe the Gospel, we will enjoy the benefits of salvation. The foundation of all our teachings is that God is love. Perfect love casts out fear.

115. The missionary embargo on plural marriages was out of date for Anglicans by a ruling of the Lambeth Conference in 1888. Many factors made monogamy difficult, not the least of which was a sense of loyalty to existing wives, and Bible study revealed the existence of polygynous Old Testament patriarchs who walked with God. Some Christians evaded the prohibition by sending different wives and their respective offspring to different churches. In 1917, ten leading men of a Lagos Methodist church were accused of polygyny. At a crowded meeting, fifty-five others said that they were guilty as well. Their dismissal led to the creation of the United African Methodist Church in Nigeria. See J. B. Webster, *The African Church among the Yoruba* (Oxford: Clarendon Press, 1964), 89–90.

116. Gerald G. Brown, *Christian Response to Change in East African Traditional Societies* (London: Woodbrooke College, 1973), 37.

117. Isiche, *Christianity in Africa*, 257.

118. Ibid.

119. de Wolf, *Differentiation and Integration*, 82–83.

120. David Throup, "The Decline of Political Debate in Kenya: Minister of Labor Okondo Threatens Bishop Muge," in *Religion & Politics in East Africa*, eds. Holger Bernt Hansen and Michael Twaddle (Nairobi: E.A.E.P, 1995), 169–70.

121. David Throup, "The Politics of Church-State Conflict in Kenya 1978-1990," in *Religion and Politics*, eds. Holger Bernt Hansen and Michael Twaddle, *Religion and Politics in East Africa* (Nairobi: E.A.E.P, 1995), 170.

122. Iklé, *How Nations Negotiate*, 72.

123. Ibid.

124. Angelique Haugerud, *The Culture of Politics in Modern Kenya* (Cambridge: Cambridge University Press, 1997),76. As Chaim Perelman put it, "To make his discourse effective, a speaker must adapt to his audience. What constitutes this adaptation, which is a specific requisite for argumentation? It amounts essentially to this: the speaker can choose as his points of departure only the theses accepted by those he addresses. In fact, the aim of the argument is not, like demonstration, to prove the truth of the conclusion from premises, but to transfer to the conclusion the adherence accorded to the premises." See Chaim Perelman, *The Realm of Rhetoric*, trans., W. Kluback (Notre Dame: University of Notre Dame Press, 1982), 21.

125. On the other hand, in the early 1990s, when there was more civil disorder apparent in Kenya than in Uganda, Ugandans were citing Kenya as an example of the type of politics to be avoided.

126. Weekly Review, "Tough Talking: President Moi Hits out at Critics of KANU," *Weekly Review* (Nairobi), May 18, 1990.

127. Daily Nation, "Multiparty System Not for Africa–Moi," *Daily Nation* (Nairobi), March 24, 1990, and "Tough Talking."

128. See October 1991 issue of *Nairobi Law Monthly*, and 1992 Parliamentary report on the ethnic clashes.

129. Haugerud, *Culture of Politics in Modern Kenya*, 77.

130. Iklé, *How Nations Negotiate*, 64.

131. Ibid.

132. Iklé believes that whether your opponent believes you to be bluffing (or to have a tendency to bluff) is one of the most important factors in a bargaining reputation. Bluffing may enable one to know and understand the kind of party one may be dealing with before any action is taken. See Iklé, *How Nations Negotiate*, 77–78.

133. Ludwig von Hohnel, *Discovery of Lakes Rudolf and Stefanie: A Narrative of Count Samuel Teleki's Exploring and Hunting Expeditions in Eastern Equatorial Africa*. Nancy Bell, trans., two volumes (London: Frank Cass, 1968 [1984]), 310.

134. The lines quoted are from a political party rally Haugerud attended in the rural Embu District, just six months after the death of the country's first president, Jomo Kenyatta, and a few months before national elections were held. See

Haugerud, *Culture of Politics in Modern Kenya*, 1. Shortly after Moi became president, he stated that the principle of *nyayo* (footsteps), a philosophy of peace, love, and unity, would lead the country on.

135. The widely used Swahili term for development is *maendeleo*, derived from *enda*, which includes a range of meanings under the general idea of motion, such as moving forward, progressing, continuing, or advancing.

136. The talk was emphatic and vigorous. Though clubs were absent, implied warnings were not. The speaker's ulterior meaning was that people were being warned to support the president's new regime, or they would be left out of its beneficence.

137. The crowds who cheered the regime and chanted official slogans could be out to entertain themselves or to flatter their leaders. In that respect, public meetings in Bukusuland are a perilous mix of ostensible respect and jocular disregard; people realize that lines spoken may not be lines lived.

138. Iklé, *How Nations Negotiate*, 66.

139. Ibid. Making a clear statement of commitment makes it more likely that an action will be carried out, but it does not make such a result certain, Iklé notes. Something may happen tomorrow that would cancel the commitment of today.

140. Iklé, *How Nations Negotiate*, 71.

141. Ibid.

142. Ibid.

143. Ibid, 68.

144. Ibid.

145. Ali A. Mazrui, *The Africans: A Triple Heritage* (Boston: Little Brown and Company, 1986), 232.

146. Ibid, .

147. Iklé, *How Nations Negotiate*, 72.

148. James F. Byrnes, *Speaking Frankly* (New York: Harper, 1947), 152–54.

149. Iklé, *How Nations Negotiate*, 72.

150. Ibid, 201. Iklé points out, "A common way of demonstrating one's commitment is to argue that domestic forces would oppose a change in one's position."

151. Richard Werbner, *Memory and the Postcolony* (London: Zed Books, 1997), 144–45.

152. The central issue that followed was to determine which law applied to the case. In the court, this was treated as a potential conflict of laws. As in all ex-colonial countries, the sources of law in Kenya are plural. There is statutory law (internal and imported); English common law; African customary law; and in appropriate instances, Islamic law. The court nevertheless found that there

were indications in the evidence that S. M. Otieno had abandoned neither his ethnic community nor its customary law, since he continued to belong to a clan association, attended some of the funerals of kinsmen, sent money to his brothers' widows, made claims to land left by his father, and paid bride wealth for his son's wife. The court, emphasizing these familial connections, simply chose to disregard all the ways in which Otieno could be said to have separated himself from Luo customs in his sophisticated urban life. The court of appeal upheld the reconstituted high court's judgment in favor of the majority Luo community and declared the permanence of ethnic identity. At present there is no way in which the African citizen of Kenya can divest himself of the association with the ethnic group of his father, if those customs are patrilineal. It is thus clear that Mr. Otieno, having been born and bred a Luo, remained a member of the Luo community and subject to the customary law of the Luo people. See Werbner, *Memory and the Postcolony*, 144–45.

153. Iklé, *How Nations Negotiate*, 3–4. See also Brett, *Negotiating Globally*, 2. When you ask people all over the world what comes to mind when you say negotiation, most describe some sort of market in which two people exchange a series of offers. Implicit in their answer is the assumption that a deal is in the making, that two parties are speaking directly (although the medium may be electronic), and that they are bargaining to divide a fixed pie of resources. Yet negotiations are not limited to direct deal making over fixed resources. In all cultures, people negotiate to resolve disputes and to make decisions in teams. When negotiators reach agreement, resources are always distributed, but the amount of resources available for distribution is not necessarily fixed. Fundamental to negotiation are the circumstances in which people negotiate and the type of agreements they reach.

154. Ibid, 2.

155. Ibid, 87–120.

156. Ibid, 87.

157. Ibid, 15.

158. Ibid.

159. Ibid, 87.

160. Ahmed, *Living Islam*, 14–15.

161. Iklé, *How Nations Negotiate*, 7.

162. de Wolf, *Differentiation and Integration*, 33.

163. Ibid.

164. Iklé, *How Nations Negotiate*, 87.

165. Abu al-'ala 'Afifi, editor, *Mishkat al-anwar*, (Cairo: Dar al-Qawmiya lil-Tab'a wa al-Nashr, 1964), 26:17.

166. Iklé, *How Nations Negotiate*, 88.

167. Ibid, 87.

168. After circumcision, it is the role of the circumciser to administer disinfectant medicine to the circumcised boys and to give them permission to eat. A day or two after circumcision, the circumciser returns for a visit to make sure that no piece of foreskin remained. If there is a remnant, he will cut it off. He then leaves the candidates without seeing them again. See Wagner, *The Bantu*, 355.

169. Iklé, *How Nations Negotiate*, 92. A Bukusu saying goes, *omurumwa sekapangwa likuma tawe*, meaning, "Never take a stick and break the messenger's head." This is similar to the Western phrase, "Don't kill the messenger because of the message."

170. Ibid.

171. James Ngugi wa Thiong'o, *A Grain of Wheat* (Nairobi: Heinemann, 1967), 10. In another version, the Swahili saying goes, *Mtumi wa kunga haambiwi maana*. This translates as, "The carrier of a secret message is not told its meaning; he is only a messenger—he is innocent."

172. Iklé, *How Nations Negotiate*, 94.

173. The Kaaba is a cube-shaped building in the middle of the courtyard of the Grand Mosque in Mecca. It is believed to be the first monument erected to a monotheistic deity and is the holiest of shrines for Muslims. The Plains of Arafat near the Mount of Mercy, where Prophet Muhammad delivered his last sermon, is a place where the pilgrim "stands" in reverent devotion from about noon to sunset. Prayers said at this time at Arafat are believed to be particularly efficacious. Muhammad said of them, "The best of the prayers is the prayer of the day of Arafat." See Zepp, *Muslim Primer*, 128–29.

174. Iklé, *How Nations Negotiate*, 95.

175. Ibid, 87.

176. In Swahili, "Usikaange mbuyu ukawaachia wenye meno watafune."

177. In Swahili, "Yaliyopita si ndwele, tugange yaliyomo na yajayo."

178. In Swahili, "Usisahau ubaharia kwa sababu ya unahodha."

179. In Swahili, "Usicheze na simba, ukamtia mkono kinywani."

180. Harold George Nicolson, *Diplomacy* (San Francisco: Jossey-Bass, 1995), 116.

181. Iklé, *How Nations Negotiate*, 114.

182. Nordstrom, *Different Kind of War Story*, 8.

183. Iklé, *How Nations Negotiate*, 102.

184. Ibid., 103.

185. Ibid.

186. Ibid, 255.

187. A concession may be defined as a revision of a negotiating position so that it will come closer to the opponent's wishes; a compromise may be classed as a way of reaching agreement through concession by both sides. Frequently, the point at which the two revised negotiating positions coincide, rather than the process of reaching this point, is referred to as "the compromise." See Iklé, *How Nations Negotiate*, 104.

188. Iklé, *How Nations Negotiate*, 105.

189. Khan, *Gardens*, 239, 1,372.

190. Iklé, *How Nations Negotiate*, 119. There are certain essential terms that are important to Islam that at times are misunderstood and judged as lies by Bukusu Christians. It is useful to acquaint ourselves with them. This is one such concept.

191. Ibid, 120.

192. Ibid, 191.

193. Angelo M. Codevilla, "Tools of Statecraft: Diplomacy and War," *Foreign Policy Research Institute*, (FPRI, 2008), http://www.fpri.org/footnotes/1301.200801. codevilla.statecraftdiplomacywar.html.

194. Ibid, 204.

195. Ibid, 206.

196. William Ury, *Getting to Peace* (New York: Viking, 1999), viii.

197. Roger Fisher and William Ury, *Getting to Yes: Negotiating Agreement without Giving In* (New York: Penguin Books, 1991), iii.

198. From the back cover of *Getting to Peace*.

199. Ury, *Getting to Peace*, ix.

200. The animals that the Bukusu and the Bushmen used to hunt included various kinds of antelopes, such as the eland, bushbuck, and impala.

201. Ury, *Getting to Peace*, xv.

202. Ibid.

203. This interdependence becomes obvious when one considers how a terrorist attack in the United States immediately affected the airlines, restaurants, and convention and tourism industries worldwide, which in turn affected the stock market, construction industry, product development, and so on. Globalization is almost synonymous with interdependence, and is a fact of modern life in Bukusuland as well as in the United States. In rural Bukusu villages, as well as in downtown Nairobi, one sees Nike shoes, Nokia cell phones, Japanese Toyotas, German BMWs, and French Peugeots. These are manifestations of the world as global village, even in Bukusuland.

204. Ury, *Getting to Peace*, 98–100.

205. Ibid, xvi.

206. Mbiti, *African Religions and Philosophy*, 3.
207. William Ury, *Getting Past No: Negotiating Your Way from Confrontation to Cooperation* (New York: Bantam Books, 1991, 1993), 3–5.
208. Ibid, 5.
209. Ibid, 4.
210. Ury, *Getting to Peace*, xix.
211. Ibid, xviii.
212. Ibid.
213. Ury, *Getting to Peace*, 3.
214. Ibid, ix.
215. Ibid, xviii.
216. Ibid, xix.
217. Ibid, 7.
218. An example of the third side, according to Ury, is the analogy of the body's immune system. He writes, "When a cell is attacked by a virus, it sends out a chemical alarm awakening the dendrite cells that lie dormant in every tissue of the body. The dendrite cells, in return, mobilize the T-cells, which come to the rescue. If the T-cells correspond roughly to the police and the peacekeepers of the world, the dendrite cells correspond to the surrounding community that must be aroused in order to stop the destructive conflict. The third side thus serves as a kind of *social immune system* preventing the spread of the virus of violence" (Ibid, 7).
219. Ibid.
220. Ibid.
221. Ibid, 4.
222. Ibid.
223. Ibid, 15.
224. Ibid, 4.
225. Ibid.
226. Ibid.
227. Ibid, 5.
228. Ibid.
229. Ibid, 6.
230. In the *siluukhi* ceremony, the convicted man is required to produce a cow, which is slaughtered in the presence of the neighbors, who act as witnesses. Then all the people attending share the meat, eating it together as a community united. The couple is then required to sleep together inside the fresh skin in front of everybody as a sign of humiliation and shame, so they will not act amorously again. In terms of Ury's concept of the third side in negotiation,

the young man survived death, the elders served as a third sider or container, and community harmony was reinforced. The parties were taught a lesson and the community avoided a conflict that might otherwise have led to rising antagonism or separation.

231. Ury, *Getting to Peace*, 23.
232. Ibid, 24.
233. Ibid, 113. A similar Swahili saying goes, "*Uzipoziba ufa utajenga ukuta*," which means, "If you do not fill up a crack, you will have to build a wall."
234. Using the analogy of a house, Ury describes the concepts of containment, resolution, and prevention: "Containment may be more urgent, like building a good roof to protect against the elements; resolving may be more apparent, like erecting the house itself; but preventing, though less visible, is more fundamental, like pouring the foundation on which both the house and roof rest" (Ibid). Prevention will obviate many would-be conflicts.
235. Ury, *Getting to Peace*, 139.
236. Ibid, 114.
237. Ibid.
238. Ibid.
239. Ibid, 115.
240. Selfishness embarrasses and shocks the Bushmen. They say, "Lions could do that, but not human beings" (Ibid, 115).
241. A man of average wealth would be expected to kill an animal of splitting at least four to six times in the course of his life. This usually begins when one is between the age of thirty-five and forty, which is the age in which a person is said to have reached the full status of manhood. Wagner, The *Bantu of Western Kenya*, 106.
242. This is a symbol of community solidarity and good relationship. The maintenance of good order is stressed during this moment of "blood pact."
243. In the case of family distribution, the meat is shared mainly among family members, with a few exceptions for outsiders. Everyone has his or her own section. The edible parts of the slaughtered animal go to the following people:
>   front legs, to the eldest wife or oldest son
>   shoulder, second wife
>   buttock, young wife or youngest son
>   back, divided up among the different wives
>   tail, herd boy
>   skin, eldest brother
>   udder, sister's son
>   heart, grandson
>   liver, wives

kidneys, sister or daughter

spleen, herd boy or the one who shuts the gate of the cattle *kraal*

lungs, grandson or old women

big stomach, butcher

small stomach, joking relative (who takes it by force)

entrails, diviner

ribs, eldest brother

diaphragm, sister's son

aitchbone, herd boys

esophagus, one half goes to the skinner, and the other half is kept by the owner

tongue, owner

chest, sister's son, mother's brother

clod, sisters

trachea, skinner or herd boy.

See Wagner, The *Bantu of Western Kenya*, 48.

244. Ibid, 106. "The slaughtering of the animal of splitting is not primarily a ritual killing," one scholar of Bukusu culture points out. Rather, "Its professed purpose is the distribution of meat among relatives and not the placating of invocation of the ancestral spirits." This does not mean, however, that the spirits are ignored. Before the first animal is slaughtered, a clan elder especially chosen by the donor dips a switch of raffia palm into a gourd of milk and, while sprinkling and stroking the cow's back, he addresses the spirits in the following words:

Spirits, you may walk quickly,

you may come and make your clan happy;

if the other spirits are laughing at you

you may pooh-pooh (for) they are poor

you may come, you may lick your blood it is here

Timbo, Songwa, Nandoli, Murembe,

you may walk quickly

your cow is here,

you may make in the belly.

245. Community within Bukusu culture is comprised of the living, "the living dead," and the yet to be born.

246. Ury, *Getting to Peace*, 115.

247. Ibid.

248. Ibid.

249. Ibid. Among the *Maanja* people of the Central African Republic, the totem for the chief is the rabbit because this unobtrusive animal has "large ears." As

is common in some parts of Africa, the chief is considered to be very close to God, to the ancestors, and to the protective spirits of the community. He does not replace the ancestors, but along with other elders, he makes them present (represents them) in his person and behavior. Like the Bushmen, the Maanja consider listening the most dominant characteristic of the chief. His "large ears" bring him closer to God, ancestors, and divinities, and closer to the conversations taking place in the community. He has the last word because he speaks after having assimilated and digested the words of the community. He is the guardian of the dynamic, life-giving word that creates and recreates the community. "Word means truthfulness, fairness, honesty, communication." See Elochkwu E. Uzukwu, *A Listening Church: Autonomy and Communion in African Churches* (Maryknoll, New York: Orbis Books, 1996), 127.

250. Ury, *Getting to Peace*, 116.

251. Ibid. The *Kung* Bushman quoted in Ury described the gift-giving custom to Anthropologist Richard Lee.

252. Personal relationships and personally centered values as they relate to community or family and close circles of friends are present in many African proverbs and sayings. For example: "Families take care of their own" (Oromo of Kenya). "A parent beats the child with a half-closed hand in order not to hurt the child too much" (Baganda of Uganda). "A letter is half as good as seeing each other" (Bukusu). "It is through people that we are people" (Swazi of Swaziland). "A person is a person because of neighbors" (Tumbuka of Malawi). "Mountains never meet but people do" (Kamba of Kenya).

253. Ury, *Getting Past No*, 68.

254. Ibid, 118. Hence, the role of the provider is to share, to protect, to respect, and to free.

255. Ibid.

256. Borrowing salt is such a typical expression of neighborliness that it is metaphorically used in that sense. A man contemplating marrying a second wife would say, "Let me marry another wife; they may beg salt from one another," meaning that his wife is longing for company.

257. A guest who imposes upon the hospitality of other people without reciprocating it is an *omususumi*, meaning a person who is lazy, doesn't work, and is like a leech looking for food in other people's houses.

258. Ury, *Getting to Peace*, 124.

259. Ibid, 131.

260. Ibid, 125.

261. Ibid.

262. Ibid, 127.

263. Khan, *Gardens*, 16.

264. Qu'ran 57:29.

265. Fazlur Rahman, *Islam* (Chicago: University of Chicago Press, 1979), 165.

266. These texts illustrate Islamic scholar John Hick's comment on covenantal relationships: "Religious pluralism implies that those who are on the other great ways of salvation are no less God's chosen people, although with different vocations." Other Qur'anic texts display an even wider openness to other monotheistic faiths. One of them declares, "Believers (Muslims), Jews, and Christians—whoever believes in God and the Last Day and does what is right will be rewarded by their Lord; they have nothing to fear." Another verse is even more inclusive: "All who commit themselves to God and do well shall be rewarded by their Lord." Commenting on this text of salvation, Muhammad Asad, an Islamic scholar, concludes, "Salvation is open to everyone who consciously realizes the oneness of God, surrenders himself to His Will, and by living righteously, gives practical effect to the spiritual attitude." See Muhammad Asad, *The Message of the Qur'an* (London: Brill, 1980), 24.

267. Amos 3:2.

268. Amos 9:7.

269. Psalm 87:5.

270. William E. Phipps, *Muhammad and Jesus* (New York: The Continuum Publishing House, 1996), 238. Increasingly popular among students of world religions is an approach that values tolerance of other faiths and commitment to their own faith. Pluralists hold to one faith while entering into dialogue with those adhering to the other faiths. William Phipps, professor of philosophy and religion at Davis and Elkins College, offers, "Meaningful dialogue involves both the honest facing of basic differences and a common searching for a truth that no group completely possesses. The goal of pluralism is not to arrive at a uniform super religion, but to improve the faith of the participants by understanding the commitments of others and sometimes adapting beneficent values proven effective elsewhere."

271. Ury, *Getting Past No*, 109.

272. Ury, *Getting to Peace*, 135.

273. Ibid, 137.

274. Ibid, 136

275. Ibid.

276. Ibid, 139.

277. Ibid, 141.

278. This same message is found in the gospels when John says, "Let him who is without sin cast the first stone" (John 8:7). This same idea is expressed in the

common American colloquialism, "People who live in glass houses shouldn't throw stones."

279. *Encyclopedia of Religion* (New York: Macmillian Publishing Company, 1987), 366.

280. (Exodus 21:23–25); (Leviticus 24:19, 20); (Deuteronomy 19:21); (Proverbs 24:29).

281. Kenneth Cloke, *Mediating Dangerously: The Frontiers of Conflict Resolution* (San Francisco: Jossey-Bass Publishers, 2001), 77.

282. See also (Lamentations 3:30), "Let him give his cheek to the smiter, let him be filled with reproach," and (Proverbs 24:29), "Do not say, I will do to him as he has done to me."

283. In the Qur'an, the law of the *talion* is similar to that found in the Hebrew Scriptures and the Code of Hammurabi. This law is further clarified in the Qur'an when it is explained that for intentional homicide, the next of kin has the right to equal retaliation. Revenge is limited to killing a free man for a free man killed, a slave for a slave, and a woman for a woman. In writing to the people in Yemen, the Prophet Muhammad also permitted that a man be killed in retaliation for murdering a woman. See Mishkat 15:2.

284. The Qur'an does not abolish blood revenge, but it provides some alternative penalties for it. For example, compensation can be paid for unintentional homicide. "Good and evil are not alike. Repel evil with that which is best and, lo, he between whom and thyself was enmity is as though he were a warm friend. But none attains to this save those who are granted a large share of good" (Qur'an 41:35–36).

285. These verses reflect a set pattern called the "Principles of Holy War." Human action will be met by a corresponding action of God at the final judgment.

286. Ury, *Getting to Peace*, 143.

287. Ibid, 146.

288. In the words of Carolyn Nordstrom, associate professor of anthropology at Notre Dame University, the mediator might approach the parties in these words: "We all know how you feel, we all sympathize. But taking revenge, killing someone else, that will just continue this war, it will certainly lead to more killing and violence and hatred. And then they will take revenge, and you may lose yet another loved one in the future. Violence would continue to define their lives. To truly defeat someone is not to act with the opponent's rules, but to institute another set of rules altogether." See Nordstrom, *Different Kind of War Story*, 232–33.

289. Ury, *Getting to Peace*, 146.

290. Each side will require a great deal of reassurance and encouragement, claims Ury, particularly from their peers, so as not to feel as though outsiders (in this case the mediator) are meddling in what they regard as their internal affairs.

291. Ury, *Getting to Peace*, 146.

292. Ibid, 149.

293. Ibid, 154.

294. Ibid.

295. Ibid.

296. Ibid, 169.

297. Ibid, 155.

298. Ibid, 162.

299. James S. Hewett, ed. *Illustrations Unlimited* (Wheaton, Illinois: Tyndale House Publishers, 1998), 38–39.

300. Ury, *Getting to Peace*, 169.

301. Ibid.

302. Ibid, 170.

303. Adelaide B. Vawter, *The Inner Fabric of My Life* (Berkeley, California: Tulip Publishing, 1990), 37.

304. Ury, 171.

305. Ibid.

306. Ibid.

307. Ibid, 173.

308. Ibid.

309. Ibid, 175.

310. Ibid.

311. Ibid, 177.

312. Ibid.

313. Ibid.

314. Ibid, 184.

315. Ibid, 186.

316. Ibid.

317. Ibid, 185.

PART IV

TRADITIONAL PATTERNS OF COMMUNICATION AND DIALOGUE IN BUKUSULAND

CHAPTER 13

•◆•

THE BUKUSU FAMILY

This section of the study presents traditional patterns of communication and dialogue experienced in Bukusu life, especially as they relate to cultural interaction and conflict resolution. In the strict sense, the Bukusu "household" is the smallest unit of the family; it consists of the children, parents, and grandparents. It is what the Babukusu worldview would call "the family at night," for it is generally at night that the household is so narrowly defined. At night, parents are with their children in the same house; they discuss private affairs of their household and educate their children in matters pertaining to domestic relationships. If a man has more than one wife, he has several households, since each wife will usually have her own house erected within the homestead property (an enclosed compound).

The family in a Bukusu homestead has a much wider circle of members than the word suggests in Europe or America. In traditional Bukusu society, the family includes children, parents, grandparents, aunts, uncles, brothers, sisters (all of whom may have children of their own), and other relatives, often living in huts or homes within the same compound.

The central courtyard of the homestead is the main place of work and worship. This is where much of the homestead's food is prepared and eaten, as the woman's hearth is located there. It is also there that the ancestors' shrines in the form of round stones are cemented into the base of a wall close to the hearth. These stones periodically are splashed with chicken blood and feathers, the remains of sacrificial requests for protection of the home and its people.

In the Bukusu way, the area occupied by two or more homesteads is called a village. It comprises houses, gardens, fields, cattle sheds, granaries, courtyards, threshing grounds, a men's outdoor fireplace, the children's playground, and family shrines. These all constitute common grounds of cultural interaction and, thus, provide opportunities for dialogue and human relationships. The social relationships that evolve in village life have an effect on the entire community, as they will be right relationships.

A child is that link of right relationship both actually and symbolically between the paternal and maternal clan families. Caring for children is, for most Bukusu women, a hard, taxing part of their lives. Generally, a woman gives birth in the house within the husband's homestead. She is attended to by a number of other women from the homestead and the neighborhood. Men, including the father of the child, are not allowed in the birthplace.

When speaking of the newborn, Bukusu people say that a "stranger" has arrived. The baby is a stranger because its prior history in the unseen world, called *kungumwiyikha*, is unknown. Coming from a place where social practices and conventions are believed to have been different, it will have to learn the habits of its parents and to develop everyday patterns that constitute a relationship of familiarity. The environment turns out to be a training ground for skills and techniques to be used later. Far from being considered a *tabula rasa*, the Bukusu newborn is thought of as already having a history, a personality, desires, and relationships beyond. It is up to the parents and the community to interpret this history as evidenced by the child and to make accommodations for it.

The Importance of the Naming Ceremony

The occasion of naming a child is one of rejoicing, feasting, and dancing. The ceremony brings together the oldest and the youngest in the community and everyone in between. These encounters across the years bear testament to the continuity of a clan's life and reaffirm its importance. The naming ceremony is also a profoundly religious event. The mission of the divinity, the sense of the ancestors' direct involvement, the prayers and blessings, are all part of a communal religious experience in which the child serves as the focus.

The naming ceremony (and subsequent name-giving events) are explained in detail here to show that dialogue between the living community and that of the living dead (the recently dead whose spirits remain present and active within the community) is preserved and strengthened. This relationship between the newborn child and the spirits of the living dead represent one way in which Bukusu people maintain a continuous dialogue with ancestors in an attempt to avoid conflicts between them. To a Westerner, being given a name may seem like a minimal act—a name is just a label—but to a Bukusu, a name is a proactive way to insert the child into the community and to help the child avoid later conflicts with spirits from the realm of the *sasa*. These spirits are believed to bring conflict to the home, and a name can appease the spirits of the living dead, transforming them into allies instead of annoyances. Any approach to conflict prevention for the Bukusu needs to include strategies that address the relationship of the living to the living dead. These strategies, and the ones that follow, all demonstrate how the Bukusu society is purposefully designed to facilitate dialogue, even at an early age.

Naming is a rite and action of protection and of defense. Intentionally ugly names are sought for children to shelter them from hostile spirits. In the same way, naming people after events, seasons, locations, and other things preserves the dialogue or connection between the rest of creation and humanity. It is also a reminder that human life and the life of nature are intertwined and inseparably rightly related.

A week after the birth of a child, the women of the village assemble to shave the baby's head and to name it. A number of considerations influence the choice of the name to be given, such as whether the baby was born in the morning, evening, or night and on which day of the week. Special circumstances related to the baby, its family, or its clan may be used in selecting its name, as well as elements such as whether the child is the firstborn and whether male or female.

In the path of life, every Bukusu individual is given at least three different types of names—a childhood name, an adolescent name, and an ancestral name. Each child is given a name associated with some circumstance of his or her birth—the place where the child was born (on the veranda, in the field, on a visit), the time of birth (as the cows were returning home, just before daybreak), a special event (during circumcision, when a plane flew overhead), some special aspect of the birth (born before full term, breech birth, the mother went to sleep after delivering), or some ordinal position of the child (a twin, following a twin, following a series of children who died). Other names may refer to the particular characteristics of the season or to a conspicuous event that occurred during the mother's pregnancy or delivery. Naming children after important events enables people to trace the time of the year in which any child was born, especially in those days when people did not read or write or follow a calendar.

Bukusu boys' names frequently take the prefix *wa*, and girls' names the prefix *na*. A child who was born during heavy rain might be named *Wafula* if a boy and *Nafula* if a girl. A boy born during harvesting season might be named *Wekesa*, and a girl *Nekesa*.[1] A child may also receive two informal names from the mother—for example, *Wanyama* and *Khaoya*. Wanyama suggests that the child was born at the time when there was plenty of meat in the house, and Khaoya means that the child was born at the time of a rinderpest epidemic.

A child born to Bukusu Muslim parents during a time of trouble might be given the name *Taabu*, meaning "trouble." Islam has been so Africanized that, in many areas, Islam has long ceased to be regarded as anything other than an African religion. Naturally, children by Muslim parents are given Arabic names associated with the Muslim religion. For example, *Yahya* means God's gift, *Tahir* means pure or clean, *Sadiki* means faithful, and *Bilal* refers to the first black convert to Islam. Among Bukusu Muslims and Christians, traditional Bukusu nicknames have been replaced by either Qur'anic or Biblical names, which have been accepted wholeheartedly by traditional believers. These names offer an example of a new cultural element that fits well into a traditional life pattern.

The second name is that given at adolescence. It is a nickname given informally by the teenager's peers. A young man is given his adolescent name by his age-mates after circumcision at age ten to eleven. A young girl receives her second name from the age-mates with whom she sleeps in a house when she reaches the age of puberty. This name is usually socially rough and to the point. Nicknames always describe the individual's perceived character or physical features and mannerisms at that age. Nicknames sometimes take over childhood names in popular usage, lasting through the people's lives.

The nickname influences community relationships, because it most often reflects shortcomings in behavior, and the individual is expected to work hard to change these weaknesses. If the person changes the behavior that inspired the name, people will drop it from common usage in recognition. If the person does not change, the name will persist and will inhibit or exclude the person from succeeding in the community and from being asked to mediate in conflict situations.

A few people are given nicknames that praise them for the good they do. In that case, the name reinforces the young person's potential for group leadership and for acting as a facilitator in helping to avoid or resolve conflict.

The most significant name a person receives is the ancestral name, although it is rarely used. The name is chosen from a person's ancestor, a long-dead spirit from the *zamani*, who is considered to be a good spirit. This ancestor becomes the person's spirit guide. When a person is in conflict, he or she will consult the ancestral spirit by approaching a soothsayer who will pass on the messages and intentions of that ancestor for the person, including suggestions for how to help resolve the conflict. In the world of the Bukusu, the relationship to the ancestral spirits is an essential factor in understanding potential strategies for establishing dialogue and resolving conflicts within the communities.

The ancestral name is ceremonially conferred upon the child, and is a necessary condition for acquiring the status of adulthood—although not necessary for the child's growth or well-being. The time for bestowing the ancestral name depends upon the child's physical condition. If the child grows up normally, without health and behavioral problems, the ancestral name is given to the boy after circumcision rites and to a girl when she is about to be married. However, if the child cries a great deal and refuses to suckle or if the child becomes very ill, the child is given the ancestral name earlier than usual. Should it be evident that the child is going to die, no ancestral name will be bestowed upon the child.

The choice of the name has to be carefully considered; the bestowal of an ancestral name upon a child should not be rushed. To reach a decision about an ancestral name, the child's father or maternal uncle consults a diviner, who finds the right name. A male person can only be named after a male ancestor, and a female after a female ancestor. According to Bukusu beliefs, men can suffer harm from and enjoy the protection of male spirits only, and women experience the protection of female spirits. Another general rule is that a child cannot be named after the spirit of a person who died having not been married or who, though married, died without leaving a child.[2] Furthermore, the number of spirits who are deemed to have a potential influence over the child, and whose names must therefore be considered, is restricted to the clans of the eight great-grandparents of the child.

The qualities of character possessed by the spirits while they were physically living are not taken into consideration when the ancestral name is being chosen. Even the names of wrongdoers who were killed by lynching or hanging might be given to the children to save them from frequent visitations by the spirits through dreams. The fact that an individual, during his or her physical lifetime, had the reputation of being a witch or a sorcerer does not stop the diviner from suggesting that name. The only ancestral names that are excluded from the choice are those of individuals who, during their lifetime, suffered from leprosy or who died from being struck by lightning. Such people are buried in swampy earth near a stream, where their spirits vanish quickly and have no more contact with the living. They cannot return to trouble the people. By interviewing the father or the maternal uncle of the child, the diviner will find out which of the spirits is likely to trouble the child. The diviner does not mention the name of a particular spirit but presents the clients with ambiguous clues, the meaning of which can be reached only by the clients, so as to respect their own ideas as to what would be the most fitting name for the child.

Should it happen that an ill child does not recover, even after the ancestral naming, it is generally believed that the spirit refused to have the child named after it or that several spirits were fighting to have the child named after them. The balancing ritual is repeated, and the child may be renamed. If the child still does not get well, the father and the uncle consult another diviner, who will suggest the name of another spirit. The diviner may discover that the illness was caused by disease, or by spirits who demand the slaughter of a cow. The parents will then kill the proper animal and put the meat out on the stick near the family ancestral shrine. At times, this process can go on for a very long time before the right ancestral name for the child is found. The acceptance of the ancestral name is realized when, at the mention of the name, the child sneezes and eventually stops crying.[3]

Once the spirit has accepted the responsibility of being a child's guardian (as indicated by the sneeze) and the child has recovered, there is no more fear of that spirit. The Bukusu people hold that a spirit never harms its namesake. If the child feels sick once again, the illness will not be attributed to the spirit of the ancestor from whom the child received the name but to a sorcerer or another spirit who is jealous as a result of the child's not having been named after him or her.

A child's ancestral name serves as a bridge between the paternal and the maternal clans. Through this type of bonding, the child is introduced to the spiritual world. It is believed that the desire of the ancestors to ensure their own immortality and the continuity of their line leads to the protection of their namesake child. The ancestors are symbolically alive in the child. Kinship continues; "it cannot die," the Bukusu people say, when contrasting kinship with other forms of relationship. Kinship and family traditions continue for endless generations with the same strength and with the same power over children they have had since time unknown.

The three names a child is given—the birth name, the nickname, and the ancestral name—all influence the way in which that person is perceived and the ways in which that person responds to interaction with others, especially in times of tension and conflict.

Life Lessons of a Bukusu Child

As a child grows up, many new developments take place between the child and the mother. The mother stops suckling the child when she realizes that she is pregnant again. When another child starts forming in the womb, as its older brother or sister is still at the breast, there is often jealousy, and it is the custom to send the older child away to live with relatives.

If a child keeps crying persistently after having been weaned, the mother puts hot pepper or tobacco juice on her nipples to discourage the child's desire to suckle. If this does not work, the child is sent to stay with its maternal grandmother, who then suckles the child until he or she gets tired of suckling the grandmother's dry breasts. The grandmother always does her best, but adult food is not as good as the mother's milk; in that way, the child suffers. These conditions reveal the way in which Bukusu parents relate to their children. A strong bond related to the traditional patterns of communication and dialogue is present between the children and their family elders.

In the village, children largely are left to their own devices. They play with toys and model animals and birds using clay—in a simple Bukusu expression, they "shape each other," with nature as their playground. They play games, such as hide-and-seek. They make diverse toys—hoops and poles, jackstones (a game in which you toss a rock upward rather than bouncing a ball), push toys with wheels made from plantain trunks, and a wheelbarrow-like wagon in which they push each other. The boys fabricate hats out of leaves and wear them for days. Anthills provide roller coasters for boys and girls. From the top of an anthill, children slide down, seated on pieces of banana trunk.

Traditionally, Bukusu children learn mainly through imitation and observation. Just as children around the world mimic their elders, Bukusu children enjoy their own versions of adult institutions. For example, boys imitate the village men's society, building small-scale replicas of the men's recreation houses in the bush outside the villages.

Children are expected to learn through imitation and emulation, not by asking questions. The number and the nature of questions that children in Europe or America expectantly ask their parents would stun a

Bukusu child. Among the Bukusu people, questions from children are not encouraged. Parents give information to their children as they consider it necessary. Here dialogue becomes the lesson simply by default. Recall the wise saying: "Sometimes silence speaks louder than words."

Between ages five and six, a child is gently guided by parents and relatives to leave the parental house at night and start sleeping in the house of a nearby grandparent or elderly relative of the same sex. Even before the child starts to go to his or her grandparents' house to sleep, the grandparents have become the focus of the child's daytime visits. After that, the child begins to establish even wider relationships beyond his or her parents, and the grandparents typically take a dominant role in the informal instruction of the child. Children are then taught everyday technical skills such as planting, herding, or grinding millet on stones. They are also taught the skills of telling stories, myths, riddles, sayings, and proverbs of their cultures and how to trace their family and clan genealogies. As a result, grandchildren come to view their grandparents not only as very kind and pleasant people, but also as teachers of clan wisdom and, above all, as the people they can depend on to help in moments of trouble and pain. This bond between grandparents and grandchildren is part of learning to dialogue.

Grandparents are usually free to enjoy their grandchildren without the stress of maintaining them. Grandparents provide a link to the past and can teach children about family traditions and history. Their love and attention play an important part in building children's self-confidence. According to psychologists, children who grow up enjoying a strong relationship with their grandparents feel more emotionally secure than children without this bond. They also have healthier attitudes about their own aging and older people. The relationship between children and their grandparents develops naturally when they live near each other. The relationship of the child and its grandparents is affectionate, almost to the point of overindulgence. Grandparents and grandchildren exchange a lot of jokes in a teasing manner. Their jokes are usually relationally toned, and expressions such as "my little wife" or "my little husband" are commonly used when talking to a grandchild of the opposite sex. The jokes and terms of endearment reflect the deep love that grandparents have for their grandchildren.

Children are trained at an early age to share in the duties of family life. Soon after they have learned to walk, boys and girls are taught to care for their younger siblings, run errands, and make themselves useful in various little ways. Between the ages of five and eight, boys become herd boys, looking after sheep, goats, and calves in the fields. This is also the time when boys learn to hunt for birds using slingshots and to gather wild honey, fruits, and mushrooms. For food, they drink milk straight from the udder of a cow while looking after the cattle. When they take the animals to the river, they learn to swim and to fish. It is the task of boys when they are young to learn how to plow the land with oxen. They are also responsible for scaring away birds and monkeys that want to eat the millet in the fields. They teach each other how to make bows and arrows and to look for areas where there is good grass for grazing and salt licks for animals to lick. These skills are essential for every rural Bukusu boy.

Similarly, at this age, girls assist their mothers in the daily work of carrying water from the spring; gathering firewood, mushrooms, wild roots, and vegetables; and above all, the weary task of grinding millet, or sorghum, for morning and evening meals. Girls are trained by their mothers. When a mother is away from home, she may leave a girl of five at home to do housework. She gives her a small pot to fetch water and tells her to sweep the house, bring firewood, collect vegetables, and look after the young children. A few years later, when the girl is six or seven, she will start to dig in the gardens. She will start to cook and make fire by the time she is eight. She is taught to do exactly as her mother does, so that when the mother goes anywhere, she will return home to find the work done. If the mother finds the work poorly done, she scolds her daughter. Mothers are concerned that their daughters learn proper skills of housekeeping so that their husbands will not beat them up for neglecting their duties and so that it will not be said that they failed to learn proper behavior from their mothers.

After early childhood, boys are much more involved with their fathers than with their mothers. A boy who spends much time at his mother's house is called "mother's tail" because he clings to her. A male child who remains at home with his mother is despised by his peers. At adolescence, the boy takes a step toward his eventual independence, moving out of his parents' house to build his own hut nearby or to share with other boys in that part of the compound. He can now freely entertain his friends, and his parents no longer closely restrict his comings and goings. It is at this point that the boy's obedience may become questionable and lead to open rebellion against the father. Boys may refuse to herd their fathers' cattle and escape to live in a friend's house or take the opportunity to visit their maternal uncles or grandparents. But frequently, a mother rises in defense of her son, seeking to protect his eventual rights to property, while the son sides with his mother if the father attacks her or if the father's favoring a co-wife threatens her position. This can be a very painful time for a boy.

A son who is on bad terms with his father may not inherit his father's wealth. In the same way, children of different co-wives sometimes receive from their father tremendously different levels of material support. The seeds of hostility between father and son are often sown early, and a boy's disobedience may well damage his later fortunes. In order that a son may be supported by his father through circumcision, he may wait until after the rite is complete to express outward hostilities or violence toward his father. If the boy were to lash out at his father prior to the rite of passage, he would not have support and, therefore, could not be circumcised with honor. Before circumcision, few demands are made on youths, who are allowed to wander freely to seek friendship with those of the same age.

Once circumcised, however, a son is obliged to go and assist his father, somewhat to the exclusion of the son's former peers. If the father refuses the son's assistance, the son simply remains his dependant, continuing to rely on the father's household food while being forced to live apart in his own hut. In such situations, the resentment of the son, together with awareness of his dishonorable position, makes violence a real possibility. The situation then becomes the interest of the clan; noticing the breakdown of normal tradition, the clan will intercede in ways to persuade the father to reconsider his decision, as it is hurtful to the community. It will come to some formal dialogue process if there is hesitancy on either the father's or the son's part. The community here becomes the collective third side that Ury discussed.

As for a girl, she continues to live in her mother's house until she marries. During this time, girls care for younger children in their mother's absence. At age eight, the girls help their mothers with housework and farming. By early adolescence, a girl is expected to cook and relieve her mother of a considerable part of the housework.

The lives of Bukusu children are shaped by customs, rituals, and taboos. These ways of life go unquestioned. Boys follow the ways laid out for them by their fathers, and girls lead lives similar to those of their mothers.

Social Life of Husband and Wife

According to the Bukusu people, marriage is a dynamic whole, the purpose of which is, among other things, to create an alliance, a gradual growing together of partners, families, and clans. That dynamism creates a bond and a communion between two families and their clans. For the marriage process to continue, all social or political animosities between the two sides must end. The order of the Babukusu worldview demands that balance and a sense of harmony be maintained if the marriage is to last. Rituals and ceremonies are intended to establish and solidify ties via harmony and mutual understanding. However, the marital relationship between husband and wife among the Bukusu people is not equally balanced. The husband enjoys superior status and expects total obedience from the wife. There are clear divisions of labor within the family. It is a rule that men cannot do what has been designed for women to do and vice versa. It is the wife's responsibility to sweep the house and the courtyard, to grind the corn or millet, to build the fire, to cook, and to clean out the cattle barn. She carries the water from the spring, takes care of the baby, buys the cooking pots, and gathers firewood. She gathers the salt (by burning the salt reeds and filtering the ashes), cleans the walls of the house and the surface of the yard with cow dung, pounds the floor of the newly built house so that it is hard and level, and maintains the food in the granary. In addition to this list of household obligations, the wife performs the greater and more strenuous part of the garden work. Cultivation is still based on hand tilling; small acreage and mountainous terrain combine to deter the use of ox plowing, except in the more open plain areas.

The responsibility for providing cash income lies with the husband. Cash crops as well as millet are his area of control (though his wife is usually expected to labor in the fields too). Other crops are the domain of the wife, particularly the vegetables, sweet potatoes, cassava, bananas, and beans.

The particular organization of household production varies from household to household. The burden of cultivation is laborious; both men and women rise before dawn to work on their fields until about ten o'clock in the morning. Then, women leave their fields and return home to make breakfast. The wife cooks for all members of the family, but family members eat in two separate groups. The mother and daughters, and sometimes young boys, eat together in the kitchen, while the father and the older boys eat their meals in the veranda of the main house. Sometimes the husband eats outside under a large, sacred tree or in the shade nearby the granary or on the top of an anthill, where in the olden days the men spent much of their time on lookout for enemies and cattle raiders. After breakfast, when it begins to get very hot, men generally leave their homes to go about their own affairs, such as taking the cows to the river or going to the beer party. The women spend the rest of the day in domestic activities, though they too may later join their husbands at a beer party in the afternoon.

Essential to the Bukusu rural economy is the institution of the "beer party." In many cases, beer is offered in exchange for labor. A man may have a banquet for his neighbors and friends who have responded to his call for help in a morning's work in his fields. Such work parties are needed for the weeding and harvesting of corn or millet. An alternative to offering beer for labor is to pay each person, in cash, the price of drinking all afternoon from a shared pot of beer. The beer parties create a pleasant atmosphere for neighbors to pass time together and to share the joys and hardships of life.

The beer party provides a milieu not only for socializing but, quite naturally, for relaxed dialoguing. At the beer party, it is the husband's privilege to own and sit on a stool (*endebe*), while women must sit on the floor between their husband's legs. When men assemble to enjoy the beer pot, they drink the beer through long, hollow reeds (*chisekhe*); the wives must crawl along the ground to pass under the reeds, while men freely step over the reeds.[4] This order of conduct represents one form of structural inequality between Bukusu men and women.

Almost every Bukusu man or woman has some skill that can be turned into a marketable commodity, especially with the commercialization of the economy today that has arisen from the success of cash crops. All services are offered on a cash basis. Building construction is a focus for many people. Each person has his or her own specialty; one brings the grass, another is a thatcher, and a third erects the framework of poles, while a fourth prepares the clay for mudding the house. The women bring in the water, as well as fill clay in the walls. Local carpenters, trained in the Christian mission schools or Islamic *madrasas*, make fitted doors and windows.

Apart from those engaged in building, there are other skilled jobs, ranging from artisans, bicycle mechanics, and tailors, to traditional potters and blacksmiths. Others take to setting up as butchers (especially Muslims), grocers, and small shopkeepers, while those with less capital take up other businesses, such as bringing dried fish for sale back from the shores of Lake Victoria and Lake Turkana.

Ritual specialists are vital to the Babukusu culture and include mediums, or diviners, who identify and treat physical and spiritual sickness, and soothsayers, who foretell the future, often by reading the entrails of sacrificed animals or the behavior of individuals. Sorcerers use incantations and curses to make life difficult for people or their crops or engage in magical acts to harm children physically; they also use poisonous ingredients put into food or drink to kill people. And there are circumcisers, who are chosen and possessed by a spirit with this initiation gift, and rainmakers, who call the rain by the use of their magical powers and rituals. The rainmakers help the communities decide when it is best to prepare their land and sow their seeds. By observing subtle changes in nature that would be undetectable to most people—in, for example, air currents, in the flowering and shedding of leaves of certain trees, in the behavior of ants, in birds' songs, in even the croaking of frogs and toads— they have been able to interpret weather patterns and provide valuable advice. These methods all point to very scientific principles well known to the Western world; for example, the technology of EEG/EKG studies on condition of the emotions and the heart bear out that such primal practices as these have validity and serve the principle of using healing dialogue for right relatedness with humankind and nature.

Most diviners are women because, as the Babukusu say, "Women see farther and deeper than men." Sorcerers can be men or women, and rainmakers and circumcisers are only men.[5] Each of these clan specialists expects payment for services and is chosen freely, based on reputation and success in performing on past occasions. A man with no special acquired skill often develops into a middleman or distributor, seeking buyers for someone's surplus millet or corn or negotiating sales of livestock. The very poorest in the community collect firewood or burn charcoal for income.

The husband and wife maintain social relationships with their respective families. Their relatives are usually given an equal level of hospitality in the family household. The wife may pay frequent visits to her parents, but the husband must give her permission to do so. The physical punishment of wives is quite common among traditional Bukusu couples. Sometimes a woman will even ask to be beaten, believing that if her husband doesn't beat her, he doesn't love her. The husband might chastise the wife for not cooking well, for not attending to a child who got hurt, or for going to see her parents without his permission. This may end the argument, and she can return to her duties. But if her husband hit her hard enough to hurt her, she might go to her mother in-law for comfort if they have a good relationship. She might go to her brother in-law, who would then speak on her behalf to the husband. If this physical abuse persists, she might move to her parental home, where the husband will have to seek her out to talk and resolve their differences, or to the home of other relatives, where she is given protection until some agreement with the husband has been reached; otherwise, the marriage might be formally dissolved by returning the bride wealth.

Today, there are educated Bukusu women who would not tolerate spousal punishment. They would argue that no woman of sound mind would tolerate someone inflicting pain on them. They would say that attitudes that are accepting of such practices are attributed to them by men. Their refusal to accept being manhandled has caused the Bukusu understanding of marriage and power relationships to move toward less physical resolution of conflict for couples.

The social place of a wife improves as she grows older and becomes a mother. She is no longer called wife but old woman, or *omukhaye*, a most honored title, which implies respect and social standing. Her change in status is also expressed in a more elaborate way. Once they are past childbearing age, both husband and wife can now receive visits from, and offer hospitality to, their parents and other people of higher social status, who would not have entered their house before. The husband and wife can now address each other by their ancestral names. Currently, the lifespan of the Bukusu ranges sixty to seventy years, with the women living longer than the men.

At this point, the marital relationship also improves by the performance of the *sitiso* rite, which is the ritual killing of an animal at the home of the wife's parents, as a thanksgiving ceremony for her new status of womanhood. The husband and wife eat a piece of raw meat together in the presence of the community, symbolizing one flesh and blood, after which they utter each other's clan names. The wife is, thereafter, known and addressed by her clan name, and she has all the honor and ability to represent her clan, especially in her role of third person in resolving conflicts.[6]

Bukusu parents desire many children. A productive wife commands more respect from her husband and his kinsmen than the wife who is barren or who bears daughters only, a fate for which the wife alone is held responsible. Neither of these two "misfortunes" is openly accepted as grounds for a divorce, especially if the husband is poor and cannot marry again without having to recover the marriage cattle that he gave for the first wife.

Many rites and sacrifices are performed to detect and remove the root cause of barrenness, which is attributed chiefly to the anger of the spirits of the dead. Impotency on the part of the husband may contribute to the breakup of a marriage for reasons of sexual incompatibility. For reasons of procreation, infertile or impotent husbands often give silent agreement to one of their brothers to step in quietly and sire children for them.

A dispute over a case of adultery arose in my village in the sixties. An impotent man in the community became extremely upset when he learned that his wife had taken another lover and become pregnant. The man went to the chief, who was also the local arbiter of disputes, to request compensation for the wrong. His case, however, was almost immediately dismissed as groundless. The chief decided that, since the complainant had paid bride wealth, the paternity of any children she gave birth to was the responsibility of the husband and not the lover. The arbiter added that the complainant should be pleased that his wife had taken up with another man, like Tamara and Judah in Genesis 38, for otherwise he would have remained childless. The husband had to accept that child.

The respective sexual rights and duties of husband and wife among the Babukusu are poorly balanced. The husband holds exclusive rights over his wife. For example, any extramarital involvement by the wife is considered adulterous, and if it takes place, the husband can demand a fine of two cows from her father and the lover. The wife, on the other hand, has no rights over her husband. Under the pretext of culturally normative polygyny, any relationship that the husband might carry on with an unmarried woman is regarded by the society as possibly leading to a second marriage. From this point of view, the husband receives the benefit of the doubt. The only exception is that if either the wife or the husband tenaciously avoids her or his marital duties, the unsatisfied partner may issue a complaint before the council of elders (who are all men), who are expected to resolve the marital conflict.

Rules of marital conduct specifically related to women also reveal another aspect of inequality between husband and wife. In the wedding ceremony, the paternal uncle speaks aloud the following advice to the newly married niece in the presence of the community:

When you are going to the river carrying a water pot and you hear your husband calling from behind because he wants to sleep with you, put the water pot down and return to the house to sleep with him. After that, you can go back to your chores. When you are working in the garden and your husband calls you, go to the house and do as he wants. When he has finished, you may return to the garden.

When you are going to fetch firewood and the husband calls you, go and follow him. When you are roasting millet on the fire and your husband wants you, do not argue, but let it burn; go and sleep with your husband. When your husband makes love to you, you must move your hips and play. When your husband copulates with you and he is near to climax, hold him tightly and embrace him, and don't lie there dormant.[7]

After this, the maternal uncle takes over and repeats the same points, emphasizing the woman's abject submission to the husband.[8]

These women are unaware that their abject behavior perpetuates gender-stereotyped attitudes that minimize the likelihood of their society changing the perception that women are created only to submit to husbands and to bear and rear children. If a culture is to recognize that women are a great asset, particularly in the realm of politics, the change must largely come through women stepping into roles not culturally ascribed to them. In our rural societies, the word "woman" provokes images of reproductive roles, and women cannot do much to alter the situation. This prevents women's gaining entrée to decision-making processes. These are the perceptions used to enforce the role of women and their inability to engage in political life. Unless women start working toward diluting such biases, the culture will continue to suppress their chances of rising to their full potential as equally human. With this going on, it is unlikely that Bukusu women can run the home and, at the same time, make major decisions concerning the lives and future of their families every day. Their potential cannot be elevated to the realm of governance, even at the local level. The male structures of control demoralize what scholars refer to as the greatest egalitarian value in any society—gender equality.

We can discern the maturity of any social group by looking at the way women are treated within it. The cultural identities of both genders influence political values and determine how gender equitability is viewed. Sadly enough, it appears that women hold with these twisted political values even more than their male counterparts. When asked what gender equality meant to her, Elizabeth Andahwa, a twenty-year-old college student in Kenya, said, "being able to do the same things that men do." Charity Chirchir, a middle aged peasant woman from the Great Rift Valley, responded to the same question differently. "To me, gender equality is defeating men at everything," she said. These answers aptly portray the gender equality scenario in many African countries. Traditional African cultures clearly stipulated the different roles of men and women in the society. Boys and girls grew up knowing what society required of them. As boys herded their livestock, girls would fetch firewood and water. As the boys hunted, older girls would perfect their cooking prowess. Then marriage would come along and young men would grow into husbands that fit the society's description of a husband. The same applied to young women. Thus would their lives be lived in this age-old pattern, more according to the norms of the society and less according to individual aspirations.[9] The situation largely has to do with how we humans are socialized.

CHAPTER 14

• ◆ •

THE BUKUSU CLAN

Another area of Babukusu relationships—one that provides unique communication patterns, as well as particular strategies of conflict resolution—is the clan. The term *clan*, or *luyia*, literally means "those gathered around the fireplace" in Lubukusu. This goes back to the period when elders used to meet every morning to warm themselves around a communal fire and discuss the events of the day, as well as to settle all-important issues of the clan. The fireplace is still the center of public life for each of the one hundred and sixty-five clans of the Babukusu.

When there is a lack of collective responsibility, there is a corresponding lack of organized governance or community leadership over the actions of individuals and families that are social detriments to the progression of the community as a whole. Group membership does not include advocacy against violence or the regulation of conflicts; nor does it provide any security for the individual or family. As a consequence, when there is no accountability to the group, individuals are free to do what they want. When something goes awry and offense has been taken, individuals take the law in their own hands and resort to retaliatory acts that lead to endless hostilities, revenge acts, and conflicts.

The Splitting of Clans

The formation, as well as splits, of clan factions often happened at beer parties—the latter, for example, when an individual under the influence of alcohol uttered a slanderous remark. The occasion of funeral rites is another place that splits occur, when a clan member attributed the death of an individual to another, igniting the hostility that led to the split of the clan.

More reasons for the split in a clan arose from the natural expansion out into what would be the buffer zone of land not contestable by any other nearby clan. The clan sees the need to split off to form new, independent sub-clans. These subclans never represent a completed development in clan evolution, but rather a dynamic process of growth and change. Subclans that had not been strong enough to stand on their own came to some affiliation with larger and stronger clans for economic and defensive alliances. With time, many splits and formations of new clans came into being. However, these splits carried long-lasting and deep-seated animosity. The dispersing of clans brought about endless conflicts that should be resolved.

CHAPTER 15

•◆•

TRADITIONAL APPROACH TO CONFLICT RESOLUTION

This section of the book provides a bridge between past and present by attempting to reconstruct the main principles that governed conflicts in the traditional Bukusu society. Relationship alliances, blood compensation, and "joking relations" are the key strategies traditional Bukusu people used for conflict resolution.

Relationship Alliances

Relationships among the Babukusu are anchored to one's locality but are also connected to geographically distant areas where a person's relatives have migrated or where one's sisters have married. These patterns of distant relationship alliances also tend to be maintained from generation to generation as the younger generations develop and relate with others at the larger clan gatherings. The geographical link is vital to understanding the nature of relationships within that clan's locality and also to the understanding of the nature of that clan's political leadership.

Traditional leaders are called *bakasa*. These are men rich in cattle and regarded as influential, who are respected for the power they could exert by virtue of their wealth, and also of their wives and, thus, their kin relationships. The *bakasa* were at one time both war leaders and formal spokesmen for peace. The Bukusu people, seeing in their leaders the potential successors to the current chiefs, tend to talk about such men as peacemakers. *Bakasa* are usually called in to solve disputes among the people of an area. However, peace and war go hand in hand. The same relational influence can be used to raise allies in war, as well as to control tempers in disputes and encourage factions to build common commitments for peace.

Blood Reparation

For the Babukusu, "blood reparation" is an aspect of reconciliation ignited by a killing. The Bukusu people's belief is that the spirits of the dead must be appeased. Instead of calling for blood revenge, however, economic compensation is made to stop the hatred. For example, if there is a killing within the clan, five head of cattle might be demanded; possibly up to eight head of cattle might be demanded for a killing outside the clan—for the hatred would have more severe and dangerous consequences if it were outside the clan.[10] The question of a spiritual, internal pollution adds further complications and demands higher rates of compensation to achieve reconciliation. Killings within the clan do not incur such pollution because one has a chance to purify oneself on the grave of the deceased, in order to guard against a vengeful spirit that might return to harm the killer. Killings outside the clan incur pollution caused by frequent visits of a foreign spirit. In this case, detailed ceremonies of reconciliation and purification are required. Failure to perform these ceremonies will result in the murderer roaming around acting crazy. For such a death, the relatives of the deceased member might demand up to twelve head of cattle before they agree to reconciliation. The payment of blood reparation was developed in the past to encourage reconciliation between the conflicting clans and to stop clan hatred and ongoing feuds. The main purpose of a blood compensation ceremony is to achieve renewed and harmonious relationships, not just momentary or superficial reconciliation.[11] Superficial reconciliation can bring only superficial healing.

Joking Relatives

Apart from blood reparation as a means of restoring relationship, the Babukusu have another unusual way of achieving peace and reestablishing relationships when a killer and the victim are distantly related. This is the institution of *bukulo*, or "joking relatives." A "joking relationship" is a relationship between two persons by which one is traditionally permitted, and in some cases required, to tease or make fun of the other, who in turn is required to take no offense but to respond in kind.[12] Joking relations represent a type of "peace pact" based on prohibited aggression under all circumstances.[13]

This phenomenon of the joking relationship is in essence what the whole world of competitive team sports appears to be for some individuals who cannot abide the concept of violent, competitive play that is accepted and loved by the world. *Encyclopedia Britannica* defines joking relationships thusly:

> Joking relationships are generally found in situations in which conflict or rivalry is possible but must be avoided. In one form, it is used as an instrument of social sanction, with the joker calling public attention to an individual or a group that has behaved in a socially unacceptable way. When such a relationship obtains between groups, the jocularity or critique, although disrespectful, expresses the separateness of the groups in a manner that averts actual conflict. The second form of joking relationship is often found in association with the avoidance relationship, which limits direct personal contact and maintains an extreme degree of respect between categories of people. In such cases, joking relationships are typically prescribed between people of opposite sex who are potential partners in marriage or sexual relations, while avoidance relations are required between persons of opposite sex for whom marital or sexual relations are forbidden. Both of these customs— viewed as points along a continuum of respectful behavior ranging from avoidance to license—act to stabilize relations that might be subject to conflict. For example, in many cultures a man must avoid his mother-in-law and joke with his sisters-in-law, while a woman must avoid her father-in-law and joke with her brothers-in-law.[14]

It appears that this phenomenon demonstrates humankind's love for battle, even mere mock battle. As to what purpose it serves, who knows? It appears that joking relationships of this order (competitive games) become a controlled testing ground to win a society away from radical individualism that, in the extreme, might be characterized as isolationist and that eschews any relatedness, thereby frustrating the mission and purpose of "community." In the Bukusu cultural environment, such individualism can have little or no part in that communal setting. The community is everything.

The African saying, "I am because we are," points to the importance of the group. It is also sometimes said, "Since we are, therefore I am." This African truism on right relatedness appears also in the wisdom words of the Western world—in Latin, Descartes' *"Cogito ergo sum"* ("I think, therefore I am.") The concept refers to that two-edged sword that forever signals strife for those who would stand apart versus those who would understand and support their community by holding its importance as paramount. Individualism holds that every person is an end in him or herself and that no person should be sacrificed for the sake of another. Community-oriented thinking holds that the needs and goals of the individual are subordinate to those of the larger group and should be sacrificed when the collective good so requires.

This struggle is the common condition of all humankind wrestling with the compulsion to assume the role of the absolute "I am." We fight the impulse to see ourselves as the god of our own world, rather than submitting to a role as one of the many, in which parity must be the ideal. I offer this explanation of why and how the experience of the Bukusu tribal traditions come so very close to the ideal for whole relatedness in a community as family, or more widely, the extended family/clan. This is the meaning of "joking relationships," in which all oppressive individualities become dissolved in forgiveness through openly dialogic communal understanding that can facilitate emotional healing for each participating individual.

Any opposing clan becomes a joking partner that has license to abuse and insult another. This license extends to the outright snatching of property from each other, even to claiming young girls and thereby making them their wives prematurely.

However, it should be noted that joking partners are neither direct kin nor linked by the performance of any mutual service, such as funeral or cleansing rites. Joking partners stand outside even this normal scheme of sociability. Effectively, they are the only non-kin in the Bukusu social world—the only people with whom one relates to whom he or she is not linked by the bond of marriage or of blood. The relationship is defined thus and has meaning solely in terms of the license given by the joking relationship.

The chief characteristic of the joking-relationship behavior is that one party delivers the most highly intentional insult, which the recipient must tolerate with no emotion. This is as distinguished from lighthearted joking and playing. Joking relationship exchanges are not lighthearted play; they are true insults, which may take no note of normal etiquette and of the restrictions of gender, age, or generation. In practice, the most extreme forms of verbal insult tend to take place only between men who are young, and they are more restrained between those of opposite sex. However, in principle, such restraints may be set aside, and any type of insult is allowed. Such insults may range from relatively innocent remarks over personal appearance to more direct accusations of witchcraft and animal pederasty and sexual obscenity—accusations that, in other circumstances, would undoubtedly result in a serious fight. Even though such insults are false, the recipient cannot respond to them physically. Parenthetically, this behavior appears to be common within almost any youthful group interchange where other cultural maturity is absent; and for these youths, not to take such "put-downs" in stride would be "losing face."

Paradoxically, the joking relationship puts those so related on the level of both foe and friend, or at least they share a peculiar combination of friendliness and hatred. Its attitude and behavior is seen as a direct expression of the virtual peace pact once culturally concluded between the overtly conflictual clans. Symbolically, such hatred is demonstrated only in the exclusion of the enemy when there is a meeting of the parties, as well as in the seriousness of the insult in mock thefts. This symbolic theme is further developed in understandings associated with snatching another's personal belongings in an obvious manner. A joking relative cannot snatch from the partner until he or she has provoked him or her into responding in kind. Fearful as to what a joking relative may take, those in the homestead usually attempt restraint because, once the joking relative has successfully picked a quarrel, he or she may snatch the object he wants and make off with it. Joking relationships are linked with destruction, and with the taking of life and the inevitable enmity such an act engenders. When the joking partner takes livestock, for example, he must slaughter the animal on the way home; it cannot be taken into his home alive and then use it for breeding.

While hatred is said to underlie the actions taken in the joking relationship, the pact equally implies a prevailing peace and friendship that is well understood. Under pain of the destruction of their lives, the joking relationship prohibits its participants from taking offense or responding with genuine hostility.[15] Nevertheless, hatred is an ever-present part of the joking relationship and is said to rise once more to the surface at times of illness and death, when joking relatives are identified once more as killers. For this reason, the joking relatives do not visit or communicate with each other during illness, for fear that if they do, the sick person will worsen and die. Moreover, it is said that the last remaining sense of the dying will be their hearing, so in their presence it is important to be careful what you say. They will likely carry your thoughts into the next world. Following a death, joking relatives practice total avoidance, again, like enemies, neither meeting nor greeting. This behavior is in deference to the "living dead," who are considered to be in a state of personal immortality.[16]

The joking relationship may be described as an explicit strategy for making peace, as a mode of past dispute settlement, or as a mechanism for turning a situation of enmity into one of friendship. It can also be seen as a continual reminder of the presence of mutually regrettable hatred continuing between longtime rivals. It requires the individual to subdue his or her anger on behalf of community and clan peace. Such a disposition toward peace, rather than toward conflict, is believed to remain with the individual's heart. Violence on one side is met with restraint and even generosity of forbearance on the other side, and natural retaliatory impulses are thus suppressed. Joking relations facilitate the positive transformation of enemies into allies, conceived in terms of enduring and absolute right relatedness (as in today's radical inclusivity preached from the Vatican).

CHAPTER 16

• ◆ •

MODERN FORMS OF COMMUNICATION

Although the past is a powerful determinant of culture, human societies selectively add to the past, subtract from it, and mold it in their own images by what they choose to remember and choose not to remember. Salah M. Hassan, professor of African art history and visual culture at the Africana Studies and Research Center at Cornell University in Ithaca, New York, pointed out that the notion of tradition should be rooted in social life understandings rather than in linear time.[17]

Traditional Bukusu people have evolved culturally, and they continue to process knowledge in facing new challenges and developing new means of social communication and adjusting traditional conflict resolution. New slogans and catchwords circulate in gatherings, in towns, and in the villages and are echoed in national radio broadcasts, on television, on the Internet, and in newspapers. Regardless of the attraction of modern means of social communication, the public gathering or *baraza* is a preferred method of acquiring information, even as it adjusts itself to the changing times.[18] The *baraza* represents a crossroad, in a sense. It offers a window into processes occurring at many levels of social interaction from local to national, from the office of a village elder to that of a cabinet minister.

The term *baraza* is a Swahili word used to refer to public assemblies, usually held outdoors. It ranges from several men, women, and children to larger gatherings. Normally, the local leaders, including chiefs, district officers, public servants, and village leaders, address smaller assemblies in the countryside. The barazas are also held in soccer stadiums, chiefs' camps, school compounds, public spaces near trading markets, or the rural villages; all are considered "the place of Sacred Trees."

The audience usually stands or sits on the grass, sometimes exposed to downpours or beating sunshine. Speakers are more comfortable under a canvas pavilion where they take chairs or wood benches at the front, on the sheltered platform. Other local leaders who may not address the assembly and who might include headmasters, school committee persons, board members, and religious leaders, share this "VIP section."

The *baraza* is one of few occasions for the public display of elite exclusivity. Among the audience, elderly men often sit near the front and women at the back. Oddly enough, the *baraza* allows for dialogue among individuals of broadly different social status—rich with poor, literate with illiterate, women with men, old with young, and strangers with locals. At a *baraza* today, farmers in patched clothing and bare feet can be seen encountering cabinet ministers in three-piece suits. Politicians park Mercedes Benzes before people who are accustomed to miles of daily travel on foot. Such meetings usually aim at achieving a popular consensus (or previously worked through agreement), rather than being only a vital debate of issues. The *baraza* may include fundraisings, rallies for a cause, and multitasking assemblies at which leaders communicate policy, explain program directives, or instruct people in agricultural techniques or health care measures.

The balance of dialogue and monologue during a gathering varies and sometimes is openly discussed. Any gathering may provoke outbursts by individuals in the audience. For example, just as a prominent speaker at a fundraising rally announces his or her generous donation to a new project, an individual in the crowd fulfilling the role of proverbial truth sayer, also known as "prophet" or whistle-blower, might shout out a question about a bounced check contributed at a previous *baraza* by the speaker him or herself. Dissident voices are not necessarily silent during these gatherings. A person in the crowd might shout out embarrassing questions or reminders of scandals associated with those on the speaker's platform, such as the corruption of local funds collected for development projects or community money embezzled. These assemblies are "revealing" insofar as they are the principal means for addressing differing opinions between ordinary (*mwananchi*) citizen and government officials.

The next chapter takes a closer look at the various elements that complicate dialogue for consensus among the Muslims, Christians, and traditional Bukusu people. These include traditional ceremonies, the council of elders, and funeral rites, as well as aspects of Islam, Christianity, and traditional religion in a shared arena. This is a prime example of current Roman Catholic thought; it is characterized as "radical inclusivity," a concept that the Babukusu have ever held dear. The Babukusu appear to have somehow always been ahead of the proverbial curve in terms of using the method of dialogue. When such radical inclusivity is embraced, every human being looks for and now is judged as deserving consideration in all things human. To paraphrase Babukusu thought, universal is well and good, but for the Babukusu, we come first. From Latin comes the similar phrase, "You cannot give what you do not have." In this context, the word *catholicity* must take on a flexible definition, one that acknowledges that all cultures are in no way in lockstep in terms of their universal understandings.

Part IV Notes

1. The prefixes *wa-* and *na-* and the initial vowel *e* of the nominal stem are contracted to *we-* and *ne-* respectively.

2. Those who die childless are given very little ceremony, and their spirits do not go to the home of the dead, *emakombe*, but are doomed to wander endlessly in the bush. They become the evil spirits of the streams, bushes, and paths. Whereas the spirits of the fertile are seen as life-giving, those of the childless are evil and bring death to anyone who unexpectedly sees them. The names of the childless are not handed on. Their corpses are tightly bound and wrapped to prevent the escape of the spirit, *sisimu*, and are often buried without a formal funeral so that family members are not shamed (by the person having no children).

3. Should the child die immediately after receiving the ancestral name, no more children will be named after this particular ancestor, for fear that the children might suffer a similar fate. Naming a child conveys a message; it is also a technique, an action, and a rite of protection and of defense. The Bukusu system of personal names is a sort of symbolic disguise to elude death, steering death away from a child by using a horrible or contemptible name. See Jean-Marc Ela, *My Faith as an African* (Maryknoll, New York: Orbis Books, 1988), 36.

4. This does not mean that husbands bully their wives. In real life, the master of the home tends to be the one who has the stronger personality. The share that a husband or wife contributes toward the family economic maintenance also affects the balance of power between them. For example, if the husband possesses no cattle and depends entirely upon his wife's garden labor, his behavior toward her tends to be meek (even though the wife will still be submissive to him).

5. Women traditionally were circumcised by female circumcisers, but this practice was ended around the 1950s.

6. This does not mean that the wife is adopted into the husband's clan; she still remains a member of her own clan.

7. See Wagner, *The Bantu of Western Kenya*, 424. These five directives are told with a solemnity and force that is similar to a Christian priest telling the parishioners

to follow the Ten Commandments or an Islamic mullah telling believers to follow the Five Pillars of Islam.

8. If the wife does not follow these commandments, she is sent home to her mother, who, along with other women in the community, teaches her to respond according to these dictums; then the wife returns to the husband appropriately "trained."

9. David John Bwakali, "Gender Inequality in Africa," *Contemporary Review*, 2001, http://findarticles.com/p/articles/mi_m2242/is_1630_279/ai_80607713/pg_2/?tag=content;col1.

10. I remember a case where, following a murder, the wife of the dead man demanded blood reparation, and when this was refused, her son tracked down his paternal uncle, the murderer, and killed him.

11. This form of practical morality is not specific to the Bukusu people. As John Mbiti suggests, it is widespread in east Africa. Mbiti writes, "What lies behind the conception of 'moral good' or 'evil' is ultimately the nature of the relationships between individuals in a given community ... It is not the act alone which would be 'wrong' as such, but the relationships involved [and impacted] in the act" (Mbiti, *African Religions and Philosophy*, 213).

12. When two clans have been engaged in a war, and each has tried in vain to overcome the other, they decide to make a compact that no man or woman would dream of breaking. A dog is brought to the boundary where so many fights have taken place and cut in two. One half is placed on the land of one clan and the other half on the land of the other clan, and the warriors of each clan march in procession between the two halves, which are then spurned by both parties. There is much hand shaking and merriment, and from that time on, the clans are friendly. This underlies the belief that whoever breaks the compact will "end like the dog—disowned, cut in two, and spurned." It is possible to extrapolate further, however, by examining the matrix of ideas and attitudes that are associated with the dog. For the Bukusu people, the dog epitomizes antisocial troublemaking. It has "bad blood" and is described as indiscriminate in all its habits and proclivities, whether sexual, aggressive, or gustatory. As such, dogs are generally despised in Bukusuland, making the Muslim abhorrence of the dog readily comprehensible. The dog is the only domesticated animal that is not eaten, a prohibition that extends to all animals that fall into the dog class (a class which includes most of the wild carnivores, leopards, and lions). All associations reinforce the idea that the dog is a hostile predator that is tolerated within human society for one purpose alone—its use as a guard animal, where its natural aggressiveness can be used to warn and fend off danger from human enemies. To this end, dogs are frequently both beaten

and starved and fed "medicines" in order to make them fiercer. The killing of a dog to cement a peace pact, thus, forcefully carries the idea of destroying "disorder" and all its associated evils. The dog represents aggressiveness and the disregard for normal conventions and rules, which leads to trouble and ill will within the community and the outcome of these qualities, hatred. Once the dog has been killed, the two parties may freely enter each other's houses, with the hatred removed, though not forgotten. See J. B. Purvis, *A Grammar of Lumasaba Language* (London: Society for the Propagation of the Gospel, 1909), 292.

13. Accounts of the origin of joking relatives among the Babukusu are rarely elucidated beyond the statement that there had been prior fighting between two clans. Alternatively, accounts of fighting between clans might conclude with the statement that they were made joking relatives. Nevertheless, we are faced with a concept of kinship and an idea of social living that is coded in terms of restraint and of submission of the self to rules laid down as right and proper. With restraint set against individualism, again and again, in the course of this section, the theme of social control merges with that of self-control, with the focus on the individual's management of self for the betterment of the community.

14. Encyclopedia Britannica, "Joking Relationship," *eb.com*, http://www.britannica.com/EBchecked/topic/305724/joking-relationship, last accessed March 15, 2011.

15. Avoidance of overt and public strife is an ideal, just as physical avoidance is seen as the main strategy for peaceful dealing with an enemy.

16. Mbiti, 83.

17. Salah M. Hassan, "Modernist Experience in African Art: Toward a Critical Understanding," in *The Muse of the Modernity: Essays on Culture as Development in Africa*, eds. Philip G. Altbach and Salah M. Hassan (Asmara, Eritrea: African World Press, 1996), 45.

18. The term *baraza* may have been introduced into Swahili from Arabic or Persian or both. Its Persian meaning is royal court. A late nineteenth century Swahili dictionary (Kraph 1882) defines *baraza* as follows: "A stone seat or bench table, either outside of the house or in the hall, where the master sits in public and receives his friends."

PART V

APPLYING DIALOGIC PRINCIPLES TO THE BUKUSU CONTEXT

CHAPTER 17

• ◆ •

CULTURAL OPPORTUNITY FOR DIALOGUE

The essential goal of this work is to consider the three dialogic concepts discussed—Martin Buber's philosophy of dialogue, Fred Iklé's strategies for dialogue, and William Ury's techniques for negotiating dialogue—in the context of traditional Bukusu cultural communication patterns, in order to identify opportunities within the Bukusu community that might serve as the basis for the promotion of intercultural respect and interreligious dialogue between Muslims, Christians, and the Bukusu people.

Here we examine traditional Bukusu life with its concerns, perspectives, and potentials so as to identify both those aspects of communication and conflict resolution that are working well and those that could benefit from implementing aspects of the philosophies of Buber, Iklé, and Ury. In Bukusu cultural life, dialogue is always potentially present; but the realms where it is lacking in actuality—among the council elders, at initiation ceremonies and funerals, and about land rights, issues of women's roles and their rights in general, and wives' rights in polygynous marriages—are all significant in terms of providing important contexts for interaction among Babukusu people. In each of these, everyone in the community has a role to play, regardless of religious affiliation, status, or gender. All Babukusu life and cultural norms come together here. They are key situations in which every Bukusu member is necessarily an actor, never a spectator! The reader will notice here that I make this exclamatory assertion for emphasis to anyone not from a native culture in Africa. The African way in right relational context is never a rigid forward mandate, but ever an opening to dialogue. However, in a genuine effort to impress the reader from outside Africa, that is the West, I employ direct language. Dialogue must always come before demands! Always!

There are many places and times in Bukusu life when the potential for dialogue and problem solving exists. Going in groups to the river to collect water or wash clothes, herding cattle and sheep, gathering for community meetings and at campfires, and attending beer parties and clan feasts—all these activities and venues afford the Babukusu the opportunity to meet, talk, and deal with life's blessings and challenges. Three aspects of Bukusu life that are especially fertile ground for conflict resolution and communion are the council of elders, initiation ceremonies, and funeral rites. Each can be seen as a microcosm of the greater Babukusu life.

Bukusu communities are guided by three interrelated systems of thought. First is the legal system, administered by a council of elders who must oversee according to traditions handed down for generations. The second is their system of beliefs that embody the spirits of the ancestors, who are thought to remain with the living to guide and enforce obedience to the traditions. Finally, there is a system of supernatural rituals that regulates conflicts within the community. These systems work in synchronism for the purpose of guiding the entire community and keeping it in compliance with all other clan communities and those people who are neighbors.

Council of Elders

Among Bukusu people, the clan leaders are generally referred to as elders. The elders are usually fifty years of age or older; however, not all elderly people belong to the council of elders. The council elders can be distinguished only by the specific functions they perform in and for the community. Within the council of elders there are herbalists, rainmakers, diviners, mediums, prayer leaders, and prophets. These are the ethical experts and spiritual leaders of the Bukusu people. They serve as teachers, counselors, and moral guides. They are expected to lead a visibly ethical life themselves so that their leadership will be both credible and useful to the people. People turn to them to learn what is wrong with a suffering individual or the community and what ought to be done in particular circumstances to set things right with life's vital forces. Since African religions are community-oriented (everyone belongs to the community by virtue of birth), religious leaders are responsible for the entire community and are answerable to it. This applies to the entire social hierarchy, from the father and mother of the family and the head of the clan to the chief of the nation (ethnic group), as well as all those who must comply in the spirit of the culture. The responsibility and accountability of each leader is seen within the context of right relatedness. Because African traditional religions embrace the whole life of the people, there can be no distinction between the religious and the secular. The responsibility of any leader includes these two aspects of life. A leader's aim is always to promote life. The leader is judged on that single criterion. Leadership is good and acceptable only if it enhances life; failure to do so means the leader will lose community effectiveness and respect.

Religious leaders are charged with the responsibility of seeing to it that things are right between the visible and the invisible worlds, and in the invisible world itself. Elders must restore balance by way of prayers, sacrifices, offerings, and right relationships, whenever creation's harmony is threatened or severed.[1] Religious leaders have the responsibility of protecting the bond between the living and the ancestors, which must remain unbroken in order for the community to continue to enjoy the preservation and continuation of life. Traditionally, the Bukusu people gathered to pray to Wele in order to address specific situations in the community and to find solutions to their challenges (such as how to deal with hunger, sickness, or enemies in case of an attack). When prayer takes place (often under the sacred tree, on a hill, or near a big rock), it is led by a chief, a counselor, or an outstanding elder in the village, with the intent of driving away the bad spirit that has caused the misfortune.[2] The qualities of being a good leader might include having a pleasing appearance, a good memory, oratorical skills, and an ability to resolve conflicts among people. Spiritual or religious beliefs are not used as criteria for leadership selection; thus, within each clan, conflicts are resolved by the most qualified governing body of the council of elders and might easily include Muslims, Christians, and traditional believers.

The council of elders is composed of men whose sons have reached warrior age; that is, the sons are post-circumcision, or twelve years of age. In theory, fathers and sons form a coalition in which the ruling group can call upon its warrior sons to support joint decisions by acting as a sort of enforcement for the community.[3]

Time and again, members in the council of elders emerge as spokesmen for their clans on specific issues of mutual concern. These spokesmen express the central position of the elders once the elders have come together to make the best decision for the clan. Moreover, clan spokesmen must resolve conflicts between clans. All decisions are collective and are promulgated by the elders in the council. Hence, resolving conflicts is regarded as the highest role for every Bukusu elder.

When the council of elders meets, the members bring to the circle their own affairs, events of the day, and the next social place where beer will be served in the afternoon. Beer brings them together for relaxation and can facilitate brainstorming about pressing issues that will be discussed later in a formal *baraza* for concerned members.

As the elders seek to make decisions that invite communal unity, they take into account the religious traditions of the collected individuals or groups involved in conflicts. Each elder has to have a religious cultural sensitivity. The elders must do everything they can to promote a culture of cooperation, understanding, appreciation, tolerance, and respect for each other's traditions and beliefs.

In meetings, formal or informal, the council of elders openly discusses issues of conflict using dialogue as the guiding principle for conflict resolution. The tradition of *barazas* provides maximum opportunity for enhancing interaction between those who outwardly appear as Muslim and Christian and traditional believers yet all together are truly the clan and the community; the elders become the Bukusu third-side presence in the *baraza*, using its influence for prevention, intervention, and resolution of interpersonal or intergroup conflict.

Initiation Ceremonies

Bukusu initiation is a rite of passage event celebrated by the immediate family and neighbors. It is a matter of the initiate's proven worthiness to move to the next life phase. Bukusu initiation rites are a discipline and an educational part of the process in which a child becomes a fully responsible adult. Initiation is a ritual transformation from one state of being to another. Testing the initiate's worthiness to enter the new phase often involves special instructions, restrictions, seclusion, and rituals.[4] One scholar, Arnold van Gennep, when discussing rites of passage, distinguishes between physiological puberty and sociological puberty. The former has to do with physical maturity, and the latter has to do with social maturity.[5] In Bukusu life, these two aspects of growth are linked, since every form of initiation has physical, psychological, and sociological components. Among the Bukusu people, the social initiation rites that follow puberty rites are part and parcel of the puberty rites of physical maturity that quite naturally are ever in process and indefinable. The maturity can be applied only virtually until the action of the individual proves his readiness in the eyes of the community.

For Bukusu boys, the process of initiation begins with the individual's physical separation from the community and from contact with the outside world. During this period, initiates have no status in the society. The community tells the initiates in a very definite way that without initiation and formal membership in the communal life, they are nothing. At this point, the candidates receive from the elders formal instruction that will help them to understand the community and its social and religious customs. The elders pass on mythology, proverbs, riddles, stories, songs, dances, and ancestral wisdom to the initiates. Within oral cultures, proverbs are an important form of symbolic thought and imagery. Equally important are the myths of traditional Bukusu people that interweave the real with the mystical and speak of archetypal heroes who are both images and symbols.

Traditional Bukusu people believe that it is essential for adults to impart strength, intelligence, willingness to work, and a respect for authority to their children in every conceivable way. Through the ritual process of initiation, initiates are taught the most essential knowledge about the life of the clan. To undergo initiation is to symbolically die and be reborn. It is a moment when initiates pass from nature (the forest) to culture (the village). In this sacred passage, they receive the secrets of the clan and are made ready to have their own children and responsibilities.

Although Bukusu boys and girls go through initiation ceremonies, the forms and objectives of the ceremonies do differ greatly. Boys are secluded and taught in the bush; for girls, a grass hut is built within the village. The reason for these differences in group preparation is that the boys' ceremony is intended to teach obedience to the discipline of the elders and endurance under hardships. For girls, the emphasis is on sexual compatibility and reproduction and the importance of household and parenting responsibilities.

Today, in the religiously diversified population of Bukusuland, traditional initiation rites are vital in generating a sense of community oneness, since all members, in one way or another, undergo the same Bukusu initiation ceremonies. The historical pattern has been for all Bukusu children, regardless of their parental faith traditions, to experience the rites of passage that the Bukusu have passed down for generations. This means that, usually, Christian Bukusu boys and girls have been taught and initiated according to the ancient and traditional ways of their Bukusu elders. Similarly, Muslim Bukusu children have participated in the traditional Bukusu initiation rites of passage. In Bukusuland, such initiation rites are not treated as counter to the beliefs and rituals of these varied religious traditions or to their worshiping communities. They all are, first and foremost, truly Bukusu. In fact, local, native Catholic priests and their bishops want to encourage, support, and be present in these ceremonies. Local, native Muslim leaders do this as well. Furthermore, within a family of mixed religious traditions among the parents or relatives, everyone, Christians, Muslims, and traditional believers alike, is expected to accept the initiation rites.

Native Muslims and Christians find ways to weave their traditions together with indigenous Bukusu conventions. For example, traditional, local Islam follows only the custom of circumcision in the rite of passage.

Because it is an important part of Bukusu tradition, local Bukusu Muslim boys attend circumcision initiation camps with the Bukusu community. For these Bukusu Muslims, the circumcision ceremony needs to be completed by the initiation event. According to Islamic custom, the initiate's reintegration into society may be recognized by the greater Islamic celebration of Qur'anic tradition.[6] In Muslim Bukusu societies, the circumciser is often a traditional elder, but the period of seclusion is under the control of the Islamic teacher. Today, a more "refined Islam" in Bukusu townships is gaining ground; where formerly beer was served at a boy's coming out of seclusion, now food with tea or soda is served to the guests.

Similarly, Catholics acclimatize their own rites to Bukusu traditions. For example, after the male circumcision operation, as the initiates are healing or after they have healed completely, they are prepared for the sacraments of baptism and confirmation. One foot is inside the Church, while another stands in the common knowledge of the traditional way of life.[7] As Aylward Shorter, a scholar at the Catholic University of Eastern Africa, Nairobi, describes it, "At Baptism, the African Christian repudiates remarkably little of his former non-Christian outlook. He may be obliged to turn his back upon certain traditional practices that, rightly or wrongly, have been condemned by the Church. Consequently, he returns to the forbidden practices on occasion with remarkable ease. Conversion to Christianity is for him sheer gain, an "extra" for which he has opted."[8]

Thus, a convert's Christian beliefs overlay his or her traditional ways. "African Christians operate out of two thought-systems at once," explains Shorter, "and each is only superficially modified by the other."[9] Initiation ceremonies act as a social magnet, pulling together people in the community who follow different spiritual traditions. In those gatherings, the conversations that take place and the relationships that are woven together usually serve as catalysts for intercultural cooperation.

However, initiation rituals can also be fertile ground for cultural and religious conflicts or misunderstandings. For example, for a traditional Bukusu, there is no initiation ceremony without beer. It is within the social sharing of the beer that the ancestors are invited to participate. This may not be acceptable by Muslim and Christian tenets. In Islam, alcohol is regarded as *haram*, or that which Allah has explicitly forbidden humans to partake of and for which he specified a penalty. It is absolutely prohibited because it hinders one from the remembrance of Allah (Qur'an 5:93–94). Similarly, Bukusu Christian Baptists also tend to resist or reject this aspect of cultural life.

As initiation is a time for potential conflict or communion between families, clans, and religious groups, these ceremonies are fertile moments for positive third-side interventions.

Funeral Rites

The history of funeral rites is a history of humankind. Funeral customs are as old as humanity itself. Every culture and civilization wants to take proper care of its dead. And every culture and civilization ever studied has three things in common relating to death and the disposition of the dead:

(1) Some type of funeral rites, rituals, and ceremonies
(2) Some sacred place for the dead
(3) Some memorialization of the dead

According to traditional Bukusu beliefs, death is an evil that forever disturbs the harmony of the living. Their funeral dancers sing, "If we knew the home of death, we would set it on fire." The gathering of relatives and friends and the proper observance of burial and funeral rituals express the belief that harmony is restored during the time of family stress through the correct rite of passage that transports the deceased to the abode of the collective immortality, the ancestors.

Funerals are one of the most important events in Bukusu communities. Marriages take place on weekends, during intervals between routine preoccupations, but when a death occurs, most routine activities stop abruptly until the funeral is concluded.

Funeral rites in a Bukusu village start shortly after one's death, as women cry out loud, signaling that someone has just died. By wailing, the women are emotionally and spontaneously growing ritually involved; even as they alert the nearby relatives and neighbors, they call for consolation and support. Since the entire village becomes involved, certain features of village structure are manifested with unusual clarity. Young men are immediately dispatched to travel to distant relations and break the news of the loss. In a case in which the deceased has been very ill for a long time, relatives will have been notified of the individual's condition, and a number will already be present in the home. Failure to attend the sickbed of a close relative may in some instances be regarded as an indication of blameworthy responsibility for that person's sickness. Thus, people make every effort to attend both the sickbed and the funeral.

A funeral consists of a burial and a commemoration ceremony. The Bukusu people believe that without the proper ritual of mourning, the spirit of the deceased will not rest peacefully in the grave but will interfere constantly in the affairs of the living. Everyone in the extended family and the village normally attends funerals. In many Bukusu Muslim and Christian families, the home of a recently deceased member is considered a holy place, where people pray and read from the Holy Scriptures. Religious leaders and family members from the clan also take turns consoling the bereaved.

A memorial ceremony is significant; it is here that a person's life history is told. How one is to be remembered in death is a crucial factor in people's lives. One looks forward with great concern to being remembered as a good Bukusu. The Bukusu hold that the spirit of the dead must travel a dangerous road. Upon arrival at the other end, the spirit has to be admitted by other spirits into the place of all right relatedness—*Zamani* is the limitless past, the dreamtime, the time before time with "the I am." As soon as the funeral rites are performed, the spirit of the dead is said to begin its long journey to the land of the "living dead." The newly deceased's acceptance into the company of the long-dead spirits depends on the nature of the life that he or she has led. Good people get across easily; for bad people, it takes years to reach the land of the ancestors. The ancestors are very powerful beings because they continue to maintain close relationship with the living. The spirits of the living dead live in the present realm of the *sasa*—the state of all things as present. The spirits, no longer remembered, pass into the *zamani* and join the community of ancestors.

Just as most cultures' funeral rituals focus on transitions, so do those of the Bukusu. Bukusu ceremonies carried out after death are expressions for making the spirit of the living dead's journey easier and for the establishment of new relationships with ancestors lost to popular memory.

If the recently dead person was a chief, a successor has to take his place. His heirs must divide the whole inheritance actually and virtually among themselves. Someone must be responsible for his debts, the fate of his widows must be decided upon, and everyone who stood in a particular relationship with him must accept where he or she stands with regard to the heirs and his successor. Before all these things can be attended to, a period of adjustment must take place. An interval in between allows the society to pass gradually from the old order to the new.

As Harold Koenig points out in *Aging and God: Spiritual Pathways to Mental Health in Mid-Life and Later Years*, "Death is a subject of relevance to everyone. It is the one fact about the future that can be counted on for certain. Indeed, death is a universal, natural, persistent, inescapable, unavoidable, and undeniable fact of life. Death's impact on human behavior does not take place in isolation; it takes place in a given social context. In other words, a person's behavior is a dynamic interaction between the person and the social context in which he or she lives."[10] A number of aspects of Bukusu funeral rites demonstrate the Bukusu people's interactions with death within their specific cultural context, in which unity is of utmost importance. These included the structure according to which people attend a funeral—attendees are known by their motives; the manner of burying a clan elder versus that of burying an ordinary member of the community; and the hair-shaving ceremony, an occasion for settling disputes that affect the family of the deceased. Each of these is a matter of great care and concern.

Motives for Funeral Attendance

In light of the concept of the third-person role, it may be pointed out that most of those who attend a funeral will be members of the dead person's clan. In the case of the deceased's being a man, the brothers and sisters of his wife will come to the funeral even if they live some distance away, whereas the husbands of his sisters and the wives of his brothers will come only if they live nearby. If a young woman dies, the number of mourners who come from her own clan is often larger than that of people belonging to her husband's clan, but if she is an old woman with many children, she is given as big a funeral in her husband's clan as she would have in her own. As a rule, neighbors attend funerals regardless of their clan or kinship affiliations with the deceased. Traditional neighborhoods are most likely to foster right relationships in everyday life.

Age group solidarity comes into play at funerals, as friends give support to the bereaved family. If the deceased is thirty-five or forty years of age, most of the mourners are approximately one's age-mates because they would have known the person well through lifelong acquaintanceships. In the case of the funeral of an old man or woman, there are far more old people present than at the funeral of a middle-aged or young person.

The chief motive for attending the funeral is to express one's feelings of sorrow over the loss sustained and the desire to see the deceased once more before the burial. Closely linked with this motive appears to be the fear of taking on the anger of the dead person's spirit by failing to be present at the funeral rites, especially in the case of close kin, as well as the anxious wish to assuage any doubt on the part of the bereaved that one may be in any way responsible for the death that has occurred. Most mourners, however, are not subject to such fear. They are part of the community in mourning the loss of the deceased person.

The same old women can be observed turning up at various Bukusu funeral gatherings, regardless of their kinship connection to the deceased. These women are often dressed in the most remarkable mourning regalia. They have assigned themselves as token mourners to support the funeral ceremony. It might appear that their display is over the top, unless one understands that, for them, this is important, as it comprises what is left of their social life.

Otherwise, the behavior of the mourners is quite informal. The old men sit together in a circle in the front yard, gossiping and drinking beer through long reed straws from a common beer pot. Young men and women stand or sit around in groups, some chewing pieces of sugarcane, which, on this occasion, is always brought along in great quantities, as the mourners are not provided with much food. Boys and girls welcome the occasion to play, to sing and dance together, to chant loudly and laugh, or even to shout from group to group. Children run all over the place, chasing one another, entirely unconcerned, and no one ever rebukes them or tells them to be quiet or show restraint.

While some of the helpers in the home assist in preparing food or bringing in water from the stream, others simply sit, watching like crows, expecting to be fed by the bereaved family for weeks. They can become a great burden to the bereaved family. Some relatives may even stay for a month.

Burial of a Clan Elder versus Burial of an Ordinary Person

The burial of a clan head differs in many respects from that of an ordinary member of the community. There is a prohibition against wailing immediately after a clan elder dies, and mourners are kept at a distance from the corpse until it has been established who will succeed the elder and play his role in the community. This prohibition is instrumental in preventing a political crisis from emerging in the clan. Upon seeing the deceased, the relatives are very likely to begin to wail. Seeing the corpse elicits violent expressions of deeply felt emotions and sorrow, which may easily lead to quarrels and mutual accusations and, finally, to a disruption of the harmony of the clan. The risk of potential violence is minimized when these passions are restrained until the deceased person's sons' and grandsons' rights of succession to their father's office have been concretely established.

The burial of a Bukusu leader is marked by the attendance of a large crowd and the full observance of all ritual details, such as anointing with a type of oil made from a cow, whose skin is used to wrap the body of the deceased for burial, and the presence of a large flock of cattle, symbolically brought to participate in the mourning. In addition, the Bukusu bury clan elders with a warrior's weapon.

In the case of an ordinary clan member, these symbolic acts and gestures are absent. These differences are important in the sense that they provoke one of the few instances between Babukusu in which social and political leadership is clearly recognized in ceremonial behavior.[11]

A few clans among the Bukusu, including the Balunda clan, bury their people in a sitting position, a practice that is observed even today. They believe that death is not a sign of defeat or conquest but a form of relaxation. To them, the dead are simply taking a rest from physical activities but continue to oversee the activities of their families and the community at large. Therefore, they need to remain vigilant in a sitting position. While all members of the community are buried in this manner regardless of sex, age, or status, in the case of elders, the Balunda people believe that this is the only way to ensure that the elders continue occupying their revered positions, from which they can direct and counsel the living. Respected elders are responsible for supervising the burial rites and ensuring that all the required rites are observed.

During times of mourning, feasting, and property settlement, people come together with mixed emotions and motives. They sense that the previous order of things in their own regard may be unsettled. There are numerous opportunities for them to speak in small and large groups, sometimes with kindred spirits and other times with people they barely know or whom they distrust because of past enmities. Consequently, such times hold crucial potential for the display of distrust.

Dialogue in such situations can be seen as a helpful remedy. Even in the national press of Kenya, this behavior is frequently described as not helpful for peaceful conflict resolution—hence, the need for dialogue. Why? Because we are all ultimately human.

With the proper assistance of the elders acting in the manner Ury noted in his studies, bridges can be built and relationships reinforced that will add to community harmony. The elders play the role Ury calls the third party. Otherwise, these gatherings can lead to unfortunate interactions, misunderstandings, or divisions. Funerals must be seen as critical times for reordering community building.

A properly conducted funeral in Bukusuland for a leader of the whole of the Babukusu tribe holding sway over a million individuals begins with the removal of the body from the house. After the death of this one, a hole is made in the side of the house. When it is time to remove the body from the house, it is taken out through the hole, feet first, instead of through a door. This is to keep the spirit of the deceased leader from finding an easy way back into the home. It is a sign that the deceased's time is through. As the body is being transported to the place of burial, thorns and sticks are placed along the way and a complicated pattern is used to confuse the spirit further. These precautions are taken so that the spirit does not come back to bother the living.

The Hair-Shaving Ceremony

Hair-shaving among the Bukusu people takes place three days after the burial. The custom of hair-shaving requires that everyone who has come into contact with the deceased member during his or her last illness must have his or her head shaved. Bukusu people believe that life is concentrated in the hair. Therefore, shaving the hair symbolizes death, and its growing again indicates the strengthening of life. This serves as a ritual purification. It is believed that the disease from which the deceased person suffered and which sprang from his or her body sticks to the hair of those persons who were in close contact with the departed, allowing the disease to spread. That is why the Bukusu people refer to the hair-shaving ceremony as the coming out of the sickness. This creates a lot of problems for women who don't want to shave their beautiful hair. Nowadays, a negotiation has been reached in which women will cut off a small symbolic lock of hair, rather than shave their heads completely. This is an indicator of the idea that cultures change according to the current needs of the members of that culture. In teaching things African, I never fail to point out in my lectures the truism that culture is a tool for human survival, as survival ability surely changes over time and with circumstances. Africa, for some time now, has been a compression of things primitive up against this world of sophistications and technical advances. To hold any older cultures in disrespect is to fail to appreciate them. The premise of this book is that the Bukusu's ability to dialogue, which Ury praises as an ideal, is a unique asset.

The hair-shaving ritual is an import opportunity to address the unresolved conflicts of all those attending the funeral and the entire community, the more self-serving motivation in clipping only a small lock of hair notwithstanding. Ritual leaders in the community, both male and female, take charge of this communal rite, during which relatives and neighbors voice various unresolved claims and issues that the dead person still has regarding cattle, cash money, grain, or other objects. This list includes any debts that the deceased member may have owed when he or she died, as well as debts that may have been owed to him or her.

After claims of this nature have been put forward and settled, clan elders distribute land and assets among the sons of the deceased person and other relatives entitled to a share, carefully managing the issues so as to avoid conflicts that could arise later.[12] In addition, the symbolic hair-shaving ritual provides an opportunity for the relatives of the deceased member to discuss the probable cause of his or her death and to voice suspicions against particular individuals.

As noted earlier, for the Bukusu, the final cause of every human death, even that of a very old person, is a mystical agent—usually by an act of sorcery brought about by a fellow human being harboring ill will against the deceased. To put it simply, all human death is the direct result of fellow human beings, not just a condition, illness, or a trauma. In most cases, these accusations give rise to a heated debate between the parties, namely the relatives of the deceased and those of the accused. Accusations of this order, uttered on the occasion of the hair-shaving ritual, have led, on several occasions, to outbreaks of open hostility and to family or clan feuds. If it happens that the accused belongs to the clan of the deceased, the accusations leveled against him or her may easily lead to quarreling and fierce fighting. It is the duty of the specially revered elder, the comforter, the third party, to prevent such quarreling by making peaceful speeches, reminding the kin of the dead person and how we must all die and that such quarreling only serves to weaken the community and throw it open to scorn. It is also the third party's duty to try to bring people into commonality by agreement. Because of his personal wisdom, a third party "comforter" will advocate to the family that they accept the changes the death has prompted. Often, the Bukusu comforter will choose to tell the following tale regarding death:

A long, long time ago, human beings did not die. One day, a chameleon came to the homestead of a certain man who was a son of *Maina* (a Bukusu elder). He was sitting outside the courtyard, eating. The chameleon asked him to give it some of his food, but the man refused. When the chameleon did not stop begging him, the man finally became angry and drove it away. Thereupon, the chameleon cursed the people and spoke: "I am leaving you now, but from now on, you shall die." Then the people began to breathe the air, get ill, and die. After the chameleon had left the man, it visited the snake, which gave it something to eat. To reward the snake for its good deed, the chameleon blessed the snake with eternal life. That is why when the snake gets old, it merely casts off its skin instead of dying. The Bukusu people hold that, even as of today, snakes die only when they are killed.[13]

However, there is no presupposition that a family or clan unit will always have a comforting (ameliorating) leader of the type just described. If no such man is in place, all the elders must take a hand, sharing in public discussions with the aim of tempering the decisions of the deficient clan leader.[14]

CHAPTER 18

• ◆ •

THE UTILITY OF CULTURAL COMPROMISE

There are four areas of Bukusu life that present Western observers, as well as worldly Bukusu, with a high potential for discomfort or conflict—circumcision, land rights, women's rights, and polygyny. This chapter deals with each of these concerns, especially as they reflect the confluence of religious traditions, in order to highlight the need for dialogue concerning these issues.

The Circumcision Ritual

The circumcision ritual is practiced across many, but not all, cultures in Africa and is one of the most resilient of all traditional African practices in the urban, industrialized environments there. The Bukusu people see male circumcision as central to their culture and defend it fiercely against opposition from churches, health organizations, and individuals within and outside the community. Despite this tension, the ritual remains an important milestone for many Bukusu young people who actively seek circumcision because they want to become adults and be accepted by their community.[15] Traditional Bukusu people consider circumcision necessary for all boys and offer several reasons for their position. The most important is that the circumcision rite proves one is a Bukusu.

Two schools of thought dominate the dispute surrounding issues of male circumcision in Bukusu society today—those of the traditionalists and those of the abolitionists. Traditionalists view circumcision and the ritual acts that go with it as a determining factor in the preservation of Bukusu customs and are convinced that any effort to stop the practice of male circumcision would undermine the entire structure of the traditional culture. For many Bukusu people, the wider ceremonial significance of circumcision, as well as its educational role, means that its gradual decline in importance even now is linked directly to the threat to traditional Bukusu culture. For example, Bukusu musicians mourn the loss of traditional circumcision songs, which speak to Bukusu aesthetics and cultural beauty. The songs always educated the people about their cultural heritage.

Abolitionists tend to focus their attention not only on the pain that surgery inflicts on the boy but also on the belief that circumcision is shocking, cruel, and unnecessary. Abolitionists are concerned with the unhygienic circumstances in which circumcision operations are often carried out, together with the minimal training of many circumcisers. Unhygienic conditions, such as the use of dirty instruments, and lack of proper follow-up can result in complications—some severe and potentially life-threatening—including severe bleeding, bacterial infections, gangrene, and mutilation of the penis. Uncontrolled bleeding is sometimes difficult to stop if a circumciser has cut too deeply or has mistakenly cut off the penis. But for the most part, the participators in this rite employ great care.

The traditionalists respond by noting that a good number of people all over the world perform circumcision. Understandably, if one were to ask them why, they would give various reasons. A Muslim would cite purity and tradition. The Muslim community believes that circumcision is a religious obligation prescribed in the Sunna and the hadith of the Prophet Muhammad.[16] For the Bukusu Muslim, circumcision symbolically purifies the boy, making possible his future participation in prayer and in the reciting of the Holy Qur'an.

Within Christianity, male circumcision has no religious significance; most Roman Catholics in Bukusuland praise the idea of traditional circumcision. Bishop Masaba of the Anglican Church, who underwent the Gishu rites of circumcision on Mount Elgon as a boy, has validated the traditional circumcision rites of his own people and affirmed their value for Anglican boys.[17]

Some Protestant Pentecostals in Kenya, however, are opposed to certain elements of the traditional Bukusu rites. They tend to believe that anyone who has embraced Christianity must do away with non-Christian traditions. Some Pentecostals are willing to observe the process of traditional preparation and training for initiation into manhood, but they send their children to a hospital for the actual circumcision to be performed under the supervision of a medical doctor. One story tells of a Protestant Pentecostal Bukusu man living in Nairobi who wished not to have his sons circumcised at all but found that he could not resist community pressure from his home three hundred miles away. He let his sons be circumcised, and as a consequence, he lost his place on the local Protestant church council.

Additional conflicts arise between boys who are circumcised in the hospital and those who are circumcised at home in the traditional way. Those who are circumcised in the hospital are excluded from the company of their male peers. They are later barred from socializing in traditional beer parties. They are also forbidden to approach a candidate in preparation for circumcision and are ridiculed through circumcision songs. At any circumcision rite or celebration, boys who were circumcised in the hospital are despised and are not included in the ceremonies by the elders, lest they inject fear into the boys who are going to be circumcised. There is no mixing at such times, and if there is, the violators are severely beaten, even to the point of death. So, then, we may ask, just how do all these distinctions of worthiness ever support the idea that the Babukusu can hold the position of having the ideal means of dialogue?

The chasm that can arise between the circumcised and the uncircumcised, between the traditionally initiated and the surgically initiated, and between the parents and families of all concerned, calls for community members who must facilitate mending dialogue, remaining mindful once again that culture is a tool for human survival. With an emphasis on dialogue and collaboration, partnered with a willingness to act in ways that reconcile differences and build alliances, the Bukusu grow in health, rather than let themselves be splintered into factions.

Land Ownership

African land ownership is another highly emotional issue. The Bukusu people cherish land with reverence and great admiration for permanence. In their lands lies a bond between the living, the dead, and those yet to be born. In the place where the ancestors are buried dwells the soul of the clan and the hopeful expectations for the life of the next generation. The umbilical cord of a newborn baby and the foreskin of a circumcised boy are buried in the land. The bloodshed in these events binds the individual to the land and to the departed members of his or her lineage. This is why Bukusu people kneel barefoot next to the grave when they want to communicate anything to their ancestors, showing thereby great respect for the land on which the ancestors lived.[18]

While land ownership is a birthright of every individual in Bukusu society, it has also a communal dimension, whereby all members of the community are expected to share its resources under some form of traditional authority. For example, communal grazing lands found along the riverbanks and along the mountains, forests, salt licks for animals, watering places, pathways, and reserves for building materials belong to the entire community. Communal rights to these lands and resources are important in people's lives. In the past, the clan head protected these lands from being compromised by cultivators, but its use for grazing was open to everyone in the community, including strangers and people residing in neighboring clans.

Now, Bukusu economic development has been tied to the centrality of land resources, as well as to cultural and traditional practices. Rituals of rainmaking, thanksgiving, and prayer services have in the past been tied to the land. The custom of asking for rain through the help of the ancestors and God is greatly featured in Bukusu tradition. Either people go to the mountain as a community or a rainmaker undertakes the process alone. The mountain on which the rituals of prayer and sacrifice take place is valued, respected, and reserved as a sacred place.

A Bukusu person cannot imagine how anyone can remain human if he or she is denied the very essential God-given mother earth, out of whose dust he or she was created. This belief of the Bukusu people that their traditional lands are a gift from God and from the ancestors is accepted as a truth. They continue to see themselves as the stewards of God-given resources, especially of communally owned land. "In land lies our future and our survival" is a famous slogan echoed by Jomo Kenyatta, the first president of the Republic of Kenya.

Land rights among the Bukusu people are based on three main principles—land-cultivation, inheritance, and clan relatedness. It may be said that the continued occupation of the land for many generations constitutes a fourth principle that confers rights equal in effect to those of an owner. Land rights refer to any land that the present Bukusu holders have acquired by inheritance. Family land is transferred to each succeeding generation, but it is progressively subdivided as each new individual family is set up. Family land is held at any given time by a single member of the family, in accordance with the rules of inheritance and succession.

Land inheritance is a source of controversy and tension in Bukusuland today. Traditionally, only men could own land, just as only men could own cattle. Daughters could not inherit any of their father's land. If a man left daughters but no sons, his brothers or his brothers' sons inherited his land. Bukusu customary law, although modified over time, continues to follow such patrilineal codes. Marriage remains the main channel by which the right of individual access to land is granted and ownership and uses of land are distributed. These rights are mediated by gender. Men gain rights to land inheritance through trans-generational patriarchal lineages of succession. Men are allocated land by their fathers upon marriage. Brothers frequently quarrel over land rights and paternal land allocations, even to the point of killing each other. Here is raw humanity without the benefit of dialogue. Among the Bukusu, this behavior goes against the grain of the tradition. Traditionally, the recognition of land ownership among the Bukusu didn't necessarily require lines drawn on a map. And when the Bukusu people did start selling plots of land, a process of drawing boundaries with one's neighbor wasn't always in place. Very often, people would buy the land,

and the seller would simply point in one direction or other and tell the new owner that his neighbor and boundary was somewhere over there. The result—many people with valid, competing claims. And that was the easy part. While much of the land in the rural areas is undeveloped, the traditional systems reserve empty land for children, grandchildren, and other relatives—making families dirt poor but land rich. What now?

The transfer of property (either cattle or land) creates certain disharmonies between men, as well as between women. While cattle herding is a responsibility of men, in the actual sense, farming is women's work, and though the men claim to own the land, the farms belong to the women in an everyday sense. Women produce 60 to 80 percent of Africa's food and contribute to the production of post-colonial/governmental managed cash crops for export.[19] Thus, while the ownership is transferred from father to son, in reality, the transfers are from a woman to her daughter in-law. Though land ownership is lawfully the men's domain, women are beginning to acquire land, in spite of traditional thinking.

Another aspect of land rights that often leads to conflict revolves around property boundaries. National and ethnic boundaries have been set only as a result of disputes over the land. When the pressures of population at first began to increase (especially after the establishment of British rule had put a stop to ethnic warfare), the British narrowed down uninhabited border zones until these zones eventually disappeared.[20] The people of Kenya were displaced, and the common recognition of natural features, such as mountains or streams, marked boundary lines. Clans planted, especially wild fig trees, to mark clan boundaries.[21] After the elders of two bordering clans had come to terms about the alignment of their common boundary, a public beer party sealed their agreement. The purpose of the party was to publicize the new and binding boundary agreement.

Factional fighting and political violence can often be traced back to the struggle for land. The Bukusu way of handling family lands makes the process particularly vulnerable to conflict, given that ownership is defined by loose and irregular boundaries and by land left fallow in the bush. Despite the density of the population in Bukusuland, the technical procedure for constructing boundaries is still comparatively loose.

Individual plots are marked off by shrub branches and sisal plants and only rarely are demarcated by barbed wire by those few who can afford it. In the course of marking one's plot, a person may add one or two feet from another person's piece of land to his original land. The disputes provoked by this kind of action are very serious, sometimes ending with bloodshed before the elders step in to settle the matter. Furthermore, in traditional Bukusu community life, an individual or family secured land rights for as long as the person or family was using it. It became family land when it was cleared, cultivated, and planted; until then, it was clan land. If a person claimed to own a fallow piece of land but did not cultivate it, his claim was invalid. This confirms the principle that it is by use of land that a permanent right of ownership can be established and not merely by staking a claim.

Tensions arising from land disputes caused ethnic massacres in the 1990s, when almost all of Kenya was plunged into land clashes. In western Kenya, tensions between the Bukusu and the *Sabaot* (Elgon Masai) people exploded into violence, and many families on both sides lost lives, homes, and farms. But land conflicts do not necessarily center on ethnicity. Some recent land disputes involved the violent evictions of the poor and squatters accused of land grabbing. In such clashes, land, livelihoods, and life itself are at stake. Individuals violently evicted from their land are drawn into struggles construed as ethnic in nature, but initially, those involved did not kill one another over ethnicity. Some of these tensions have deep historical roots, such as threats of violence among various groups over the reallocation of land in former White Highlands (land appropriated by colonial, white settlers) during Kenya's transition to independence. As the importance of ethnic identity increased, open conflicts broke out throughout almost the entire country.

As to the influence of religious beliefs or practices on land rights and property disputes, priests and mullahs are seldom called upon to facilitate conflict resolution in these matters. Instead, clan elders are so honored, if anyone is called at all.[22] This is an area of potential concern, as outside religious leaders (Muslim and Christian) have been kept from asserting influence or authority toward making peace among Babukusu.

The implication is that, in attempts to initiate dialogue about this subject, such outside religious leaders now may well provide a service, acting as a third side in conflict resolution.

Women's Rights

What does the Bukusu culture expect of women? Ali A. Mazrui describes traditional gender beliefs in sub-Saharan Africa, which are true for traditional Bukusu women also: "Rural African women are custodians of fire (in charge of firewood), custodians of water (ensuring its supply in the home), and custodians of earth (cultivating the land)."[23] Bukusu men, on the other hand, are in charge of defending the land and managing cattle, goats, and sheep. Men cut down trees so that women can use branches for firewood.

In domestic policy, a Bukusu woman is ruled by a system that is entirely male dominated. Theoretically, traditional Bukusu women remain inferior to men throughout their lives, coming first under their fathers' authority and secondly under that of their husbands. Furthermore, Bukusu women are excluded by tradition from the council of elders. With few exceptions, women are not even allowed to address the council. Often you hear women make remarks such as, "Let me speak even if I am a woman." Such statements sanction the notion that women aren't leadership material.

If women are to have their concerns heard, their only recourse is to lobby privately, behind the scenes, at the house or among friends. The reason for this exclusion, claim the men, is that women do not have enough *wisdom* to sit on the council of elders. Men maintain that a woman's function is to bear children and look after the home. Having been excluded from traditional council of elders' decision-making, women are expected, nonetheless, to comply with any and all council decisions and to assist in their implementation.

In Bukusu village society, a woman suffers; she is discriminated against and oppressed, to quote African feminist scholar Mercy Amba Aduyoye, a leader in the World Council of Churches, "even before she has uttered her first cry."[24] The announcement of the birth of a baby, for example, is greeted with the common question as to whether the child is male or female. Aduyoye shows what happens when a family is expecting a baby. She articulates the basic difference between male and female in African cultures:

"Oh, mother, I heard good news today. My wife has given birth."
"What did she get?"
"A girl."
"Welcome, source of water, she will give us water to drink."

Juxtaposed with this is the response one might hear at the birth of a boy:

"Oh, mother, I heard good news today. My wife has given birth."
"What did she get?"
"A boy!"
"Oh, mighty man of valor, stay on if you have come."[25]

Aduyoye continues, "The girl, the giver of water, and mighty man of valor are both welcome. She brings us the water of life and he will put our enemies to rout. But when there are no enemies to fight, he turns to fight the women. That is a predominant expression of patriarchy."[26] Women still suffer from violence in every African society. In few places, however, is the abuse more entrenched than in sub-Saharan Africa. It is an accepted thing for women to be treated by their husbands as if they were punching bags.

As a reaction to these cultural attitudes and limitations, many young women have resolved to flee rural villages to escape to the cities. Without diplomas or special skills, they join the already crowded ranks of those attempting to survive through "off-the-books" economic endeavors.[27] Many of these young women are forced to exchange sexual services for money as a means of survival. Such behavior, which has always involved substantial health risks, is now, with the presence of the HIV/AIDS epidemic, virtually a death sentence.[28]

Bukusu cultural discourse cannot be viewed outside the context of gender relations or of patriarchy, since male domination is part of the central ideology in Bukusuland. Patriarchal domination is observable in action, in ideas, and within the gender politics of conjugal relations. Not only does such gender inequity have real effects on social behavior and gender relations, but it also places very real limits on what is negotiable and what is not by non-tribal law (civil law). Bukusu cultural attitudes toward women are now seen as comprising an oppressive system stemming from long before the arrival of European philosophies.

The emergence of a capitalistic form of culture in Bukusuland has reinforced the sexist system because of the benefits it affords. It legitimizes the domination of women by men.[29] The main aspects of Bukusu law that enforce male dominance are rooted in the holding of all property in the hands of men (not only the livestock but also the land where women work) and the bride wealth payments, which render a woman's father and brothers reluctant to support her when she is in conflict with her husband. It is argued by some that the husband buys and pays for his wife and that her relatives give up their duty of protection when they accept the bride wealth.[30]

Many minor regulations and cultural norms reinforce this standard of preserving male authority and demeaning the woman. For example, the husband's sitting stool is almost sacred, and a woman may not sit on it. For a wife to pass wind in front of her husband is a great insult to him. She may not step over the spear or walking stick of her husband. Many of these expectations apply to the young children as well; and a woman must always serve her husband first. So goes tradition. These mores are less firmly enforced in the cities and among educated spouses than in rural Africa. From the Western perspective, as well as from the modern African point of view, and even from Muslim and Christian perspectives, patriarchal dominance is oppressive and wrong.[31] The Bukusu people need to overhaul their whole society. They are becoming aware of this need, which has them polishing their skills at dialogue. In regard to the status of women, it is the Islamic euphemism that has it that all people are "equal as the teeth of a comb."

There is another side to gender relations. In practice, the freedom granted to men to manage their own affairs is also being granted to women now. Today, in some Bukusu villages, a woman has a recognized right to choose her own husband and the initiative in divorce also may (and often does) come from the wife.

That Bukusu women are not without power may be understood by the two weapons of parity—the tongue and the ability to fight physically— often referred to by the Kiswahili word *kali*, meaning "fierce." Women do use their tongues effectively to insist on their rights and to press their points of view. No husband would be willing to deny a *kali* wife her specified rights. Bukusu women are known to fight back physically. In such fights, women seek to grab the man by his genitals, a matter of great psychological concern among men, who believe this betrays weakness on their part—they will appear stupid and useless and without command in the home. It may come as a surprise to some that the strategy is scriptural. In (Deuteronomy 25:11), we read, "If two men are fighting and the wife of one of them comes to rescue her husband from his assailant, and she reaches out and seizes him by his private parts, you shall cut off her hand. Show her no pity." The Bukusu remedy is, of course, less harsh, though the Bukusu still regard the implications quite seriously. When a man has his genitals grabbed in such a way—either by his own wife or another man's wife—he must slaughter a goat before he can enter his wife's house again or have intercourse with her.

Women are also believed to possess magical means of controlling their husbands. This knowledge is given to them in secret sessions during the initiation ritual cycle of womanhood.[32] When they learn the "way of the leopard," for example, they receive their age-group membership and are taught the nature of medicine. The skills they are taught can be used for good or evil, to protect or attack. This power is secret and powerful; other than when it is passed down from mother to daughter, generation after generation, it is unspoken. Bukusu men know that they dare not say anything about this ritual out of fear for their lives. The belief is that if a man speaks of this rite, termites will come through his head, and he will die a horrible death.[33] Further, men do hesitate to mistreat their wives out of fear of (high regard for) the women's powers of retribution, dialogue notwithstanding. Dialogue of course is closer to mutual love than primitive fear.

Many a Bukusu woman boasts that she knows potions that could make her husband love her, make him stop beating her, and make him grant her the favors she asks of him. Men complain that a woman may do magic against a man by urinating in his food, by putting a bit of her excrement or some menstrual blood in his gourd of milk, or by passing wind into it. Such acts are believed to drain the man's strength or make him ugly in the face. Bukusu men do not know for sure what women experience and are taught. Similarly, Bukusu women do not know what Bukusu men are taught in their most sacred and secret rites of passage. Consequently, each must begin the marriage relationship with a basic fear of the other, while later forming a strong bond with the mate.

Thoughtful attention to efforts toward peace and justice and toward equality and liberation for all human beings, needs to characterize the endeavors of all persons and groups who view religion as a positive factor in Africa. To what extent is this striving for humanization by interaction in the realm of gender relations extended to women and to men in Africa or Bukusuland? Bukusu women, for two decades or so now, have begun to claim what is positive in Islam, in Christianity, and in Bukusu traditional cultures, and, to question all that is in the way of their progress as individuals and as a respected community of women. Yet things have only begun to change for the traditional Bukusu. Women should not have to flee their houses or villages for the freedom of the cities. Men should not continue to miss the opportunity to genuinely understand and develop more complete relationships with the women in their lives. Furthermore, children should be raised in more gender equitable ways, so that they will be able to meet the challenges and needs of the twenty-first century world and of their community locally. The majority of African communities, clans, and families and individual Bukusu men and women work to stimulate and feed dialogue on these issues rather than stifle them. They strive to address perceived and real inequities with a spirit of collaboration and confirmation.

Polygyny

Although the belief in the merits of polygyny is a well-established cultural bias, this practice has declined significantly in recent years. Still, the reality of one man with two or more wives is a significant ground for fostering dialogue, as well as conflict.

Before examining issues relating to this cultural heritage, we need to correct a common mistake: People often refer to the practice of a man having more than one wife as polygamy. Technically, this is an error. Such an arrangement, in the Bukusu case, is more correctly described as *polygyny*. Polygamy is the practice of having more than one wife *or* husband at the same time, whereas polygyny is a marriage rule that allows a man to be married to more than one wife simultaneously. (Polyandry is the condition of one woman having two or more husbands simultaneously.) Polygyny is a marriage rule found in many cultures, and it is widely accepted in African and Middle Eastern societies, among both Muslims and followers of traditional African religious beliefs. The number of men who are actually able to practice polygyny, however, is usually limited to a small minority of individuals in any given society. Polygyny is the form of marriage frequently practiced among rural Bukusu communities. Noel King, a scholar of East African history of religions, describes polygyny in sub-Saharan Africa: "It really amounted to a few women bringing up children, each with a husband who was also the husband of the other women. Often, each woman had her own granary, cooking place, and house, and definite privileges and responsibilities with regard to the husband."[34]

In the Bukusu rural setting, the practice of polygyny means the formation of a number of separate but linked households run by individual wives who have a husband in common.[35] The preference given by most husbands to a favored wife constitutes a frequent occasion for jealousy and strife among co-wives. Socially, the first wife, called "the great wife," enjoys a higher status. Her house is usually the largest one. Her homestead is surrounded by an enclosure and occupies the favored position opposite the entrance gate. The husband also keeps his personal belongings in her house—his weapons, special stool, beer straws, and medicine. The favored wife, on the other hand, has no formal privileges, as in fact, her status may not be permanent but depends upon the changing moods and dislikes of the husband. For example, a second wife, in some sense, displaces the first, particularly when the second marriage follows the first wife's failure to bear any sons. A wife's failure to bear a son compels a Bukusu man to take another wife, in order to bear a son to inherit his property. This is the case not just in Bukusuland but in any country with patrilineal leadership. Patriarchy continues to exist in this world. In many places around the world, males are simply thought to be the better choice as heirs.

Polygyny is a custom found all over Africa. Up until the very recent past, chiefs and other wealthy men typically had four, five, or even more wives. One famous Bukusu chieftain, Sudi Namachanja, was known to have had ninety-nine wives. In political terms, the more wives a man had, the more political alliances he would form, and therefore, he would become an authoritative power broker and effective politician, national leader, chief, or king.

Out of ignorance or unfamiliarity, most individuals tend to pass judgment on polygyny without understanding it. It is worth making an attempt to understand the institution before condemning it. To do so necessitates hearing the pros and cons of the practice.

Two primary rationales are given for the practice of polygyny in Bukusuland. Proponents of the sociocultural perspective assert that polygyny provides a balance and equal distribution of social, material, and security benefits to both men and women. A key responsibility of culture is the establishment of social institutions that will maintain the orderly existence of a society. Secondly, central cultural social systems serve to promote a system of values, and these values are a set of ideas, concepts, and practices in which people believe strongly, as is the case with polygyny. As Kenyan scholar Ali A. Mazrui explains:

Culture provides lenses of perception, the way of looking at reality, a worldview; culture provides standards of evaluation; what is good and what is evil; what is legitimate and what is illegitimate are rooted in criteria provided by culture. Culture conditions motivations; what motivates individuals to act or refrain from acting, what inspires individuals to perform well or to really exert themselves is partly inspired by cultural factors. Culture is the medium of communication; the communicative aspects range from language in the literal sense to physical gestures and modes of dress. Culture provides a basis of stratification, a pecking order in society. Status, rank and class are partly the outcome of a cultural order.[36]

One can hardly appreciate the origin of polygyny unless one sees the need to understand the role culture plays in a given society. Culturally, in the Bukusuland of the past, women and children were safer in large households, where they were better protected from aggressors. Men preferred polygyny because it provided more sexual gratification and diversity among mates.[37] Within a Bukusu village society, there was a concern for the well-being of unmarried and widowed women. Clan elders believed that if these women's needs went unmet, the women may engage in adultery or prostitution. As human beings, their sexual, social, psychological, and economic well-being had to be taken care of. Polygyny was seen as the solution to this problem. In addition, the number of a man's wives, as well as the number of his children and livestock, measured his wealth. It was prestigious to be polygynous. Pride was associated with a larger family, and shame and low self-esteem were associated with small families, which were symbolic of poverty.

Proponents of the economic rationale argue that polygyny was established to address the prevailing economic issues of the time. In order to establish a mode of production that was going to be beneficial to the community, the polygynous form of marriage was preferred, as it stressed collective responsibilities, the communal ownership of land and wealth, and the economic benefits of the extended family.[38] In addition, in the agricultural life of the Bukusu, human labor is essential, and polygyny provided more hands to work the fields to produce more food and cash crops for sale. Thus, polygyny not only represented but also *produced* wealth for the family group.

In the long-established Bukusu communities where this arrangement was widespread, a man who had four wives was obligated to provide a section of the family farm for each of his wives. Thus, the suffering of the childless woman in Bukusuland was somewhat mitigated by polygyny, as no woman was without a man, and the children of other wives became like her own.[39] Furthermore, under this system, the additional woman (or women) was protected by the husband's security, and the husband, in return, had another woman (women) to share his labor and his love.

In argument against polygyny, many people who have experienced polygynous families—as husbands, wives, or children—bemoan polygyny's miseries for a number of reasons. Essentially, the existence of co-wives creates distinct problems and restrictions in terms of allocation of resources. Co-wives and their children compete for the man's affection and attention and for shares of cash, which he controls, to cover school fees, food, clothing, and other material goods and for portions of his inheritance wealth. Conflict also arises over the distribution of power and the escalation of gender politics within the homestead.

The relationship between husband and wife in the polygynous family differs from that in the monogamous family, mainly because in the polygynous family, the wife has to share her sexual and economic claims upon her husband. In theory, the polygynous husband is supposed to devote an equal amount of sexual, relational, and economic attention to all his wives. In practice, however, this expectation is often unfulfilled, leading to relational imbalances, jealousies, and conflicts. A perception of neglect or unfair treatment on the part of one co-wife can initiate a cycle of ill feelings or bitter quarrels that can lead to poisoning or accusations of sorcery among the wives. A Bukusu proverb says, "Two wives are two pots of poison." This can be interpreted both metaphorically and literally. Metaphorically, this refers to the challenge men feel in keeping two wives happy and avoiding poisonous jealousies and battles. More literally, there are times when a husband may not feel free to eat food other than that which has been cooked by the great wife, as he fears being poisoned by the other wives. Even though this idea is seldom confirmed by facts, it supports the cultural norm that the bond linking the husband to his first wife is more stable and trustworthy than that binding him to those whom he has married later.

The meticulous fairness demanded of the husband in such marriages is difficult to achieve; jealousy and quarrels between co-wives are endemic.

Such quarrels lead to accusations by one wife that the other is using love charms to lure away the husband's affections or is bewitching her children. The man also fears that his younger wives might have lovers on the sly, adding to the precariousness of the arrangement. Women fight among themselves, and their husband is caught in the middle trying to mediate or force resolution.[40]

Thus, polygyny has its positive and negative aspects. It is both a sign of status and prestige for a husband and a possible source of conflict for all concerned. It can even become an unintended invitation to poverty. Today, with a cash economy predominant in Bukusu villages, polygyny is possible only for those in affluent circumstances; it is not a reality for ordinary Bukusu people nowadays, though some men like to think it should still be so. Consequently, polygyny is decreasing in Bukusuland, not so much because of Western or religious influence, but more because of the changing economy and the prevailing cultural climate, which are rapidly rendering polygyny problematic at best.

Many within the Catholic tradition and the Islamic faith find it difficult to condone polygyny as found among the Bukusu people today. Consequently, when members of polygynous Bukusu families have official dealings with these religious bodies, significant and deeply held differences of opinion arise. When matters that are so important to a people or faith tradition are discussed, debates or battles may readily ensue. People with opposing views may disregard or demean the meaning and value of the position other persons are putting forth. The confluence of dissonant opinions at times like this can be fertile ground for misunderstandings and critical judgments. For example, if a Christian Bukusu man who has a family decides to marry the widow of his deceased brother, such a decision automatically goes against the Christian faith but would likely be tolerated by Muslims and African traditional religions. As members of the families, the community, and various religious leaders discussed the man's decision, their opposing beliefs could surface and be difficult to discuss amicably. That is when constructive dialogue would be useful but also when it could be difficult to achieve. Yet these differences of beliefs and religious ways of being cannot be ignored; they cannot be silenced. They must be addressed sensitively and constructively.

CHAPTER 19

• ◆ •

APPROPRIATE STRATEGIES AND TECHNIQUES
FOR THE BUKUSU CONTEXT

The challenge before Bukusu communities today—Muslim, Christian, and traditional—is to develop ways of living together as a community in peace and harmony. This challenge raises nearly unavoidable questions: How can Bukusu people learn to deal with their differences while neither suppressing them nor having conflicts over them? How can the Bukusu community create a culture of coexistence and conflict resolution in their villages, at work, and with their neighbors? These are crucial questions that call for answers. Too often, answers are contextually dependent. One answer doesn't fit all circumstances.

The following presents the perspectives of Martin Buber, Fred Iklé, and William Ury as suggestions—more as general understandings than as specific strategies—that can be of value in advancing positive and collaborative intercultural interaction.

Martin Buber's Potential Contribution

Buber's primary emphasis is understood to focus mostly on relations between individuals. The goal, he suggests, is to overcome social distance by genuine or dialogic relation. "All real living is meeting," he counsels.[41] Through this interpersonal relating, Buber reports, individuals confirm one another.

Inclusion becomes the key to genuine relationship and mutual dialogue. For Buber, everyone counts and no one is left out. Buber argues for an ethic that does not think of or use other people as objects of one's own personal needs or gratification. Instead, he writes, "We must learn to consider everything around us as 'you' speaking to 'me,' and requiring a response."[42]

Applying Buber's perspective to Bukusu life might be especially relevant in terms of the role of women. Women are not treated well in Bukusu society; they are neither included nor confirmed. Instead, they are manipulated, used, silenced, shut out of the council of elders, and prevented from being taken seriously in many community issues and decisions.

Buber's philosophy stands in direct opposition to such a reality. Buber calls for the valuing and inclusion of all people, and for confirmation of each person's ideas and points of view. There is a yearning within each person to be accepted and affirmed and to be respected for what he or she is and can be. There is a need within each person to share his or her way of being with others, to have it welcomed, honored, and given full consideration. Bukusu women express such yearnings and deserve such treatment. Their perspectives and experience need to be part of the communal wealth.

Buber narrates an old Jewish tale that relates to this belief. He tells of a man who searched around the world for buried treasure, only to discover it could be found in his own backyard:

Rabbi Bunam used to tell young men who came to him for the first time the story of Rabbi Eizik, son of Rabbi Yekel of Cracow. "After many years of great poverty, which had never shaken his faith in God, he dreamt someone bade him look for a treasure in Prague, under the bridge, which leads to the king's palace. When the dream recurred a third time, Rabbi Eizik prepared for the journey and set out for Prague. But the bridge was guarded day and night and he did not dare to start digging. Nevertheless he went to the bridge every morning and kept walking around it until evening. Finally, the captain of the guards, who had been watching him, asked in a kindly way, whether he was looking for something or waiting for somebody. Rabbi Eizik told him of the dream that had brought him here from a faraway country. The captain laughed: 'And so to please the dream, you poor fellow wore out your shoes to come here! As for having faith in dreams, if I had had it, I should have had to get going when a dream once told me to go to Cracow and dig for treasure under the stove in the room of a Jew, Eizik, son of Yekel. I can just imagine what it would be like, how I should have to try every house over there, where one half of the Jews are named Eizik and the other Yekel!' And he laughed again. Rabbi Eizik bowed, traveled home, dug up the treasure from under the stove, and built the house of prayer, which is called Reb Eizik Reb Yekel's Shul.

"Take this story to heart," Rabbi Bunam used to add, "and make what it says your own: There is something you cannot find anywhere in the world, not even at the Zaddik's, and there is, nevertheless, a place where you can find it. Here where one stands."[43]

This story can be understood to suggest that our life offers richness, regardless of the circumstances. But it can also be taken to suggest that each person is a treasure. People do not have to try to be like someone they are not; they do not have to deny their own richness. In the life to come, you will not be asked why you were not Moses; you shall not be asked why you were not Zusye. You need to be yourself; you can't be anyone else. With this interpretation of the story, the importance of each woman's reality becomes evident, and the expectation that Bukusu husbands and elders need to honor and include women becomes obvious.[44] Taking this idea one step further, an individual's social location determines his or her worldview. Things look different depending on where one is. Buber wrote, "The desire to influence the other then does not mean the effort to change the other, to inject one's own rightness into him; but it means the effort to let that which is recognized as right, as just, as true (and for that very reason must also be established there, in the substance of the other) through one's influence take seed and grow in the form suited to individuation."[45]

Buber's story of the Hasid and the above quote also help to explicate the position of those who are marginalized in Bukusu communities, especially women. According to the feminist focus on the politics of perspective, where one stands on certain issues determines both how one sees things and how one is seen by others. Feminists say women have a particular standpoint; but kept outside the circles of Bukusu patriarchy and religious powers, women's voices and perspectives traditionally have been ignored by men.

Buber's approach suggests a paradigm shift in community and clan consciousness so that marginalized people at least receive attention. More significantly, the central patriarchy would evolve to include and confirm women's vision as well as men's.

Bukusu women's liberation movements have been slowly gaining momentum, especially in the cities and among educated communities. Women's viewpoints are now being taken more seriously nationally, and their voices are being included in the centers of power—African governments and churches. Although the reality is that the resolution is far from complete, women, political organizations, and educational institutions are discussing these issues throughout the continent. Progress is at hand; African men and women are following the global trends toward gender equity.

Furthermore, if all leaders of and adherents to Islam, Christianity, and traditional Bukusu religion were to embrace the *I-Thou* principle in gender relations, intercultural respect would be manifest and religious disagreements and segregation would be minimized. However, each of these traditions in Bukusuland has its own problems with embracing gender equity; for example, the local Catholic Church resists placing women in significant leadership positions, going against the true teaching of the Catholic Church, which holds women in very high regard. Currently in the United States and throughout much of the Western world, women serve as pastoral administrators for many parishes. Their contributions in ministry and administration are greatly valued and appreciated in their communities. In Bukusuland, this is still unheard of. For Kenyan bishops, as well as Bukusu priests and laity, to have women in such positions would be seen as an affront, or at least as an anomaly and a questionable sharing of communal responsibilities. It is reasonable to assume that there are still evolutionary changes taking place regarding the role of women within Bukusu religious communities. A dialogic respect, as Buber suggests, may be needed to facilitate these changes that will bring greater transcultural respect and collaboration.

One way proponents of social change might encourage this reality is to educate youth about dialogic ways of community. Catholic, Muslim, and traditional communities of Bukusuland could design youth programs in which the interpersonal meanings of communion would be explored from Buber's dialogic perspective. These programs or seminars could be designed to be appropriate for the training of youth leadership to develop community service and educational programs. The youth could volunteer in neighborhood organizations to learn about community challenges and develop their own ideas and strategies for bringing about dialogue, conflict resolution, and positive social change.

Community activists could design a similar program for priests, catechists, and lay leaders active in the Bukusu community. Such programs may well be planned to deepen and enhance Church members' faith, while adding deeper meaning to their understanding of Christ's message of love for one another and Saint Paul's message of peace and respect for other cultures. This may become a positive vehicle for the furtherance of the conversation that is already taking place regarding the role and involvement of women in the Church and the community.

Similarly, Muslim members of the community could design and implement training programs appropriate for Muslim leadership. These measures would encourage and empower Christian and Muslim leaders to take the message of grassroots dialogic relations to their religious communities. The seeds of mutual respect in every personal encounter could thus be planted.

Fred Iklé's Potential Contribution

Fred Iklé's perspectives on negotiation and peacemaking also have great potential for the Bukusu community. Iklé's concerns are essentially two questions: How can conflict stop once it arises? And how can communities preserve peace? Iklé answers these questions in a number of ways, but most valuable to the Bukusu is his emphasis on accommodation and community spirit.

Accommodation is the solution to negotiation in Iklé's approach. Iklé asserts that accommodation makes the negotiating process more efficient because it increases the chances for agreement on specific and immediate issues. When one accommodates, he or she comes to terms or adapt to his or her situation with a positive attitude. Accommodation reduces hostility between warring groups and stimulates friendly feelings between leaders or influential officials of each side. These improved attitudes can help to minimize conflict and make future agreements more likely.[46]

In order to negotiate successfully, Iklé suggests, a positive or collaborative community spirit has to exist. As he puts it, "The life of our community also depends on everyone looking upon and treating community matters as matters of real joint responsibility."[47] What helps to preserve the community spirit is the interest of each member in reciprocation. When groups are engaged in a long-term common effort, each community needs the future collaboration of its partners and remains dependent on their goodwill. This awareness makes it possible to regard an act of generosity today as establishing a credit for tomorrow. This perspective also makes it safe for negotiators to accept an agreement in principle—provided all partners have the same understanding of it—and to leave the details to the experts or technicians. [48]

Iklé adds that community spirit permits negotiators to dispense with some of the more rigid rules of accommodation that may seem necessary between less friendly communities. Instead, there is strong emphasis on the common objectives, and, ideally, none of the parties are keeping motives hidden motives from each other. In emphasizing the role of community spirit, Iklé suggests that people follow the advice of Jean Monnet, whom many think of as the primary facilitator of European unity. Iklé reports that, according to Monnet, "The participants are reminded regularly to act in accordance with the community spirit, *l'espirit communautaire*, and to focus on the common interest, rather than on trades between conflicting interests, and to maximize the advantages of their joint undertaking, rather than to exchange separate gains and losses with each other."[49]

Applied to the Bukusu context, problems of land rights and women's rights could be ameliorated by embracing these aspects of Iklé's perspective. Disputes over land between Bukusu communities and their neighbors are still a source of conflict and hatred. Such disputes can provide an opportunity for women to influence positive negotiations among clans. This was evidenced in the land clashes of the early1990s at Mount Elgon between the Bukusu and the neighboring Sabaot people. Men of both sides took up arms and made war, leaving many dead and others wounded and displaced. Amid these ethnic clashes, many women were adversely affected because they had intermarried with the other ethnic groups; thus, they felt attacked from both sides by clan antagonisms and hatred.

In conflicts like this, women are often among the most ardent voices for a resolution to the conflict—not only because of the suffering caused by the violence, but because they are caught between their loyalties to the clans of their fathers and mothers and those of their husbands and children. In times of mounting ethnic or interclan tensions, women are sent to their childhood clan to state grievances and requests and to carry back the responses of the elders to their husbands' clans, often helping to resolve conflict without violence. Similarly, during times of open conflict, women serve as messengers between the clans, carrying messages of peace and gifts of negotiation and reconciliation to the opposing groups. Women play this role because of their interclan ties.

However, Bukusu women are usually not part of formal peace negotiations and reconciliation meetings. A far more common way for women to make their views known during negotiations is indirectly, through their fathers, husbands, or brothers. Women at home discuss issues freely with their men, who then carry their ideas and input to the formal negotiation of the council of elders. Iklé's approach suggests that women are, thereby, acting as primary peacemakers—for one might conclude that women plant the seeds of the community spirit as they inconspicuously, yet determinedly, encourage wisdom, cooperation, and reconciliation at the council of elders.

Thus, a Bukusu woman is involved at many levels of conflict resolution in Bukusuland. She resolves disputes in the family and in the extended family by preserving harmony between herself and her husband, by ensuring good relationships between her children and their spouses, and even by bringing clans back into peaceful accord.

One advantage that can be gained from Iklé's approach pertains to times when there is a lack of reciprocal willingness to seek common ground and agreements. It is possible that respected elders among the Bukusu community, especially those on the council of elders, could be encouraged to discuss the elements of negotiation and conflict resolution that Iklé advocates. Religious groups or government officials could initiate this process, with the intention of empowering the elders by giving them more options for adjudicating problems. In this way, elders could combine the wisdom of their experience with the tradition of their authority, enhanced by the knowledge of those experienced in conflict resolution in other environments. They would gain additional tools and skills for handling conflicts and bringing about negotiation. The elders' position of authority would not be challenged by this approach but rather would be honored and strengthened.

In a situation in which there is an apparent and irresolvable enmity between groups, it is possible that the Church, Christian groups, Islamic leaders, or government officials could set up mediation and arbitration boards that could provide free services to those in need of negotiation assistance. Christians, Muslim, and local community leaders would need to sensitively choose the composition of these boards, and the boards would need to secure confidentiality of negotiation by mutual agreement. Ideally, the people on these boards would be trained in the principles and perspectives of Buber, Iklé, and Ury; but it is my opinion that Ury's belief in assigning implicit trustworthiness to the parties becomes something of a weakness. Community empowerment is the goal we have for these programs and not "parties" as illustrated by Ury. For Iklé, empowering people helps them gain control over their own lives. It is a process that fosters power in people that they can use in their own lives, their communities, and their society at large by acting on issues they define as important. During this process, then, the third party would want to yield to the dialogue principles of Iklé, even while considering those of Ury beneficial. This position would provide a new and flexible alternative for the community in dealing with any potentially volatile situation.

William Ury's Potential Contribution

William Ury, like Iklé, tackles the most critical challenge facing every culture today—getting to peace. The presumption among so many that human beings have always warred (and always will) has been unchallenged from person to person and from parent to child (recall here the Bukusu people's knife-sharpening prayer in which they invoke Wele's help, viewing war as a demonstration of the divine power intervening on their behalf). Ury argues that fighting is *not* an inevitable part of human nature. If peoples of like mind decide to reclaim their responsibility for avoiding conflict, then peace must be an alternative. No one should hold the belief that fighting is either desirable or inevitable. The "naturalness" of fighting is no longer an acceptable excuse for so misbehaving. In negotiation that includes third-party negotiators, it is recognized that abandoning this old-fashioned thinking is the ultimate benefit of negotiation.

Ury argues that a people's tranquility, productivity, and very lives depend on getting at peace. For the Bukusu, each individual must, by this understanding and life application, act as teacher, healer, and mediator to achieve fair and nonviolent conflict resolution, whether the dispute takes place during innocent play or under the auspices of other considerations. Parents can assist their children in learning how to deal with conflicts at play constructively. A teacher may bring a conflict resolution issues into the classroom. A religious leader can help people to appreciate apology and forgiveness. A journalist can spotlight a potential conflict for the public's attention. It should be concomitant with any police officer's role to mediate local conflict by finding the cause before applying the heavy hand of the law, as the most basic law is as follows: Peace is the only way. Segments within the community ought to put their talents to use as bridge builders to peace for peaceful conflict resolution.

The conflicts and differences of the past and the present must make way for better community relations, on into the future. If the challenges are great, says Ury, the opportunity and the conditions are also great. More importantly, these serve as opportunities ripe for communal learning.[50] Such an opportunity is what, in education and psychology, is termed "the teachable moment." A lot of learning does take place among the Bukusu people. Even as the Bukusuland population, by Ury's estimation, is comparatively advanced in conflict resolution by dialogue, he still finds that all Bukusu community members must learn to act as optimally sensitive facilitators whenever people with Muslim, Christian, or Bukusu traditional beliefs meet. After all, humans do not genetically inherit such considerate behaviors. Each generation, singularly and severally, must work through the processes of communal dialogue to learn how to live in peace.

Rites of passage, such as circumcisions and funerals, serve to heighten people's awareness of dialogue's capacity to bind, yet because of differences in their faiths and their cultural traditions, adherents to one faith or another may become uncomfortable in a ceremony. Bukusu facilitators do well to help lighten and enlighten the assemblage, promoting acknowledgements that facilitate friendly exchanges among all gathered instead of merely standing by, idly watching the ceremony fall apart. They can pull people and faith communities together out of awkward instances rather than watch them harden their hearts with displays of standing apart. In doing so, the presiding elder must redirect the assemblage back to some commonality that would lead to mutual respect and consideration.

Some might believe that the third party that could help the Bukusu people would be an outside agency or person. However, this would go against the deeper meaning of Ury's admonition; the third-side involvement from *within* the Bukusu community is ever to be preferred.

One practical possibility for implementing this notion would be to have schoolchildren learn at the earliest opportunity that all persons are equally human. Teachers, professional development leaders, community groups, and parents would design educational programs for simple children's reading matter and classroom role-playing activities to heighten awareness in the children regarding the need for conflict resolution in the community. Such learning strategies would promote more effective friendships and diminish intimidation, ridiculing, and overtly hostile behaviors. The seed planted in young children in their public and religious school setting naturally becomes the root structure for their deeper and growing commitment to community harmony. Such programs might be initiated by the government, by religious groups, by nongovernmental institutions (NGOs) that have played important roles in the past during famines and wars in alleviating poverty and helping disadvantaged people, or simply by the local community.[51] Based on his international experience, Ury allows that these groups will, in time, become vehicles for the dissemination of conflict resolution strategies for the world. Since any group similar to the Bukusu in this regard tends to be esteemed by their neighbors and ultimately imitated, such conflict resolution practices serve to reinforce the essential thrust for humanity's overall well-being. If people live in peace, the need for NGOs will diminish. Ultimately, teaching programs focusing on conflict resolution education and Ury's third-side philosophy could become a win-win strategy for positive human coexistence, bearing in mind that the continuance of peaceful coexistence is dependent on each generation's passing on this philosopher's ideas.

When we take into consideration all of these concerns and potentials, a model arises that surely can benefit more than Bukusu people and their three religious disciplines. An institute jointly sponsored by Christian, Muslim, and traditional Bukusu factions ultimately would be established. Such an institute would focus on leadership training and community education on building dialogue and resolving conflicts. Members from each of these supportive communities (both men and women) ideally would share in the program design, implementation, and evaluation on a cyclic basis for fine-tuning at a given time and place. The process would not only teach collegiality, but it would also model it. Such institutions might be started in small pilot projects to ascertain what works and to fine-tune its projects. On this basis, a model would evolve that could serve to encourage peace and empower peacemakers not only among the Bukusu communities, but among all who stand in awe of their accomplishments.

The Bukusu people have a saying in their oral tradition that is reflected in the famous Chinese proverb, "A journey of several miles begins with the first step." That is, the journey begins not by leaps and bounds but by the first step. In this life, every step must lead to another step. This is how people will find their way to any goal, and so it must be with peace. Based on this common wisdom, Ury tells a story: "A Chinese nobleman once asked his gardener to plant the seed of a rare and beautiful tree. When the gardener protested, 'But sir, that tree will take a hundred years to flower,' the nobleman replied, 'Then we'd better plant it this afternoon.'" [52] When we apply this to the situation at hand, we see that, because the task of creating a genuine new co-culture may take a generation or more, there is no better time for us to begin than now.

The time to begin working for mutual respect and cooperation is ever the present moment. Traditional Bukusus, Christian Bukusus, Islamic Bukusus, and all other people living in Bukusuland are compelled by tradition itself to find ways to embrace community and to support each other for the good of all. Elsewhere in diversely cultured populations, as for example in the United States of America, this quality of communality is considered national patriotism. In the contemporary world, we all must see this attitude as a universal stance as so many move across the margins of the world.

Conclusion

• ◆ •

The challenge is to find ways to establish cultural respect and cooperation worldwide, as well as among Muslims, Christians, and traditional clan peoples of the Bukusu. Taking into consideration their appropriate relatedness for Bukusu culture and tradition, Buber's philosophy of dialogue, Iklé's strategies for dialogue, and Ury's techniques for negotiating dialogue serve well to promote intercultural respect and interreligious dialogue. If we keep this goal in mind and focus on an understanding of Bukusu culture, we will have a proper context for gaining an increasingly profound understanding through which we can integrate alternative points of view.

I have presented the history of Islam and Christianity in Bukusuland and their more current interaction with traditional Bukusu people, followed by the approaches of Buber, Iklé, and Ury, delineating both their theoretical and practical observations.

After presenting communication patterns that are part and parcel of the Bukusu life and culture, I have focused in the last section on a number of areas in Bukusu life in which conflicts, potential or actual, exist. My goal was to demonstrate how the collective wisdom of these three outsiders, with their perspectives on dialogue, adds to the appreciation of the dialogue traditional among the Bukusu people, over and above any religious differences among their cultures. These suggestions were meant neither to solve all problems nor to imply that doing so is possible. Rather, I offer them as kindling for the fires of research, providing for future community campfires.

My hope and expectation is that such conversations and dialogues will help to clear the way for positive growth among all communities worldwide that might resonate with the traditional example the Bukusu oral tradition communicates by their message—the importance of drumming up dialogue for sharing humanity's journey toward all mutual understandings, respect, and collaboration.

This has been the story of my people. I know my people, both young and old, will read it and think deeply about its meaning. I pray to God, Allah, and Wele (which are all names for the One Divine and Guiding Spirit) that my words and these ideas will serve each of these communities well and bring about positive dialogue as we face common challenges in blending the futures of these three great traditions.

Part V Notes

1. J. Ferguson McLennan, "The Nature of Tribal Religion," in *Traditional Religion in West Africa*, ed. Adegbola (Nairobi/Kampala: Uzima/CPH, 1983), 242–43.

2. A typical example of this is the method the Babukusu employ in driving away an evil spirit from the vicinity of a homestead. Two small huts or shrines are erected on the newly paved path from the home leading to the stream, where the spirits are believed to dwell at nighttime. The section of the path is carefully cleaned and several twigs, as well as feathers of a chicken that has been killed and roasted, are stuck into the ground beside the two huts. If the evil spirits come along that path, they will be terrified at seeing the two sacrificial huts and will turn back again.

3. Male youth are trained to be warriors and, thus, are believed to be "hot-blooded," emotional, violent, selfish, and in need of being controlled. Girls often encourage and instigate fighting among the boys. They sing the warriors songs and taunt them by saying, "If you are afraid, leave it to us; we will show you that we are not cowards." Youth create conflict within the community that only the elders can resolve. The elders' role, therefore, is to resolve the conflicts raised by young people. Restoring social harmony is required for the survival of the community.

4. As one African theologian explains, "Initiation is not only a decisive experience bringing about a new state of being, a mode of existence in the world with reference to the ancestors; it is also a true language in itself, which is composed of gestures and words" Ela, *My Faith*, 40.

5. van Gennep, *Rites of Passage*, 65ff.

6. King, *Christian and Muslim*, 68.

7. For some Bukusu Christians, this leads them to feel as if they are in what one scholar calls a "religious concubinage," by claiming, "Mass in the morning, diviner at night! Amulet in your pocket, and scapular around your neck!" This reveals the cultural tension some Bukusu Christians face. For many of those baptized, conversion to the Gospel may be experienced as an "ambiguous adventure." See Ela, *My Faith*, 139.

8. Aylward Shorter, "Problems and Possibilities for the Church's Dialogue with African Traditional Religion," in *Dialogue with the African Traditional Religions*, ed. A. Shorter, (Kampala: Gaba Publications, 1975), 7.

9. Ibid.

10. Harold G. Koenig, *Aging and God: Spiritual Pathways to Mental Health in Mid-Life and Later Years*, (Bing-hamton, New York: Haworth Pastoral Press, 1994), 441.

11. In regard to religious beliefs of the parties involved, conflicts can occur when two religious groups insist that their particular burial religious rite must be observed.

12. This results in lands being cut and parceled again and again, resulting in smaller and smaller family properties.

13. A familiar and traditional folktale of the Bukusu people.

14. The positive potential for intercultural communication during funeral ceremonies can also be recognized when religious leaders share in their ceremonies or when religious prayers and symbols from different traditions are included. During the meals and the communal mourning that takes place, significant opportunities arise for people of different faiths and traditions to interact and bond. Similarly, when religious leaders offer ecumenical prayers, taking turns leading the group, a sense of recognition on the part of the other may evolve.

15. Because of the cultural and social significance of circumcision, hospital circumcision operations were frowned upon by Bukusu people in the past. Now, because of the extra expense of school fees, less money is being spent on the ceremony, and hospital circumcisions are becoming more acceptable. Traditional circumcision ceremonies are costly. A big feast is prepared and plenty of beer is brewed. At least three head of cattle for every candidate are slaughtered, and an enormous amount of food is prepared for the attendees, which can frequently number up to four hundred people. Such an event can cost the equivalent of many years of one's savings. However, in recent years, Bukusu parents' priorities have been changing. Along with these changes have come new priorities in spending. Their discretionary funds are being used more for education, health care, and school fees. Parents are now dedicating such amounts of time, energy, and money to these more modern priorities that they are gradually losing interest in or willingness to fund such extravagant circumcision events as in the past. These rites are still being held, but the magnitude and expense of the events are decreasing significantly.

16. Muslims consider genital circumcision necessary for all normal children. Almost invariably, the immediate explanation offered is that circumcision is

a religious obligation prescribed in the hadith of the Prophet Muhammad. However, it is worth noting that circumcision is not once alluded to in the Qur'an. This omission is remarkable, and Muslim writers do not attempt any explanation of it. Circumcision is held to be founded on the Sunna, or the customs of the prophet, thereby dating the circumcision codes from the time of Abraham. There is no authentic account of the circumcision of Muhammad, but some writers assert that he was born circumcised. Most eminent scholars deny this. In the *sabihu l' Bukhari*, a short chapter is devoted to the subject of *khitan*, or circumcision, in which there are three traditions:

1) Abu Hurairah relates that the prophet said that one of the observances of *Fitra* is circumcision.

2) Abu Hurairah relates that the prophet said that Abraham was circumcised when he was eighty years old.

3) Said Ibn Jubair relates that it was asked of Ibn Abbas, "How old were you when the Prophet died?" He said, "I was circumcised in the days when it occurred." And Jubair says they did not circumcise in those days until men were fully grown.

See Thomas Patrick Hughes, *A Dictionary of Islam* (London: W. H. Allen and Co., 1888), 57. On the other hand, one Muslim scholar notes, "To be a Muslim, it is believed, is to be circumcised" H. Ammar, *Growing up in an Egyptian Village* (London: Routledge and Kegan, 1954), 120.

17. King, *Christian and Muslim*, 95.

18. There are many African creation myths that tell about the origins of human beings. The Fon people of Dahomey, for example, believe that when God had set the universe in order and had created animals and plants, he then formed the first human beings from clay and water. A striking common characteristic of these stories, including the one from the book of Genesis in the Bible, is that they all point to the earth or the soil as the source of human origin. Looking at land from a theological point of view, it is usually believed that the earth is the basis without which creation could not have been possible, that human life is not possible without being connected to the land, and that the violation of people's rights to land is tantamount to violating the very image of God in which humanity was created. For African creation myths, see John S. Mbiti, *Concepts of God in Africa* (London: SPCK, 1970), 163.

19. C. Newbury and B. G. Schoepf, "State, Peasantry and Agrarian Crisis in Zaire: Does Gender Make a Difference?" in *Women and the State in Africa*, ed. Kathleen A. Staudt (Boulder: Lynne Rienner, 1989), 151.

20. Ury's ideas provide a context for explaining the development of land conflicts in Bukusuland: "When our ancestors settled down, the increasing number

of hungry mouths created a squeeze on land and food. There was constant pressure to expand the lands under cultivation. As farmers spread out, they came into conflict with others who needed the same land or with hunters or gatherers who saw their game driven off. Droughts and shortages tempted groups to attack their neighbors and seize their crops in order to survive. The new way thus increased not only the amount but the intensity of conflicts" (Ury, *Getting to Peace*, 64).

21. This displacement took place from the late nineteenth century onwards, at least from the more desirable land. The cooler and more fertile parts of Kenya were part of what became known as the "White Highlands" With independence, politically well-connected rich took these lands, rather than needy Kenyans. This displacement and the resulting resentment is part of the root of today's violence. This is paraphrased from a TIME magazine article, "KENYA: Open the Highlands," and the date is June 20, 1955, and the URL is http://www.time.com/time/magazine/article/0,9171,861593,00.html

22. The Kenyan government has formally given this power to the elders.

23. Ali A. Mazrui, "The Black Woman and the Problem of Gender: An African Perspective," in *The Global African*, ed. Omari H. Kokole (Asmara, Eritrea: African World Press), 237.

24. Mercy Amba Aduyoye, *Daughters of Anowa: African Women and Patriarchy* (Maryknoll, New York: Orbis Books, 1995, 88.

25. Ibid, 87–88.

26. Ibid, 87.

27. This is true for traditional Bukusu, Muslim, and Christian women, in spite of the fact that it strongly conflicts with their religious beliefs.

28. Newbury and Schoepf, "State, Peasantry, and Agrarian Crisis," 105.

29. Rosemary Edet and Bette Ekeya, "Church Women of Africa: A Theological Community," in *With Passion and Compassion: Third World Women Doing Theology*, eds. Virginia Fabella and Mercy Amba Aduyoye (Maryknoll, NY: Orbis, 1988), 5.

30. This is not the norm, but it has some truth for many Bukusu. Husbands tend to believe they own their wives, but wives know that, in extreme cases, they can still flee to their relatives for refuge.

31. This is not true in the case of extreme fundamentalist groups. However, an essay on the possibility of a new image for the African woman by Rosemary Nthamburi, a Kenyan scholar, opens with the following statement: "The African states have been through the traditional society, colonialism, and have now entered into a state of independence. As they experience these historical events and changes, African women labor under disabilities in employment, law, and

sad to say, in church." Nthamburi goes on to claim that, when analyzing the women's present experience, one cannot ignore the fact that, in the realm of religious leadership, Africa has Muslims, Christians, and traditional believers, all of whom are attempting to move side by side, affecting and authenticating one another's concepts—mostly in ways that are unfavorable to women. See Rosemary Nthamburi, "On the Possibility of a New Image for an African Woman," a paper submitted to the Continental Consultation on Theology from Third World Women's Perspectives (EATWOT Women's Commission), Port Harcourt, Nigeria, August 19–23, 1986.

32. There is a similar ritual for Bukusu men, which carries an entirely different meaning. This ritual also needs to remain in the realm of the unspoken and should not be described.

33. This belief is so deeply held that I am the first to write of it in any way and, in fact, am unwilling to explain any additional rites or beliefs of the actions or belief references behind this central ritual for Bukusu women.

34. Noel Q. King, *Religions of Africa* (New York: Harper & Row, Publishers, 1970), 75.

35. Some Bukusu individuals are flexible in allowing unofficially and nonsexual joined arrangements. A Bukusu woman who is unable to have children is sometimes married as a "husband" to another woman who is made pregnant by a man who is secretly chosen by the first woman. She and her female partner are then considered the official parents of the child. The barren woman thus becomes the socially recognized "father" and thereby adds members to *her* father's patrilineal kinship group.

36. Mazrui, *Africans*, 7.

37. Further, as it is taboo for a couple to engage in sexual intercourse during pregnancy, polygyny provided a solution to this dilemma. Polygyny also provided a form of birth control, in the sense that it would allow the spacing of children, by virtue of the sexual taboos attached to sex during breast-feeding.

38. A practical challenge to both the social and the economic rationales depended on the amount of dowry a man's family could afford for additional wives.

39. King, *Religions of Africa*, 75.

40. Such quarreling reflects badly not only on the wives but also on the husband. It is often the husband who is blamed by neighbors for troubles in the man's household.

41. Buber, *I and Thou*, 20–21, 11.

42. Buber, *Knowledge of Man*, 108.

43. Martin Buber, *The Way of Man: According to the Teaching of Hasidism* (New York: The Citadel Press, 1966), 37.

44. Although Buber doesn't use the phrase, his philosophy suggests a social equity, a "justice among genders," that enables and encourages a dialogic community.

45. Martin Buber, *Knowledge of Man*, 69.

46. Iklé, *How Nations Negotiate*, 87–88.

47. Ibid, 120.

48. Ibid.

49. Ibid, 119.

50. William Ury, *The Third Side* (New York: Penguin Books, 2000), 199.

51. NGO stands for Non-Governmental Organizations, such as the Red Cross, Catholic Relief Services, and World Vision International.

52. Ury, *Getting to Peace*, 107.

BIBLIOGRAPHY

•◆•

Abdalati, Hammaduh. *Islam in Focus.* Delhi: Crescent Publishing Company, 1988.

Abu al-'ala 'Afifi, ed. *Mishkat al-anwar.* Cairo: Dar al-Qawmiya lil-Tab'a wa al-Nashr, 1964.

Abu-Bakr, Ali, ed. *National Museums of Kenya-Fort Jesus Museum.* March 22, 2001. http://www.experiencekenya.co.ke/museums.php.

Abu-Lughod, Lila. *Writing Women's Worlds.* Berkeley: University of California Press, 1993.

Achebe, Chinua. *Arrow of God.* New York: Anchor Books/Doubleday, 1974.

_____. *Things Fall Apart.* Johannesburg, South Africa: Heinemann Publishers (Pty) Ltd., 1996.

Aduyoye, Mercy Amba. *Daughters of Anowa: African Women and Patriarchy.* Maryknoll, New York: Orbis Books, 1995.

Ahmed, b. Abd al-Rahman Alawi. *Manaqib al-Sayyid Muhammad b. Ahmad b. Abi Bakr al-Shadhili al-Yashruti.* Cairo: Mustafa al-Babi al-Halabi, 1934: Martin, 1976.

Ahmed, Akbar S. *Discovering Islam: Making Sense of Muslim History and Society.* London: Routledge, 1988.

————. *Living Islam: From Samarkand to Stornoway*. London: BBC Books Ltd., 1993.

Ahmed, Salahuddin. *A Dictionary of Muslim Names*. New York: New York University Press, 1999.

Ajayi, J. F. A. *Christian Missions in Nigeria 1841–1891*. London: Longmann, 1965.

Algar, Hamid. *The Sunna: Its Obligatory and Exemplary Aspects*. Oneonta, New York: Islamic Publication International, 2000.

Ali, Maulana Muhammad, Ali. *Muhammad The Prophet*. The Ahmadiyya Anjuman Isha'at Islam Lahore-U.S.A., 1993.

Allen, James De Vere. *Swahili Origins*. Ohio: Ohio University Press, 1993.

Ammar, H. *Growing up in an Egyptian Village*. London: Routledge and Kegan, 1954.

Amin, Duncan Willetts, and Brian Tetley. *Spectrum Guide to Kenya*. Nairobi: Camerapix Publishers International, 1989.

Anderson, Benedict. *Imagined communities: Reflections on the Origin and Spread of Nationalism*. London: Verso Press, 1993.

Anderson, M. David, and Douglas H. Johnson, eds. *Revealing Prophets: Prophecy in Eastern African History*. Nairobi: E.A.E.P, 1995.

Ani, Marimba. *An African-centered Critique of European Cultural Thought and Behavior*. Trenton, NJ: Africa World Press, 1994.

An-Na'im, Abdullahi Ahmed, ed. *Proselytization and Communal Self-determination in Africa*. Maryknoll, New York: Orbis Books, 1999.

Appiah, Kwame, Anthony. *In My Father's House: Africa in the Philosophy of Culture*. New York: Oxford University Press, 1992.

Asad, Muhammad. *The Message of the Qur'an.* London: Brill, 1980.

Ashcroft, Bill, Gareth Griffiths, and Helen Tiffin. *The Empire Writes Back.* London: Routledge Press, 1989.

Ayandela, E. *The Missionary Impact on Modern Nigeria 1842-1914.* London: Longmann, 1966.

Babatunde, Emmanuel. *Women's Rights versus Women's Rites.* Trenton, NJ: Africa World Press, Inc., 1998.

Baines, John D., Egan, Victoria, and Bademan, Graham. *The Encyclopedia of World Geography: A Country by Country Guide.* Santiago, California: Thunder Bay Press, 2003).

Bhabha, Homi K. *The Location of Culture.* London: Routledge Press, 1994.

Bamyeh, A. Mohammed. *The Social Origins of Islam: Mind, Economy, Discourse.* Minneapolis, Minnesota: University of Minnesota Press, 1999.

Barthes, Roland. *The Responsibility of Forms.* Translated by Richard Haward. New York: Hill and Wang, 1985.

Barrett, B. David, ed. *World Christian Encyclopedia: A Comparative Survey of Churches and Religions in the Modern World, AD 1900–2000.* Nairobi: Oxford University Press, 1982.

Barzun, Jacques. *From Dawn to Decadence: 500 Years of Western Cultural Life, 1500 to the Present.* New York: Harper Collins Publishers, 2000.

Battaglia, Debra, ed. *Rhetoric of Self-making.* Berkeley: University of California Press, 1995.

Baur, John. *The Catholic Church in Kenya: A Centenary History.* Nairobi: Saint Paul's Publications-Africa, 1990.

_____. *2000 Years of Christianity in Africa*. Nairobi: Daughters of Saint Paul-Africa, 1994.

Bayart, Jean-Francois. *The State in Africa: The Politics of the Belly*. London: Longman Press, 1993.

Bings, Tony. *Tropical Africa*. London: Routledge Press, 1994.

Bohm, David. *On Dialogue*. Edited by Lee Nichol. London: Routledge Press, 1998.

Boxer, C. *The Portuguese Seaborne Empire, 1415–1825*. London: Hutchinson, 1969.

Bratton, Michael. "Civil Society and Political Transitions in Africa." In *Civil Society and the State in Africa*, edited by John W. Harberson, Donald Rothschild, and Naomi Chazan, 66–67. Boulder, Colorodo: Lynne Rienne, 1994.

Brett, M. Jeanne. *Negotiating Globally*. San Francisco: Jossey-Bass Press, 2001.

Brown, G. Gerald. *Christian Response to Change in East African Traditional Societies*. London: Woodbrooke College, 1973.

Buber, Martin. *A Believing Humanism: My Testament, 1902–1965*. Translated by Maurice Friedman. New Jersey: Humanities Press International, 1967, 1990.

_____. *A Land of Two Peoples: Martin Buber on Jews and Arabs*. Edited with commentary by Paul R. Mendes-Flohr. Oxford: Oxford University Press, 1994.

_____. *Between Man and Man: With an Afterward by the Author on* "The History of Dialogical Principle." Translated by Ronald Gregor Smith. London: Routledge & Kegan Paul, 1947; Macmillan, 1965.

_____. *I and Thou*. A new translation with a prologue "I and You" and notes by Walter Kaufman. New York: Charles Scribner's Sons, 1970.

_____. *The Knowledge of Man: A Philosophy of the Interhuman.* Edited with an introductory essay by Maurice Friedman. Translated by Maurice Friedman and Ronald Gregor Smith. San Francisco: Harper & Row Publishers, 1966.

_____. In *On Intersubjectivity and Cultural Creativity Heritage of Sociology.* Edited by S. N. Eisenstadt. Chicago: University of Chicago Press, 1992.

_____. *The Way of Man: According to the Teaching of Hasidim.* New York, New York: The Citadel Press, 1966.

Burden, Jean. "Howard Thurman," *Chicken Bones: A Journal for Literary and Artistic African-American Themes.* From *The Atlantic Monthly* (1953), http://www.nathanielturner.com/howardthurman.htm.

Bujo, Benezet. *African Theology in Its Social Context.* Maryknoll, New York: Orbis Books, 1992.

Burgman, Hans. *The Way the Catholic Church Started in Western Kenya.* Nairobi: Mission Book Service, 1990.

Bwakali, David John. "Gender Inequality in Africa." *Contemporary Review.* 2001 On Bnet, http://findarticles.com/p/articles/mi_m2242/is_1630_279/ai_80607713/pg_2/?tag=content;col1.

Byrnes, F. James. *Speaking frankly.* New York, New York: Harper & Row, 1947.

Cabral, Amilcar. "National Liberation and Culture." http://www.panix.com/~lnp3/quotes/amilcar_cabral.htm).

Cain, Hope, Felder, ed. *The Original African Heritage Study Bible* (King James Version). Nashville, Tennessee: Winston Publishing Company, 1993.

Callaway, Barbara, and Lucy Creevey. *The Heritage of Islam: Women, Religion, & Politics in West Africa.* Boulder & London: Lynne Rienner Publishers, 1994.

Casto, Dalton L. *The Dilemmas of Africanization: Choices and Dangers for Sub-Saharan Africa*. Moraga, California: African Ways Publishing, 1998.

Chittick, Neville. *Kilwa: An Islamic Trading City on the East African Coast* Vol.1 (History and Archeology). Nairobi: British Institute in Eastern Africa, 1974.

Cloke, Kenneth. *Mediating Dangerously: The Frontiers of Conflict Resolution*. San Francisco: Jossey-Bass Publishers, 2001.

Codevilla, Angelo M. "Tools of Statecraft: Diplomacy and War." *Foreign Policy Research Institute*. FPRI, 2008, http://www.fpri.org/ footnotes/1301.200801.codevilla.statecraftdiplomacywar.html.

Cohen, David, ed. *The Circle of Life: Rituals from the Family Album*. London: Aquarian Press, 1991.

Constantin, Francois. "Muslims and Politics." In *Religion and Politics in East Africa*, edited by Holger Bernt Hansen and Michael Twaddle, 23 and 202. Nairobi: E.A.E.P. 1995.

Cox, Harvey. *Fire from Heaven: The Rise of Pentecostal Spirituality and the Reshaping of Religion in the Twenty-First century*. London: Cassel, 1996.

Daily Nation. "Multiparty System Not for Africa—Moi." *Daily Nation* (Nairobi), March 24, 1990.

de Wolf, Jan J. "A Quaker Account from 1926 Reports." Quoted in *Differentiation and Integration in Western Kenya*: A Study of Religious Innovation and Social Change among the Bukusu. The Hague: Mouton, 1977.

_____. *Differentiation and Integration in Western Kenya*. The Hague: Mouton & Co., 1977.

Desai, R, ed. *Christianity in Africa as Seen by the Africans*. Denver: Allan Swallow, 1962.

Donders, Joseph G. *Non-Bourgeois Theology*. New York: Orbis Books, 1985.

———. *Praying and Preaching the Sunday Gospel*. Maryknoll, NY: Orbis Books, 1990.

Edet, Rosemary and Ekeya, Bette. "Church Women of Africa: A Theological Community." In *With Passion and Compassion: Third World Women Doing Theology*, edited by Virginia Fabella and Mercy Amba Aduyoye. Maryknoll, NY: Orbis, 1988.

Edgerton, Robert B. *The Individual in Cultural Adaptation*. Berkeley: University of California Press, 1971.

Ela, Jean-Marc. *My Faith as an African*. Maryknoll, New York: 1993.

Ellen, Gruenbaum. *The Female Circumcision Controversy: An Anthropological Perspective*. Philadelphia, Pennsylvania: University of Pennsylvania Press, 2001.

Elochukwu, E. Ozukwu. *A Listening Church: Autonomy and Communion in African Churches*. Maryknoll, New York: Orbis, 1996.

Emery, James. "Short Account of Mombasa and the Neighboring Coast of Africa." *Journal of the Royal Geographical Society*, 1883.

Encyclopedia Britannica. "Joking Relationship." *eb.com*. http://www.britannica.com/EBchecked/topic/305724/joking-relationship.

Encyclopedia of Religion. New York: Macmillan Publishing Company, 1987.

Erny, Pierre. *Childhood and Cosmos: The Social Psychology of the Black African Child*. New York: New Perspectives, 1973.

Esack, Farid. "Muslims Engaging the Other and the Humanum." In *Proselytization and Communal Self-Determination in Africa*, edited by An-Na'im and Ahmed Abdullahi. Maryknoll, New York: Orbis Books, 1999.

Esposito, John L. *Islam: The Straight Path*. New York: Oxford University Press, 1988.

Fadiman, Jeffrey A. *When We Began, There Were Witchmen: An Oral History from Mount Kenya*. Berkeley: University of California Press, 1993.

Fanon, Frantz. *Black Skin, White Masks*. New York: Grove Weidenfeld, 1967.

Farah, Caesar E. *Islam*. New York: Barron's Educational Series, Inc., 1968.

Farsi, S.S. *Swahili Sayings: Erevuka na Yaliyomo*. Nairobi: Kenya Literature Bureau, 1993.

Farrant, Jean. *Mashonaland Martyr: Bernard Mizeki and the Pioneer Church*. Cape Town: Oxford University Press, 1966.

Ferguson, Brian R., and Neil Whitehead, eds. *War in the Tribal Zone*. Santa Fe, NM: School of American Research Press, 1992.

Ferdinando, Keith. *The Triumph of Christ in African Perspective*. Great Britain: Paternoster Press, 1999.

Firestone, Reuven. *Jihad: The origin of Holy War in Islam*. New York: Oxford University Press, 1999.

Fisher, Robert B. *West African Religious Traditions*. Maryknoll, New York: Orbis Books, 1997

Fisher, Roger, and William Ury. *Getting to Yes: Negotiating Agreement without Giving In*. Boston: Penguin Books, 1983.

Fisher, Roger, and Scott Brown. *Getting Together: Building Relationships as We Negotiate*. Boston: Penguin Books, 1989.

Ford, Clyde W. *The Hero with an African Face: Mythic Wisdom of Traditional Africa*. New York: Bantam Books, 1999.

Friedman, Maurice. *Martin Buber: The Life of Dialogue.* New York: Harper & Row, 1955, 1960.

G. Merrick. *Hausa Proverbs.* New York: Negro Universities Press, 1969.

Garfield, Robert. *The Concise History of Africa.* Acton, Massachusetts: Copley Publishing Group, 1994.

Gibbs, L. James Jr., ed. *People of Africa: Cultures of Africa South of the Sahara.* Prospect Heights, Illinois: Waveland Press, Inc., 1988.

Geertz, Clifford. *The Interpretation of Cultures.* Princeton, NJ: Basic Books, 1973.

Gilliland, S. Dean. *African Religion Meets Islam.* New York: University Press of America, 1986.

Goldschmidt, Walter. *Culture and Behavior of the Sebei: Study in Continuity and Adaptation.* Berkeley: University of California Press, 1976.

Gray, John. *Early Portuguese Missionaries in East Africa.* London: Macmillan, 1958.

Gree, Christina, ed., *The Role of Publishing in the Subjugation and Reawakening of African Culture,* June 1997. http://www.brookes.ac.uk/schools/apm/publishing/culture/cree.html.

Greene, Sandra E. *Gender, Ethnicity, and Social Change on the Upper Slave Coast: A History of the Anlo-Ewe.* Portsmouth, NH: Heinemann, 1996.

Habermas, Jürgen. *Moral Consciousness and Communicative Action.* Cambridge, MA: The MIT Press, 1996.

Haddad, Yvonne Yazbeck, and Wadi Z. Haddad, eds. *Christian-Muslim encounter.* Florida: University of Florida Press, 1995.

Haafkens, J. "Christian-Muslim Relations in Africa: A Pan-African View." In *Islam in Africa: A Perspective for Christian-Muslim Relations.* Edited by H. S. Wilson, 12. Geneva: Printshop of Ecumenical Center, 1995.

Hassan, Sallah M. "Modernist Experience in African Art: Toward a Critical Understanding." In *The Muse of the Modernity: Essays on Culture as Development in Africa*. Edited by Phillip G. Albach and Salah Hassan. Asmara, Eritrea: African World Press, 1996.

Haugerud, Angelique. *The Culture of Politics in Modern Kenya*. Cambridge: Cambridge University Press, 1997.

Haule, G. S. "The Entrepreneur." In *Modern Tanzania*, edited by J. Illiffe. Dar es Salaam: Historical Association of Tanzania, 1973.

Haynes, Jeff. *Religion and Politics in Africa*. Nairobi: Zed Books, 1996.

Herald, Suzette. *Controlling Anger*. Kampala: Fountain Publishers, 1988.

Hewett, James S., ed. *Illustrations Unlimited*. Wheaton, Illinois: Tyndale House Publishers, 1998.

Hillman, Eugene. *Polygamy Reconsidered: African Plural Marriage and the Christian Churches*. Maryknoll, New York: Orbis Books, 1975.

Hiskett, Mervyn. *The Course of Islam in Africa*. Edinburgh: Edinburgh University Press, 1994.

Hoare, Timothy D. "Some Basic Concepts in Primal Religion." http://staff.jccc.net/thoare/primal.htm.

Hodgson, Dorothy L., ed. *Rethinking Pastoralism in Africa*. Nairobi: EAEP, 2000.

Hohnel, von Ludwig. *Discovery of Lakes Rudolf and Stefanie: A Narrative of Count Samuel Teleki's Exploring and Hunting Expeditions in Eastern Equatorial Africa*. Translated by Nancy Bell, Vol. 2. London: Frank Cass, 1968.

Holway, James D. "Islam in Kenya and Relations with the Churches." In *Kenya Churches Handbook*, edited by David B. Barrett, George K. Mambo, Janice McLaughlin, and Malcolm J. MacVeigh. Kisumu, Kenya: Evangelical Publishing House, 1973.

Hughes, Thomas Patrick. *A Dictionary of Islam*. London: W. H. Allen and Co., 1888.

Humphrey, Harman. *Men of Masaba*. New York: Viking Press, 1971.

Idries, Shah. *The Way of the Sufi*. London: Arkana/Penguin, 1990.

Iklé, F. Charles. *How Nations Negotiate*. New York: Harper & Row, 1987.

_____. *Every War Must End*. New York: Columbia University, 1991.

Iliffe, John. *Africans: The History of A Continent*. Cambridge: Cambridge University Press, 1995.

Isichei, Elizabeth. *A History of Christianity in Africa*. Lawrenceville, NJ: Africa World Press, 1995.

Jenkins, Orville Boyd, "The Nubi of Kenya and Uganda." In *Thoughts and Resources on Culture, Language, Communication and Worldview*, 1996, 2000, 2006, 2008: http://orvillejenkins.com/profiles/nubi.html.

_____. "People Profile: The Swahili People." In *Thoughts and Resources on Culture, Language, Communication and Worldview*, 1996, 2008, http://strategyleader.org/profiles/swahili.html.

Jomier, Jacques. *How to Understand Islam*. New York: Crossroad, 1991.

Kasozi, A. B .K. "Christian-Muslim Inputs into Public Policy Formation in Kenya, Tanzania & Uganda." In *Religion and Politics in East Africa*, edited by Holger Bernt Hansen and Michael Twaddle. Nairobi: E.A.E.P, 1995.

Kennedy, John, ed. *Nubian Ceremonial Life*. Berkeley: University of California Press, 1978.

Kenyatta, Jomo. *Facing Mount Kenya*. Vintage Books, 1965.

Kerr, David A. "Questions and Answers about Islam." In *A Muslim Primer*, edited by Zepp, Ira G., Jr. Westminster, Maryland: Wakefield editions, 1992.

King, Noel Q. *African Cosmos*. Belmont, California: Wadsworth Publishing Company, 1986.

———. *Christian and Muslim in Africa*. New York: Harper & Row, 1971.

———. *Religions of Africa*. New York: Harper & Row, Publishers, 1970.

Kinoti, Hannah W. "Religious Fragmentation in Kenya." In *Proselytization and Communal Self-Determination in Africa*, edited by Ahmed Abdullahi Na'im, 282. New York: Orbis Books, 1999.

Kleinman, Arthur. *The Illness Narratives: Suffering, Healing and the Human Condition*. New York: Basic Books, 1988.

Koenig, Harold G. *Aging and God: Spiritual Pathways to Mental Health in Mid-Life and Later Years*. Bing-hamton, New York: Haworth Pastoral Press, 1994.

Krapf, J. L. *Travels, Researches and Missionary Labors*. Cass, London: 1968.

Kung, Hans. *Global Responsibility: In Search of New World Ethic*. New York: Crossroad, 1991.

Kurian, George Thomas Kurian, ed. *Encyclopedia of the Third World, fourth edition*, volume III. New York: Facts on File, 1992.

Kwame, Anthony Appiah. *In My Father's House: In the Philosophy of Culture*. New York: Oxford University Press, 1992.

Lacunza-Balda, Justo. "Translation of the Qur'an into Swahili." In *African Islam and Islam in Africa*, edited by David Westerlund and Eva Evers Rosander. Athens, Ohio: Ohio University Press, 1997.

Landau, Paul S. *The Realm of the Word: Language, Gender, and Christianity in a Southern African Kingdom*. Portsmouth, NH: Heinemann, 1995.

Lau, Joe and Chan, Jonathan. Critical Thinking Web. "Identifying Hidden Assumptions." *Argument Analysis*. http://philosophy.hku.hk/think/arg/hidden.php.

Lawson, E. Thomas. *Religions of Africa: Traditions in Transformation*. Prospect Heights, Illinois: Waveland Press, 1985.

Levtzion, Nehemia and Randall L. Pouwels, eds. *The History of Islam in Africa*. Athens, Ohio: Ohio University Press, 2000.

Lemu, Aisha B. *Laxity, Moderation and Extremism in Islam*. Hemdon, Virginia: International Institute of Islamic Thought, 1996.

Lewis, B, V. L. Menage, C. H. Pellat, and J. Schcht, eds. *Encyclopedia of Islam Vol. 3*. London: Luzac and Co, 1971.

Lewis, Bernard. *The Origins of Ismailism*. Cambridge: Cambridge University Press, 1940.

Lings, Martin. *Muhammad: His Life Based on the Earliest Sources*. Rochester, Vermont: Inner Traditions, Ltd., 1983.

_____. *The Eleventh Hour: The Spiritual Crisis of the Modern World in the Light of Tradition and Prophecy*. Lahore: Sohail Academy, 1984.

Magesa, Laurenti. *African Religion: The Moral traditions of Abundant Life*. Maryknoll, New York: Orbis Books, 1997.

Mair, Lucy. *Primitive Government*. Bloomington, Indiana: Indiana University Press, 1962.

_____. *Witchcraft*. London: World University Library, 1969.

Makila, F.E. *An Outline History of Babukusu of Western Kenya*. Nairobi, Kenya: Kenya Literature Bureau, 1978.

Malinowski, Bronislaw. *Malinowski and the Work of Myth*. NJ: Princeton University Press, 1986.

Marwick, M. *Witchcraft and Sorcery.* Harmodsworth: Penguin Books, 1982.

Mazrui, A. Ali. *Cultural Forces in World Politics.* Nairobi: Heinemann, 1990.

————. *The Africans: A Triple heritage.* Boston: Little, Brown and Co., 1986.

————. "The Black Woman and the Problem of Gender: An African Perspective." In *The Global African,* edited by Omari H. Kokle. Asmara, Eritrea: African World Press.

Mbiti, John. *African Religions and Philosophy.* Nairobi: Heinemann Press, 1980.

————. *The Concepts of God in Africa.* London: SPCK, 1970.

————. "A History of the Kenya Churches." In *Kenya Churches Handbook.* Edited by D. B. Barrett. Kisumu, Kenya: Evangel Publishing House, 1973.

McLennan, John Ferguson. "The Nature of Tribal Religion." In *Traditional Religion in West Africa,* edited by E. A. A. Adegbola. Nairobi/Kampala: Uzima/CPH, 1983.

McMahon, Elisabeth. "A Solitary Tree Builds Not": Heshima, Community, and Shifting Identity in Post-emancipation Pemba Island." *International Journal of African Historical Studies* 39, no. 2 (2006): 197-219.

Memmi, Albert. *Dependence.* Translated by Philip A. Facey, MA: Beacon Press, 1984.

Miller, Norman, and Roger Yeager. *Kenya: The Quest for Prosperity.* San Francisco: Longmann, 1994.

Menkiti, Ifeanyi. In Net Industries, "Communitarianism in African Thought-Menkiti On Communitarianism." http://science.jrank.org/pages/8771/Communitarianism-in-African-Thought-Menkiti-on-Communitarianism.html#xzz1EwAtIgMB, 1994, 2011.

Msigala, Kolumbo. Quoted in T. Ranger, "Missionary Adaptation of African Religious Institutions: The Maasai Case." In *The Historical Study of African Religion*, edited by T. Ranger and I. Kimambo. London: Heinemann, 1972.

Nakuma, Constancio, ed. *African Culture as a Culture of Diversity within a Multilingual Society.* http://web.utk.edu/~csms/nak97.html.

Nasr, Seyyed Hossein, ed. *Islamic Spirituality Foundations.* New York: Crossroad, 1991.

Newbury, C. and B.G. Schoepf. "State, Peasantry and Agrarian Crisis in Zaire: Does Gender Make a Difference?" In *Women and the State in Africa*, edited by Kathleen A. Staudt. Boulder: Lynne Rienner, 1989

Ngugi, wa Thiong'io. *A Grain of Wheat.* Nairobi: Heinemann, 1967.

_____. *The River Between.* London: Heinemann, 1975.

Nicolson, Harold. *Diplomacy.* San Francisco: Jossey-Bass, 1995.

Njau, Philip. "Aus meinem Leben." Quoted in Illiffe, *A Modern History of Tanganyika.* Cambridge: Cambridge University Press, 1979.

Nordstrom, Carolyn. *A Different Kind of War Story.* Philadelphia: University of Pennsylvania Press, 1997.

Nouwen, J. M. Henri. *Reaching Out.* New York: Doubleday, 1975.

Nthamburi, Rosemary. "On the Possibility of a New Image for an African Woman," a paper submitted to the Continental Consultation on Theology from Third World Women's Perspectives (EATWOT Women's Commission), Port Harcourt, Nigeria, August 19–23, 1986.

Nzibo, Yusuf A. "Islam and the King's African Rifles," In *Islam in Kenya.* Edited by Bakari Muhammad and Saad Yahya. Nairobi: Mewa Publications, 1995

————. "Islamization in the Interior of Kenya: A General Overview." In *Islam in Kenya*. Edited by Bakari Muhammad and Saad Yahya. Nairobi: Mewa Publications, 1995.

O'Brien, Donal B. Cruise. "Coping with Christians: The Muslim Predicament in Kenya." In *Religion and Politics in East Africa*, edited by Bernt Holger Hansen and Michael Twaddle. London: James Curry, 1995.

————. "The Muslim Predicament in Kenya." In *Religion and Politics in East Africa*, edited by Holger Bernt Hansen and Michael Twaddle. Nairobi: E.A.E.P, 1995.

Occhiogrosso, Peter. *The Joy of Sects*. New York: Doubleday, 1996.

Ojike, Mbonu. *My Africa*. New York: John Day, 1946.

Okaya-Lakidi, Dent. "Manhood, Warriorhood and Sex in Eastern Africa: Perspectives from the 19th and 20th Centuries," *Journal of Asian and African Studies*, 1979.

Olupona, K. Jacob, ed. *African Traditional Religions in Contemporary Society*. St. Paul, Minnesota: Paragon House, 1991.

Opuku, Asare Kofi. In *African Roots*, edited by N. I. Michael Dash, Rita Dixon, Darius L. Swann, and T'Ofori-Atta Ndugu. Lithonia, Georgia: World Literature Publishing House, 1994.

Osogo, John. "Superstitions and Taboos Observed among the Luhya." *Luhya Culture*, http://www.luhya.net/HTML_files/taboos.html.

Osahon, Naiwu. "Arabs Mortal Hatred and Enslavement of the Black Race." *The Nigerian Voice*, 2009. http://www.thenigerianvoice.com/nvnewsp/10876/1/pagenum3/arabs-mortal-hatred-and-enslavement-of-the-black-r.html.

————. "Arabs in Africa." *Edofolks.com*, 2009, http://www.edofolks.com/html/arabs_in_africa.htm.

p'Bitek, Okot. *African Religions in Western Scholarship.* Kampala: Uganda Literature Bureau, 1990.

Paris, Peter J. *The Spirituality of African Peoples: A Search for a Common Moral Discourse.* Minneapolis: Fortress Press, 1995.

Parrinder, Geoffrey. *African Mythology.* London: The Hamlyn Publishing Group, 1986.

_____. *African Traditional Religion.* London: Hutchinson's University Library, 1962.

Pavitt, Nigel. *Kenya: The First Explorers.* New York: St. Matthew's Press, 1989.

Perelman, Chaim. *The Realm of Rhetoric.* Notre Dame, Indiana: University of Notre Dame, 1982.

Phillips, E. William. *Muhammad and Jesus: A Comparison of the Prophets and Their Teachings.* New York: A Paragon House Book, 1996.

Pins, A. H. J. *The Swahili-speaking Peoples of Zanzibar and the East African Coast.* London: International Institute (IAI), 1967.

Piot, Charles. *Remotely Global: Village Modernity in West Africa.* Chicago: University of Chicago Press, 1999.

Pipes, Daniel. *In the Path of God: Islam and Political Power.* New York: Basic Books, 1996.

Pobee, John S. "African Instituted (Independent) Churches." From the revised edition of the *Dictionary of the Ecumenical* Movement. World Council of Churches and the Wm. Eerdmans, 2002, World Council of Churches, 2011, http://www.oikoumene.org/en/member-churches/church-families/african-instituted-churches/dictionary-of-the-ecumenical-movement-african-instituted-independent-churches.html.

Pouwels, R. *Horn and Crescent: Cultural Change and Traditional Islam.* Cambridge: Cambridge University Press, 1987.

Prins, Gwyn. *The Hidden Hippopotamus. Reappraisal in African History: The Early Colonial Experience in Western Zambia.* Cambridge: Cambridge University Press, 1980).

Przyluski, J. *La Participation.* Paris: 1949.

J. B. Purvis. *A Grammar of Lumasaba Language.* London: Society for the Propagation of the Gospel, 1909.

Rahman, Fazlur. *Major Themes of the Qur'an.* Minneapolis: Bibliotheca Islamica, 1989.

———. *Islam.* Chicago: University of Chicago Press, 1979.

Rappaport, Roy A. *Pigs for the Ancestors: Ritual in the Ecology of a New Guinea People.* New Haven: Yale University Press, 1968.

———. *Ecology, Meaning, & Religion.* Berkeley, California: North Atlantic Books, 1979.

Read, Margaret. "The Ngoni and Western Education." In *Colonialism in Africa 1870—1960: III Profile of Change: African Society and Colonial Rule.* Cambridge: Cambridge University Press, 1971.

Robinson, Richard. "Leakey Family." *Biology Reference.* http://www.biologyreference.com/La-Ma/Leakey-Family.html.

Said, Ahmed Salim. "An Outline History of Islam in Nyanza Province," *Islam in Kenya*, Edited by Bakari Muhammad and Saad Yahya. Nairobi: Mewa Publications, 1995.

Scheub, Herold. *A Dictionary of African Mythology.* New York: Oxford University Press, 2001.

Schoepf, B. G. "AIDS and Society." In *Women and the State in Africa*, edited by Jane L. Parpart and Kathleen A. Staudt. Boulder: Lynne Rienner, 1989.

_____. "Women, Health and Economic Crisis." In *Women and the State in Africa*, edited by Jane L. Parpart and Kathleen A. Staudt. Boulder: Lynne Riener, 1989.

Senghor, L. S. "Preface" to Amadou Koumba, *Les nouveaux contes*; A. Hampate Ba, *Aspects de la civilization Africaine*.

Shiloah, Ammon. *Music in the World of Islam: A Socio-Cultural Study*. Detroit: Wynne State University Press, 1995.

Shorter, Aylward. "Problems and Possibilities for the Church's Dialogue with African Traditional Religion." In *Dialogue with the African Traditional Religions*, edited by A. Shorter Kampala: Gaba Publications, 1975.

Shue, Henry. *Basic Rights*. Princeton, NJ: Princeton University Press, 1980.

Sivan, Emmanuel. *Radical Islam*. London: London University Press, 1990.

Smith, Dan. *The State of War and Peace*. London: Penguin Group, 1997.

Spear, Thomas, and Richard Waller, eds. *Being Maasai: Ethnicity and Identity in East Africa*. Nairobi: EAEP, 1993.

Spencer, William. *The Middle East*. Connecticut: The Dushkin Publishing Group, Inc., 1994.

Spero, D. "Patent Protection or Piracy: ACEO Views Japan." *Harvard Business Review*, 68, no. 5.

Sperling, C. David. "The Beginning and Growth of Rural Islam." In *The History of Islam in Africa*.

_____. "The Coastal Hinterland and Interior of East Africa." In *The History of Islam in Africa*. Edited by Nehemiah Levtzion and Randall L. Pouwels. Athens, Ohio: Ohio University Press, 2000.

Stevens, L. "Religious Change in a Haya Village, Tanzania." *Journal of Religion in Africa*, 1991.

Susser, Bernard. *Existence and Utopia: The Social and Political Thought of Martin Buber*. Rutherford, NJ: Fairleigh Dickinson University Press, 1981.

Thomas, Gerholm. "The Islamization of Contemporary Egypt." In *African Islam and Islam in Africa*. Edited by Westerlund David and Eva Evers Rosander. Athens, Ohio: Ohio University, 1997.

Tariq, "Who Are the Nubians," *Afraka.com*, http://www.afraka.com/showthread.php?208-Who-Are-the-Nubians.

Throup, David. "The Decline of Political Debate in Kenya: Minister of Labor Okondo threatens Bishop Muge." In *Religion and Politics in East Africa*. Edited by Holger Bernt Hansen and Michael Twaddle. Nairobi: E.A.E.P, 1995.

Thurman, Haward. *For the Inward Journey: The Writings of Howard Thurman*. Richmond, Indiana: Friends United Press, 1984.

_____. *The Luminous Darkness*. Richmond, Indiana: Friends United Press, 1989.

_____. *The Search for Common Ground*. Richmond, Indiana: Friends United Press, 1986.

Trimingham, Spencer J. *Islam in East Africa*. London: Clarendon Press, 1964.

Turner, Victor. *The Forest of Symbols: Aspects of Ndembu Ritual*. Ithaca: Cornell University Press, 1967.

_____. *The Ritual Process: Structure and Anti-Structure*. New York: Aldine de Gruyter Press, 1969.

Ueland, Brenda. "Tell Me More." *Utne Reader* (November/December, 1992).

Ury, William. *Getting Past No: Negotiating Your Way from Confrontation to Cooperation*. New York: Bantam Books, 1993.

_____. *Getting to Peace*. New York: Penguin Books, 1999.

_____. *The Third Side*. New York: Penguin Books, 2000.

Utalii Travel and Safari, http://www.utalii.com/Off_the_normal_path/kilwaruins.htm.

Uzukwu, Elochkwu E. *A Listening Church: Autonomy and Communion in African Churches*. Maryknoll, New York: Orbis Books, 1996.

Van Gennep, Arnold. *The Rites of Passage*. London: Routledge, 1960.

_____. *The Rites of Passage*. Translated by M.B. Vicedom and G.L. Caffee. Chicago: The University of Chicago Press, 1960.

Van Heist, M. *Land Unit Map of Mount Elgon National Park*. IUCN Technical Report, unpublished, 1994.

Vawter, Adelaide B. *The Inner Fabric of My Life*. Berkeley, California: Tulip Publishing, 1990.

Verma, Ritu. *Gender, Land, and Livelihoods in East Africa through Farmers' Eyes*. Nairobi: International Development Research Center, 2001.

Vikors, Knut. "Sufi Brotherhoods in Africa." In *The History of Islam in Africa*. Edited by Nehemiah Levtzion and Randall L. Pouwels. Athens, Ohio: Ohio University Press, 2000

Waines, David. *An Introduction to Islam*. New York: Cambridge University Press, 1996.

Wagner, Günter . *The Bantu of Western Kenya* Vols. 1 & 2. London: Oxford University Press, 1970.

Walakira, P. "Part of Establishment: Catholicism in Uganda." In *African Reactions to Missionary Education*. Edited by E. Bernard. New York: Teacher's College Press, 1975.

Walji, R. Shirin. "Ismailis in Kenya: Some Perspectives on Continuity and Change." In *Islam in Kenya*. Edited by Bakari Muhammad and Saad Yahya. Nairobi: Mewa Publications, 1995.

Webster, J. B. *African Church among the Yoruba*. Oxford: Clarendon Press, 1964.

Weening, Hans, ed. *World Quaker Website*, 1995. http://www.quaker.org/fwcc/EMES/booklet.html#1.

Weiner, Robert Paul. *Creativity and Beyond*. New York: State University of New York Press, 2000.

Wells, Spencer. *The Journey of Man: A Genetic Odyssey*, Princeton, NJ: (Princeton University Press, 2002), 56–58.

Werbner, Richard, ed. *Memory and the Post Colony*. London: Zed Books, 1997.

Were, S. Gideon. *A History of the Abaluhyia of Western Kenya*. Nairobi: East Africa Publishing House, 1967.

Weekly Review. "Tough Talking: President Moi Hits out at Critics of KANU." *Weekly Review* (Nairobi), May 18, 1990.

Wipper, A. *Rural Rebels: A Study of Two Protest Movements in Kenya*. Nairobi: Oxford University Press, 1977.

Wood, Clive, Boy, Gordon, and Allan, Iain. *Snowcaps on the Equator: The Fabled Mountains of Kenya, Tanzania, Uganda and Zaire*. London: Bodley Head Press, 1988.

Wood, James and Guth, Alex. "East Africa's Great Rift Valley: A Complex Rift System." *Geology.com*, 2000–2011. http://geology.com/articles/east-africa-rift.shtml.

Young, J. U. "Out of Africa: African Traditional Religion and African Theology." In Cohn-Sherbok, *World Religions and Human Liberation*. Maryknoll, New York: 1992.

Zahan, Dominique. *The Religion, Spirituality, and Thought of Traditional Africa*. Chicago: University of Chicago Press, 1979.

Zafrulla, Muhammad Khan. *Gardens of the Righteous*. New York: Olive Branch Press, 1975.

Zepp, Ira G. Jr. *A Muslim Primer*. Westminster, Maryland: Wakefield Editions, 1992.

Zuesse, Evan M. *Ritual Cosmos: The Sanctification of Life in African Religions*. Athens, Ohio: Ohio University Press, 1979.

Scriptural References in the Manuscript
All references from the Qur'an are from Muhammad Ali, Maulana. *Holy Qur'an*. With English Translation and Commentary (English and Arabic Edition). 1991. Dublin, Ohio: Ahmadiyya Anjuman Isha'at Islam Lahore, 2002.

All references from the Bible are from *The Jerusalem Bible*. 2000. New York, NY: Doubleday.

An Online Scholarly Information Database
African Culture as a Culture of Diversity within a Multilingual Society. Edited by Constancio Nakuma. http://web.utk.edu/~csms/nak97.html.

Circumcision Quote. Edited by James Prescott, July/August 1989. net/burness//birthing_spirit/cirquote.html.

Country Reports on Human Rights Practices–2000 Released by the Bureau of Democracy, Human Rights, and Labor. February 2001. http://www.state.gov/g/drl/rls/hrrpt/2000/af/index.cfm? docid=841.

Dictionary of Ecumenical Movement Online, 1999. http://www.wcc.org/wcc/what/ecumenical/aic-e.html

"Great Rift Valley," Microsoft Encarta Online: Encyclopedia 2000, http://encarta.msn.com, (c) 1997-2000 Microsoft Corporation.

Kenya Government History: July 1998.
http://www.worldrover.com/vital/kenya.html.

Kenyalogy Online: General information, 2000–2001,
http://www.kenyalogy.com/.

Members-International Coalition for Genital Integrity: January 1997.
http://www.icgi.org/ICGImemberTable.html.

The Nubi of Kenya: http://www.grmi.org/~jhanna/obj33.htm.

National Museums of Kenya – Fort Jesus Museum: ed. Ali Abu-Bakr, March 22, 2001. http://www.Museums.or.ke/regftjes.html.

Recent History. Edited by Chris Kreger, September 28, 2000.
http://www.cotf.edu/ete/modules/rift/rvrescenthistory.html.

Teso Online: J.C.D. Lawrence 2000.
http://www.kenyaweb.com/people/nilotes.html.
The Role of Publishing in the Subjugation and Reawakening of African Culture: June 1997. Edited by Christina Gree.
http://www.brookes.ac.uk/schools/apm/publishing/culture/cree.html.

The Swahili People of East Africa. http://www.org/~jhanna/obj49.htm.

Theory of Cognitive Dissonance Online. Edited by Leon Festinger.
http://www.comm.cornell.edu/comm116/cdlecture.html.

World Quaker Website. Edited by Hans Weening, 1995.
http://www.quaker.org/fwcc/EMES/booklet.html#1.

INDEX

Anderson, William, 97
Anglican Church Missionary
  Society, 97
animal sacrifice
  animal of splitting tradition,
    228–31, 263n241, 263n243,
    264n244
  in circumcision rites, 38
  of dogs, 303n12
  in peace ceremony, 34
  siluukhi ceremony, 262n230
  sitiso rite, 286
  for spilling of blood, 55n65
ants, in listening metaphor, 151
Appiah, Anthony Kwame, 35
"Arabs Mortal Hatred and
  Enslavement of the Black Race"
  (Osahon), 77
arbiter role, in conflict resolution, 240
army units, 85, 135n83
arranged marriages, 41–42
Arrow of God (Achebe), 48
assimilation issues, 24
assumptions, 146–48, 150–51
audience, discourse role, 257n124
avoidance relationships, 295

B

Babukusu peoples
  clan structure, 27–35
  community characteristics, xii
  cultural groups, 10
  origin and migration of, 115–19
  symbolic identity, 22–26
  term definitions, xi
bad omens, 125, 142n182
Baganda people, 99
Bailey, Sue, 150
Bakikayi clan cluster, 22

Balunda clan, 318
Bamalaba clan cluster, 22
Bamwalie clan cluster, 22
Banambayi clan cluster, 22
Baneala clan cluster, 22
Bang'oma people, 29
Bantu language group, 5–6
Bantu people, 50n11
Baraza, Patrick, xiv, 30, 352–53
Barrett, David, 101
Barthes, Roland, 152, 249n16
basic needs, 228–30, 232–33
Basilikwa clan cluster, 22
Baur, John, 96–97, 98
Beecher Report, 107
beer/beer parties, 283–84, 313–14
Between Man and Man (Buber), 153
Bible, The, 100, 234–35, 237–38,
  248n1, 266n278, 333–34
blame, 237, 240
blood
  in animal of splitting tradition,
    229, 263n242
  spilling of, atonement ceremony,
    55n65
  symbolism of, 38–39
blood reparation, 293
bluffs, in conflict rhetoric, 192–94,
  257n132
Bohm, David, 146, 147–48, 150–51
borders and boundaries
  in land ownership, 328–30
  national, 4–5
Bouma, Father, 103–4
boys. *See* male circumcision rites;
  men and boys
bride wealth, 202–3, 285, 332
bridge-builder role, in conflict
  prevention, 235–36
Britain. *See* Great Britain

Brown, Gerald, 186
Buber, Martin. *See also I-Thou*
  relations
  on center, 253n77
  on community relationships,
    166–73
  on culture, 175–76
  on dialogue forms, 161–66
  I-It relations, 153–55, 249n20
  implications of philosophy, 340–44
  importance of, 177–78
  on individual/group, 253n72
  on negotiability, 173–75
  on politics, 176–77
building practices, 284
Bukusu Education Society, 111–12
Bukusu homeland, xv, 3–4, 10–11,
  50n3
Burgman, Hans, 103
burial rites, 186, 198–99, 318–20
Bushmen, of Kalahari Desert, 216,
  224, 228, 230–31, 247
butchers, Muslims as, 83–84
Byrnes, James F., 197

C
cabinet ministers, speeches of,
  190–92
Cabral, Amilcar, 18
Cabral, Pedro Alvares, 88–89
Carter, Jimmy, 216
cash crops, 196
cash income, 283, 284, 328
catechists, in spread of Christianity,
  104, 105, 106
Catholics and Catholicism
  conflict with Protestants, 108–11
  gender roles in, 343
  in Kenya, 8–9, 93–99

marriage and, 186
mission appeals system, 197
radical inclusivity, 301
traditional religion and, 313
cattle enclosures (*kraals*), 11
ceremonies and rituals. *See also*
  circumcision; rites of passage
  blood reparation, 293
  dhikr, in Sufism, 71
  elders' role in, 128
  function/significance of, 35, 46
  funerals, 122–23, 141n169, 186,
    314n22, 355n14
  hair-shaving, 320–21
  for leaders, 28
  naming ceremonies, 275–77
  for peace, 34
  tooth removal rites, 15
  weddings, 287–88
chameleons, stories regarding, 322
change
  in conflict resolution, 227
  culture and, 120–22
  in negotiation strategy, 194–95
chiefs. *See* leaders
childhood names, 274
childlessness, 302n1
children
  clan relationships and, 272
  conflict resolution and, 349–50
  importance of, 157, 286–87
  infants and newborns, 272,
    273–77
  informal teaching of, 230–31,
    278–82. *see also* education
  naming of, 302n3
  parental relationships, 281–82
  polygyny and, 335–36
  sons, preference for, 335–36
China, traditional stories from, 241

necessity of, 17–21
relationships in, 13–14, 130, 167, 212–13, 231, 265n252, 317
rites of passage and, 47–49
shared experiences and, 166–69
as third side in conflict resolution, 223–31
transient forms of, 254n85
communal spirit, 345
communication. *See also* dialogue
in negotiation, 201
traditional forms, xi, 299–301
"Communitarianism in African Thought" (Menkiti), 48
community. *See* communal life; culture
competitive games, 294–95
compromise, 261n187
concessions, in negotiation, 205, 211–12, 261n187
confirmation, as element of dialogue, 160–61
conflict. *See also* conflict negotiation; conflict resolution
among clan members, 291
approaches to, 200
containment of, 243–47, 263n234
culture of, 221–22
escalation causes, 232, 238, 243
fatalism and, 221–22
as invitation to negotiation, 182, 200, 245–46
prevention of, 227–36, 263n234, 273
sources of, 14, 179–80, 323–30
conflict containment, 243–47, 263n234
conflict negotiation
agreements in, 213–14

end state objectives, 183–84
ground rules for, 199–204
third parties in, 17, 222–31, 240, 262n218, 310, 319, 347–48, 349
vocabulary of, 184–99
conflict resolution
children and, 349–50
opportunities for, 348
overview of, 263n234
roles in, 238–43
strategies for, 227, 236–43
traditional practices, 292–98, 320–21
women's role, 346–47
Consolata Missionaries, 99
construction, 284
cooperation, Ury on, 217–18
cooperative negotiation, 217–19
corruption, 255n112
council of elders (*baraza*), 105, 110, 308–10
counting systems, 31–32
Cox, Harvey, 109
creation myths, 119–20, 356n18
credibility, in negotiation, 201, 202
culture. *See also* communal life
Buber on, 175–76
change and, 120–22
of conflict, 221–22
environment and, 121
experiential view of, 19
history and, 18
Mazrui on, 336–37
negotiation and, 181–83
as term, 19
culture of diversity, 19
Cushite peoples, 50n12
Cushitic language group, 5–6

D

Daily Nation, The, 69
dancing, 104, 109
deadlines, in negotiation strategy, 196–97
death
  of elders, 127, 318–20
  funeral rites, 122–23, 141n169, 186, 314–22, 355n14
  joking relatives and, 297
  Koenig on, 316
  ritual killing, 15, 29
  traditional practices/beliefs, 122–23, 321
dehumanization, 155
dependence, 164–65
de Wolf, Jan, 10, 17–18, 107, 109
dhikr ritual, 71, 73
dialects, 7, 10, 13, 15, 18
dialogue
  among groups, 178
  audience in, 257n124
  author on, 352–53
  beer parties and, 283–84
  in bridge-building, 235–36
  civility in, 208–10
  equality in, 152
  forms of, 161–66
  at funerals, 319
  gender roles and, 333–34
  listening in, 148–52, 166
  purpose of, 145–48
  time and, 33
  in traditional culture, 122–23, 307–22
diet, 11. *See also* meals and food
Dini ya Musambwa (DYM), 137n110, 186–88
diplomacy, 194, 206–7, 209–10, 346
discrimination, 69, 77–78, 87

divination, 39–40
diviners, 91, 126, 163, 276, 284, 285
dogs, sacrifice of, 303n12
domestic violence, 285–86
drums and drumming, xi, 109, 244–45

E

early warning signals, of conflict, 244, 245
education. *See also* learning
  Christian churches and, 90, 92–93, 99, 102, 106–11
  vs. practical knowledge, 188
Egypt, Bukusu in, 115
elders
  ancestors as, 127–28
  conflict resolution role, 310, 319, 329
  council of, 105, 110, 308–10
  death/burial of, 127, 318–20
  history of term, 27–28
  leadership qualifications, 26
Elgon, Mount (*Mount Masaba*), 12–13
Elgon Maasai, 14, 17, 52n32
Emery, James, 76
emotionality, in negotiation, 208–10
emulation, 278–79
England. *See* Great Britain
entrails, divination and, 39–40
environment, culture and, 121
equality, dialogue role, 152
equalizer role, in conflict resolution, 240–41
equivocal language, in negotiation, 201
ethnicity/ethnic identity, 19, 20–21, 32

religious vs. political, 131n12
rural, 80–81
term definitions, 59
tolerance in, 233–34, 266n266
traditional religion and, xii, 79,
80–87, 274, 312–13, 350–51
Ismaili sect, of Shiism, 68
I-Thou relations
community and, 170–73, 174,
254n78, 254n79, 254n80
elements of, 158–61
gender relations and, 343
overview of, 155–58, 252n55

J

Jackson, Michael, song lyrics, 8
Jesus, teachings of, 235, 238, 248n1
jihad, concept of, 64–65
John Paul II, Pope, 95
joking relatives (*bukulo*), 293–98,
304n13
Jomier, Jacques, 67
Junaid of Baghdad, 72

K

Kaaba, 260n173
Kabras people, 15–16, 17–18
Kalenjin people, 14, 17, 52–53n32
Kananach age-set, 30
Kapuye, John, 91
Kazozi, A. B. K., 107
Kennedy, John F., 194–95
Kenya
Christianity in, 88–98
ethnic massacres in, 329
geography, 3–4
human diversity, 4–6, 8
language groups in, 5–8

map of, xv
police in, 247
religious affiliations in, 8–9
Kenya, Mount (*Kirinyaga*), 5
Kenya African National Union
(KANU), 191–92
Kenya African Rifles (KAR), 85
Kenyan Christian Church, 104
Kenyatta, Jomo, 193
Kenya-Uganda railway, 97
Kerre, Henry, 111
Khayo people, 16, 18
Khomeini, Ayatollah Ruhollah, 202
Khrushchev, Nikita, 194–95
KIKI (booklet), 103–4
Kikuyu peoples, 198–99
King, Noel, 335
Kipkwamet age-set, 30
Kipnyikeu age set, 30
Kiswahili language, 5–8
Kluckholhn, __, 128
Knowledge of Man (Buber), 153
Koenig, Harold, 316
Kolongolo age-set, 30
Krapf, Johann Ludwig, 7, 90, 94–95

L

Lake Victoria, 3–4
land
clan conflicts and, 291
colonialism and, 12, 99
as community resource, 14
Iklé's philosophy and, 346
ownership conflicts, 326–30,
332, 337–38, 356n20
as source of human origin,
356n18
languages, in Kenya, 5–8. *See also*
dialects

law of the talon, 237–38
leaders
  for ceremonies, 35
  conflict resolution role, 292–93,
    310, 319, 329
  councils of, 308–10
  death/killing of, 15, 29, 316
  qualifications of, 26
  role of, 123
  succession of, 68, 127, 316, 318
  women as, 343–44
Leaky family, 97
learning
  communal, 348–49
  formal. *see* education
  informal, 278–82, 311–12
legal practices, 62, 65–67, 198,
  237–38, 258n152
leprosy, attitudes toward, 276
Lex Talionis, 237–38
"Liberian Girl" (Jackson), 8
lightning, people struck by, 276
liminal phase, of rites of passage, 48
Lion King, The (movie), 8
listening
  active, 230–31, 236, 249n16
  in dialogue, 148–52, 166
  traditional stories regarding,
    264n249
literacy, 92–93, 108, 111
living center, Buber on, 170, 173,
  174
living dead ancestors (*bimakombe*),
  37, 125, 128, 142n179, 273–77,
  315–16
Logoli people, 16
long-dead ancestors (*kimisambwa*),
  125, 142n181, 242, 264n244
love, God as, 256n114
Lubukusu dialect, 10

Luhyia people, 4, 10, 15, 18
Lulogoli dialect, 10
Lumboka (village), 28
Lunyala dialect, 10
Luo people, 4, 198–99, 258n152
Luwanga dialect, 10
Lwaijumba, Edward, 93
lying, in negotiation, 201

M

Maanja people, 264n249
Maasai people, 4–5
Maben, Clyde Kay, 128
Magesa, Laurenti, 157
Maina (Bukusu elder), 225–26
Maina (son of Mubukusu), 25
Maina age set, 30
Mair, Lucy, 128
Makila (historian), 22, 115, 122–23
male circumcision rites
  age-sets and, 26, 28–32
  face-saving in, 205–6
  family relationships and, 281–82
  Islamic influences, 86
  in oral tradition, 116–17
  overview of, 15, 32, 36–38
  phases of, 38–45
  significance of, 45–47
Malikites, 66
Mango (son of Bwayo), 117
Mango (son of Mubukusu), 25
Marach people, 16
marriage
  among groups, 18
  arranged, 41–42
  bride wealth, 202–3, 285, 332
  land ownership and, 327–28
  polygyny, 185–86, 256n113,
    256n115, 334–39, 358n37

self-introduction and, 23
status and, 39
traditional practices, 225–27,
  262n230, 282–89, 302n3,
  358n35
martyrs, 65
Ma'ruf, Muhammad, 70–71
Masaba, Bishop, 324–25
Masinde, Elijah, 137n110, 187, 188
Mazrui, Ali A., 330, 336–37
Mbayi clan, 53n45
Mbiti, John S., xiv, 9, 19, 218,
  303n11
meals and food
  at funerals, 317–18, 355n15
  sharing of, 228–31, 232–33,
    263n241, 263n243, 264n244
  traditional roles regarding, 283
Mecca, 260n173
media, conflict warning role, 245
mediator role, in conflict resolution,
  239–40, 267n288, 267n290
medicine. See health care
meetings
  of elders, 105, 110, 308–10
  informal, 231
  public, 299–301, 301n18
  sites for, 207, 236
Memmi, Albert, 165
memorial ceremonies. See funerals
men and boys
  initiation rites, 311. see also male
    circumcision rites
  naming conventions, 274
  rules of conduct for, 44–45
  sons, preference for, 335–36
  traditional roles, 280–82, 282–
    89, 302n3
Menkiti, Ifeanyi, 47–48
mentoring, 146

messengers, 206–7, 346
Mijikenda people, 90
millet, in Bukusu agriculture, 196
Mill Hill Missionaries, 96, 99,
  102–5, 106
mission appeals system, 197
missionaries and mission work
  biographical tradition, 112
  education and, 90, 92–93, 99,
    102, 106–11
  exclusion warnings, 185–86
  informal, 85
  in Kenya, 93–99
Molotov, Yvachelsav, 197
Mombasa, 76
Monnet, Jean, 345
monogamy, 186
monologue, vs. dialogue, 162–63
moral codes, 129, 157–58, 198–99,
  255n112, 303n11
Mrenge of Rabai, 91
Mubukusu (mythic ancestor), 10,
  25, 115
Muge, Alexander, 188–90
Muhammad, 60–61
multiparty politics, 191–92
Mumia, Chief, 79
Mungoma (son of Mubukusu), 25
murder, 123, 293–98
Murunga of Wanga, Chief, 109, 111
Musa Mbuto, 111
music
  communal life and, 73
  dancing, 104, 109
  drums and drumming, xi, 109,
    244–45
  in promotion of education, 72
  in Sufism, 73
mutuality, as element of dialogue,
  159, 163–64, 174–75

mutual understanding, in
negotiation, 203–4
Mwambu (first man), 120
myth, 118–19

N

Nabongo Mumia (king), 15
Nabwana, Pascal, 109–10, 111
Nakuma, Constancio, 19
naming ceremonies, 272–77, 302n3
National Council of Churches of
Kenya (NCCK), 93–98
"National Liberation and Culture"
(Cabral), 18
nation-states, 4–5, 214. *See also*
colonialism; politics; *individual
countries*
negotiation. *See also conflict entries*
Buber on, 173–75
communal life and, 212–13
conflict as invitation to, 182,
200, 245–46
cooperative, 217–19
culture and, 181–83
need for, 179–81
positional bargaining, 236
public opinion and, 198–99
term definitions, 194–95,
259n153
third parties in, 17, 222–31, 240,
262n218, 310, 319, 347–48, 349
neighborhood relationships, 13–14,
130, 167, 317
neutral ground, in negotiation, 207,
236
Ngai (supreme being), 5
Ngoni people, 90
nicknames, 275
Nicolson, Harold, 209

Nilotic language group, 5–6
Nilotic people, 10, 15, 18, 29, 51n13
Njau, Filipo, 93
nongovernmental organizations
(NGOs), 350
Nordstrom, Carolyn, 32, 267n288
Nouwen, Henri, 150
Nthamburi, Rosemary, 357n31
Nubia people, 80
numbers, 31, 54n53
Nyala people, 18
Nyange Lumuli age-set, 30
Nzibo, Yusuf A., 80, 81

O

objectification, 154–55
O'Brien, Donal Cruise, 77
Ocaya-Lakidi, Dent, 46–47
Okondo, Peter, 189–90
Omubukusu, xi
oneness, of Allah, 60. *See also*
holistic worldview
one-sided dialogue, 163–65
oral traditions, xii–xiii, 22, 115–19,
311–12
Osahon, Naiwu, 77
Otieno, S. M., 198, 258n152
Ouko, Robert, 189

P

paradise, in Islam, 62–63
parallel conversations, 161–63
parent/child relationships, 281–82
Paris Peace Conference, 197
Parrinder, Geoffrey, 114–15, 250n27
past, xiii–xiv, 5, 30–31
patriarchy, 330–34, 336. *See also*
gender roles

patrol concept, in conflict
 containment, 244–45
patronymic relationship systems,
 24–26
peace
 ceremonies for, 34
 as norm, 222
 pacts, 303n12
peacekeeper role, in conflict
 containment, 246–47
peacemakers, women as, 346–47
Pentecostals and Pentecostalism,
 109, 325
personal experience, 19. See also
 individual
"Person and Community in African
 Traditional Thought" (Menkiti),
 47–48
Phipps, William, 266n270
Pierre, Erny, 9
pilgrimage, in Islam, 64, 260n173
pluralism, 266n270
plural marriage. See polygyny
police, perception of, 247
politics
 Buber on, 173–75, 176–77
 conflict vocabulary, 184–99
 gender roles and, 288–89
 multiparty, 191–92
polygamy, vs. polygyny, 335
polygyny, 185–86, 256n113,
 256n115, 287, 334–39, 358n37
Portugal, 136n90
positional bargaining, 219–21, 236
power, equalization of, 240–41
prayer
 Buber on, 175
 in Islam, 63
 from Sufism, examples, 71–72
 in traditional religion, 125, 309

predestination, 221–22
presence, as element of dialogue,
 158–59, 162–63
Prins, Gwyn, 137n96
Program on Negotiation, Harvard
 University, 216
promises, in negotiation, 201
property. See land
proselytizing. See missionaries and
 mission work
Protestants and Protestantism, 8–9,
 93–98, 108–11, 325
protests, 137n110, 246
provider role, in conflict prevention,
 232–33
puberty. See initiation rites
public gatherings, 299–301, 301n18
public opinion, in negotiation, 198–99
punishment
 warfare imposed as, 183
 of women, 285–86
purification and cleansing rituals
 in blood reparation, 293
 for boys/men, 43–45
 circumcision as, 324
 for girls/women, 39
 hair-shaving, 320–21
 in Islam, 63–64

Q

Qadiriyya sect, of Islam, 70–71
Quakers, 100–101, 109–10, 138n111
questions, asked by children, 278–79
Qur'an
 blasphemy and, 202
 on revenge, 238, 267n283,
  267n284
 role of, in Islam, 60
 on tolerance, 234, 266n266

seclusion phase, of circumcision rite, 42–43
secret knowledge, 333–34
secular
  in Islam, 65
  legal practices, vs. traditional religion, 198–99
Sela (first woman), 120
self-introduction, 23–25
Seventh Day Adventists (SDA), 96
sexual rights, 286–87
Shadhiliyya sect, of Islam, 70–71
Shafi'i School, of Islamic law, 66, 67
Shahadah (declaration of faith), 63
shaming, 255n112
Shar'iah law, 62, 65
sharing, of food, 228–31, 232–33, 263n241, 263n243, 264n244
Shiite beliefs, 67–68
Shorter, Aylward, 313
shrines, 125, 128, 354n2
Shugwaya Empire, 74
Sieng'eniesi age-set, 30
signals
  of conflict, 244, 245
  in warnings, 184–85
Silikwa clans, 53n44
siluukhi ceremony, 262n230
Simiyu Daniel, 111
sin, 95
singing, 92
sitiso rite, 286
slavery, spread of Islam and, 74, 77–78
snakes, significance of, 158
social immune system, 262n218
society. *See* communal life; culture
Society of Saint Joseph. *See* Mill Hill Missionaries
soft rules, of Iklé, 200–201, 204–13

songs, 92
Sperling, David, 75, 76
spirit, Buber on, 174–75
spirits, in Islam, 81, 87. *See also* ancestral spirits
Stam, Nicholas, 102–3
strangers, self-introduction of, 23–24
street vendors, 239–40
succession, 68, 127, 316, 318
Sudi, Chief, 82, 140n138, 336
Sufism, 71–73, 241
Sunna, 60–62
Sunni beliefs, 65–67, 131n2
surgical circumcision, 325, 355n15
Swahili
  languages and language groups, 5–8
  people, 75–76

T
taboos, 127, 157–58, 250n27, 358n37
Tachoni people, 15, 17–18
Tanzania, 4–5, 80
tash ahhud (declaration of faith), 63
taxation, by colonial administrators, 195–96
teacher role, in conflict prevention, 233–35
teaching. *See* education; learning
technical dialogue, 161, 163
Teso people, 10, 15, 18, 29, 51n13
"Thigh of an Elephant" metaphor, 22–26
Thiong'o, Ngugi wa, 206
third parties
  as comforters, 321
  in conflict resolution, 17, 222–31, 240, 262n218, 310, 319, 347–48, 349

violence, 233–34, 285–86. *See also* conflict; war
vitalism, 9

W

Wagner, Günter, 17, 27, 33, 82, 124
Walakira, P., 92
Walji, Shirin R., 68–69
walled villages, 27–28
Waluchio, Chief, 110
Wanga people, 15, 18
Wanyika people, 90
war. *See also* conflict
  circumcision rite and, 46–47
  as community event, 210
  concept of, 33–35
  holy, in Islam, 64–65
  Iklé on, 181, 182–83
  Ury on, 348
warnings, in conflict rhetoric, 184–88
Wataita people, 98
water, 14, 121, 164
Way the Catholic Church Started in Western Kenya, The (Burgman), 103
Webuye Falls (*Mwikhupo*), 12
wedding ceremonies, 287–88
Wele Khakaba, xii, 120, 124. *See also* Allah; God
Were, Gideon S., 15
Whitehead, Neil, 34
White Highlands, 105, 329, 357n21
wholeness. *See* holistic worldview
wilderness, as site of initiation, 20
witchcraft and sorcery, 125–26, 128–29, 157–58, 276, 284–285. *See also* diviners
Witlox, Father, 104
witness role, in conflict containment, 243–45

women and girls
  Buber's philosophy and, 341–44
  in Bukusu stories, 164
  Iklé's philosophy and, 346
  initiation rites, 14, 39, 312
  leadership opportunities, lack of, 357n31
  as messengers, 346
  naming conventions, 274
  Pentecostalism and, 109
  punishment/abuse of, 285–86
  purification and cleansing rituals, 39
  rights of, 330–34
  traditional roles, 11, 280, 282–89, 302n3, 328, 331
  widowed, as Christian converts, 91
World War I, 85

X

Xavier, Francis, Saint, 89

Y

youth
  conflict and, 354n3
  programs for, 344

Z

Zahan, Dominique, 114, 121, 130
Zaidi sect, of Shiism, 68
zakat (alms-giving), 63
Zamani period, 37, 142n179. *See also* long-dead ancestors (*kimisambwa*)
Zambia, Christianity in, 94

CPSIA information can be obtained at www.ICGtesting.com
Printed in the USA
LVOW12s0921311214

420965LV00002B/62/P

9 781462 016204